Quantum Computing and Communications

An Engineering Approach

Quantum Computing and Communications

An Engineering Approach

Sándor Imre and Ferenc Balázs

Both of
Budapest University of Technology and Economics, Hungary

John Wiley & Sons, Ltd

Other Wiley Editorial Offices

John Wiley & Sons Inc., 111 River Street, Hoboken, NJ 07030, USA

Jossey-Bass, 989 Market Street, San Francisco, CA 94103-1741, USA

Wiley-VCH Verlag GmbH, Boschstr. 12, D-69469 Weinheim, Germany

John Wiley & Sons Australia Ltd, 33 Park Road, Milton, Queensland 4064, Australia

John Wiley & Sons (Asia) Pte Ltd, 2 Clementi Loop #02-01, Jin Xing Distripark, Singapore
129809

John Wiley & Sons Canada Ltd, 22 Worcester Road, Etobicoke, Ontario, Canada M9W 1L1

British Library Cataloguing in Publication Data

A catalogue record for this book is available from the British Library

ISBN 0-470-86902-X

This book is printed on acid-free paper responsibly manufactured from sustainable forestry in
which at least two trees are planted for each one used for paper production.

To my father who taught me the way of thinking and to my mother who showed me how to endure to the end.

Sándor Imre

P.S. and of course to my children Sanyus, Marci, Orsi, Andris and their mother Adel.

Contents

Part I Introduction to Quantum Computing

Part II   Quantum Algorithms

Preface

Quantum computing and communications is one of the promising new fields of the new millennium. This emerging topic has reached the age when not only physicists and mathematicians but also engineers are becoming more and more interested in it. This book is based on the first semester of a two-semester subject dedicated to Ph.D. students and undergraduates in electrical engineering and computer sciences at Budapest University of Technology and Economics. This first semester covers a thorough basic introduction to the quantum computing world and discusses *quantum-assisted* computing and communications where we use the new paradigm to improve (assist) the performance of classical systems (e.g. searching in an unsorted database or strengthening communication security). In addition the second semester deals with *quantum-based* communications or more precisely with quantum information theory (e.g. channel capacity, error correction). After six semesters of experience we decided to prepare a book which can be used both as lecture notes and as a standalone learning aid for colleagues with engineering practice.

Although there are several good books on the market none of them has been written by engineers to engineers. The so-called 'engineering' approach has minor and major differences compared to materials authored by experts of physics, despite the fact that they cover more or less the same topic. As a simple example for the former category let us mention that engineers use j rather than i to denote the imaginary part of a complex number. However, it is not only conventions that make the discussion different. A presented sophisticated solution of a certain problem and the proof of its correctness do no satisfy an engineer. She/he always wants to know the way leading from the definition of the problem via system model construction and a logical chain of thoughts before reaching an answer to the original problem. If this 'special' viewpoint is omitted, which happens often when the authors are not familiar with engineers' everyday lives, then it always leaves behind a lack of completeness.

Another important aspect for engineers can be summarized as the 'need for practical applications'. A new theory or even an algorithm in itself has limited value. One has to prove and show that their implementation constraints, such as computational complexity, required memory, etc., can be fulfilled in the case of certain practical applications. Furthermore an unambiguous mapping of theoretical and real-life parameters has to be provided.

Finally, working as an engineer means the permanent study of the science of making compromises. The outcome of a design process must be precise enough *and* cheap enough *and* manageable enough *and* etc. and not the most precise *or* the cheapest *or* the most manageable *or* etc. Hence error analysis must always be kept at the focus of investigations.

All these endeavors are motivated by the fact that engineers should learn how to *design* new practical solutions. We always have this philosophy in sight when addressing various topics of quantum computing and communications. Of course we do not want to rank the engineering approach above those of physicists and mathematicians, we simply state that they are different (and not better or worse) in some sense. Due to this fact learning and understanding are much easier if explanations follow the way we are used to.

From a background mathematics' point of view we assumed a typical curriculum of engineers and computer scientists, however, the required math has been summarized in the appendix.

Because of the limited size of this book there are some aspects that are not discussed in detail. We did not devote an individual chapter to the implementation questions of quantum computers. Instead at the end of each chapter in the *Further Reading* we give a state-of-the-art survey of the current status of implementation and provide up-to-date references for interested readers. Philosophical questions and answers are also beyond the scope of this book but we suggest reading e.g. [84, 145] if the reader has time and would like to widen his/her knowledge.

Now we invite the reader to join us on the journey which is going to pass sometimes interesting, sometimes strange and sometimes challenging lands of the quantum world. Do not hesitate, the new world is waiting for you...

The Authors

How to use this book

According to ancient legend, one day Alexander the Great, conqueror of the 'that time known world' (Greece, Egypt, Persia), asked Menaikhmos the famous mathematician to teach him geometry in an easier and faster way. Menaikhmos smiled at this wish and answered: '*Oh king, you ordered your engineers to build distinct roads for citizens and for messengers and the army of the king all around your empire, but there is only one road for all in geometry!*'[1]

Basically we agree with Menaikhmos: learning and understanding quantum computing and communications need time and effort from the reader. However, we are convinced that if the way the knowledge is served is chosen carefully and fits more or less to previous studies of the reader, then high spirits can be maintained at hard portions of the topic. Before starting the voyage we would like to provide some useful hints and tools similarly to seamen who check their maps and compasses before sailing out to sea.

This book can be divided logically into three well-defined parts. Part I explains the basics of quantum computing and communications. As the next level Part II introduces well-known quantum algorithms while advanced readers can find several quantum assisted solutions for state-of-the-art infocom problems in Part III. The book has been equipped with several special features intended to help the reader.

- A dedicated web site can be found at **www.mcl.hu/qcc** containing useful information related to this book.

---

[1] The same story is known with Euclid and King Ptolemy.

- All the used notations, acronyms and abbreviations are summarized at the beginning of this book so that the reader can turn to this list at any time.

- We prepared plenty of exercises from easy to hard-to-answer types, which allow the reader to test whether his/her understanding is appropriate. The solutions of exercises can be downloaded from the web site of this book or a hard copy can be obtained from the publisher. We do not claim, however, that the proposed solutions are the simplest and shortest ones. Therefore we encourage diligent readers to find more attractive solutions and send them to the authors (imre@hit.bme.hu) in latex format. Appropriate alternatives will be included with the names of their solver into the solutions file.

- As a life belt the reader may find a summary of corresponding mathematical background in the appendices.

- In order to allow the reader to widen his/her knowledge beyond the scope and size of this book a carefully selected large list of references has been attached. We took special care to choose – if possible – such publications that can be accessed electronically on the Internet so that the reader may save time (and money).

- The book is amended with a list containing links to the web pages of the most important leading institutes and laboratories where additional information can be found or even current activities can be followed.

- Obviously the probability of writing a book without any error is fairly low. Therefore we ask the reader to address any comments or found errata to the authors (imre@hit.bme.hu). A regularly updated and downloadable list of errata is maintained on the book's web site.

Acknowledgments

The authors gratefully acknowledge the comments and helpful advice of Prof. Katalin Friedl from the Computer and Automation Research Institute of the Hungarian Academy of Sciences. Pressure from and interest of students attending the corresponding courses were the most motivating issues that helped us keep the deadlines. We thank our boss Prof. Laszló Pap for the permanent encouragement and allowing us enough free time to complete the work.

Certain results introduced in this book were prepared in the frames of OTKA F042590, COST 289.

List of Figures

Acronyms

BER	Bit Error Ratio
BPSK	Binary Phase Shift Keying
CAC	Call Admission Control
CDMA	Code Division Multiple Access
DES	Data Encryption Standard
DCT	Discrete Cosine Transform
DFT	Discrete Fourier Transform
DNS	Domain Name Server
DS-CDMA	Direct Sequence-Code Division Multiple Access
FDM	Frequency Division Multiplexing
FDMA	Frequency Division Multiple Access
FFT	Fast Fourier Transform
HLR	Home Location Register
GSM	Global System for Mobile communications
GUT	Great Unified Theory
IETF	Internet Engineering Task Force
IP	Internet Protocol

LSB	Least Significant Bit
MSB	Most Significant Bit
pdf	probability density function
MAC	Medium Access Control
MAP	Maximum *A Posteriori*
ML	Maximum Likelihood
MLS	Maximum Likelihood Sequence
MUD	Multiuser Detection
NMR	Nuclear Magnetic Resonance
PG	Processing Gain
QC	Quantum Computation/Quantum Computing
QFT	Quantum Fourier Transform
QMUD	Quantum-based Multiuser Detection
SDM	Space Division Multiplexing
SDMA	Space Division Multiple Access
SIM	Subscriber Identity Module
SRM	Square-Root Measurement
SS	Spread Spectrum
TDM	Time Division Multiplexing
TDMA	Time Division Multiple Access
UMTS	Universal Mobile Telecommunication System
URL	Uniform Resource Locator
WCDMA	Wideband Code Division Multiple Access
WLAN	Wireless Local Area Network
WWW	World Wide Web
$\tilde{a}$	Measured/estimated value of variable a
$\breve{a}$	Technical constraint/demand for variable a, e.g. a must be less than $\breve{a}$
$\forall$	for all
j	$\sqrt{-1}$
$\lvert\cdot\rangle$	Vector representing a quantum state, its coordinates are probability amplitudes
$\mathbf{x}$	Traditional vector, e.g. $\mathbf{x} \in \{0,1\}^n$ refers to the vector representation of n-bit binary numbers

$\lvert\cdot\rangle_N$	State of an N-dimensional quantum register, i.e. the qregister contains $n = \mathrm{ld}(N)$ qbits
$\lvert\mathbf{0}\rangle$	Special notion for the more than one-qbit zero computational basis vector to distinguish it from the single qbit $\lvert 0\rangle$
U	Operator
$U^{\otimes n}$	n-qbit (2^n-dimensional) operator
$\mathbf{U}$	Matrix of operator U
$P(\alpha)$	Phase gate with matrix $\begin{bmatrix} 1 & 0 \\ 1 & e^{j\alpha} \end{bmatrix}$
H	Hadamard gate with matrix $\frac{1}{\sqrt{2}}\begin{bmatrix} 1 & 1 \\ 1 & -1 \end{bmatrix}$
X	Pauli-X (bit-flip) gate with matrix $\begin{bmatrix} 0 & 1 \\ 1 & 0 \end{bmatrix}$
Y	Pauli-Y gate with matrix $\begin{bmatrix} 0 & -j \\ j & 0 \end{bmatrix}$
Z	Pauli-Z (phase-flip) gate with matrix $\begin{bmatrix} 1 & 0 \\ 0 & -1 \end{bmatrix}$
$\otimes$	Tensor product; this notation is often omitted, it is used only if the tensor product operation has to be emphasized
$\oplus$	Modulo 2 addition
$(\cdot)^*$	Complex conjugate
$\langle\cdot\lvert\cdot\rangle$	Inner product
$\lvert\cdot\rangle\langle\cdot\rvert$	Outer product
$\dagger$	Adjoint
$(\cdot)^T$	Transpose
$*$	Convolution
$\triangleq$	Definition
$\equiv$	Equivalence
$\wedge$	Logical AND operator
$\vee$	Logical OR operator
$\mid$	Logical IF operator
$\mathbb{Z}$	Set of integer numbers

$\mathbb{Z}_2 \equiv \{0, 1\}$ Set of binary numbers

$(\mathbb{Z}_2)^n \equiv \{0, 1\}^n \equiv \{0, 1\}^n$

                 Set of n-bit binary numbers

$\mathbb{Z}_N \equiv \{0, 1, \ldots, N-1\}$

                 Set of positive integer numbers between 0 and $(N-1)$, i.e. set belonging to the modulo N additive group

$\mathbb{Z}^+$	Set of natural numbers, i.e. positive integer numbers
$\mathbb{Z}^-$	Set of negative integer numbers
$\mathbb{Z}_p^*$	Set of positive integers belonging to the modulo N multiplicative group
$\mathbb{C}$	Set of complex numbers
$\mathrm{ld}(\cdot)$	*Logarithmus dualis*, $\log_2(\cdot)$
$\lceil \cdot \rceil$	Smallest integer greater than or equal to a number
$\lfloor \cdot \rfloor$	Greatest integer less than or equal to a number
$\lfloor \cdot \rceil$	Rounds to the nearest integer
$\gcd(a, b)$	Greatest common divisor of a and b
$\delta(x - x_0)$	Dirac function, it is 1 if its argument equals zero i.e. $x = x_0$ else it is zero everywhere
$\mathbb{E}(x)$	Expected value of random variable x
$f(x)$	Function continuous in x
$f[x]$	Function discrete in x
$\Re(x)$	Real part of complex number x
$\Im(x)$	Imaginary part of complex number x
$\#(\cdot)$	Number of, counts the occurrence of its argument
Thin line	Quantum channel
Thick line	Classical channel

Part I

Introduction to Quantum Computing

1

Motivations

1.1 LIFE CYCLE OF A WELL-KNOWN INVENTION

Every invention/technology has its own life cycle, similar to a human being. It can be shorter or longer but all of them have common phases and stages. Let us summarize this evolution using the well-known example of steam engine. First, scientists spend lots of time to find out something new. In our case Heron, a most famous experimenter, designed and implemented a steam-engined ball named Heron's ball (see Fig. 1.1).

Once a new idea has been born a long period of time is required until the stage when size, cost, efficiency, etc. of pieces of this equipment reach a minimally required and acceptable level. Many amateurs and experts devote their life to fulfil these requirements representing the childhood of the technology. The way is paved with many failures and rare successes therefore most of them remain anonymous forever. However, one day a clever guy manages to combine the small pieces of former results and adds something to them thus finally he/she succeeds. Concerning our example James Watt built the first working steam engine in 1765. Thanks to Mr. Watt steam technology attained its majority.

In the third phase the technology emerges from the deep of dark and mysterious laboratories and begins spreading among everyday people. Fulton's ship *Clermont* in 1807 irreversibly ended the glorious age of sailing ships and men of war while Stephenson's *Rocket* in 1829 convinced the skeptics that railway would be the leading transportation solution on land in the future. Human, sail and animal power had been replaced by steam engines during some decades from the kitchens via workshops up to enormously large ships such as *Titanic* or the battleships of World

Quantum Computing and Communications   S. Imre, F. Balázs
© 2004 John Wiley & Sons, Ltd   ISBN 0-470-86902-X (HB)

Fig. 1.1 Heron's ball about 100 B.C.

War I. The efficiency of the largest steam engine reached 22000 kW in 1941. Of course to achieve this level of popularity geniuses have to overcome strong resistance from those who exert the power. For instance William Symington built a steam-engined towboat on the Thames and presented her capabilities. Unfortunately the officials prohibited Symington from using the boat because they were afraid that the waves generated by the boat might damage the river-bank.

The size/power in itself is, however, not enough to survive (cf. dinosaurs or large empires). After a certain point *efficiency* becomes as important as power. It was foreseen and proven theoretically – long before steam-powered systems reached the top – that the efficiency of any steam-engine is limited and not enough for example for flight. If the new demand cannot be satisfied by means of a certain technology then other, even very young ideas are brought to light while the old one will be squeezed gradually. The reader may guess the name of the new pretender: yes, it was the internal combustion engine.

1.2 WHAT ABOUT COMPUTERS AND COMPUTING?

Now let us turn to our 'home' science which focuses on computers, computing and communications. The most important steps towards an electronic computer were done during World War II when the large number calculations in the Manhattan project required an elementary new equipment which was fast enough and adaptive (programmable). Many clever scientists were engaged with this problem. We mention here the polymath Neumann because he will appear several times in this book. As we will see later he played important role in quantum mechanics as well but at this moment we say thank you to him for the invention of the 'control by stored program' principle.[1] This principle combined with the vacuum tube hardware which formed the basis of the first successful computers.[2] Unfortunately the tubes strongly limited the possibilities of miniaturization hence the first computers filled up a whole room, which strongly restricted their wide applications. Therefore scientists paid attention to the small-scale behavior of matter. Fortunately the invention of semiconductors and the appearance of the transistor in 1948 by Bardeen, Brattain and Schockley opened the way to personal computers and other handheld equipment.

One day in 1965 when Gordon Moore from Intel was preparing his talk and started to draw a plot about the performance of memory chips he suddenly observed an interesting rule called Moore's law. As it is depicted in Fig. 1.2 he concluded that since the invention of the transistor the number of transistors per chip roughly doubled every 18–24 months, which means an exponential increase in the computing power of computers. Although it was an empirical observation without theoretical proof the law seems to be still valid nowadays. However, similar to the case of steam engine farseeing experts tried to determine the future of this technology. They estimate serious problems around 2015. What reasons may stand behind this prophecy?

No matter how surprising it sounds this trend can be traced back simply to drawing lines. The growth in processors' performance is due to the fact that we put more and more transistors on the same size chip. This requires smaller and smaller transistors, which can be achieved if we are able to draw thinner and thinner – even much thinner than a hair – lines onto the surface of a semiconductor disk. Next current technology enables us to remove or retain parts of the disk according to the line structure evolving to transistors, diodes, contacts, etc. Apart from the technical problem of drawing such thin lines one day our lines will leave our well-known natural environment with well-known rules revealed step by step during the evolution of human race and enter into a new world where the traveler must obey new and strange rules if he/she would like to pass through this land. The new world is called nano-world, the new rules are explained by quantum mechanics and the border between the worlds lies around nanometer (10^{-9}m) thickness. Fortunately scientists have already performed many reconnaissance missions in the nano-scale region thus we have not only theoretical but also technology-related knowledge in our hands called nanotechnology.

From a computer scientist's point of view, who has algorithms and programs in his/her mind, the growth in the capabilities of the underlying hardware is vital. If we have an algorithm which is not efficient often enough time alone solves the problem due to the faster new hardware. We can say that we got used to Moore's law during the last decades and forgot to follow what is happening and what will happen with the hardware. For decades, this attitude was irrelevant but the deadline to change it is near to its expiration. Fortunately experts called our attention to the fact that we

---

[1] The third area where he is counted among the founding fathers is called game theory.
[2] As an interesting story we mention here that Neumann was talented in mental arithmetic, too. The correct operation of the computer under construction was tested by multiplying two 8-digit numbers. Typically Neumann was the fastest.

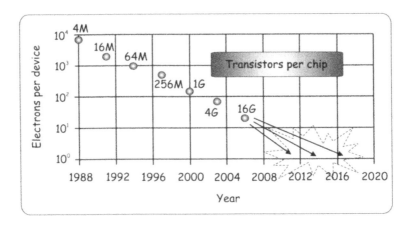

Fig. 1.2 Moore's law

will have to face serious problems if this trend cannot be maintained. One thing is sure, however, the closer we are to the one-electron transistor (see Fig. 1.2) disturbing quantum effects will appear more often and stronger. Hence either we manage to find a new way of miniaturization or we have to learn how to exploit the difficulties and strangeness of quantum mechanics. Independently from the chosen way we must do something because *Computing is a must* or as ancient Romans said *"Navigare necesse est!"*

In compliance with the latter concept Feynman suggested a new straightforward approach. Instead of regarding computers as devices working under the laws of classical physics – which is common sense – let us consider their operation as a special case of a more general theory governed by quantum mechanics. Thus the way becomes open from the hardware point of view. On the other hand hardware and software always influence each other. Since new hardware concepts require and enable new software concepts we have to study quantum mechanics from a computer science point of view. Moreover it is worth seeking algorithms which are more efficient than their best classical counterparts thanks to the exploited possibilities available only in the quantum world. These software-related efforts are comprehended by *quantum computing*. Once we familiarized ourselves with quantum-faced computing why keep communications away from the new chances. May be the capacity of a quantum channel could exceed that of classical cable or we could design more secure protocols than currently applied ones. *Quantum communications* or *quantum information theory* tries to answer these questions.

Realization issues are out of the scope of this book thus we mention here that there are fairly promising results in certain areas e.g. implementation of secure quantum-based communications but we do not want to conceal that desktop quantum personal computers are far from introduction to the market. Concerning the subject of our book, quantum computing and communications have passed several important milestones. Top experts have experimentally validated algorithms which overcome the classical competitors. For instance we are able to find an item in an unsorted database or factorize large numbers very quickly. Quantum principles allow solving easily a long discussed problem, namely random number generators e.g. [21]. Furthermore as we mentioned before, implementation of certain algorithms reached such a stage that one can buy corresponding equipment in an appropriate shop. Fortunately many questions are waiting to be answered thus the reader will find not only solutions but open questions in this book. Nothing shores up more convincing the spreading of the new paradigm than the fact that more and more publications appear in popular science magazines and journals [38, 22, 110, 115].

Remark: Moore's law has several interpretations depending on which side of the market it has been phrased

- Rock's law: *"The cost of capital equipment to build semiconductors will double every four years."* by Arthur Rock (industry)

- Machrone's law: *"The machine you wants always costs $5000."* by Bill Machrone (customer)

- If the reader is familiar with other versions of Moore's law we ask him/her to post it to the authors (imre@hit.bme.hu) so that we will share them on the book's web page.

1.3 LET US PLAY MARBLES

Playing games is as old as humankind. To give further motivations to study quantum computing and communications and to read the remaining more then 250 pages of this book we suggest playing a simple but interesting game. First let us introduce our virtual friends who are always ready to participate in games or any other experiment. They are *Alice*, *Bob* and *Eve*. Since Eve is often inclined to act the young rascal any time when we need an eavesdropper or negative hero she will be happy to play this role.

Alice and Bob decide to join. We explain the rules of the game to them (cf. Fig. 1.3). We have a sack full of marbles. First we put 0, 1, 2, 3 or 4 marbles into a blue colored box. Our choice is uniformly random. Next we take a red box and flip a coin. In compliance with the result if we got a tail we put marbles from the sack into this box such that the total number of marbles in the two boxes will be 4 else we complement them to 6. Now we ask Alice and Bob to enter two perfectly separated rooms which prevent any type of communications between them i.e. they are shaded from voice, electromagnetic radiation, etc. Both of them are only allowed to take one of two identical, previously prepared devices each having an integer input and a one-bit output. When our players have seated themselves comfortably we give Alice the blue box while Bob obtains the red one. Now they are allowed to open the boxes and feed the device with the number of marbles. Next each of them has the possibility to give a one-bit sign according to the device's output, for instance via setting a flag in

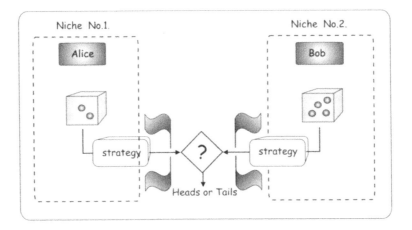

Fig. 1.3 Alice and Bob are playing marbles

an up or down position. If they are able – based on this sign and their own marbles – to design a perfect device (i.e. strategy or mapping) which makes obvious to the audience whether the coin has fallen onto heads or tails then they win this turn and are rewarded with a pair of cinema or theatre tickets.

Alice and Bob are clever and wily hence they investigate first the existence of such a strategy which provides success with probability 1. Let $(x; y)$ denote a certain configuration, where x refers to the number of Alice's marbles while y to that of Bob. If the total number of marbles equals 4 then one of the following five combinations has been prepared: $\{(0; 4), (1; 3), (2; 2), (3; 1), (4; 0)\}$. On the other hand Alice and Bob have to face one element of the following set: $\{(0; 6), (1; 5), (2; 4), (3; 3), (4; 2)\}$.[3]

It is easy to see that no classical strategy exists which ensures certain success. However, interestingly as we will present at the end of Part I a simple quantum protocol allows Alice and Bob to make any combination unambiguous for the audience. This seems to be in total contradiction to our classical theory of probability or more generally how nature works. We hope that the reader is eager to learn this protocol and we ask him/her to read the basics before turning to those pages. In the meantime we call the reader to participate in the quest of the most efficient classical strategy that results in the largest probability of success if the game is repeated many times. Please, post your candidate strategy with derivation of the corresponding probability of success to the authors (imre@hit.bme.hu) in ps or pdf format. Correct strategies will be published on the book's web page.

---

[3]Configurations $(5; 1)$ and $(6; 0)$ are trivially excluded since Alice is given at most 4 marbles.

2

Quantum Computing Basics

This chapter is devoted to the basic information, techniques and skills required to travel around the quantum world safely. First we introduce quantum phenomena using the strange sounding probabilistic $\sqrt{I}$ gate in Section 2.1. Quantum computing is rooted in quantum mechanics therefore Section 2.2 explains the postulates of quantum mechanics which form the solid base of any further discussion. Next we build bridges between classical and quantum computing in Section 2.3 and 2.4 where generalization of registers and logic gates are investigated. The following Section 2.5 analyzes an interesting quantum circuit called quantum interferometer. Quantum mechanics offers certain possibilities which are not present in classical computing. The most important one which connects pieces of quantum information very tightly is referred to as entanglement and is introduced in Section 2.6. As in everyday life everything has its price. The price of entanglement has some restrictions e.g. we can use the COPY command in quantum computing as explained in Section 2.7. Finally we show how to prepare an arbitrary quantum state in a quantum register in Section 2.8.

2.1 MYSTERY OF PROBABILISTIC $\sqrt{I}$ GATE

We propose to start getting acquainted with quantum computing and communications by means of a thought experiment leading to a fairly surprising result. Let us investigate coin tossing using scientific apparatus. If one flips a coin she/he will

Quantum Computing and Communications   S. Imre, F. Balázs
© 2004 John Wiley & Sons, Ltd   ISBN 0-470-86902-X (HB)

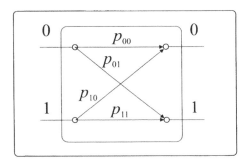

Fig. 2.1   Scientific model for coin tossing

obtain a head or a tail randomly. When we have a legal coin[1] tossed enough times then statistically both results occur about half of the times. This operation can be modeled by means of a device depicted in Fig. 2.1 where heads and tails are represented by logical 0 and 1, respectively. Transition probabilities are defined in the following manner

$$p_{kl} \triangleq P(out = l \mid in = k); \quad k, l \in \{0, 1\},$$

and obviously $\sum_l p_{kl} = 1$. Moreover our model is able to handle counterfeiters with illegal coins demanding p_{kl} different from 0.5. However, from the scientific point of view we have constructed the most general binary memoryless probabilistic function $f : \{0, 1\} \rightarrow \{0, 1\}$. Its operation becomes deterministic only either if $p_{00} = p_{11} = 1, p_{01} = p_{10} = 0$, which models an identity transformation (shortcut) or when $p_{00} = p_{11} = 0, p_{01} = p_{10} = 1$ implements an inverter.

Now we make the experiment more difficult by tossing a certain coin two times successively, which can be modelled by concatenating two boxes according to Fig. 2.2. Furthermore we are interested in the transition probabilities P_{kl} of a special single gate which is equivalent to the two-gate configuration. It is reasonable to assume that the two tossings are independent thus basic probability theory advises us how to calculate different P_{kl}

$$
\begin{aligned}
P_{00} &= p_{00}p_{00} + p_{01}p_{10}, \\
P_{01} &= p_{01}p_{11} + p_{00}p_{01}, \\
P_{10} &= p_{11}p_{10} + p_{10}p_{00}, \\
P_{11} &= p_{11}p_{11} + p_{10}p_{01}.
\end{aligned}
\tag{2.1}
$$

Interestingly if $p_{00} = p_{11} = p_{01} = p_{10} = 0.5$ then $P_{00} = P_{11} = P_{01} = P_{10} = 0.5$, that is using two concatenated gates provides the same result as a single one which

---

[1] Readers from telecom may consider binary symmetric channel as an equivalent problem.

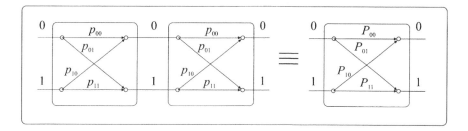

Fig. 2.2 Scientific model for concatenated coin tossing

is in full harmony with our everyday experiences, namely flipping a coin twice produces random results similarly to a single tossing.

   With this point our view of nature proved to be round and complete. However, readers who are not familiar with quantum mechanics are kindly asked to steel their hearts. *There exist devices which operate in full compliance with the random coin tossing model if only one of them is investigated, but when concatenating two of them the output becomes suddenly deterministic!* Deterministic means here that the two gates together look as if they implemented an identity transform.

   Maybe probability theory is able to provide a reassuring answer to this paradox. Identity means that P_{01} and P_{10} must be equal to zero. Unfortunately the corresponding equations in (2.1) contradict this demand because identity requires nonzero p_{00} and p_{11}, thus to achieve $P_{01} = P_{10} = 0$ one needs $p_{01} = p_{10} = 0$ since negative probabilities are not allowed. On the other hand individual random behavior cannot be imagined with $p_{01} = p_{10} = 0$. Our well-known and well-tried classical probability theory seems to be in real trouble. Is the situation really that serious? Fortunately not, at least in terms of everything we have learned in the frame of classical probability theory remain valid provided one does not want to extend his/her journey to the nano-scale world. Unfortunately we have just started such a visit therefore we need a new theory to explain this surprising identity operation *and* to be general enough to describe traditional coin tossing as well.

   This new theory is called *quantum mechanics*. Before revealing our strange device which will be referred as probabilistic $\sqrt{I}$ (square root identity) gate[2] let us illustrate a potential mathematical apparatus which is able to handle this unusual phenomenon. Roughly speaking Schrödinger suggested assigning so-called *probability amplitudes* to nano-scale events instead of classical probabilities. Unlike classical probability p which should be real and can have values between 0 and 1 probability amplitudes c are complex numbers. Probability amplitudes can be handled in the same way as classical probabilities when considering e.g. alternative or independent events. Moreover the observed classical probability can be determined in a very simple way namely $p = |c|^2$. Unfortunately we are able to access probability amplitudes

---

[2]$\sqrt{I}\sqrt{I} = I.$

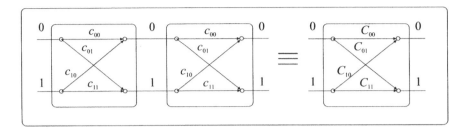

Fig. 2.3 Concatenated probabilistic $\sqrt{I}$ gates

only indirectly via measurements (observations) representing the bridge between the macro-scale classical and nano-scale quantum worlds. It has to be emphasized that only one world exists which obeys the rules (postulates) of quantum mechanics but our everyday strongly limited observation possibilities show a certain 'projection' of it. This is maybe the most disturbing consequence of quantum mechanics. So we ask the reader not to be worried at this stage since we are going to return to this strangeness several times within the introduction so that he/she can accept[3] it easier.

In possession of the notion of probability amplitudes we are able to design suitable probabilistic $\sqrt{I}$ gates and concatenate two of them, see Fig. 2.3. If one would like to define the quantum equivalent of the legal coin tossing then $c_{00} = c_{01} = c_{10} = \frac{1}{\sqrt{2}}$ and $c_{11} = -\frac{1}{\sqrt{2}}$ has to be set up. Let us check the transition probability amplitudes of the equivalent single gate

$$C_{00} = c_{00}c_{00} + c_{01}c_{10} = \frac{1}{\sqrt{2}}\frac{1}{\sqrt{2}} + \frac{1}{\sqrt{2}}\frac{1}{\sqrt{2}} = 1,$$

$$C_{01} = c_{01}c_{11} + c_{00}c_{01} = \frac{1}{\sqrt{2}}\left(-\frac{1}{\sqrt{2}}\right) + \frac{1}{\sqrt{2}}\frac{1}{\sqrt{2}} = 0,$$

$$C_{10} = c_{11}c_{10} + c_{10}c_{00} = \left(-\frac{1}{\sqrt{2}}\right)\frac{1}{\sqrt{2}} + \frac{1}{\sqrt{2}}\frac{1}{\sqrt{2}} = 0,$$

$$C_{11} = c_{11}c_{11} + c_{10}c_{01} = \left(-\frac{1}{\sqrt{2}}\right)\left(-\frac{1}{\sqrt{2}}\right) + \frac{1}{\sqrt{2}}\frac{1}{\sqrt{2}} = 1. \qquad (2.2)$$

The experienced classical probabilities can be calculated by the 'squared absolute value' function that is $P_{00} = P_{11} = |1|^2$ and $P_{01} = P_{10} = |0|^2$, which is the identity transform.

A plausible explanation of this surprising result can be given if the reader considers the arrows in Fig. 2.3 as waves (sinusoid signals) with amplitudes c_{kl} and these waves interfere with each other causing total wipe out or maximal gain. This

---

[3] Unfortunately either we accept it or not as with the axioms of Euclidian geometry, which are based on the reasonable argument that everything that contradicts the experimental results has to be rejected while those statements which prove to be in harmony with them can be accepted.

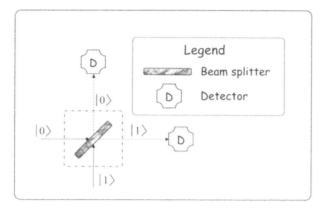

Fig. 2.4 Implementation of probabilistic $\sqrt{I}$ gate – the half-silvered mirror

reasoning is much closer to the truth than one may expect because our mysterious equipment which contradicts the classical probability theory is a half-silvered mirror (or beam splitter). It operates in the following way (see Fig. 2.4). When a great amount of photons are shot onto the beam splitter about half of them hits the vertical detector and the remaining half arrives at the horizontal detector. Next we connect the outputs of such a device by means of traditional mirrors to the inputs of an identical half-silvered mirror. Surprisingly the horizontally launched photons always hit the vertical detector (see Fig. 2.5). It is hard to interpret this result using our classical view of nature. If we consider the photon as a small marble whose way is chosen randomly at each beam splitter then it is impossible to explain why the photon is directed each time to the same detector. Maybe deploying a detector onto one of the paths between the two beam splitters can answer which way the photon was travelling? However, the photon does not accept this trick. Because of the extra detector the operation of the configuration loses its deterministic nature and becomes random as if only the second half-silvered mirror were used alone. This is another important lesson. *Measurements typically influence the observed system and thus the measurement results themselves.* A more successful attempt if the photon is regarded as a marble before arriving the first beam-splitter is that it turns into a wave which propagates on both paths. At the second half-silvered mirror the two waves (the photon) interfere(s) (with itself) and convert back to a marble before striking the detector. This explanation highlights why the concatenated probabilistic $\sqrt{I}$ gates are referred as *quantum interferometer*.

Finally we would like to emphasize that *there is no sense in thinking about the state of the photon (which path it is taking), it must be considered as being in both states (both paths) at the same time and the measurement force it to collapse (select) into one of them.* This differs fundamentally from our classical approach which assumes that the photon always travels along a single path hidden to the eyes of the observer and measurements only reveal this path instead of deciding

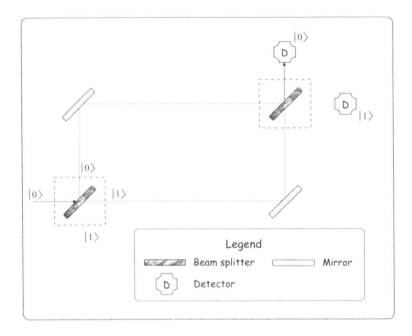

Fig. 2.5 Concatenated half-silvered mirrors as identity transformation

it. We will analyze the interferometer more scientifically in Section 2.5 and discuss measurements in Chapter 3.

Remark: Let us throw some light upon the close connection between the measuring apparatus and the measured object using the widely known microscopy. Optical microscopes use the reflected photons from the object's surface. To achieve reflection the half-wavelength of the photon (more precisely light is considered as a wave at this point) has to be smaller than the unevenness of the surface. Therefore in order to observe smaller and smaller details we need shorter and shorter wavelengths e.g. X-rays. On the other hand the light can be regarded as a series of photons. Each photon has its mass and thus its energy which depends on the frequency of the light. The higher the frequency then the higher the corresponding energy. Since frequency and wavelength are in inverse relation the reflecting photon transfers more and more energy to the observed object, that is the photon influences it more and more radically.

2.2 THE POSTULATES OF QUANTUM MECHANICS

Nobody knows how the physical world really operates. The only thing we can do is to model it. A given model/theory can be regarded as a suitable tool for the description of events all around us if the difference/error between expectations originating from the theory and the observations remain below a certain limit. For instance different models were developed for *throwing* during the history of the human race. First cavemen formed some simple rules based on experiences related to the power and angle of throwing. Although this approach ensured a high percentage hit on a mammoth it proved to be insufficient for cannon-balls. Later Isaac Newton introduced gravity and more sophisticated formulas which enable more or less precise hits on the enemy's castle if the shell is regarded as a zero-sized elementary mass and the trajectory is calculated in advance. Unfortunately in order to enter the spaceflight and advanced astronomical age Newtonian theory had to be replaced by relativity theory, which provides a high probability of survival for astronauts fired out towards the moon. This proposal handles the spaceship as a marble rolling ahead in the elastic textile of space-time curved by planets and stars. These models represent different viewpoints about nature therefore they give different explanations of how the world operates but what they have common is that they do not answer why the world operates that way.

Each theory is based on several assumptions that cannot be verified theoretically, only experiments shore up that they are in consonance of the nature. For example Euclidian geometry has so-called axioms e.g. the sum of angles in a triangle equals 180°. However, these assumptions can be replaced by other ones, for instance the sum of angles in a triangle is less or greater than 180° leading to Riemanian (elliptic) or Bolyaian (hyperbolic) geometry.

In the case of quantum mechanics we have four assumptions called postulates which form a solid base for the theory. According to our state-of-the-art knowledge most of the rules in the universe can be traced back to these postulates and only a few effects such as the long-range gravity seem to be an exception. Thousands of scientists are spending their scientific life trying to discover the so-called *great unified theory* (GUT) which is able to squeeze these two theories, i.e. relativity theory and quantum mechanics, into a single one.[4]

Because not only the universe but also the content of this book are based on these postulates let us summarize them from a quantum computing point of view.

First Postulate (state space): *The actual state of any closed physical system can be described by means of a so-called <u>state vector</u> v having complex coefficients and unit length in a Hilbert space V, i.e. a complex linear vector space (state space) equipped with an inner product.*

A two-dimensional Hilbert space can be regarded as the simplest example of a closed physical system. The state of the system can represented by means of a two-dimensional vector $\mathbf{v} = [a, b]^T = a\mathbf{0} + b\mathbf{1}$, where $\mathbf{0} = [1, 0]^T$ and $\mathbf{1} = [0, 1]^T$ stand for the orthonormal basis vectors of the Hilbert space V and $a, b \in \mathbb{C}$. In order to preserve the unit length constraint the following relation binds together the coefficients $|a|^2 + |b|^2 = 1$. The coordinates of a quantum

---

[4]Roughly speaking the problem can be focused on the geometry of space and time or space-time, which is handled in totally different ways in relativity theory and quantum mechanics.

state vector are often referred as *probability amplitudes* because they play the role of amplitudes in Schrödinger wave functions describing the location of particles.

Second Postulate (evolution): *The evolution of any closed physical system in time can be characterized by means of unitary transforms depending only on the starting and finishing time of the evolution.*

According to the previously introduced physical system the second Postulate can be interpreted as $\mathbf{v}'(t_2) = U(t_1, t_2)\mathbf{v}(t_2)$ and $\mathbf{v}' \in V$.

The above definition describes the evolution between discrete time instants, which is more suitable in the context of quantum computing, however, we cite here its original continuous-time form known as the Schrödinger equation

$$H\mathbf{v} = i\hbar\frac{\partial \mathbf{v}}{\partial t},$$

where $\hbar$ denotes the *Planck's constant*[5] and $H/\hbar$ represents the so-called Hamiltonian, a Hermitian operator characterizing the evolution of the system. Comparing H to U the former is time invariant. The connection between the two approaches can be bridged by means of the following relation

$$U(t_1, t_2) = e^{\frac{-iH(t_2 - t_1)}{\hbar}}.$$

Those readers who are not familiar with operator functions are advised to read Section 12.2.6.

The linear algebraic representation of a unitary operator U is a quadratic matrix $\mathbf{U}$ which consists of elements U_{ij} denoting the conditional probability amplitude connecting input orthonormal basis vector $\mathbf{j}$ with vector $\mathbf{i}$. Unitarity has several equivalent definitions which are summarized in Section 12.2.5.

Third Postulate (measurement): *Any quantum measurement can be described by means of a set of* measurement operators *$\{M_m\}$, where m stands for the possible results of the measurement. The probability of measuring m if the system is in state $\mathbf{v}$ can be calculated as*

$$P(m \mid \mathbf{v}) = \mathbf{v}^\dagger M_m^\dagger M_m \mathbf{v},$$

and the system after measuring m goes to state

$$\mathbf{v}' = \frac{M_m \mathbf{v}}{\sqrt{\mathbf{v}^\dagger M_m^\dagger M_m \mathbf{v}}}.$$

Because classical probability theory requires that

$$\sum_m P(m \mid \mathbf{v}) = \sum_m \mathbf{v}^\dagger M_m^\dagger M_m \mathbf{v} \equiv 1,$$

---

[5]$h = 6.6260755 \cdot 10^{-34}$ Js.

measurement operators have to satisfy the following <u>*completeness relation*</u>

$$\sum_m M_m^\dagger M_m \equiv I.$$

Measurements are obviously not reversible and therefore they represent the only exception under the unitarity constraint. We can say that measurements connect the quantum and classical worlds[6] or measurements are the only tools which allow taking a look at what happens in the quantum world. Unfortunately they prove to be very coarse, like an elephant in a porcelain store, i.e. they influence the system itself under measurement as the second part of the third Postulate and our former discussion about microscopes claim.

The completeness relation is very useful when designing measurements because it allows checking whether all the possible outcomes were taken into account.

Fourth Postulate (composite systems): *The state space of a composite physical system W can be determined using the tensor product of the individual systems $W = V \otimes Y$. Furthermore having defined $\mathbf{v} \in V$ and $\mathbf{y} \in Y$ then the joint state of the composite system is $\mathbf{w} = \mathbf{v} \otimes \mathbf{y}$.*

2.3 QBITS AND QREGISTERS

The postulates of quantum mechanics introduced in the previous section provide exact mathematical formulations of the basic rules of nature. However, they are far from everyday computer scientist or engineering practice. We would rather prefer a higher level abstraction which hides real physical particles and processes and allows the application of such notions as bit, register, gates, circuits and last but not least communication channels because they represent our homely environment. Therefore this section is devoted to building up a similar level of abstraction for the quantum universe.

The smallest information-bearing unit is called a *bit*. It contains either 0 or 1 but only one of them at the same time. A coin is a good classical realization of a bit. It has two sides, a head and a tail, and one can assign logical values 0 and 1 to them. In compliance with the first Postulate the simplest quantum system can be described by means of a two-dimensional complex valued vector in a two-dimensional Hilbert space. We call it a *qbit* and the reader may think of an electron or photon as physical implementations. Column vector $\mathbf{v}$ will be denoted by $|v\rangle$ and pronounced as 'ket v' according to Dirac and the literature.

A qbit has two 'computational basis vectors' $|0\rangle$ and $|1\rangle$ of the Hilbert space corresponding to the classical bit values 0 and 1 and an arbitrary state $|\varphi\rangle$ of a qbit is

---

[6]A coarse definition of a *classical world* is that part of the universe which can be observed by means of the five original senses. Or in a more compact form everything which is above the nanometer scale.

nothing else than a linearly weighted combination of the computational basis vectors

$$|\varphi\rangle = a|0\rangle + b|1\rangle = a \begin{bmatrix} 1 \\ 0 \end{bmatrix} + b \begin{bmatrix} 0 \\ 1 \end{bmatrix} = \begin{bmatrix} a \\ b \end{bmatrix}, \tag{2.3}$$

where the weighting factors $a, b \in \mathbb{C}$ are the so-called probability amplitudes, thus they must satisfy $|a|^2 + |b|^2 = 1$. This is in full harmony with the third Postulate which states when measuring a qbit we will obtain $|0\rangle$ with probability $|a|^2$ and $|1\rangle$ with $|b|^2$, respectively. *We strongly emphasize here again that before the measurement the qbit has both logical values, i.e. it is in both computational basis states at the same time and the measurement allows the qbit to collapse into one of them. This completely differs from the classical approach which assumes that the coin is in one of the logical states before the measurement and the measurement only reveals this fact.*

Computational basis states are orthogonal therefore from a practical point of view the computational basis vectors of a photon can be represented by horizontal and vertical polarization or for an electron, spin up and spin down can play these roles. The terminology widely used in the literature, which refers to the linearly weighted superposition of computational basis vectors (even for more than two-dimensional Hilbert spaces), is *superposition*.

We will denote the row vector corresponding to $|\varphi\rangle$ as $\langle\varphi|$ using the pronunciation 'bra φ'. The relation between column and row vectors are $|\varphi\rangle = (\langle\varphi|)^\dagger$.

The inner (scalar) product of two vectors $|\varphi\rangle$ and $|\psi\rangle$ gives the explanation of these strange names. It has to be written as $\langle\varphi|\psi\rangle$ and as the reader has already guessed we will say 'braket' or more precisely 'bracket' φ and ψ.[7]

Before building more complex systems from qbits let us introduce a spectacular geometrical representation of a single qbit. This requires us to rewrite (2.3) into a more plausible form

$$|\varphi\rangle = e^{j\gamma} \left[\cos\left(\frac{\alpha}{2}\right) |0\rangle + e^{j\beta} \sin\left(\frac{\alpha}{2}\right) |1\rangle \right], \tag{2.4}$$

where $\alpha, \beta, \gamma \in \mathbb{R}$. Factor $e^{j\gamma}$ is called the *global phase*. Since its absolute value equals 1 the global phase does not influence the measurement statistics which rely on the $|\cdot|^2$ function of the probability amplitudes. Due to this reason the global phase is often omitted during the analysis of quantum algorithms and circuits.

While (2.3) can be viewed as a vector in a two-dimensional Descartes (orthogonal) coordinate system whose axes are complex planes requiring four geometrical axes to draw the vector, (2.4) without $e^{j\gamma}$ hides the description of a vector in a three-dimensional polar coordinate system. Polar coordinate systems need two real angles α, β and the length of the vector which is trivially 1 in our case thanks to the first Postulate. This special visualization is linked to Felix Bloch, thus we call the coordinate system in Fig. 2.6 the Bloch sphere. We can convert the polar

---

[7] Dirac had a colorful and witty personality, didn't he?

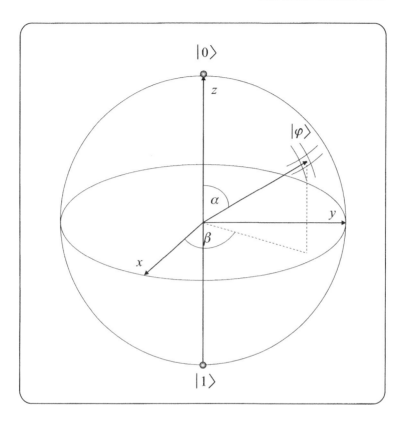

Fig. 2.6 Geometrical visualization of one qbit in the Bloch sphere

coordinates into three-dimensional Descartes coordinates in the following manner

$$|\varphi\rangle = [x, y, z]^T = [\cos(\beta)\sin(\alpha), \sin(\beta)\sin(\alpha), \cos(\alpha)]^T. \qquad (2.5)$$

Finally we emphasize that the Bloch sphere gives visualization up to a global phase $e^{j\gamma}$. If we decide for another γ then $|\varphi\rangle$ will point to another position on the surface.

Similarly to classical computer science a collection of n qbits is called a *qregister* of size n. It may contain any of the $N = 2^n$-dimensional computational basis vectors, n qbit of size, or arbitrary superposition of these vectors. If the content of the qbits of a qregister is known then the state of the qregister can be computed by means of a tensor product in compliance with the fourth Postulate in the following way $|\varphi\rangle = |qbit_{N-1}\rangle \otimes |qbit_{N-2}\rangle \otimes \cdots \otimes |qbit_1\rangle \otimes |qbit_0\rangle$.

Let us consider a simple example with two qbits

$$|\varphi_1\rangle = \frac{|0\rangle + |1\rangle}{\sqrt{2}}, \quad |\varphi_2\rangle = \frac{|0\rangle + |1\rangle}{\sqrt{2}}.$$

When we join the two qbits we yield a four-dimensional qregister $|\varphi\rangle$

$$|\varphi\rangle \equiv |\varphi_1\rangle|\varphi_2\rangle \equiv |\varphi_1, \varphi_2\rangle \equiv |\varphi_1 \varphi_2\rangle$$
$$= \frac{|0\rangle \otimes |0\rangle + |1\rangle \otimes |0\rangle + |0\rangle \otimes |1\rangle + |1\rangle \otimes |1\rangle}{2} = \frac{|00\rangle + |01\rangle + |10\rangle + |11\rangle}{2}.$$

This result explains that the state of a two-qbit register consists of four, linearly weighted (by probability amplitudes) computational basis vectors. These vectors – 00, 01, 10 and 11 – are nothing else than the potential contents of a classical two-bit register. However, in our quantum case all of them are squeezed into a single qregister. States which can be produced from individual lower dimensional states by means of tensor product are called *product states*.

What happens if we measure the first qbit? Let us assume $|\varphi_1\rangle = |0\rangle$ as the measurement outcome. The state of the qregister changes because of the measurement to

$$|\varphi\rangle = |0\rangle \otimes \frac{|0\rangle + |1\rangle}{\sqrt{2}} = \frac{|00\rangle + |11\rangle}{\sqrt{2}},$$

which highlights the fact that a qregister does not contain necessarily all the basis vectors. More precisely we should say that the missing computational basis states are present in the superposition but with zero probability amplitudes.

If we generalize this simple example with two gbits to an n-gbit register then its general state can be characterized by

$$|\varphi\rangle = \sum_{i=0}^{2^n - 1} \varphi_i |i\rangle,$$

where φ_i represents the probability amplitude belonging to the computational basis state $|i\rangle$. Wait! Is it true than that such a qregister contains 2^n different classical numbers at the same time? The answer is unanimously *yes*. The consequences prove to be really dizzying. Provided $n = 500$ the corresponding qregister comprises more classical numbers than the number of all atoms in the known universe! In order to picture how large this 2^{500} is we assume an extraterrestrial being which decided shortly after the big bang to move *only* a point of a pencil made of black lead from one place on her desk to another, carbon atom by carbon atom. She started this persistence-requiring hobby about 15,000,000,000 years ago. If she takes an atom each second then she has only completed $\frac{1}{100,000}$ of the job although only a small point of pencil has been considered. . .

Furthermore we are able to perform a mathematical operation in a single step on all the numbers, which can be regarded as an extraordinary parallel processing capability. Unfortunately as we will see later only one of the numbers can be accessed when asking (measuring) about the content of the qregister. Therefore the real challenge is not the usage of quantum parallelism, but to design suitable gates or algorithms which are able to increase the probability amplitude of the wanted result as close to 1 as possible thus ensuring almost certain success during the measurement.

Finally we mention here that our attempts to give geometrical visualization of quantum systems has ended with the one-qbit Bloch sphere because the organs of senses of human race are confined to three space dimensions.

2.4 ELEMENTARY QUANTUM GATES

We have outlined the analogy between classical and quantum computing in terms of how to describe information-storing entities called *registers*. The next obvious question is how to generalize classical operations (logic gates and circuits) on classical registers to their quantum counterparts. The second Postulate clearly explains that time evolution of the states of quantum registers can be modelled by means of unitary operators which are often referred to as quantum gates. Therefore a *quantum gate* can be regarded as an elementary quantum-computing device which performs a fixed unitary operation on selected qbits in a fixed period of time. One-qbit quantum gates are called *elementary quantum gates*. Since unitary operators have several interesting and useful properties we suggest the reader jumps to Section 12.2.5 for a few moments.

Before getting acquainted with some widely used simple quantum gates let us take a short detour to clarify an apparent paradox. We know that unitary operators are *reversible* and they are implementing a *distance-preserving mapping*. Furthermore we have learned that the quantum description of nature is more general than the classical one, that is there may exist quantum phenomena that cannot be explained using the classical theory but quantum mechanical postulates have to fit to all classical events. However, even the reader is able to list classical logic gates which are not reversible such as AND, XOR, etc. For instance if an XOR gate[8] emits a 1 we cannot be sure whether the inputs were (0,0) or (1,1). The situation seems to be very hard, maybe quantum mechanics is not complete? In order to banish the storm-clouds we suggest reading again the corresponding postulate. It begins with 'The evolution of any *closed physical system...*', which gives the key. AND and XOR gates are not closed systems. If we extended the XOR gate with an extra output bit (e.g. it is enough to connect one of the inputs to this extra output) then we would be able to reveal both input bits unambiguously. In full compliance with this conclusion unitary gates have quadratic matrices i.e. they have the same number of inputs and outputs.

Now the time has come to introduce several basic, one-qbit quantum gates U. We will present their operation on most general one-qbit state $|\varphi\rangle = a|0\rangle + b|1\rangle$ and the outcome state will be referred as $|\psi\rangle = U|\varphi\rangle$. We start with the quantum analogy of

---

[8] Irreversibility of the XOR gate can also be originated from the fact that it has two input bits but only a single one-bit output.

the classical inverter called the *bit-flip gate* or Pauli-X gate

$$|\psi\rangle = X|\varphi\rangle = \begin{bmatrix} 0 & 1 \\ 1 & 0 \end{bmatrix} \begin{bmatrix} a \\ b \end{bmatrix} = b|0\rangle + a|1\rangle.$$

It is easy to see that the bit-flip gate exchanges the probability amplitudes of the computational basis states. Considering the classical case, that is $|\varphi\rangle = |0\rangle$ or $|1\rangle$, $|\psi\rangle$ will be the inverse of $|\varphi\rangle$.

Our next quantum gate has no classical predecessor but it is rather motivated by the bit-flip gate. The Pauli-Z or *phase-flip gate* flips the phase of the input state

$$|\psi\rangle = Z|\varphi\rangle = \begin{bmatrix} 1 & 0 \\ 0 & -1 \end{bmatrix} \begin{bmatrix} a \\ b \end{bmatrix} = a|0\rangle - b|1\rangle.$$

As a simple rule of thumb one can realize that the phase-flip gate multiplies the probability amplitude of computational basis state $|1\rangle$ by -1.

To make the set of Pauli-gates complete we define the Pauli-Y gate in the following way

$$|\psi\rangle = Y|\varphi\rangle = \begin{bmatrix} 0 & -j \\ j & 0 \end{bmatrix} \begin{bmatrix} a \\ b \end{bmatrix} = \begin{bmatrix} -jb \\ ja \end{bmatrix} = -jb|0\rangle + ja|1\rangle,$$

which results in exchanged probability amplitudes multiplied by j.

The effect of Pauli gates can be easily visualized exploiting the Bloch sphere from the previous subsection. Rotations around the x, y and z axes can be generated by Pauli gates. For instance a rotation by angle α around the x axis can be expressed as

$$e^{-j\frac{\alpha}{2}X} = \cos\left(\frac{\alpha}{2}\right) I - j \sin\left(\frac{\alpha}{2}\right) X,$$

where we exploited the definition of operator functions discussed in Section 12.2.6.

A simple sheet of glass can behave as an elementary quantum gate as we will see soon in Section 2.8. Its quantum logic name is *phase-rotator gate* or *phase gate* and it performs the following operation

$$|\psi\rangle = P(\alpha)|\varphi\rangle = \begin{bmatrix} 1 & 0 \\ 0 & e^{j\alpha} \end{bmatrix} \begin{bmatrix} a \\ e^{j\alpha}b \end{bmatrix} = a|0\rangle + e^{j\alpha}b|1\rangle.$$

Finally we discuss the so-called Hadamard gate. For a general input it produces

$$|\psi\rangle = H|\varphi\rangle = \frac{1}{\sqrt{2}}\begin{bmatrix} 1 & 1 \\ 1 & -1 \end{bmatrix}\overbrace{\begin{bmatrix} \frac{a+b}{\sqrt{2}} \\ \frac{a-b}{\sqrt{2}} \end{bmatrix}}^{\begin{bmatrix} a \\ b \end{bmatrix}} = \frac{a+b}{\sqrt{2}}|0\rangle + \frac{a-b}{\sqrt{2}}|1\rangle. \quad (2.6)$$

It is easy to see taking a look at the related matrix that the Hadamard gate is not only unitary but it is Hermitian ($H^\dagger = H$), too. Furthermore $HH = I$ as the reader can deduce in **Exercise** 2.1. Pauli gates and the Hadamard gate have special connections explained in **Exercise** 2.2, $HXH = Z$, $HYH = -Y$ and $HZH = X$. The first and the third relations highlight the fact that the bit-flip and phase-flip gates can substitute for each other when Hadamard gates are available i.e they are equivalents up to the Hadamard transform.

Because Hadamard gates are often initialized with classical inputs in many quantum-computing algorithms we provide here the corresponding outputs

$$H|0\rangle = \frac{|0\rangle + |1\rangle}{\sqrt{2}},$$

$$H|1\rangle = \frac{|0\rangle - |1\rangle}{\sqrt{2}}. \quad (2.7)$$

Both results suggest that a *Hadamard gate feeded with classical states creates a uniformly distributed superposition of all the computational basis vectors and only the sign of the amplitudes may vary.* This simple observation can be easily generalized for n-qbit registers whose each individual qbit is connected to a one-qbit Hadamard gate. First we present the outcome provided an all-zero input $|\varphi\rangle = |000\ldots0\rangle$

$$|\psi\rangle = H^{\otimes n}|\varphi\rangle = \frac{1}{\sqrt{2^n}}\sum_{i=0}^{2^n-1}|i\rangle, \quad (2.8)$$

where $H^{\otimes n}$ stands for the joined n-qbit Hadamard gate. If we use an arbitrary computational basis state $|k\rangle, k = 0, 1, \ldots, 2^n - 1$ as the input then the output superposition can be computed in the following manner

$$H^{\otimes n}|k\rangle = \frac{1}{\sqrt{2^n}}\sum_{i=0}^{2^n-1}(-1)^{ik}|i\rangle, \quad (2.9)$$

where ik refers to the binary scalar product of the two decimal numbers considering them as binary vectors (sum of bitwise products modulo 2).

Next we use the Hadamard gate to emphasize the *superposition principle* which proves to be often very useful when analyzing quantum circuits or algorithms. We applied the matrix-vector operation to compute the outcome of the Hadamard gate assuming arbitrary initial superposition in (2.6). The same results can be achieved if the gate is feeded with each computational basis state individually and the results are added together. Equations (2.7) presented the requested individual output states thus

$$|\psi\rangle = H|\varphi\rangle = a\frac{|0\rangle + |1\rangle}{\sqrt{2}} + b\frac{|0\rangle - |1\rangle}{\sqrt{2}} = \frac{a+b}{\sqrt{2}}|0\rangle + \frac{a-b}{\sqrt{2}}|1\rangle,$$

which reinforces (see (2.6)) the applicability of the superposition principle.

We close this subsection with some useful definitions. A *quantum network* or *quantum circuit* is a quantum-computing device consisting of quantum logic gates whose computational steps are synchronized in time. The outputs of some of the gates are connected by wires to the inputs of others. The size of the network is its number of gates. A *quantum computer* will be viewed in this book as a quantum network (or a group of quantum networks). The term *quantum computation/computing* is defined as a unitary evolution of the network which takes its initial input state to some final output state.

Exercise 2.1. Prove in several different ways that $HH = I$.

Exercise 2.2. Prove that $HXH = Z$, $HYH = -Y$ and $HZH = X$.

2.5 GENERAL DESCRIPTION OF THE INTERFEROMETER

We have provided a plausible explanation based on complex valued probability amplitudes in Section 2.1 when the $\sqrt{I}$ gate were explained. Now, in possession of the Postulates of quantum mechanics and having gathered some experiences with simple quantum transformations it is worth describing the operation of the interferometer. Fig. 2.7 depicts a more general architecture than the previously discussed one, that is two sheets of glass were deployed into the ways of photons. Their role is to introduce different delays into the propagation along the two paths and thus enabling a more general description of the interferometer.

Since this is our first quantum circuit analysis we use the linear algebraic approach and follow the operation step by step. On the other hand we ask the reader to perform the analysis by means of the plausible *superposition principle* in **Exercise** 2.3.

First we define the transforms implemented by hardware elements providing a quantum-computing type abstraction. The matrix describing a beam splitter can be easily produced taking into account the block diagram of the probabilistic $\sqrt{I}$ gate and assigning logical in- and outputs while having in sight Fig. 2.7 and considering that H_{ij} stands for the conditional probability amplitude connecting the input computational basis state $|j\rangle$ to output $|i\rangle$, $i, j \in \{0, 1\}$

$$\mathbf{H} = \frac{1}{\sqrt{2}}\begin{bmatrix} 1 & 1 \\ 1 & -1 \end{bmatrix}$$

which is nothing else than the Hadamard gate. The two sheets of glass are functioning as phase shifters acting on different computational basis vectors thus

$$\mathbf{P} = \begin{bmatrix} e^{j\alpha_0} & 0 \\ 0 & e^{j\alpha_1} \end{bmatrix}.$$

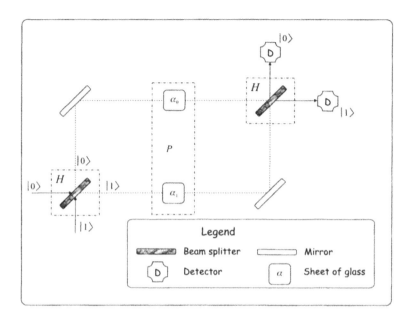

Fig. 2.7 Generalized interferometer

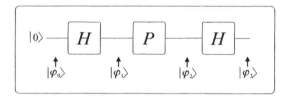

Fig. 2.8 Abstract quantum circuit of the generalized interferometer

For the sake of practicing what we have learned let us calculate the input and output states of each gate in detail, only this time in compliance with Fig. 2.8. Shooting photons horizontally onto the first half-silvered mirror means an initial state $|\varphi_0\rangle = |0\rangle$. The beam splitter carries out a Hadamard transform

$$|\varphi_1\rangle = H|\varphi_0\rangle = \frac{1}{\sqrt{2}} \begin{bmatrix} 1 & 1 \\ 1 & -1 \end{bmatrix} \begin{bmatrix} 1 \\ 0 \end{bmatrix} = \begin{bmatrix} \frac{1}{\sqrt{2}} \\ \frac{1}{\sqrt{2}} \end{bmatrix}.$$

Next the phase shifter has to be applied

$$|\varphi_2\rangle = P|\varphi_1\rangle = \begin{bmatrix} e^{j\alpha_0} & 0 \\ 0 & e^{j\alpha_1} \end{bmatrix} \begin{bmatrix} \frac{e^{j\alpha_0}}{\sqrt{2}} \\ \frac{e^{j\alpha_1}}{\sqrt{2}} \end{bmatrix}.$$

Finally the second beam splitter takes care of interfering the two paths

$$|\varphi_3\rangle = H|\varphi_2\rangle = \frac{1}{\sqrt{2}} \begin{bmatrix} 1 & 1 \\ 1 & -1 \end{bmatrix} \begin{bmatrix} \frac{e^{j\alpha_0}+e^{j\alpha_1}}{2} \\ \frac{e^{j\alpha_0}-e^{j\alpha_1}}{2} \end{bmatrix}.$$

In order to understand the operation of the interferometer it is worth converting $|\varphi_3\rangle$ into a more illustrative form

$$|\varphi_3\rangle = \frac{e^{j\alpha_0} + e^{j\alpha_1}}{2}|0\rangle + \frac{e^{j\alpha_0} - e^{j\alpha_1}}{2}|1\rangle$$

$$= e^{j\frac{\alpha_0+\alpha_1}{2}} \left(\frac{e^{j\frac{\alpha_0-\alpha_1}{2}} + e^{-j\frac{\alpha_0-\alpha_1}{2}}}{2}|0\rangle + \frac{e^{j\frac{\alpha_0-\alpha_1}{2}} - e^{-j\frac{\alpha_0-\alpha_1}{2}}}{2}|1\rangle \right).$$

The term $e^{j\frac{\alpha_0+\alpha_1}{2}}$ can be omitted during further analysis because it represents the global phase and thus it does not influence the final measurement statistics. Moreover let us introduce $\Delta\alpha \triangleq \alpha_0 - \alpha_1$. With respect to the well-known relations $\frac{e^{j\Delta\alpha}+e^{-j\Delta\alpha}}{2} = \cos(\Delta\alpha), \frac{e^{j\Delta\alpha}-e^{-j\Delta\alpha}}{2j} = \sin(\Delta\alpha)$ we reach

$$|\varphi_3\rangle = \cos\left(\frac{\Delta\alpha}{2}\right)|0\rangle + j\sin\left(\frac{\Delta\alpha}{2}\right)|1\rangle.$$

Now, we are able to determine the probabilities of hitting the photon with the horizontal or vertical detector

$$P_0 = \cos^2\left(\frac{\Delta\alpha}{2}\right) = (1 + \cos(\Delta\alpha))\frac{1}{2},$$

$$P_1 = \sin^2\left(\frac{\Delta\alpha}{2}\right) = (1 - \cos(\Delta\alpha))\frac{1}{2}.$$

If $\Delta\alpha = 0$ then we yield the idealistic scenario (i.e. no phase shifters) that is one of the paths is cancelled due to the interference and the operation becomes fully deterministic. Provided a $\frac{\pi}{2}$ difference exists between the two paths both detectors are hit equiprobable. Obviously the operation depends only on $\Delta\alpha$ which represents the difference in the thickness of the sheets placed into the two paths in our experiment. This harmonizes with the fact that the global phase can be omitted from the outcome statistics point of view.

Exercise 2.3. Perform the analysis of the generalized interferometer using the superposition principle.

2.6 ENTANGLEMENT

2.6.1 A surprising quantum state – entanglement

If we ask the reader to determine the individual one-qbit states of a 2-qbit quantum register $|\varphi\rangle = a|00\rangle + b|01\rangle$, then recalling the 4th Postulate, which advises us how to handle individual and corresponding merged system, one can easily calculate $|\varphi_1\rangle = |0\rangle$ and $|\varphi_2\rangle = a|0\rangle + b|1\rangle$, where $|\varphi\rangle = |\varphi_1\rangle \otimes |\varphi_2\rangle$.

Now we are interested in the decomposition of $|\varphi\rangle = a|00\rangle + b|11\rangle$. Interestingly this effort proves to be fruitless because no individual one-qbit states exist at all. One may think at first sight that such a $|\varphi\rangle$ is not allowed by quantum mechanics. However, if we consider that $|\varphi\rangle$ can be regarded as a special two-qbit superposition having zero probability amplitudes for computational basis states $|01\rangle$ and $|10\rangle$ then this simple answer seems to be more than doubtful. As we will see soon such special states can be produced easily but of course not by means of joining two single qbits (see Section 2.6.2).

Let us investigate the potentialities hidden in $|\varphi\rangle$. If we decide to measure the first qbit then either $|0\rangle$ or $|1\rangle$ will be obtained randomly with corresponding probabilities $|a|^2$ and $|b|^2$, respectively. However, provided the measuring equipment answers 0 then a measurement on the second qbit can lead only to 0. Similarly a 1 on the first qbit results in 1 with sure success on the second one. It looks like there is a mysterious connection between the two qbits! Carefully designed experiments proved that this interesting effect remains valid even if the qbits of $|\varphi\rangle$ is delivered onto two distant locations. Furthermore surprisingly the propagation of this binding effect between the two qbits after the first measurement takes zero time, i.e. it is much faster than the speed would need. Wait! This effect seems to be in total contradiction of Einstein's relativity theory with bounded speed of any signal or effect.[9] Not surprisingly Einstein had never accepted in his life this consequence of quantum mechanical description of the Nature. But experiments (see Section 2.6.5) performed after his death disproved Einstein's belief...

Bowing to the arguments of experimental physicians we turn to exploit this strange property of nature, but first let us introduce the related terminology. States whose decomposition comprise one-qbit states are called *product states* while

---

[9]It is worth citing Einstein's interpretation of relativity theory: "When a man sits with a pretty girl for an hour, it seems like a minute. But let him sit on a hot stove for a minute and it's longer than any hour. That's relativity."

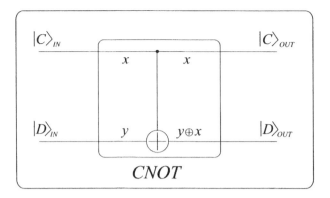

Fig. 2.9 Controlled NOT gate

qbits/qregisters bounded together by this special phenomenon are referred to as *entangled states*. What if our two assistants Alice and Bob share an entangled pair and Bob travels to another city. If Alice were able to influence the results of her measurement then she could transmit a binary encoded message to Bob faster than any communication device, even those ones using light or electromagnetic radiation. Fortunately (at least from a relativity theory point of view) as we will see soon in Section 2.6.5 it is out of her possibilities. However, the reader should not be disappointed about our first unsuccessful attempt. Although Alice and Bob failed with the faster than light communications, entanglement still remains one of the most efficient tools of quantum computing and communications enabling e.g. teleportation (see Section 4.2) and is thus often mentioned as a basic resource. In order to be able to exploit this strange gift of Nature we need to learn first how to produce it and what disadvantageous consequences should be taken into account. Therefore the forthcoming sections are devoted to discussing different aspects of entanglement.

2.6.2   The CNOT gate as classical copy machine and quantum entangler

Let us now focus on the exciting question of how to produce an entangled pair of qbits if a tensor product does not lead to it. As the first step we introduce a simple but very important two-qbit gate called *controlled NOT* or CNOT. If we use classical inputs then it operates in the following manner. One of its inputs is referred as *data* and the other as *control*. Both inputs can be fed with 0 or 1. If the control has been initialized with 0 then the CNOT gate simply connects the data input to the data output. Conversely a control with 1 results in an inverted data output. Thus the name of the gate becomes obvious for the reader.

For the sake of being precise this set of rules has been summarized in a circuit implementing the functionality of CNOT and is depicted in Fig. 2.9 with the

Table 2.1 Truth table of controlled NOT gate

IN		OUT	
x	y	x	$y \oplus x$
0	0	0	$0 \oplus 0 = 0$
0	1	0	$1 \oplus 0 = 1$
1	0	1	$0 \oplus 1 = 1$
1	1	1	$1 \oplus 1 = 0$

corresponding truth table (see Table 2.1) and master equation

$$CNOT : |x\rangle|y\rangle \rightarrow |x\rangle|y \oplus x\rangle. \tag{2.10}$$

We strongly emphasize here that x and y are classical values (i.e. computational basis states 0 and 1).

As a next step let us derive the matrix of the CNOT gate. We can follow two ways. On one hand the truth table advises us that the CNOT gate connects the input and output classical dibits in the following manner $|00\rangle \rightarrow |00\rangle$, $|01\rangle \rightarrow |01\rangle$, $|10\rangle \rightarrow |11\rangle$ and $|11\rangle \rightarrow |10\rangle$ thus

$$\mathbf{CNOT} = \begin{bmatrix} 1 & 0 & 0 & 0 \\ 0 & 1 & 0 & 0 \\ 0 & 0 & 0 & 1 \\ 0 & 0 & 1 & 0 \end{bmatrix}, \tag{2.11}$$

where we remind the reader that it is enough to consider the computational basis states when deducing the matrix of a unitary transform thanks to the superposition principle. A bit more pragmatic way to write up the matrix is if one realizes that the CNOT gate is nothing more than a controlled Pauli-X gate, hence we need an identity matrix in the upper left corner and a matrix $\mathbf{X}$ in the lower right-hand side corner.

The CNOT gate is obviously unitary, which fact can be easily recognized using that definition which states that the rows/columns of its matrix should form an orthogonal set of unit vectors.

The COPY command is a fairly common one often used by computer scientists and programmers. It is worth pointing out that the CNOT gate can be regarded as a one-bit copy machine. Provided its data input is initialized permanently with $|0\rangle$ then the CNOT gate emits a copy of the control input on each output.

Now let us try to make a copy of $|C\rangle_{IN} = a|0\rangle + b|1\rangle$. The input joint state is $|C\rangle_{IN} \otimes |D\rangle_{IN} = a|00\rangle + b|10\rangle$. Using the superposition principle one gets $a|0, 0 \oplus 0\rangle + b|1, 1 \oplus 0\rangle = a|00\rangle + b|11\rangle$ at the output which is nothing less than an *entangled pair*! The same result can be achieved using an algebraic matrix-vector operation.

Our mood is a bit ambivalent. On one hand we learned how to produce an entangled pair but on the other hand we have failed with copying an arbitrary

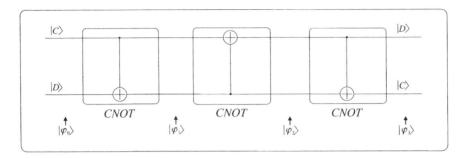

Fig. 2.10   SWAP gate made of CNOTs

quantum state. As we will see in Section 2.7 our worry is not groundless. However, at this moment we are satisfied with our entangler gate.

Finally before discussing several special entangled pairs we introduce an interesting application of the CNOT gate. Many sophisticated quantum algorithms require a gate which is able to reverse (swap) the sequence of quantum wires. The gate implementing this useful functionality is called a SWAP gate. Fig. 2.10 presents three concatenated CNOT gates swapping two quantum wires.

Thanks to the superposition principle it is enough to investigate the operation of the SWAP gate assuming computational basis state inputs $|i\rangle$ and $|k\rangle$ where $i, k \in \{0, 1\}$. Instead of exploiting the matrix definition of the CNOT gate let us rely on Fig. 2.9. The system is initialized with $|\varphi_0\rangle = |i\rangle \otimes |k\rangle$. The output of the first CNOT is simply $|\varphi_1\rangle = |i\rangle \otimes |i \oplus k\rangle$. When computing the output of the middle CNOT gate we take into account that the roles of control and data wires have to be swapped thus

$$|\varphi_2\rangle = |i \oplus (i \oplus k)\rangle \otimes |i \oplus k\rangle = |k\rangle \otimes |i \oplus k\rangle.$$

Finally the third CNOT gate produces

$$|\varphi_3\rangle = |k\rangle \otimes |(i \oplus k) \oplus k\rangle = |k\rangle \otimes |i\rangle.$$

We give the opportunity to the reader to prove that he/she really managed to understand how the SWAP gate operates in **Exercise** 2.4 where we ask the reader to calculate its matrix.

Exercise 2.4. Calculate the matrix of the two-qbit SWAP gate.

2.6.3   Bell states

Obviously an infinite number of different entangled pairs can be defined by only varying probability amplitudes of $|\varphi\rangle = a|00\rangle + b|11\rangle$. Moreover computational basis states $|01\rangle$ and $|10\rangle$ also form a suitable subset of all possible two-qbit basis

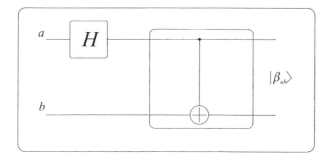

Fig. 2.11 Bell state generator quantum circuit

vectors. There are four distinguished entangled pairs called *Bell states* or *EPR pairs*

$$|\beta_{00}\rangle = \frac{|00\rangle + |11\rangle}{\sqrt{2}},$$

$$|\beta_{01}\rangle = \frac{|01\rangle + |10\rangle}{\sqrt{2}},$$

$$|\beta_{10}\rangle = \frac{|00\rangle - |11\rangle}{\sqrt{2}},$$

$$|\beta_{11}\rangle = \frac{|01\rangle - |10\rangle}{\sqrt{2}}.$$

For the sake of memory a compact formula can be derived

$$|\beta_{ab}\rangle = \frac{|0, b\rangle + (-1)^a |1, NOT(b)\rangle}{\sqrt{2}}, \tag{2.12}$$

where $a, b \in \{0, 1\}$. The corresponding quantum circuit which can be used to produce the Bell states can be seen in Fig. 2.11.

Bell states have an often exploited important property, namely they form an orthonormal vector set which is equivalent to the fact – as we will see later – that they can be distinguished unambiguously.

Obviously entangled pairs can be generalized to entangled triplets, e.g. $\frac{|000\rangle + |111\rangle}{\sqrt{2}}$, which are often referred to in the literature as *Greenberg–Horne–Zeilinger states* (GHZ states). The generator quantum circuit for n-qbit orthogonal entangled states is depicted in Fig. 2.12 that has to be fed with n-qbit computational basis states. Fig. 2.12 has an important lesson. If we have say an entangled pair divided between two parties and a third player would like to entangle his/her qbit with the other ones then it is enough to meet with the player holding the Hadamard gate and what is more it can be easily shown that not only the first quantum wire is suitable for control purposes but any entangled wire can be used, too. Therefore to spread entanglement it is enough to access one of the entangled qbits. Unfortunately

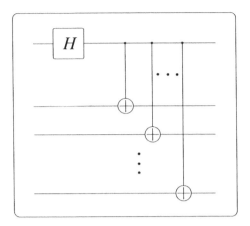

Fig. 2.12 Generalized quantum entangler

this concession cannot be further softened i.e. by means of classical communication only we are not able to entangle two qbits.

2.6.4 Entanglement with the environment – decoherence

The interferometer and entanglement
Every real system, whether it is quantum or classical is in contact with an external environment – a noisy collection of particles whose state can never be perfectly known. Of course the system and the environment together form a closed quantum system for which the postulates of the quantum mechanics are valid. This entanglement between the system and the environment in which it is embedded leads the system to change its state over time randomly from the observer point of view. This process is known as *decoherence*. In order to illustrate this unwanted effect we turn to the interferometer whose operation was exhaustively analyzed in Section 2.5.

The system in question will be the photon travelling through the interferometer while the environment contains the whole universe except the photon. As we discussed earlier (see Fig. 2.7) we shoot the photon horizontally into the system represented by $|0\rangle$ while the initial state of the environment is denoted by $|\Omega\rangle$. The photon passes a beam splitter (i.e. a Hadamard gate) which is followed by a phase shifter producing

$$|\varphi_2\rangle = \frac{e^{j\alpha_0}|0\rangle + e^{j\alpha_1}|1\rangle}{\sqrt{2}}|\Omega\rangle = |\varphi_2\rangle = \frac{e^{j\alpha_0}|0\rangle|\Omega\rangle + e^{j\alpha_1}|1\rangle|\Omega\rangle}{\sqrt{2}}.$$

for the closed system (photon + universe) according to Fig. 2.8.

At this point suddenly an intelligent quantum butterfly incarnates the entanglement between the photon and the universe in the following manner. If the system (photon) is in state $|0\rangle$ then it flies to a white flower causing the universe to change to $|\Omega_0\rangle$ else it lands on a red flower resulting in the environment in state $|\Omega_1\rangle$. This simple rule can be described more precisely, namely

$$|0\rangle|\Omega\rangle \rightarrow |0\rangle|\Omega_0\rangle, |1\rangle|\Omega\rangle \rightarrow |1\rangle|\Omega_1\rangle.$$

Therefore the butterfly changes $|\varphi_2\rangle$ to

$$|\varphi_2'\rangle = |\varphi_2\rangle = \frac{e^{j\alpha_0}|0\rangle|\Omega_0\rangle + e^{j\alpha_1}|1\rangle|\Omega_1\rangle}{\sqrt{2}}.$$

The second Hadamard gate makes the two paths interfered

$$
\begin{aligned}
|\varphi_3\rangle &= \frac{e^{j\alpha_0}\frac{|0\rangle+|1\rangle}{\sqrt{2}}|\Omega_0\rangle + e^{j\alpha_1}\frac{|0\rangle-|1\rangle}{\sqrt{2}}|\Omega_1\rangle}{\sqrt{2}} \\
&= |0\rangle\frac{e^{j\alpha_0}|\Omega_0\rangle + e^{j\alpha_1}|\Omega_1\rangle}{2} + |1\rangle\frac{e^{j\alpha_0}|\Omega_0\rangle - e^{j\alpha_1}|\Omega_1\rangle}{2} \\
&= e^{j\frac{\alpha_0+\alpha_1}{2}}\left(|0\rangle\frac{e^{j\frac{\alpha_0-\alpha_1}{2}}|\Omega_0\rangle + e^{-j\frac{\alpha_0-\alpha_1}{2}}|\Omega_1\rangle}{2}\right. \\
&\qquad\qquad \left. + |1\rangle\frac{e^{j\frac{\alpha_0-\alpha_1}{2}}|\Omega_0\rangle - e^{-j\frac{\alpha_0-\alpha_1}{2}}|\Omega_1\rangle}{2}\right).
\end{aligned}
$$

Omitting the global phase and using $\Delta\alpha \triangleq \alpha_0 - \alpha_1$ again we obtain

$$|\varphi_3\rangle = |0\rangle\frac{e^{j\frac{\Delta\alpha}{2}}|\Omega_0\rangle + e^{-j\frac{\Delta\alpha}{2}}|\Omega_1\rangle}{2} + |1\rangle\frac{e^{j\frac{\Delta\alpha}{2}}|\Omega_0\rangle - e^{-j\frac{\Delta\alpha}{2}}|\Omega_1\rangle}{2}.$$

When deducing the probability of measuring $|0\rangle$ or $|1\rangle$ we must be careful because $|\Omega_0\rangle$ and $|\Omega_1\rangle$ are not orthogonal by all means, i.e. $\langle\Omega_0|\Omega_1\rangle \neq 0$. $|\Omega_1\rangle$ can be expressed by means of its projection onto $|\Omega_0\rangle$ and onto an orthogonal vector $|\Omega_0^\perp\rangle$ in the form of

$$|\Omega_1\rangle = \langle\Omega_0|\Omega_1\rangle|\Omega_0\rangle + \sqrt{1 - |\langle\Omega_0|\Omega_1\rangle|^2}\,|\Omega_0^\perp\rangle,$$

where for the sake of simplicity we assumed that $|\Omega_0\rangle$ and $|\Omega_1\rangle$ are unit length states and $\langle\Omega_0|\Omega_1\rangle$ is real thus

$$
\begin{aligned}
|\varphi_3\rangle &= \frac{e^{j\frac{\Delta\alpha}{2}} + \langle\Omega_0|\Omega_1\rangle e^{-j\frac{\Delta\alpha}{2}}}{2}|0\rangle|\Omega_0\rangle + \frac{e^{-j\frac{\Delta\alpha}{2}}}{2}\sqrt{1 - |\langle\Omega_0|\Omega_1\rangle|^2}\,|0\rangle|\Omega_0^\perp\rangle \\
&\quad + \frac{e^{j\frac{\Delta\alpha}{2}} - \langle\Omega_0|\Omega_1\rangle e^{-j\frac{\Delta\alpha}{2}}}{2}|1\rangle|\Omega_0\rangle - \frac{e^{-j\frac{\Delta\alpha}{2}}}{2}\sqrt{1 - |\langle\Omega_0|\Omega_1\rangle|^2}\,|1\rangle|\Omega_0^\perp\rangle.
\end{aligned}
$$

Now we are able to calculate the probability of hitting the detector belonging to state $|0\rangle$

$$P_0 = \left|\frac{e^{j\frac{\Delta\alpha}{2}} + \langle\Omega_0|\Omega_1\rangle e^{-j\frac{\Delta\alpha}{2}}}{2}\right|^2 + \left|\frac{e^{-j\frac{\Delta\alpha}{2}}}{2}\sqrt{1 - |\langle\Omega_0|\Omega_1\rangle|^2}\right|^2.$$

Having in sight that for any $z \in \mathbb{C} : |z|^2 = zz^*$ and substituting $\frac{e^{j\Delta\alpha} + e^{-j\Delta\alpha}}{2}$ with $\cos(\Delta\alpha)$ one gets

$$P_0 = (1 + \langle \Omega_0|\Omega_1 \rangle \cos(\Delta\alpha)) \tfrac{1}{2}.$$

Using similar techniques we obtain

$$P_1 = (1 - \langle \Omega_0|\Omega_1 \rangle \cos(\Delta\alpha)) \tfrac{1}{2}.$$

These results differ from the unentangled scenario discussed in Section 2.5 only in term $\langle \Omega_0|\Omega_1 \rangle$, that is we managed to concentrate the effect of the entanglement into a single quantity which can be easily interpreted. Obviously if $\langle \Omega_0|\Omega_1 \rangle = 1$, i.e. the two states of the environment are parallel/equal then entanglement disappears and the interferometer operates deterministically. The opposite extreme scenario happens if $\langle \Omega_0|\Omega_1 \rangle = 0$, which belongs to orthogonal environmental states. $P_0 = P_1 = 0.5$ represents a maximally entangled photon and environment, namely the interferometer becomes fully random. Of course there are many intermediate scenarios introducing more or less randomness into the operation. Thus we can conclude that an observer placed in the system will experience entanglement as happening random events while from the closed system point of view we see that events in the environment influence the system in a well-defined way. Therefore reducing the effects of entanglement with the environment (decoherence) is crucial when designing and building quantum mechanics based computers or communication devices.

Schrödinger's cat
Although Schrödinger's equation was an important step leading to the theory of quantum mechanics, Schrödinger[10] was sure that several contradictions still remained open between the classical and quantum description of Nature. In order to show that quantum superpositions make sense, he suggested the following thought-experiment.

Let us put an everyday *macroscopic* cat into a metal box together with a devilish equipment that consists of a *microscopic* radioactive atom, a hammer and a cyanide capsule. We know that the atom decays with certain probability. This effect triggers the hammer to hit the capsule, which kills our poor cat. When we start the experiment everything is clear. The cat is alive and we close the box. The atom can be represented as a qbit being in state $|not - decayed\rangle$. However, after closing the box the state of the atom turns to a superposition of $|not - decayed\rangle$ and $|decayed\rangle$. Than Schrödinger asks us whether the cat is dead or still alive? Obviously we can answer this question via opening the box and making sure with our eyes about the result. But if we are not allowed to look into the box we can say in possession of quantum theory that the cat is in a special superposition of states $|alive\rangle$ and $|dead\rangle$. The next forthcoming question is very obvious: when does the cat die?

---

[10]"I do not like it, and I am sorry I ever had anything to do with it." Erwin Schrödinger, speaking of quantum mechanics.

According to Bohr's approach conscious observation is what causes real events to happen. He thought there is an aspect of the world described by the evolution of probabilities in quantum mechanics and another aspect of the world that we observe. Whenever we open the box, i.e. make a measurement, we obtain some definite result and not just a probability. However, if we do not look there then no events happen and only probabilities are changing. Thus Bohr's interpretation assumes that the observer and the observed system cannot be dissociated.

Bohr's idea is called the *Copenhagen interpretation* of quantum mechanics. It is important to highlight that this is an *interpretation* and not a *theory*. This means that we are not able to test it using sophisticated measurements, it gives only a philosophical explanation. Another popular *interpretation* assumes that a large amount of parallel universes (worlds) exist, one for each possible measurement outcome (thus we have two cats one dead and another one alive) and when measuring the system we only select one of them. Independently from the interpretations one consequence is very important, namely the *measurement* represents the bridge between the quantum and classical worlds.

Accepting one of these interpretations the reader my still remain discontented: how can a macroscopic animal be in a superposition? During the history of the human race probably nobody has met such a frightening creature. In any case Schrödinger himself said, later in life, that he wished he had never met that cat.

We have demonstrated in the previous subsection that entanglement with the environment can be very unpleasant when using quantum devices. Now, it provides a life belt to escape from Schrödinger's trap. The rate of decoherence depends on the size of the quantum system. Physicists are now able to create and maintain quantum particles such as atoms or single photons in superpositions for significant periods of time, provided that the coupling to the environment is weak. However, for a system which is as big as a cat and which comprises billions upon billions of atoms, decoherence happens almost instantaneously, so that the cat can never be both alive and dead for any measurable instant.

Remark: If the reader is still not satisfied with the reasoning then it is not his/her fault. Clearly speaking how Nature works in the case of Schrödinger's cat has never been explained to everyone's satisfaction, but quantum information theory discussed in the second volume of this book gives a more or less plausible explanation based on *mixed states*.

Remark: In spite of the above more or less reassuring explanation the probability of meeting such a cat is still nonzero... remember the salutation of the boy scouts "Be prepared!".

2.6.5 The EPR paradox and the Bell inequality

The strangeness of quantum principles does not end with Schrödinger's cat. Although Einstein, similarly to Schrödinger, was one of the initiators of the big quest for quantum theory, later they formed the 'conservative' group of physicists together with de Broglie. After a promising start they got frightened or became dizzy from the consequences of what they had launched, hence they insisted on connecting the new theory to classical physics and never had the courage to leave the safe harbor. This can be a bit surprising in the case of Einstein considering his relativity theory with combined space and time which was strange enough at his time, but if we consider that quantum mechanics seemed to be in heavy contradiction with relativity theory (as we will see soon) we should understand his obstinacy. Please, do not regard this comment as criticism. We agree with the ancient Greeks who said that the balance of judicious elderly and courageous young people ensures the guaranty of dynamic development.

Einstein had never accepted that randomness can act as a basic organizing principle of nature. This belief led to his famous objections[11] stating that God does not play dice with the universe, which mirrors the fundamental conviction that quantum mechanics is an incomplete theory when describing the state of a particle only by means of a superposition (i.e. using 'ket' vectors). He believed that the probabilistic behavior of a measurement on a one-qbit superposition is only virtual and in reality there are variables hidden from physicists whose control enables them to make measurements deterministic. Thus it is enough to find these variables – sooner or later it has marginal importance. Of course the connection between variables (small goblins sitting in the depths of the matter) and our experiences about the measurement results can be quite complex but if you can add these goblins to the list of your friends then the wanted result can be achieved with sure success.

In the meantime while others were searching for the hidden variables Einstein, Podolsky and Rosen came forward with a thought-experiment – called the *EPR paradox* according to the initials of the authors – which seemed to validate their theory.

They proposed to share an entangled pair of particles e.g. a spin-up and a spin-down electron[12] between Alice and Bob. By means of our notations this pair can be described as $\frac{|01\rangle - |10\rangle}{\sqrt{2}}$ if $|0\rangle$ represents a spin-up and $|1\rangle$ a spin-down electron respectively. Next Alice measures her qbit in the $|0\rangle$ and $|1\rangle$ basis and yields any of them with the same probability. One thing is sure if Alice's device shows 0 then Bob will obtain 1 if he measures his own qbit. Similarly if Alice gets 1 then Bob's result will be 0. This happens even if they run the measurements at the same time or more precisely in a causally disconnected way, that is only a faster than light medium could transfer the information about Alice's result to Bob. Einstein called this surprising phenomenon 'spooky action at a distance'. Provided we accept relativity theory with its limited speed of light then quantum mechanics must be wrong or as Einstein politely said *incomplete*. In this case by means of hidden variables one can easily explain the experienced effect. The fans of quantum mechanics stuck into the EPR paradox since quantum (nanoscale) description of Nature *must* contain our classical (macroscopic) everyday experiences as well, since the macroscopic world consists

---

[11]"Quantum mechanics is very impressive. But an inner voice tells me that it is not yet the real thing. The theory yields a lot, but it hardly brings us any closer to the secret of the Old One. In any case I am convinced that He doesn't play dice."

[12]The same can be done with polarized photons.

of nanoscale particles. Relativity theory is a well-known, more or less user-friendly and experimentally many times proven description of nature hence nothing stands in the way of accepting the reasoning of the EPR triumvirate. Unfortunately (at least from Einstein's point of view) there is a minor problem in the form of the Bell inequality which allows us to check experimentally which theory provides the proper description. As we are going to see Einstein made a mistake...

The Bell inequality in its original form is not practical enough for experimental validation thus several alternatives were proposed and it is better to use the plural i.e. Bell inequalities. Because Bell inequalities are going to play an important role in this book later in connection with certain infocom applications (see Section 10.3), we introduce here its so-called CHSH[13] version. In order to become more plausible we explain first the CHSH inequality using an everyday example (for more precise mathematical formulation see *Further Reading*) and next we apply it to particles as if they were classical objects obeying our best classical theory (i.e. relativity theory) of nature.

We invite our friends Alice and Bob to participate in an experiment. We ask them to go up to the bookshelf full of different books in the room. We take books from the shelf randomly and Alice's task is to check one of the following two properties: Does the title of the book contain character 'a' or not and does it contain character 'b' or not? Similarly Bob has to check the same with characters 'c' and 'd'. Because we are suspicious about their correctness we instruct them to select between the measurements with probability $\frac{1}{2}$, and to avoid their cooperation we make an identical copy of each book and ask Bob to follow us to another room which is far away enough from Alice's room such that information exchange about their results would require faster than light communication.

Let us denote the event when Alice decides for checking (measuring) character 'a' (property a) with M_a and similarly for other characters M_b, M_c, M_d. Thus four different scenarios can happen $M_a \wedge M_c, M_a \wedge M_d, M_b \wedge M_c$ and $M_b \wedge M_d$.

Furthermore we know their thirst for excitement therefore we propose the following offer: they get 1 virtual[14] cent for every successful measurement, e.g. if Alice decides to check character 'a' in the next title and the title really contains 'a' then Alice and Bob can harvest 1 virtual cent. However, if the measurement fails then Alice loses 1 virtual cent. This regrettable event will be denoted by earning -1 virtual cent. The *real* winnings[15] are the product of virtual cents in each turn when $M_a \wedge M_c, M_a \wedge M_d, M_b \wedge M_c$ except $M_b \wedge M_d$ when we introduce a small trick, namely the real winning is multiplied by -1. Assuming total number of L attempts the aggregate earning can be calculated as

$$S_L \triangleq \sum_{l=1}^{L} (AC)_l + (AD)_l + (BC)_l - (BD)_l = \sum_{l=1}^{L} S_l,$$

---

[13] After the initials of Clauser, Horne, Shimony and Holt.
[14] We use here the word *virtual* to the fact that their real winnings are calculated from the virtual ones.
[15] The reader may reproduce the experiment with small coins of his/her country.

where $A, B, C, D \in \pm 1$ denote the virtual winnings and l is indexing the sequence number of the turns. Despite the fact that only one of the above terms is obtained in each turn based on our classical view of nature, Alice and Bob can be sure that also the other three terms also exist because all the four properties exist independently whether we measure them or not. In order to be fair with them we also perform the remaining three measurements, and calculate S_L in a correct way. Obviously S_l is an observable for Alice and Bob, which depends on the actually observed term and on three hidden variables in each turn, similarly to Einstein's expectations.[16]

Alice and Bob utilize their knowledge about basic probability theory (see Section 12.1) to estimate their revenues. First they realize that they can either win or lose 2 cents per turn according to **Exercise** 2.5. Their long-term success depends on the sign of the expected revenue in a certain turn i.e. $\mathbb{E}(s) = \mathbb{E}(AC + AD + BC - BD)$. To calculate this the joint probability density function of the properties represented by $P(A = \alpha \wedge B = \beta \wedge C = \gamma \wedge D = \delta) \triangleq P_{\alpha,\beta,\gamma,\delta}$ is needed, which describes the probability of having the values denoted by Greek letters before the measurement. Roughly speaking this probability can be computed as a product of individual probabilities $P(A = \alpha)$, etc., but if we asked a linguist he/she would call our attention to certain correlations between the occurrences of different characters[17] therefore we insist on the general approach. Now applying the rule of calculating expectation values they get

$$\mathbb{E}(s) = \mathbb{E}(AC + AD + BC - BD)$$
$$= \sum_{\alpha} \sum_{\beta} \sum_{\gamma} \sum_{\delta} (AC + AD + BC - BD) P_{\alpha,\beta,\gamma,\delta}$$

and conclude that before starting the game they have to chose books written in such a language that the gambling will be profitable.

Let us suppose that they accept the rules. Next we observe that since the peak value(s) of a random variable is always greater than or equal to its expected value hence $\mathbb{E}(s) \leq 2$. Now we ask Alice and Bob to check this obvious inequality experimentally. Unfortunately they are allowed to measure one of the terms in s but this is not a real problem because we have already learned that the expected value of a sum is the sum of expected values that is

$$\mathbb{E}(AC + AD + BC - BD) = \mathbb{E}(AC) + \mathbb{E}(AD) + \mathbb{E}(BC) - \mathbb{E}(BD),$$

hence the used 'sampling' of terms during the experiment gives the same result from the expected value point of view as if we had measured all the terms. Thus we reached the so-called CHSH inequality

$$\mathbb{E}(AC) + \mathbb{E}(AD) + \mathbb{E}(BC) - \mathbb{E}(BD) \leq 2. \tag{2.13}$$

---

[16]"I think that a particle must have a separate reality independent of the measurements. That is an electron has spin, location and so forth even when it is not being measured. I like to think that the moon is there even if I am not looking at it." Albert Einstein

[17]These correlations follow different rules in the case of different languages but in the case of a homemade experiment the product approach is satisfactory.

Not surprisingly if the patient reader performs the above experiment the obtained result will fit the theoretical ones.

Remark: As advice we suggest the reader writes a simple C program during 10 minutes and run it for 1 second, which is equivalent to a one-hour book sorting (and no duplicated libraries are required).

Because Alice and Bob are ardent admirers of quantum mechanics they decide to reproduce the above experiment using nanoscale particles. To build the analogy it is enough to replace the identical pairs of books with entangled quantum bits, e.g. with photon or electron pairs where polarization or spin represents the quantum behavior. Surprisingly by applying suitable measurements (observations) Alice and Bob measure

$$\mathbb{E}(AC) = \mathbb{E}(AD) = \mathbb{E}(BC) = -\mathbb{E}(BD) = \frac{\sqrt{2}}{2}. \tag{2.14}$$

If one substitutes these values into the CHSH inequality then he/she starts turning pale because

$$\mathbb{E}(AC) + \mathbb{E}(AD) + \mathbb{E}(BC) - \mathbb{E}(BD) = 2\sqrt{2}, \tag{2.15}$$

which is in total contradiction to (2.13)! The derivation of this result will be discussed later in Section 3.2.5 where we will have the required formalism in our hands.

What is wrong with our classical perception of nature? We used three implicit axioms during the above reasoning which are called together the *local realism* picture of nature:

- Either our *locality* axiom is wrong where 'local' means everything that is bounded by the relativity theory, that is we assume that the speed of light is limited and nothing can exceed this limit. To show that hurting this axiom is not unimaginable we ask the reader to take a simple sheet of paper and put randomly two crosses onto it, say cross A and B. Next please connect them together drawing a line with a ruler. It is easy to calculate the required time of a two-dimensional super-advanced being travelling from point A to B with the speed of light. Now, we ask the significantly less advanced three-dimensional reader to bend the sheet such that the two crosses fit to each other. Than simply by punching the paper by the point of the pencil allows us to overtake the two-dimensional alien.

- We can fail with our *realism* axiom, too. It states that every physical parameter exists independently whether it is observed or not. When we were explaining the CHSH inequality we assumed that different properties of a book exist permanently and do not change when observing the book. However, as we have already seen in connection with Schrödinger's cat, the Copenhagen interpretation says that physical properties of particles depend on the observation or more strangely there is no sense in assuming the existence of a physical property until we observe the particle. This line of thought leads far away to the ocean of philosophy which is full of interesting and surprising ideas, e.g. the anthropomorphic approach assumes that only those universes exist which are observed by a conscious being such as the human race or as a generalization, is it possible that the human race with our universe exists because somebody (God?) is observing us? Now, we stop here and advise the reader to turn to one of the professional books of Stephen Hawking or Paul Davies.

- Finally we assumed that logic is an appropriate tool for reasoning. Unfortunately Gödel proved that any logic system (except if we strongly limited it) will contain statements which are neither false nor true but simply unprovable.

Remark: Let us mention here two responses to Einstein's 'dicing God' from the 'revolutionary' group[18] of physicists. Bohr was the more concise: "Quit telling God what to do!" and Born was the more striking: "If God has made the world a perfect mechanism, He has at least conceded so much to our imperfect intellect that in order to predict little parts of it, we need not solve innumerable differential equations, but can use dice with fair success".

Remark: It can be said in Einstein's justification that experimental validation of quantum mechanics does not mean that relativity theory become obsolete. On the contrary both theories are appropriate according to our state of the art knowledge but they describe nature on different scales. The big quest for the Great Unified Theory (GUT) aims to reconcile the two theories. Maybe quantum gravity can be the interfacing point.

Exercise 2.5. Show that $AC + AD + BC - BD = \pm 2$.

2.7 NO CLONING THEOREM

We have already investigated the operation of the CNOT gate feeded with superposition in Section 2.6.2. Although we expected to realize the COPY command we reached entanglement instead. On one hand we were delighted with this surprising outcome but on the other hand we started to have suspicions about the limits of copying in the quantum world. Now it is time to explore the possibilities.

Let us assume that there exists a transformation Q which implements the COPY function for arbitrary quantum superpositions denoted by $|\varphi\rangle$. In order to be as general as possible we do not require its unitary nature our only demand is that Q can be extended to an unitary operator U acting on a closed system, which comprises the state $|\varphi\rangle$ to be cloned and a suitable environment (even the whole universe). The quantum COPY machine extended with the environment is depicted in Fig. 2.13. The input $|0\rangle$ state is used to ensure the same number of input and output quantum wires, which is essential for unitary matrices. If we were able to construct such a U

---

[18]Heisenberg with his uncertainty principle belonged to this group, too.

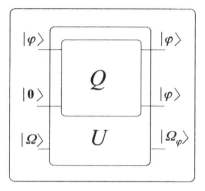

Fig. 2.13 Quantum COPY machine

our hope for a quantum cloning device Q would still be saved. So let us check the existence of U and than the design leading to Q.

Considering our special problem the most suitable definition of unitary nature is the one which claims that unitary operators keep the inner product. To exploit this definition we select two arbitrary superpositions $|\varphi\rangle$ and $|\psi\rangle$. Making a copy of each means

$$U : |\varphi\rangle|\mathbf{0}\rangle|\Omega\rangle \rightarrow |\varphi\rangle|\varphi\rangle|\Omega_\varphi\rangle,$$
$$U : |\psi\rangle|\mathbf{0}\rangle|\Omega\rangle \rightarrow |\psi\rangle|\psi\rangle|\Omega_\psi\rangle,$$

where $|\Omega_\varphi\rangle$ and $|\Omega_\psi\rangle$ describe the states of the environment after the successful cloning. The inner product of the inputs is

$$\langle\Omega, \mathbf{0}, \psi|\varphi, \mathbf{0}, \Omega\rangle = \langle\psi|\varphi\rangle\langle\mathbf{0}|\mathbf{0}\rangle\langle\Omega|\Omega\rangle = \langle\psi|\varphi\rangle$$

while for the outputs we obtain

$$\langle\Omega_\psi, \psi, \psi|\varphi, \varphi, \Omega_\varphi\rangle = \langle\psi|\varphi\rangle\langle\psi|\varphi\rangle\langle\Omega_\psi|\Omega_\varphi\rangle = \langle\psi|\varphi\rangle^2\langle\Omega_\psi|\Omega_\varphi\rangle.$$

These two quantities on the right-hand side can be equal if

- $\langle\psi|\varphi\rangle = \pm1$ which is equivalent to $|\varphi\rangle = |\psi\rangle$ or

- $\langle\psi|\varphi\rangle = 0$ which represents the orthogonality between $|\varphi\rangle$ and $|\psi\rangle$

and no other chance to satisfy the equality. The reader may propose to set $\langle\psi|\varphi\rangle = \frac{1}{\langle\Omega_\psi|\Omega_\varphi\rangle}$, which seems to be an appropriate scenario. Unfortunately we are working with unit vectors hence their inner products must be less or equal to 1. Thus only $\langle\psi|\varphi\rangle = \langle\Omega_\psi|\Omega_\varphi\rangle = 1$ is allowed which has been taken previously into account.

As a conclusion of the above investigation the *no cloning theorem* of quantum computing claims that only orthogonal quantum states can be copied. Fortunately classical states are widely used in computers today and processors are orthogonal therefore quantum description of nature – which is more general than the classical theories – proved to be in harmony with our everyday experiences. This property is fairly useful for a theory that aspires to be the most (almost) general one.

2.8 HOW TO PREPARE AN ARBITRARY SUPERPOSITION

Quantum computing aims to solve computationally hard problems by means of devices based on quantum mechanical principles. The majority of this book is devoted to the techniques which explain *how to design such circuits and algorithms/protocols*. However, human organs match the classical world therefore we need interfaces between the user and the equipment. The interface at the output is responsible for *how to transform the quantum state of the system into classical states*. It is called *measurement* and discussed in detail in Chapter 3. Now we are concentrating on the input interface, namely *how to produce an arbitrary input superposition* to initialize the device? Since we have learned that multi-qbit states can be realized partly or entirely as tensor products of one-qbit states and/or using CNOT to bind them together via entanglement, we will show here how to prepare an arbitrary one-qbit state $|\varphi\rangle = a|0\rangle + b|1\rangle$ starting from classical $|0\rangle$.

The appropriate quantum circuit is depicted in Fig. 2.14 whose evolution is investigated gate by gate. We begin with

$$|\varphi_0\rangle = |0\rangle,$$

from which the first Hadamard gates produces

$$|\varphi_1\rangle = H|0\rangle = \frac{|0\rangle + |1\rangle}{\sqrt{2}}$$

in accordance with (2.7). The first phase gate rotates the probability amplitude belonging to computational basis state $|1\rangle$ by an angle α

$$|\varphi_2\rangle = P(\alpha)|\varphi_1\rangle = \frac{|0\rangle + e^{j\alpha}|1\rangle}{\sqrt{2}}.$$

The following second Hadamard gate acts on $|0\rangle$ and $|1\rangle$ in a different manner having in sight (2.7) again

$$|\varphi_3\rangle = H|\varphi_2\rangle = \frac{\frac{|0\rangle+|1\rangle}{\sqrt{2}} + e^{j\alpha}\frac{|0\rangle-|1\rangle}{\sqrt{2}}}{\sqrt{2}} = \frac{1 + e^{j\alpha}}{2}|0\rangle + \frac{1 - e^{j\alpha}}{2}|1\rangle.$$

The second phase gate only rotates the coefficient of $|1\rangle$ again

$$|\varphi_4\rangle = P(0.5\pi + \beta)|\varphi_4\rangle = \frac{1 + e^{j\alpha}}{2}|0\rangle + e^{j(0.5\pi+\beta)}\frac{1 - e^{j\alpha}}{2}|1\rangle.$$

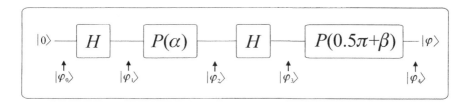

Fig. 2.14 Abstract quantum circuit of the generalized interferometer

In order to bring $|\varphi_4\rangle$ into a more treatable form we ask the reader to show in **Exercise** 2.6 that $\frac{1+e^{j\alpha}}{2} = e^{j0.5\alpha}\cos(0.5\alpha)$ and $e^{j0.5\pi}\frac{1-e^{j\alpha}}{2} = e^{j0.5\alpha}\sin(0.5\alpha)$. Substituting these results into $|\varphi_4\rangle$ we obtain

$$|\varphi_4\rangle = e^{j\alpha}\left[\cos\left(\frac{\alpha}{2}\right)|0\rangle + e^{j\beta}\sin\left(\frac{\alpha}{2}\right)|1\rangle\right],$$

which is nothing more than the most general one-qbit state introduced in (2.4). The only minor deviation appears in the global phase factor which is in our case not independent from the other two angles but this fact does not mean a real restriction because global phase has no influence on the classical result yielded on the output interface. Thus we managed to produce $|\varphi\rangle$ in the form of $|\varphi_4\rangle$.

If the reader compares Fig. 2.14 with Fig. 2.8 then it is easy to recognize that the optical implementation of the quantum initializing circuit consists of a generalized interferometer extended with another sheet of glass delaying the photon by $e^{j(0.5\pi+\beta)}$.

Exercise 2.6. Show that $\frac{1+e^{j\alpha}}{2} = e^{j0.5\alpha}\cos(0.5\alpha)$ and $e^{j0.5\pi}\frac{1-e^{j\alpha}}{2} = e^{j0.5\alpha}\sin(0.5\alpha)$.

2.9 FURTHER READING

The idea of introducing probability amplitudes by means of probabilistic gates emerged first in [48]. However, we modified it reasonably in order to create consistency between interferometer experiments and the corresponding abstract quantum computing description.

Readers interested in a more detailed view of quantum mechanics are directed to several appropriate books e.g. [23].

The quantum computing based description of the interferometer originates from [9] which has been slightly modified to ensure the harmony between the probabilistic $\sqrt{I}$ gate and the interferometer.

Schrödinger proposed [135] his cat-threatening equipment in 1935 causing serious headaches for physicists engaged with quantum mechanics and the interpretation of how nature really operates. Einstein, Podolsky and Rosen [4] published their thought-experiment known as the EPR paradox in 1935. After long discussions Bell proposed his famous inequality [29] in 1964 providing the key to an experiment which decided the debate. CHSH inequality yielded its name after the initials of its inventors Clauser, Horne, Shimony and Holt [83]. Because experimental testing of Bell inequalities was crucial to decide whether local realism or quantum mechanics gave the more suitable description of nature, large amount of efforts were invested see e.g. [2, 157, 155, 151] most of them voting for the latter one.

Our technique to produce an arbitrary one-qbit state is based on the brilliant idea discussed in [9].

3

Measurements

Measurements as tunnels between the quantum and classical worlds play an important role. Carefully designed measurements allow access to information with high probability or even with sure success, while clumsy constructions select according to uniform distributions among the possible results. Recalling our example – the Euclidian geometry – referenced when we were introducing the postulates of quantum mechanics, the authors are sure that except for a few very talented readers the majority was not able to invent Pythagoras' theorem after having a short look at the axioms in primary school although it is an evident consequence of them provided readers are familiar with the required simple steps. Therefore this chapter is devoted to the 3rd Postulate of quantum mechanics and derives practical rules for designing measurements. First we reformulate the 3rd Postulate representing the general measurement according to the applied notations in the literature in Section 3.1. Next, Section 3.2 focuses on the special case of orthogonal measurement operators (projectors). Construction rules for general measurements are discussed in Section 3.3 while we summarize the connections between the different measurement approaches in Section 3.4. Finally we design a quantum computing based efficient solution for a game with marbles in Section 3.5.

3.1 GENERAL MEASUREMENTS

Measurements can be modelled as defining a finite or infinite set of possible outcomes and than selecting one of them according to a predefined (measurement) rule. Quantum measurements are controlled by the 3rd Postulate (see Section 2.2).

Quantum Computing and Communications   S. Imre, F. Balázs
© 2004 John Wiley & Sons, Ltd   ISBN 0-470-86902-X (HB)

First let us rephrase them using the 'ket' notations that is any quantum measurement can be described by means of a set of measurement operators $\{M_m\}$, where m stands for the possible results of the measurement. The probability of measuring m provided the system is in state $|\varphi\rangle$ can be calculated as

$$P(m \mid |\varphi\rangle) = \langle\varphi|M_m^\dagger M_m|\varphi\rangle, \tag{3.1}$$

and the system after measuring m gets the state

$$|\varphi'\rangle = \frac{M_m|\varphi\rangle}{\sqrt{\langle\varphi|M_m^\dagger M_m|\varphi\rangle}}. \tag{3.2}$$

Definition (3.2) is fairly similar to a unitary transformation of a given state except that we need a denominator different from 1 in order to normalize the resulted state. This modification can be regarded as the compensation of the vanished information because of the non-reversible measurement operator. Since classical probability theory requires that

$$\sum_m P(m \mid |\varphi\rangle) = \sum_m \langle\varphi|^\dagger M_m^\dagger M_m|\varphi\rangle \equiv 1, \tag{3.3}$$

the following *completeness relation* has to be fulfilled by the measurement operators

$$\sum_m M_m^\dagger M_m \equiv I. \tag{3.4}$$

We would like to emphasize that the completeness relation *must be* always checked when all the measurement operators are believed to be constructed, because it prevents us from forgetting one or more potential measurement outcomes on the indicator dial of the measurement equipment.

Finally it is easy to see that consecutive measurements can be combined: Assuming measurement $\{M_m\}$, which is followed by another one $\{Q_q\}$, they can be merged into a single measurement with operators $R_{qm} = M_m Q_q, \forall q, m$.

The above definitions do not advise us how to construct a given measurement, they only allow us to predict the outcome of the measurement and the post-measurement state of the system. From a practical point of view we need a cookery book to build our own measuring devices. Therefore the forthcoming sections are dedicated to some recipes allowing typical sets of states to be distinguished.

3.2 PROJECTIVE MEASUREMENTS

When we were invoking measurements in the previous sections we always used the set of orthonormal computational basis states and the measuring device selected one of them. Therefore rules for the construction of measurement operators are discussed in the case of orthonormal vectors. This type of measurement is called *projective measurement* or von Neumann measurement.

3.2.1 Measurement operators and the 3rd Postulate in the case of projective measurement

Let us consider a simple example of two orthonormal states $|\varphi_m\rangle = |0\rangle$ or $|1\rangle$, which allows us to form the rules for an arbitrary large set of such vectors. The problem is the following. We are given a single qbit prepared in $|\varphi_0\rangle = |0\rangle$ or $|\varphi_1\rangle = |1\rangle$ without any hint about which of them was chosen, and we have to guess the right answer whether $m = 0$ or $m = 1$.

In order to achieve a proper decision with probability 1 assuming $|0\rangle$ has been received we turn to (3.1) that requires

$$
\begin{aligned}
1 &= \langle 0|M_0^\dagger M_0|0\rangle, \\
0 &= \langle 1|M_0^\dagger M_0|1\rangle.
\end{aligned}
\tag{3.5}
$$

Provided we are seeking for M_0 in the form of

$$
\mathbf{M}_0 = \begin{bmatrix} a & b \\ c & d \end{bmatrix}
$$

then equation system (3.5) is reduced to

$$
\begin{aligned}
1 &= |a|^2 + |c|^2, \\
0 &= |b|^2 + |d|^2.
\end{aligned}
$$

For the sake of simplicity we choose $a = 1$ and $c = 0$ in the first equation and from the second one obviously $b = d = 0$, thus

$$
\mathbf{M}_0 = \begin{bmatrix} 1 & 0 \\ 0 & 0 \end{bmatrix}.
\tag{3.6}
$$

The same technique can be applied for $|\varphi_1\rangle$ resulting in

$$
\mathbf{M}_1 = \begin{bmatrix} 0 & 0 \\ 0 & 1 \end{bmatrix}.
\tag{3.7}
$$

As we were advised in Section 2.2 we check whether the completeness relation is satisfied or not using (3.4)

$$
\sum_m \mathbf{M}_m^\dagger \mathbf{M}_m = \begin{bmatrix} 1 & 0 \\ 0 & 0 \end{bmatrix} + \begin{bmatrix} 0 & 0 \\ 0 & 1 \end{bmatrix} = \begin{bmatrix} 1 & 0 \\ 0 & 1 \end{bmatrix} = \mathbf{I}.
$$

Although we have both measurement operators in our hands it is worth taking another glance at them and realizing that $M_0 = |0\rangle\langle 0|$ and $M_1 = |1\rangle\langle 1|$.

Thus we reached a very simple and practical rule of thumb: *When we have a set of orthonormal states $\{|\varphi_m\rangle\}$ then the corresponding measurement operators which provide exact differentiation among them can be produced by $M_m = |\varphi_m\rangle\langle\varphi_m|$.*

The previously defined operators M_m belong to a special family of linear operators called *projectors* (see Section 12.2.5) and have several interesting and important properties. First of all to emphasize their special nature we will denote them from this point on by P_m according to the literature:

1. Obviously they are self-adjoint operators $P_m^\dagger \equiv P_m$ since $(|\varphi_m\rangle\langle\varphi_m|)^\dagger = \langle\varphi_m|^\dagger|\varphi_m\rangle^\dagger = |\varphi_m\rangle\langle\varphi_m|$.

2. Furthermore $P_m P_m = |\varphi_m\rangle \underbrace{\langle\varphi_m||\varphi_m\rangle}_{\equiv 1} \langle\varphi_m| = P_m$.

3. Finally they are orthogonal which means $P_m P_n = |\varphi_m\rangle \underbrace{\langle\varphi_m||\varphi_n\rangle}_{\equiv 1 \text{or} 0} \langle\varphi_n| = \delta(m-n)P_m$.

We emphasize that orthogonality was exploited only at the third property.

Based on these recognitions we can adapt the general equations of the 3rd Postulate to the projective measurement

$$P(m \mid |\varphi\rangle) = \langle\varphi|P_m|\varphi\rangle, \qquad (3.8)$$

$$|\varphi'\rangle = \frac{P_m|\varphi\rangle}{\sqrt{\langle\varphi|P_m|\varphi\rangle}}, \qquad (3.9)$$

and finally the completeness relation reduces to

$$\sum_m P_m \equiv I. \qquad (3.10)$$

Remark: The construction rule of the projective operators can be interpreted in two different ways:

- In the case of a *direct approach* we start from (3.8) and we would like to ensure $P(m \mid |\varphi_m\rangle) = 1$ if $|\varphi_m\rangle$ is received. This can be done using parallel vectors to $|\varphi_m\rangle$ in the outer product representation of P_m thus $P(m \mid |\varphi_m\rangle) = \underbrace{\langle\varphi_m||\varphi_m\rangle}_{\equiv 1} \underbrace{\langle\varphi_m||\varphi_m\rangle}_{\equiv 1} = 1$. Using the same technique for all possible m we form the set of measurement operators.

- According to the *indirect approach* we start from (3.8) again but we would like to ensure $P(n \mid |\varphi_m\rangle) = 0, \forall n \neq m$ if $|\varphi_m\rangle$ is received. This can be achieved by applying orthogonal vectors to $|\varphi_m\rangle$ in the outer product representation of P_m thus $P(n \mid |\varphi_m\rangle) = \underbrace{\langle\varphi_m||\varphi_n\rangle}_{\equiv 0} \underbrace{\langle\varphi_n||\varphi_m\rangle}_{\equiv 0} = 0, \forall n \neq m$ and because $\sum_l P(l \mid |\varphi_m\rangle) = 1$, $P(m \mid |\varphi_m\rangle) = 1$. Using the same technique for all possible m we form the set of measurement operators.

Exercise 3.1. Construct the measurement operators providing sure success in the case of the following set $|\varphi_0\rangle = \frac{|0\rangle+|1\rangle}{\sqrt{2}}$ and $|\varphi_1\rangle = \frac{|0\rangle-|1\rangle}{\sqrt{2}}$.

3.2.2   Measurement using the computational basis states

It may happen that our partner in the above discussed simple example tries to cheat by using an arbitrary unit length vector $|\varphi\rangle = a|0\rangle + b|1\rangle$ instead of the agreed computational basis states $|0\rangle$ or $|1\rangle$. Let us calculate the probability of receiving $|0\rangle$ and $|1\rangle$

$$P(0 \mid |\varphi\rangle) = \langle\varphi|P_0|\varphi\rangle = \begin{bmatrix} 1 & 0 \\ 0 & 0 \end{bmatrix} \begin{matrix} \begin{bmatrix} a \\ b \end{bmatrix} \\ \begin{bmatrix} a \\ 0 \end{bmatrix} \\ \begin{bmatrix} a^* & b^* \end{bmatrix} \ |a|^2 \end{matrix},$$

$$P(1 \mid |\varphi\rangle) = \langle\varphi|P_0|\varphi\rangle = \begin{bmatrix} 0 & 0 \\ 0 & 1 \end{bmatrix} \begin{matrix} \begin{bmatrix} a \\ b \end{bmatrix} \\ \begin{bmatrix} 0 \\ b \end{bmatrix} \\ \begin{bmatrix} a^* & b^* \end{bmatrix} \ |b|^2 \end{matrix},$$

and our qbit falls into the following states due to the measurement in compliance with (3.9)

$$|\varphi_0'\rangle = \frac{P_0|0\rangle}{\sqrt{P(0 \mid |\varphi\rangle)}} = \frac{a|0\rangle}{|a|^2},$$

$$|\varphi_1'\rangle = \frac{P_1|0\rangle}{\sqrt{P(1 \mid |\varphi\rangle)}} = \frac{b|1\rangle}{|b|^2}.$$

The above results fully correspond to the interpretation of the probability amplitudes, namely if a qbit were measured then we would receive basis state $|0\rangle$ with probability $|a|^2$ and $|1\rangle$ with probability $|b|^2$, respectively.

   If we are playing the game with qregisters n qbits of length then we have to prepare ourselves for two kinds of cheating. The first one is the simple generalization of the previous one-qbit scenario, that is instead of selecting one of the elements from $\{|k\rangle\}$ we are given an arbitrary superposition $|\varphi\rangle = \sum_k \varphi_k|k\rangle$. Analogously to the previous result we will measure m with probability $P(m \mid |\varphi\rangle) = |\varphi_m|^2$ and the register will end in this case in state $\frac{\varphi_m}{|\varphi_m|^2}|m\rangle$, which equals $|m\rangle$ up to a global phase.

   Finally another trick can be applied if we have an orthonormal set $S = \{|\varphi_k\rangle\}$ but not all the basis vectors are included. Then our unfair partner may give us a $|\varphi_m\rangle$ which is orthogonal to the elements of S but does not belong to it. What will happen? If the measurement operators are constructed as $P_k = |\varphi_k\rangle\langle\varphi_k|, k \in S$ and implemented carefully an extra operator $P_{cheating} = I - \sum_{k\in S} P_k = I - \sum_{k\in S} |\varphi_k\rangle\langle\varphi_k|$, then for any $|\varphi_m\rangle, m \notin S$ the measuring device will point to scale value *cheating* in the dial.

   Remark: Orthogonal states can always be distinguished via constructing appropriate measurement operators (projectors). This is another explanation why orthogonal (classical) states can be copied as was stated in Section 2.7 because being in possession of the exact information about such states we can build a quantum circuit producing them.

3.2.3 Observable and projective measurement

We learned with regard to normal operators (see Section 12.2.5) that they are diagonizable, i.e. their spectral decomposition always exists. Since projectors are Hermitian and thus normal, $\{|\varphi_m\rangle\}$ forming $\{P_m\}$ can be regarded as eigenvectors of an operator K representing an *observable*

$$K = \sum_m mP_m, \tag{3.11}$$

where the measurement outcomes m are the eigenvalues of K. Let us calculate the expected value of this observable if the measurement is repeated several times (of course not on the same qregister)

$$\mathbb{E}(K) = \sum_m mP(m \mid |\varphi\rangle) = \sum_m m\langle\varphi|P_m|\varphi\rangle = \langle\varphi|\left(\sum_m mP_m\right)|\varphi\rangle = \langle\varphi|K|\varphi\rangle. \tag{3.12}$$

3.2.4 Repeated projective measurement

Before leaving the projective measurement it is worth investigating the effect of repeated measurements on the same qregister. Provided we defined a set of orthogonal measurement operators (projectors) P_k to the set $\{|\varphi_k\rangle\}$ and outcome m has been chosen by the device feeded by arbitrary $|\varphi\rangle$ then the qregister after the first measurement is with respect to (3.9) in state

$$|\varphi_m\rangle = \frac{P_m|\varphi\rangle}{\sqrt{\langle\varphi|P_m|\varphi\rangle}},$$

up to a global phase factor. Applying again this measurement on $|\varphi_m\rangle$ and replacing $P_m = |\varphi_m\rangle\langle\varphi_m|$

$$|\varphi_m\rangle' = \frac{P_m|\varphi_m\rangle}{\sqrt{\langle\varphi_m|P_m|\varphi_m\rangle}} = \frac{|\varphi_m\rangle\langle\varphi_m||\varphi_m\rangle}{\sqrt{\langle\varphi_m||\varphi_m\rangle\langle\varphi_m||\varphi_m\rangle}} = |\varphi_m\rangle,$$

which claims that $P(m||\varphi_m\rangle) = 1$, i.e. repeated measurements do not change the status of the register.

Remark: Mindful readers may reach this result from the discussion in Section 3.2.1, i.e. if we receive one of the vectors from the orthonormal set then the projective measurement always gives back the corresponding index with sure success.

3.2.5 CHSH inequality with entangled particles

When we were discussing the EPR paradox and the CHSH inequality in Section 2.6.5 we promised to derive the quite surprising result (2.15). Instead of using two copies of a library we apply Bell states. The entangled qbits represent two identical copies if we use e.g.

$$|\beta_{00}\rangle = \frac{|00\rangle + |11\rangle}{\sqrt{2}}.$$

However, for both historical and practical reasons we use $|\beta_{11}\rangle$ which can be produced much easier in an experiment

$$|\beta_{11}\rangle = \frac{|01\rangle - |10\rangle}{\sqrt{2}}. \tag{3.13}$$

Let us denote the four observables with A, B, C and D similarly to the classical case. Furthermore we need four matrices describing the observables O_A, O_B, O_C and O_D. According to Section 3.2.3 the measurement results correspond to the eigenvalues of these matrices. Since $A, B, C, D \in \{\pm 1\}$ we have to keep this fact in view when designing the measurements. After some discussions Alice and Bob decide to use the following observables

$$\mathbf{O}_A = \begin{bmatrix} 1 & 0 \\ 0 & -1 \end{bmatrix}, \quad \mathbf{O}_B = \begin{bmatrix} 1 & 0 \\ 0 & 1 \end{bmatrix},$$

$$\mathbf{O}_C = \frac{1}{\sqrt{2}} \begin{bmatrix} -1 & -1 \\ -1 & 1 \end{bmatrix}, \quad \mathbf{O}_D = \frac{1}{\sqrt{2}} \begin{bmatrix} 1 & -1 \\ -1 & -1 \end{bmatrix}. \tag{3.14}$$

Matrices of these observables have two different eigenvalues, namely ± 1. Now, we have to evaluate

$$\mathbb{E}(s) = \mathbb{E}(AC) + \mathbb{E}(AD) + \mathbb{E}(BC) - \mathbb{E}(BD), \tag{3.15}$$

which can be reformulated bearing in mind (3.12)

$$\mathbb{E}(s) = \langle \beta_{11}|O_{AC}|\beta_{11}\rangle + \langle \beta_{11}|O_{AD}|\beta_{11}\rangle + \langle \beta_{11}|O_{BC}|\beta_{11}\rangle + \langle \beta_{11}|O_{BD}|\beta_{11}\rangle, \tag{3.16}$$

where O_{XY} stands for the joined observables, i.e. product of X and Y.

In order to compute (3.16) first we show how to determine the expected value of the product of two observables belonging to two qbits, say for observable A and C. We know from (3.11) that an observable can be expressed using the potential measurement results and the corresponding projectors, i.e.

$$O_A = \sum_{\alpha} \alpha P_{\alpha}, \quad \mathbb{E}(A) = \langle \varphi_1|O_A|\varphi_1\rangle,$$

$$O_C = \sum_{\gamma} \gamma P_{\gamma}, \quad \mathbb{E}(C) = \langle \varphi_2|O_C|\varphi_2\rangle, \tag{3.17}$$

if the input states of the two measurement apparatus are $|\varphi_1\rangle$ and $|\varphi_2\rangle$ respectively. Furthermore P_α and P_γ denote the projectors belonging to the measurement results α and γ. On the other hand if we regard these two independent measurements as a single combined one we can calculate the expected value in the following way

$$\mathbb{E}(AC) \triangleq \sum_\alpha \sum_\gamma \alpha\gamma P(A = \alpha \wedge C = \gamma || \psi\rangle) = \sum_\alpha \sum_\gamma \alpha\gamma \langle\psi|P_{\alpha,\gamma}|\psi\rangle,$$
$$= \langle\psi| \sum_\alpha \sum_\gamma \alpha\gamma P_{\alpha,\gamma}|\psi\rangle, \qquad (3.18)$$

where $|\psi\rangle$ stands for the input two-qbit register, $P(A = \alpha \wedge C = \gamma || \psi\rangle)$ is the joint probability distribution and $P_{\alpha,\gamma}$ refers to the joint projector working on the two-qbit register.

Since the two measurements are independent on different qbits we can write $P_{\alpha,\gamma} = P_\alpha \otimes P_\gamma$. Therefore we obtain from (3.18)

$$\mathbb{E}(AC) = \langle\psi| \sum_\alpha \sum_\gamma \alpha\gamma (P_\alpha \otimes P_\gamma)|\psi\rangle = \langle\psi| \left(\sum_\alpha \alpha P_\alpha \right) \otimes \left(\sum_\gamma \gamma P_\gamma \right) |\psi\rangle$$
$$= \langle\psi|O_A \otimes O_C|\psi\rangle. \qquad (3.19)$$

Now we are able to calculate $\mathbb{E}(s)$, which leads to the surprising result of (2.15) that is $2\sqrt{2}$ which is obviously greater than the classical result 2.

Remark: Here we introduced the most serious violation of the CHSH inequality, in practice, however, if the observables are chosen not so carefully the difference between the classical and quantum results may be smaller.

3.3 POSITIVE OPERATOR VALUED MEASUREMENT

As we have seen in the previous section if an orthonormal set of vectors is used and our partner is correct then the game does not cause any excitement. Let us therefore consider a set of non-orthogonal states. Obviously projective measurement will fail with certain probability in accordance with (3.8). In order to control this uncertainty *positive operator valued measurement* (POVM) is proposed in the forthcoming discussion.

For the sake of simplifying the analysis we merge $M_m^\dagger M_m$ into a single operator D_m. Equation (3.1) in the 3rd Postulate requires that the probability of measuring m must be nonnegative, which presses $M_m^\dagger M_m$ and thus D_m for being positive semi-definite (see Section 12.2.5). Now the reader can realize the origin of the name of this type of measurement.

The previously defined operators D_m have several interesting and important properties:

1. Obviously they are self-adjoint operators because $D_m^\dagger = \left(M_m^\dagger M_m \right)^\dagger = M_m^\dagger M_m = D_m$.

2. Any operator in the form of $|\varphi_m\rangle\langle\varphi_m|$ is positive semi-definite since for all $|\psi\rangle$, $P(m\mid|\psi\rangle) = \langle\psi||\varphi_m\rangle\langle\varphi_m||\psi\rangle = \langle\psi|\varphi_m\rangle(\langle\psi|\varphi_m\rangle)^* = |\langle\psi|\varphi_m\rangle|^2 \geq 0$. Because both $|\psi\rangle$ and $|\varphi_m\rangle$ are unit length vectors thus $P(m\mid|\psi\rangle) \leq 1$.

3. This latter statement is also true from the opposite direction because D_m is constructed in the form of $M_m^\dagger M_m$.[1]

Finally applying D_m the definitions in the 3rd Postulate become

$$P(m\mid|\varphi\rangle) = \langle\varphi|D_m|\varphi\rangle, \tag{3.20}$$

and we are typically not interested in the post-measurement state in the case of POVM because for a given D_m one cannot solve the equation system $D_m = M_m^\dagger M_m$ unambiguously. Finally the completeness relation turns to

$$\sum_m D_m \equiv I. \tag{3.21}$$

Before presenting how to determine the members of a POVM operator set it is worth thinking about the expected result if we would like to distinguish vectors from a non-orthogonal set $\{|\varphi_k\rangle\}$. Let us take first $|\varphi_m\rangle$. To ensure sure success of measuring m if $|\varphi_m\rangle$ is received then with respect to the direct approach in Section 3.2.1 we define $D_m = P_m = |\varphi_m\rangle\langle\varphi_m|$. Thus exploiting (3.20) $P(m\mid|\varphi_m\rangle) = \langle\varphi_m|D_m|\varphi_m\rangle = \langle\varphi_m||\varphi_m\rangle\langle\varphi_m||\varphi_m\rangle \equiv 1$ and indirectly any other $P(k\mid|\varphi_m\rangle) = 0, k \neq m$ because of the completeness relation. Now if we were sent $|\varphi_n\rangle$ angular to $|\varphi_m\rangle$, which means $0 < \langle\varphi_m|\varphi_n\rangle < 1$ then $|\varphi_n\rangle$ can be decomposed into a parallel $|\varphi_m^{||}\rangle$ and an orthogonal $|\varphi_m^\perp\rangle$ component to $|\varphi_m\rangle$, that is $|\varphi_n\rangle = |\varphi_m^{||}\rangle + |\varphi_m^\perp\rangle$. Calculating the probability of measuring m

$$P(m\mid|\varphi_n\rangle) = \langle\varphi_n|D_m|\varphi_n\rangle = ((\langle\varphi_m^{||}| + \langle\varphi_m^\perp|)|\varphi_m\rangle\langle\varphi_m|(|\varphi_m^{||}\rangle + |\varphi_m^\perp\rangle))$$

$$= \underbrace{\langle\varphi_m^\perp||\varphi_m\rangle}_{\equiv 0}\underbrace{\langle\varphi_m||\varphi_m^\perp\rangle}_{\equiv 0} + \underbrace{\langle\varphi_m^{||}||\varphi_m\rangle}_{\neq 0}\underbrace{\langle\varphi_m||\varphi_m^{||}\rangle}_{\neq 0}$$

$$+ \underbrace{\langle\varphi_m^\perp||\varphi_m\rangle}_{\equiv 0}\underbrace{\langle\varphi_m||\varphi_m^{||}\rangle}_{\neq 0} + \underbrace{\langle\varphi_m^{||}||\varphi_m\rangle}_{\neq 0}\underbrace{\langle\varphi_m||\varphi_m^\perp\rangle}_{\equiv 0} \neq 0. \tag{3.22}$$

Although the first term equals zero the second one proves to be always positive, hence we can deduce the following lesson: *No set of measurement operators exists which is able to distinguish non-orthogonal states unambiguously. This is another explanation why non-orthogonal states cannot be copied as was stated in Section 2.7 because of lack of exact information about such states we cannot build a quantum circuit to produce them.*

---

[1] However, it has to be emphasized that not only rank-one Hermitian operators can be positive semi-definite in general.

3.3.1   Measurement operators and the 3rd Postulate in the case of POVM

We turn to our one-qbit example once more retaining $|\varphi_0\rangle = |0\rangle$ but replacing $|\varphi_1\rangle = |1\rangle$ with $|\varphi_1\rangle = \frac{|0\rangle+|1\rangle}{\sqrt{2}}$. Obviously the two vectors are non-orthogonal, i.e. $\langle\varphi_0|\varphi_1\rangle = \frac{1}{\sqrt{2}} \neq 0$.

In order to form the members of the POVM set we exploit the indirect construction approach used for projective measurements in Section 3.2.1, which means that we would like to prevent the measurement device from answering $m = 1$ if $|\varphi_0\rangle$ and $m = 0$ if $|\varphi_1\rangle$ was given to us, respectively. More precisely we would like to ensure

$$P(1 \mid |\varphi_0\rangle) = \langle\varphi_0|D_1|\varphi_0\rangle = 0,\ \ P(0 \mid |\varphi_1\rangle) = \langle\varphi_1|D_0|\varphi_1\rangle = 0.$$

To achieve this goal we choose D_0 orthogonal to $|\varphi_1\rangle$ and D_1 orthogonal to $|\varphi_0\rangle$ as if we were designing a projective measurement

$$D_0 = \alpha\frac{|0\rangle - |1\rangle}{\sqrt{2}}\frac{\langle0| - \langle1|}{\sqrt{2}},\ \ \ D_1 = \beta|1\rangle\langle1| \tag{3.23}$$

with the corresponding matrices

$$\mathbf{D}_0 = \begin{bmatrix} \frac{\alpha}{2} & \frac{-\alpha}{2} \\ \frac{-\alpha}{2} & \frac{\alpha}{2} \end{bmatrix},\ \ \ \mathbf{D}_1 = \begin{bmatrix} 0 & 0 \\ 0 & \beta \end{bmatrix}, \tag{3.24}$$

where $\alpha, \beta \in \mathbb{C}$. Because we are well trained in using the 3rd Postulate we introduce a third operator with respect to the completeness relation

$$D_2 = I - D_0 - D_1 \Rightarrow \mathbf{D}_2 = \begin{bmatrix} 1 - \frac{\alpha}{2} & \frac{\alpha}{2} \\ \frac{\alpha}{2} & 1 - \beta - \frac{\alpha}{2} \end{bmatrix}. \tag{3.25}$$

Obviously D_0 and D_1 are positive semi-definite because of the outer product based construction. Regarding D_2 we will investigate this property later.

Before turning to setup α and β it is worth analyzing the operation of D_m. Let us compute the probabilities of measuring $m = 0, 1, 2$ in the case of $|\varphi_0\rangle$ or $|\varphi_1\rangle$

arriving at the measuring equipment with respect to $P(m \mid |\varphi_k\rangle) = \langle\varphi_k|D_m|\varphi_k\rangle$

$$P(0 \mid |\varphi_0\rangle) = \begin{bmatrix} \frac{\alpha}{2} & \frac{-\alpha}{2} \\ \frac{-\alpha}{2} & \frac{\alpha}{2} \end{bmatrix} \begin{bmatrix} \frac{\alpha}{2} \\ -\frac{\alpha}{2} \end{bmatrix}, \quad P(1 \mid |\varphi_0\rangle) = \begin{bmatrix} 0 & 0 \\ 0 & \beta \end{bmatrix} \begin{bmatrix} 0 \\ 0 \end{bmatrix},$$

$$P(2 \mid |\varphi_0\rangle) = \begin{bmatrix} 1 - \frac{\alpha}{2} & \frac{\alpha}{2} \\ \frac{\alpha}{2} & 1 - \beta - \frac{\alpha}{2} \end{bmatrix} \begin{bmatrix} 1 - \frac{\alpha}{2} \\ \frac{\alpha}{2} \\ 1 - \frac{\alpha}{2} \end{bmatrix}, \quad P(0 \mid |\varphi_1\rangle) = \begin{bmatrix} \frac{\alpha}{2} & \frac{-\alpha}{2} \\ \frac{-\alpha}{2} & \frac{\alpha}{2} \end{bmatrix} \begin{bmatrix} 0 \\ 0 \\ 0 \end{bmatrix},$$

$$P(1 \mid |\varphi_1\rangle) = \begin{bmatrix} 0 & 0 \\ 0 & \beta \end{bmatrix} \begin{bmatrix} 0 \\ \frac{\beta}{\sqrt{2}} \\ \frac{\beta}{2} \end{bmatrix}, \quad P(2 \mid |\varphi_1\rangle) = \begin{bmatrix} 1 - \frac{\alpha}{2} & \frac{\alpha}{2} \\ \frac{\alpha}{2} & 1 - \beta - \frac{\alpha}{2} \end{bmatrix} \begin{bmatrix} \frac{1}{\sqrt{2}} \\ \frac{1-\beta}{\sqrt{2}} \\ 1 - \frac{\beta}{2} \end{bmatrix}.$$

It is easy to see that to our satisfaction the completeness relation (3.3) has been fulfilled

$$\sum_{m=0}^{2} P(m \mid |\varphi_0\rangle) = 1, \quad \sum_{m=0}^{2} P(m \mid |\varphi_1\rangle) = 1.$$

Now, in possession of the above probabilities we can design different strategies (parameter setups). The most obvious one seems to cancel $P(2 \mid |\varphi_0\rangle)$ and $P(2 \mid |\varphi_1\rangle)$ to zero because in this way $P(0 \mid |\varphi_0\rangle) = 1$ and $P(1 \mid |\varphi_1\rangle) = 1$ and we are able to differentiate $|\varphi_0\rangle$ and $|\varphi_1\rangle$ unambiguously. It requires $\alpha = \beta = 2$. Wait! We have just claimed the very opposite at the end of the previous section. When and where did we make the mistake? Remember we postponed checking whether D_2 is positive semi-definite or not. It is easy to see that our current parameter setup for α and β does not provide this property. We are searching for D_2 in the form of $|\varphi_2\rangle\langle\varphi_2|$ because it guarantees that D_2 is positive semi-definite. Provided $|\varphi_2\rangle = [a, b]^T$ with real parameter a and b we infer

$$D_2 = |\varphi_2\rangle\langle\varphi_2| = \begin{bmatrix} a \\ b \end{bmatrix} \begin{bmatrix} a & b \end{bmatrix} \begin{bmatrix} 1 - \frac{\alpha}{2} & \frac{\alpha}{2} \\ \frac{\alpha}{2} & 1 - \beta - \frac{\alpha}{2} \end{bmatrix},$$

from which

$$a = \sqrt{1 - \frac{\alpha}{2}}, \quad b = \sqrt{1 - \beta - \frac{\alpha}{2}},$$

and we have the following constraint

$$\frac{\alpha}{2} = \sqrt{1 - \frac{\alpha}{2}}\sqrt{1 - \beta - \frac{\alpha}{2}} \Rightarrow \beta = \frac{1 - \alpha}{1 - \frac{\alpha}{2}}.$$ (3.26)

Unfortunately setup $\alpha = \beta = 2$ does not satisfy (3.26).

3.3.2 How to apply POVM operators

Equation (3.26) allows some freedom when designing the POVM set. Therefore the free parameters should be adjusted according to the demand of the technical problem under consideration. However, before dealing with these parameters let us explain how to use the previously defined POVM operators.

If $|\varphi_0\rangle$ were received then according to the probabilities $P(m \mid |\varphi_0\rangle)$ we would never measure $m = 1$, thus if the measuring device shows $m = 1$ we can be sure that $|\varphi_1\rangle$ was fed to the equipment. Similarly if $|\varphi_1\rangle$ were sent to us then we would never measure $m = 0$, hence if the equipment shows $m = 0$ then obviously $|\varphi_1\rangle$ was the selected state. Of course in certain cases the device responds with $m = 2$, then we can only guess the chosen vector from the set. Although we are not able to make uncertainty disappear there is a qualitative difference compared to the projective measurement. Unlike observing an outcome as in the projective measurement we can never be sure about the input, however, POVM enables – not in all cases – to give the correct answer with probability 1. Now we are ready to turn to the free parameters.

Keeping in view (3.26) first we assume that measuring 2 instead of the sent 0 or 1 has the same importance. Therefore we adjust $P(2 \mid |\varphi_0\rangle) = P(2 \mid |\varphi_1\rangle)$, which requires $\alpha = \beta = 2 \pm \sqrt{2}$. Because $\alpha = \beta = 2 + \sqrt{2}$ leads to $P(2 \mid |\varphi_0\rangle) < 0, P(2 \mid |\varphi_1\rangle) > 1$ we decide to set $\alpha = \beta = 2 - \sqrt{2}$. When we have *a priori* information about the statistics of $|\varphi_0\rangle$ and $|\varphi_1\rangle$ we can compensate different rates of occurrence by means of α.

However, all these tunings are controlled by an important rule which keeps us away from unambiguously distinguishing non-orthogonal states. Therefore as the second attempt we try to minimize the probability of measuring $m = 2$, that is to minimize the uncertainty of our decisions

$$P(m = 2) = P(2 \mid |\varphi_0\rangle)P(|\varphi_0\rangle) + P(2 \mid |\varphi_1\rangle)P(|\varphi_1\rangle).$$

Assuming uniformly distributed *a priori* probabilities $P(|\varphi_k\rangle) = \frac{1}{2}$ (which is also the best decision if one has no information about $P(|\varphi_k\rangle)$), we get

$$P(m = 2) = -\frac{1}{4}\frac{\alpha^2 - 4\alpha + 6}{\alpha - 2}.$$

$P(m = 2)$ is depicted vs. α in Fig. 3.1 together with $P(m = 2) = 1$ which shows the region where acceptable values of α are located. We know furthermore that α, β have to be nonnegative and less or equal to 2 in order to ensure $P(0 \mid |\varphi_0\rangle) \geq 0$ and

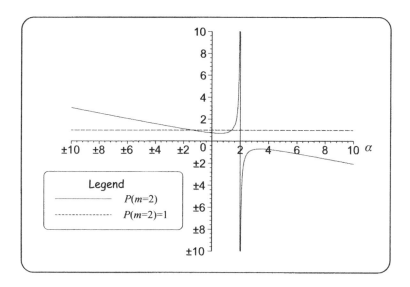

Fig. 3.1 $P(m = 2)$ and $P(m = 2) = 1$ vs. α

$P(1 \mid |\varphi_1\rangle) \geq 0$. In order to find its minimum point we calculate

$$\frac{dP(m = 2)}{d\alpha} = -\frac{1}{4}\frac{\alpha^2 - 4\alpha + 2}{(\alpha - 2)^2} = 0,$$

which advises us to chose $\alpha = \beta = 2 - \sqrt{2}$. Thus both aims can be fulfilled. The related $P(m = 2)$ equals $\frac{1}{\sqrt{2}}$ and as we expected $P(m = 2)$ cannot be reduced to zero, or in a much plausible form: we are restricted in moving probabilities between the certainty ($P(m = 0)$, $P(m = 1)$) and uncertainty ($P(m = 2)$) cases.

Our third endeavor aims to handle the so-called *false alarm – not happen alarm* problem. From an engineering point of view there are problems where making errors has different costs. For instance if the fire brigade visits a spot with nothing to do because no emergency situation has occurred the cost is less than sitting in the fire-station while a warehouse is burning down. Hence we assume that detecting $|\varphi_1\rangle$ correctly is much more important. We know already that there are some limitations for moving probabilities between $P(2 \mid |\varphi_1\rangle)$ and $P(1 \mid |\varphi_1\rangle)$ but maybe we can do the same between $P(0 \mid |\varphi_0\rangle)$ and $P(1 \mid |\varphi_1\rangle)$. Although Fig. 3.2 emphasizes that $\lim_{\alpha \to -\infty} P(2 \mid |\varphi_1\rangle) = 1$ unfortunately we need $\alpha \geq 0$, therefore $\alpha = 0$ is the best setup which provides $P(1 \mid |\varphi_1\rangle) = 0.5$. Hence asymptotically in half of the cases we will be able to give a correct answer if $|\varphi_1\rangle$ has been fed to the measuring device unlike the first two strategies where this value was only about 0.3. Of course we have to pay the price for this improvement, namely $P(0 \mid |\varphi_0\rangle)$ becomes 0 and equivalently always $m = 2$ is detected if $|\varphi_0\rangle$ has been sent.

Finally we emphasize a two-step generalization of the above example. First if we use a set of n-bit long linearly independent states $\{|\varphi_k\rangle\}$ with N elements

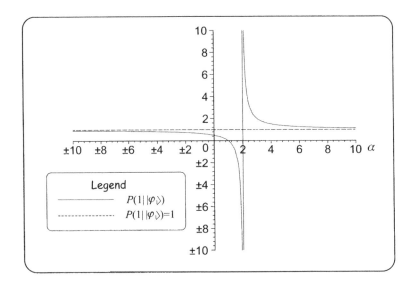

Fig. 3.2 $P(1 \mid |\varphi_1\rangle)$ and $P(1 \mid |\varphi_1\rangle) = 1$ vs. α

($k = 0, 1 \ldots N - 1$) where obviously $N \leq 2^n - 1$, then in compliance with the above explained technique one can form corresponding POVM operators D_m, $m = 0, 1 \ldots N$ which enables correct answers if the measuring equipment indicates $m < N$ and we become indecisive only when $m = N$. Of course while expanding the number of dimensions the number of free parameters is also increasing providing weighting among the measurement outcomes. Moreover, if the linear independency is not fulfilled for the members of the vector set then decision uncertainty will be increased but still one can optimize according to some demands (e.g. squared norm) based on the free parameters. For useful references see the *Further Reading* of this chapter.

3.4   RELATIONS AMONG THE MEASUREMENT TYPES

As we discussed in Section 3.2.1 projector P_m is constructed using the outer product representation $|\varphi_m\rangle\langle\varphi_m|$, where $|\varphi_m\rangle$ belongs to an orthonormal set $\{|\varphi_k\rangle\}$. Furthermore any operator in the form of $|\varphi_m\rangle\langle\varphi_m|$ proves to be positive semi-definite thus it can be regarded as a member of a POVM set (see Section 3.3.1). Consequently any projector is also positive semi-definite, therefore each projective measurement means at the same time a POVM while the POVM becomes projective measurement if $D_m \equiv P_m$, that is they are defined over an orthonormal set.

While projective measurements can be regarded as special cases of general measurements, clearly speaking POVM should be considered as watching general measurements via special spectacles. Therefore for any POVM set $\{D_m\}$ we can

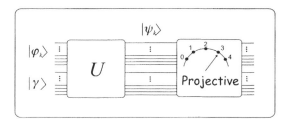

Fig. 3.3 Implementing general measurement by means of a projective one

define $M_m = \sqrt{D_m}$ and vice versa. However, the connection between $\{D_m\}$ and M_m is not unambiguous, that is we can define several different M_m to a certain D_m. All of them result in the same measurement statistic but they produce different post-measurement states. This is the reason why we omit dealing with the second statement of the 3rd Postulate.

The connection between the two types of measurements is based on Neumark's theorem. Assuming a set of non-orthogonal states n-qbit of length each and a general measurement acting on them, we can ensure their orthogonality by extending them with several auxiliary qbits. This means nothing more than increasing the number of dimensions and within a larger space the states can be orthogonalized. To achieve this goal we need a so-called ancilla qregister $|\gamma\rangle$ initialized with any classical state (say $|0\rangle$) and a unitary transformation U which produces the orthogonal states $|\psi_k\rangle$ in the larger space, see Fig. 3.3. In possession of $|\psi_k\rangle$ we can define a projective measurement $P_k = |\psi_k\rangle\langle\psi_k|$ for the extended system which results in the measurement outcomes of the original system as if we had performed the general measurement.

3.5   QUANTUM COMPUTING-BASED SOLUTION OF THE GAME WITH MARBLES

Now, we are in possession of all the knowledge that is required to design a sure-success strategy for Alice and Bob in the game introduced in Section 1.3. If the reader recalls the rules of this simple game it becomes obvious that Alice and Bob need to decide between two properties, namely whether the aggregate number of marbles equals 4 or 6 (or equivalently we get a head or a tail). Furthermore we concluded that when using classical approaches certainty cannot be achieved. Therefore we need something really 'quantum'. Let us try Einstein's *spooky action at a distance*, namely the entanglement. Hopefully it will supply us with the missing surplus. We suggest that Alice and Bob prepare and share a Bell state say $|\beta_{00}\rangle = \frac{|00\rangle + |11\rangle}{\sqrt{2}}$. They will modify this state according to their observations by means of appropriate quantum gates. The possible outcomes of these operations should be such that they allow distinguishing the 4- and 6-marbles scenarios. As we have learned in this chapter states can be distinguished unambiguously only if they are orthogonal. Hence we take say $|\beta_{01}\rangle = \frac{|00\rangle - |11\rangle}{\sqrt{2}}$ as the other quantum state beside $|\beta_{00}\rangle$ because Bell states ensure the required orthogonality. Now we have two problems to solve when designing the new quantum computing based strategy:

- First we should give transformations to Alice and Bob which ensures that marble combinations belonging to tail keep state $|\beta_{00}\rangle$ while those which are forming the set of head lead to $|\beta_{01}\rangle$.

- Once we have achieved our first goal an appropriate measurement apparatus should be constructed. Theoretically there is no obstacle in our way. Generation of Bell states is very simple (cf. Fig. 2.11) we need only a Hadamard and a CNOT gate. If we reverse these gates then we will yield either $|00\rangle$ or $|01\rangle$. The second bit belongs to Bob thus by signalling this one-bit information the original question related to the coin can be answered trivially. Interestingly Bob obtained the answer without any communication – neither quantum nor classical – with Alice. Hence if the roles were replaced faster than light communication would be implemented. At least at first sight. The inverse of the Hadamard gate is itself and exploiting the definition of unitary transforms we need to calculate the adjoint of the matrix of a CNOT gate. Unfortunately there is a minor practical problem between us and the devastation of relativity theory. The CNOT gate operates on both qbits at the same time thus its inverse does the same. However, the rules of our game do not enable the usage of such a common equipment for Alice therefore we should find out how to surmount this difficulty. We require independent transforms and measurements for our players.

Let us first tackle the former problem. $|\beta_{01}\rangle$ can be reached from $|\beta_{00}\rangle$ in a single step using a phase gate $P(\alpha)$ with parameter $\alpha = \pi$

$$\mathbf{P}(\alpha) = \begin{bmatrix} 1 & 0 \\ 0 & e^{-j\alpha} \end{bmatrix}.$$

If we consider that in the case of tail we have all together 4 marbles while head results in 6 of them then obviously setting $\alpha = \frac{\pi}{2}$ and performing such a phase gate successively as many times as many marbles Alice and Bob hold in their hands the common state of the two qbits will fit our expectations.

Concerning the second problem we follow a pragmatic approach. Let us skip the inverse of the CNOT gate and apply only the Hadamard gate on the first (Alice's) qbit and check what happens with the qbits

$$(H \otimes I)|\beta_{00}\rangle = |\beta_{10}\rangle = \frac{|01\rangle + |10\rangle}{\sqrt{2}}$$

while

$$(H \otimes I)|\beta_{01}\rangle = |\beta_{00}\rangle = \frac{|00\rangle + |11\rangle}{\sqrt{2}}.$$

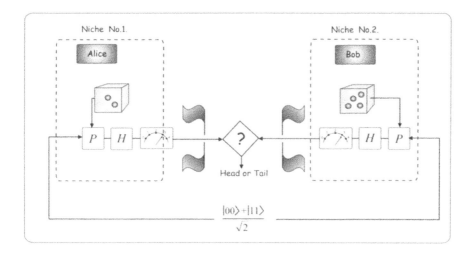

Fig. 3.4 Alice and Bob are playing marbles using quantum strategy

Thus if Alice and Bob perform separated measurements in the $|0\rangle$, $|1\rangle$ basis then the result can be distinguished easily without the application of the inverted CNOT gate. Alice and Bob signal their outcomes using the flags to the audience who makes the following simple mapping: they announce head if the two qbits are the same else head has to be reported.

Having finished the design process we emphasize that another interesting (slightly more difficult game) can be found at [80].

Finally we call the reader to design similar motivation games and post it to the authors (imre@hit.bme.hu) in ps or pdf format. New games will be collected and shared on the book's web page.

3.6 FURTHER READING

The technique we used to introduce POVM for distinguishing non-orthogonal states is based on Peres' work [119] which was further refined in [17]. Extension of the two-states one-qbit example for multiple, linearly independent states scenario was considered in [93]. Hausladen *et al.* discussed the general problem which aims at the differentiation among the states of an arbitrary set with the constraint that the number of states is less or equal to the dimension of the space they span [116]. The measurement they defined is referred to as *square-root measurement* (SRM) in the literature. The operators of a SRM can be easily produced using the states in question and we can minimize the probability of error if the states possess certain symmetries [103]. As one may expect SRM performs fairly well if the states are near orthogonal and their *a priori* probabilities follow uniform distribution [117] and it can be proven that it is asymptotically optimal [116]. A very sophisticated survey of these achievements and the proof of optimality of SRM in least-square sense can be found in [154].

Concerning the Neumark extension we advise the reader to read [120].

Eldar and Oppenheim introduced an interesting and straightforward special framework for classical signal processing with borrowed ideas related to quantum measurements in [153]. Dušek and Bužek proposed a programmable quantum measurement device for POVM in [106].

Part II

Quantum Algorithms

4

Two Simple Quantum Algorithms

The majority of this book focuses on quantum algorithms which are significantly more efficient than their best-known classical alternatives. There are no magic formulas about designing appropriate quantum algorithms to solve a certain problem. As we will see later several often used and fairly useful tools can be attained when studying available quantum algorithms systematically. However, before staring this interesting but time-consuming process we present two simple algorithms that can be understood without effort based on our (at this point) limited available skills in quantum computing. They typically excite beginners and give enough stimulation to get through some hard topics. We show how to use quantum communication channels to achieve higher information transfer rates by means of superdense coding in Section 4.1. Next the dream of all science fiction fans will be fulfilled when we design a quantum-based teleportation device in Section 4.2.

4.1 SUPERDENSE CODING

The science that is responsible among others for investigating theoretical limits of communication over an erroneous channel is called information theory. It was founded by Claude Shannon [136] in the 1940s. This science has since been flourishing not only in terms of theory but also the results have been transplanted into equivalent everyday practice and built in all communication devices. The corresponding quantum equivalent – called quantum information theory – forms the backbone of the second volume of this book. Here we would like to present only a

Quantum Computing and Communications   S. Imre, F. Balázs
© 2004 John Wiley & Sons, Ltd   ISBN 0-470-86902-X (HB)

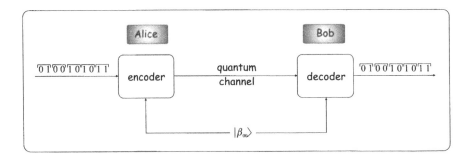

Fig. 4.1   The superdense coding scenario

simple but very stimulating example referred to as superdense coding in the literature that highlights the jewels hidden in the quantum world.

Being frustrated with the everyday phone conversations our assistants Alice and Bob decided to exchange information over an error-free quantum channel instead of using a pair of copper wires, where *quantum* refers to the capability of being able to deliver superpositions instead of classical states. The major steps can be followed in Fig. 4.1.

First Alice and Bob prepare several $|\beta_{00}\rangle$ Bell states and Bob slips one qbit of each pair in his pocket before leaving. Later when they begin the conversation Alice converts the analogous speech signal into binary strings consisting of classical 0s and 1s. Next she encodes each dibit (pair of two consecutive bits) into a superposition using special transformations on the half pair being in her possession. The coding rules are listed in the first two columns of Table 4.1. Alice then sends her qbit over the quantum channel to Bob. Now Bob has to find an appropriate decoding scheme to restore the original classical information. Since Bob was a keen student during the previous chapters he calculates the possible joint states of the two-qbit system in his hands and writes them into the third column. After a short cogitation Bob realizes (hopefully together with the reader) that the listed states are nothing more than the Bell pairs introduced in Section 2.6.3. We learned there their important property, namely they are orthogonal thus they can be cloned and distinguished unambiguously. Let us help Bob to design such a decoding equipment. Bell states can be produced by means of a Hadamard and a CNOT gate according to Fig. 2.11. Therefore in order to obtain the classical inputs in this figure from the outputs we have to reverse i.e. invert this circuit. Because of the unitary nature of the Bell gate its inverse can be computed as its adjoint

$$((H \otimes I)CNOT)^{-1} = ((H \otimes I)CNOT)^{\dagger} = CNOT^{\dagger}(H \otimes I)^{\dagger}.$$

Since both $(H \otimes I)$ and *CNOT* are Hermitian operators Bob has to implement these gates in the reverse order to build the decoder. We ask the reader to validate this result in **Exercise** 4.1.

Having clarified all the technical questions related to the quantum-assisted classical information transfer we turn to the evaluation of its advantages. If Alice and Bob were using classical digital telephones then they would need to send and receive both classical bits of each dibit. The quantum computing based solution utilizes two quantum bits, too. However, unlike the classical approach, at the time of the conversation only half the amount of qbits has to be sent revealing why this algorithm is called superdense coding.

Table 4.1 Encoding rules for Alice and the corresponding two-qbit states

dibit	transform	joint state
00	I	$\dfrac{\lvert 00\rangle + \lvert 11\rangle}{\sqrt{2}}$
01	Z	$\dfrac{\lvert 00\rangle - \lvert 11\rangle}{\sqrt{2}}$
10	X	$\dfrac{\lvert 10\rangle + \lvert 01\rangle}{\sqrt{2}}$
11	jY	$\dfrac{\lvert 01\rangle - \lvert 10\rangle}{\sqrt{2}}$

Exercise 4.1. Check whether the $CNOT(H \otimes I)$ gate really returns the wanted classical states.

4.2 QUANTUM TELEPORTATION

There is an often-repeated scene in most popular science fiction novels and movies. The space traveller enters a cabin on the board of a space ship than he/she suddenly disappears accompanied by colorful lighting effects. A few moments later our astronaut appears in another cabin located on a planet hundreds of light-years away from the starting point. Let us analyze this futuristic scene scientifically. There are two alternatives about how to carry out teleportation in practice.

On one hand we can break the traveller into smaller parts, say to elementary particles such as electrons, protons, etc., in the departure cabin. As we have learned earlier these particles obey quantum mechanics and thus each of them can be represented as a one-qbit superposition. Therefore we need a quantum communication channel between the two locations to transfer the components of our daring astronaut. Finally he/she has to be rebuilt in the arrival cabin from the original particles. This approach requires an error-free channel (more precisely error-free communication protocol) unless we would like to meet with a monster. Communications over a quantum channel together with other aspects of quantum information theory belong to the main part of the second volume of this book. However, we can reveal in advance that this job proves to be very hard.

On the other hand we are able to replace quantum communications with a classical one and utilize our related broad knowledge. To follow this way we have to measure and encode the state of each particle and only this classical information will be delivered between the two cabins. In the destination cabin a stockpile of particles are required from which the traveller can be rebuilt in compliance with the transferred assembly manual. Unfortunately this idea also suffers some drawbacks. The most challenging one is how the states of the particles can be measured? Theoretically we need an infinite number of measurements to estimate the corresponding probability amplitudes with arbitrary small inaccuracy. Finally we can conclude that neither method seems to be mature enough for practical implementation, if only...

If only we exploit our skills in quantum computing. Our assistants Alice and Bob are going to demonstrate a suitable protocol. They decided to teleport an apple in commemoration of Newton between Alice standing on the Earth and Bob spending the weekend on the Moon. For the sake of simplicity they will present the teleportation of a single particle because if it works then an apple requires only solving some minor technological problems.

Let us denote the arbitrary quantum state of the particle to be teleported by $|\psi\rangle = a|0\rangle + b|1\rangle$. The operation of the teleporting device can be followed step by step in Fig. 4.2. First Alice and Bob share a $|\beta_{00}\rangle = \frac{|00\rangle + |11\rangle}{\sqrt{2}}$ Bell pair and Bob puts his qbit in his pocket before leaving for the Moon. To make it easier to follow the operation we refer to Alice's quantum wires as A_1 and A_2 and to Bob's half pair as B. The initial input joint state is trivially

$$|\varphi_0\rangle = |\psi\rangle|\beta_{00}\rangle = \frac{1}{\sqrt{2}}\left[a|\overset{A_1}{0}\rangle\left(|\overset{A_2B}{0\,0}\rangle + |\overset{A_2B}{1\,1}\rangle\right) + b|\overset{A_1}{1}\rangle\left(|\overset{A_2B}{0\,0}\rangle + |\overset{A_2B}{1\,1}\rangle\right)\right].$$

Next Alice applies a CNOT gate onto the qbits in her hands. However, instead of using matrix-vector operations we exploit the superposition principle, that is a control with 0 leaves the data qbit unchanged while a 1 on the upper wire inverts the lower output (see Section 2.6.2). In order to highlight the modifications due to the CNOT gate we have boldfaced the corresponding qbit ($\mathbf{A_2}$)

$$|\varphi_1\rangle = \frac{1}{\sqrt{2}}\left[a|\overset{A_1}{0}\rangle\left(|\overset{A_2B}{0\,0}\rangle + |\overset{A_2B}{1\,1}\rangle\right) + b|\overset{A_1}{1}\rangle\left(|\overset{\mathbf{A_2}B}{\mathbf{1}\,0}\rangle + |\overset{\mathbf{A_2}B}{\mathbf{0}\,1}\rangle\right)\right].$$

The forthcoming Hadamard transform on the topmost quantum wire implements the well-known rule: $H|0\rangle \to \frac{|0\rangle + |1\rangle}{\sqrt{2}}$ and $H|1\rangle \to \frac{|0\rangle - |1\rangle}{\sqrt{2}}$ leading to

$$|\varphi_2\rangle = \frac{1}{\sqrt{2}}\frac{1}{\sqrt{2}}$$
$$\times\left[a\left(|\overset{A_1}{0}\rangle + |\overset{A_1}{1}\rangle\right)\left(|\overset{A_2B}{0\,0}\rangle + |\overset{A_2B}{1\,1}\rangle\right) + b\left(|\overset{A_1}{0}\rangle - |\overset{A_1}{1}\rangle\right)\left(|\overset{A_2B}{1\,0}\rangle + |\overset{A_2B}{0\,1}\rangle\right)\right].$$

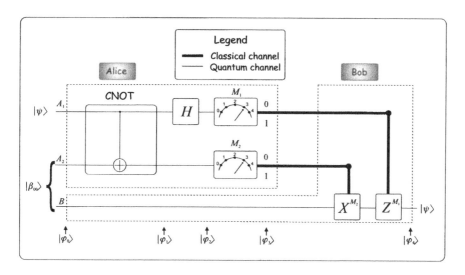

Fig. 4.2   The teleportation scenario

Before performing the measurements Alice regroups the terms in $|\varphi_2\rangle$ according to her two qbits to produce a more readable form

$$|\varphi_2\rangle = \frac{1}{2}\left[\overset{A_1 A_2}{|0\;0\rangle}\left(a\overset{B}{|0\rangle} + b\overset{B}{|1\rangle}\right) + \overset{A_1 A_2}{|0\;1\rangle}\left(a\overset{B}{|1\rangle} + b\overset{B}{|0\rangle}\right) \right.$$
$$\left. + \overset{A_1 A_2}{|1\;0\rangle}\left(a\overset{B}{|0\rangle} - b\overset{B}{|1\rangle}\right) + \overset{A_1 A_2}{|1\;1\rangle}\left(a\overset{B}{|1\rangle} - b\overset{B}{|0\rangle}\right) \right]. \tag{4.1}$$

Obviously Alice obtains one of the four possible two-bit results among 00, 01, 10 or 11 as measurement outcome. Each of them is in close connection with the state of Bob's qbit hence Alice sends these two classical bits to Bob. After a short hesitation Bob compares $|\psi\rangle$ to the potential states of his half Bell pair. It is easy to realize the following relations

$$
\begin{array}{ccccc}
A_1 A_2 & \rightarrow & B & = & U|\psi\rangle \\
00 & \rightarrow & \frac{a|0\rangle+b|1\rangle}{2} & = & I|\psi\rangle \\
01 & \rightarrow & \frac{a|1\rangle+b|0\rangle}{2} & = & X|\psi\rangle \\
10 & \rightarrow & \frac{a|0\rangle-b|1\rangle}{2} & = & Z|\psi\rangle \\
11 & \rightarrow & \frac{a|1\rangle-b|0\rangle}{2} & = & ZX|\psi\rangle.
\end{array}
$$

Therefore Bob has only to apply the inverse of the appropriate transform(s) in compliance with the received classical bits. Since our Bob read Part I carefully he knows that all these operators are unitary thus their inverses can be calculated simply by building their adjoint. Moreover it is easy to see that they are Hermitian too, which explains why the original gates are used in Fig. 4.2 as gates controlled by measurement results M_1 and M_2. Thus finally Bob obtains the original $|\psi\rangle$.

The reader may wonder where the information really travelled between Alice and Bob? Trivially the classically sent two bits were not enough to carry almost arbitrary a and b complex pairs. We would rather say that Alice encodes the difference between $|\psi\rangle$ and the half Bell pair into the classical bits. Since the other half is in Bob's possession he is able to reproduce $|\psi\rangle$ by means of the difference.

Another straightforward approach to explain the surprising operation of the teleporting device is if the reader recalls what we have learned about preparing entanglement in Section 2.6.3. If one managed to produce a Bell pair successfully then a third qbit can be entangled with the other two having only one of them in our hands. Alice's CNOT gate operates as an entangler machine thus the information has been transferred via the indirect entanglement between $|\psi\rangle$ and Bob's qbit.

There are several important aspects and consequences of the above explained teleportation technique:

- Alice needs no information about $|\psi\rangle$ to teleport it.

- Without Alice's classically transferred bit pair Bob is not able to produce $|\psi\rangle$ thus no 'faster than light' communication is possible in this way, which is in full harmony with the relativity theory.

- In order to encode and transfer a and b, i.e. $|\psi\rangle$ classically, Alice may require a very large amount of classical bits let alone the measurement problem about how to gain them. Conversely teleportation needs only two classical and two quantum bits altogether.

Exercise 4.2. Using teleportation Bob obtains a replica of an arbitrary one-qbit state in Alice's hand. Explain why quantum teleportation cannot be used in this way as a cloning machine.

4.3 FURTHER READING

Superdense coding was proposed by Bennett and Wiesner [41] in 1992. The first idea of how to carry out theoretically quantum teleportation originated from Charles Bennett and his international team [40, 152] in 1993. The first experimental realization was accomplished by the team of Anton Zeilinger [47] in Insbruck in 1997. A popular description of their work can be found in [22]. Braunstein and Kimble expanded the Insbruck experiment in 1998 and showed [141, 142] that the input and output states of teleportation are the same. An NMR-based realization was carried out by Nielsen and his colleagues [102] in the same year. Impressive results on successful long-distance teleportation is related to Nicolas Gisin and his Geneva team. They use teleportation as a building block of quantum cryptography protocols for references see Chapter 10. Since these very first results the topic is becoming very popular both from the algorithmic and implementation point of view. Interested readers are suggested to read [79].

5

Quantum Parallelism

Quantum parallelism is one of the major driving forces of quantum computing and can be referred to as a solid basis of most quantum-based algorithms alongside entanglement. This special kind of parallel computation allows solving classically complex problems such as searching an unstructured database or finding prime factors of large numbers while breaking ciphering protocols during an astonishing short period of time. In order to lay dawn the foundations of sophisticated quantum algorithms mathematical formulation of quantum parallelism (Section 5.1) with simple practical examples of Deutsch–Jozsa and Simon algorithms (Section 5.2 and 5.3) are provided within this chapter.

5.1 INTRODUCTION

Let us assume that we have an unknown function $f(x) : \{0,1\}^n \rightarrow \{0,1\}^1$. In order to determine the exact rules of its operation classically we have to substitute all the potential inputs $x = 0, 1, \ldots, 2^n - 1$, which requires either a large amount of evaluation of f sequentially or we need to buy $N = 2^n$ pieces of parallel switched elementary gates implementing f.

We try to exploit the special features of the quantum world to build a quantum gate which is able to perform this job in a single step. First we solve this problem for $f(x) : \{0,1\}^1 \rightarrow \{0,1\}^1$, which will be followed by the generalization of the binary result to n.

When we consider the master equation of the CNOT gate (2.10) with control input $|C\rangle_{IN} = \frac{|0\rangle + |1\rangle}{\sqrt{2}}$ and data input $|D\rangle_{IN} = |0\rangle$ i.e., we produce Bell pair $\frac{|00\rangle + |11\rangle}{\sqrt{2}}$,

Quantum Computing and Communications S. Imre, F. Balázs
© 2004 John Wiley & Sons, Ltd ISBN 0-470-86902-X (HB)

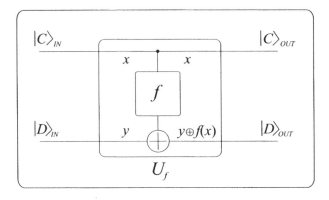

Fig. 5.1 f-controlled CNOT gate

Table 5.1   Truth table of f-controlled CNOT gate

IN		OUT	
x	y	x	$y \oplus f(x)$
0	0	0	$0 \oplus f(0) = f(0)$
0	1	0	$1 \oplus f(0)$
1	0	1	$0 \oplus f(1) = f(1)$
1	1	1	$1 \oplus f(1)$

we can observe apart from entanglement that data output contains both possible data input values. Now we introduce a little modification of the master equation (2.10) in the following way

$$U_f : |x\rangle|y\rangle \rightarrow |x\rangle|y \oplus f(x)\rangle, \tag{5.1}$$

where variables x and y are depicted in Fig. 5.1 and they refer to computational basis vectors instead of arbitrary superpositions. Therefore $x, y \in \{0, 1\}$ and the corresponding truth table is presented in Table 5.1, which allows us to apply the superposition principle for arbitrary superpositions at the inputs of the new gate.

Assuming the same inputs as for the CNOT gate and considering truth Table 5.1 we can easily calculate the output of the f-controlled CNOT gate

$$U_f \frac{|00\rangle + |10\rangle}{\sqrt{2}} = \frac{|0\rangle|f(0)\rangle + |1\rangle|f(1)\rangle}{\sqrt{2}}, \tag{5.2}$$

which comprises both $f(0)$ and $f(1)$ after a single run of the gate. We emphasize that in this binary case $|C\rangle_{IN}$ contains $|0\rangle$ and $|1\rangle$, i.e. all the possible values of x.

Remark: It is worth emphasizing that U_f is reversible independently from the fact whether f is reversible or not. It has been achieved by retaining the corresponding input $|x\rangle$ beside $|f(x)\rangle$ at the output.

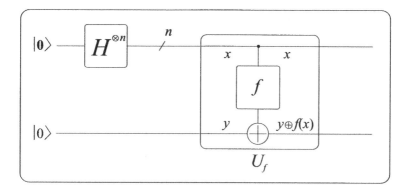

Fig. 5.2 f-controlled CNOT gate with N-dimensional control input implementing parallel evaluation of f

Since we know from (2.9) that the output of an n-qbit Hadamard gate contains a superposition of all the possible x of n bit length if it was fed with $|0\rangle_{2^n}$, hence when generalizing the binary result to an input control register n bit of size we have to start with a quantum state $|0\rangle_N$ which is connected to an N-dimensional Hadamard gate $H^{\otimes n}$, i.e. on each control wire a one-qbit H is deployed (see Fig. 5.2). The output of the Hadamard gate has to be connected to the input control register and a $|0\rangle$ to the data input, respectively. Generalizing master equation (5.1) to multiqbit control input we get

$$U_f : |x\rangle_N|y\rangle \rightarrow |x\rangle_N|y \oplus f(x)\rangle, \qquad (5.3)$$

where by applying the binary notation $x \in \{0,1\}^n$ we are going to highlight the fact that a qregister n bit of length is used as the control input. Therefore the output of the generalized f-controlled CNOT gate can be expressed as

$$U_f \frac{1}{\sqrt{2^n}} \sum_{x \in \{0,1\}^n} |x\rangle|0\rangle = \frac{1}{\sqrt{2^n}} \sum_{x \in \{0,1\}^n} |x\rangle|0 \oplus f(x)\rangle$$

$$= \frac{1}{\sqrt{2^n}} \sum_{x \in \{0,1\}^n} |x\rangle|f(x)\rangle = \frac{1}{\sqrt{2^n}} \sum_{x=0}^{2^n-1} |x\rangle|f(x)\rangle, \quad (5.4)$$

which means that we have a special superposition: each member of this superposition consists of a control output emitting one of the possible arguments x and a data output which represents the corresponding $f(x)$. So $f(x)$ has been evaluated for all the x in a *single* step independently from the size of N! We mentioned at the end of Section 2.3 that $n = 500$ qbit forming a quantum register may contain more integer numbers than the number of atoms in the known universe. Now we designed a quantum gate which is able to evaluate a given function for all these numbers in a single step.

Unfortunately there is a non-subsidiary fact which cannot be omitted. When we try to access the result register containing all the values of $f(x)$ independently from the applied measurement technique we are able to get back only one of them. The price we must pay seems to be too high because taking into account this constraint one may put the following obvious question: is it worth using quantum parallelism at all? Fortunately we have a straightforward and reassuring answer to this question. On one hand while we run quantum operators without measurements, advantages of quantum parallelism can be exploited without any difficulties. On the other hand apart from quantum parallelism we possess a brain which is able to construct such quantum gates that perform so-called *amplitude amplification*, i.e. they increase the probability amplitude of a given $f(x)$ near or equal to 1. This fact results that an appropriate measurement will give back the requested $f(x)$ value with probability $O(1)$ or in certain cases with sure success.

Remark: Amplitude amplification referred originally to a recursive technique related to the generalization of the Grover algorithm (see Chapter 7). However, we use it in a more generalized sense, denoting any techniques aiming to increase target probability amplitudes before measurement. Perhaps the plainest example of amplitude amplification is the operation of the idealistic quantum interferometer (see Section 2.5), where the second beam splitter (half-silvered mirror), while interfering the two branches of the interferometer, ensures that the photon always hits the same detector, i.e. the probability amplitude of striking that detector was amplified to 1. Therefore this notion is also often referred to as *constructive interference*. In the case of constructive interference amplitude amplification comprises only a single iteration step.

Presumably the reason now becomes clear for the reader why we mentioned at the beginning of this chapter that quantum parallelism is *only one* of the major driving forces of quantum computing. It is similar to an everyday tool whose handling must be learned in order to use it efficiently. The essence of the further sections in this chapter – beyond introducing several simple problems and their quantum solutions – can be regarded as a training on how to exploit quantum parallelism.

Exercise 5.1. Prove that $U_f : |x\rangle_N |y\rangle \rightarrow |x\rangle_N |y \oplus f(x)\rangle$ is unitary.

5.2 DEUTSCH–JOZSA ALGORITHM

People who are familiar with old tales and legends know that these stories contain pieces from a large common set of patterns which originate from the ancient heritage of the human race. It is typical that the young hero/prince has to stand several tests during his long journey before winning the love of the beautiful princess and/or the kingdom of the old king.[1] One often-mentioned episode is when the prince arrives at

---

[1] E.g. If the reader is living in the northern hemisphere and takes a look at the starry sky she/he can easily recognize several constellations (in italics) telling the story of Greek *Perseus* who killed the evil *Medusa* liberating *Pegasos* the winged horse and finally rescued the beautiful *Andromeda* daughter of *Kepheus* and *Kassiopeia*.

a crossroad which either leads to Hell or to the castle of the princess and the hero has to decide which of them to choose (this *good way-bad way* situation often occurs in the third millennium too when we are trying to reach our workplace by car during the morning rush hours). Fortunately there are usually two tramps/witches offering their services and the prince has to answer some tricky questions/puzzles in exchange of information about the right way.

Now during our journey in the quantum world, which is full of strange phenomena and rules, we arrive at our crossroad where we have to encode our questions to the witches into n-bit long binary vectors $x \in \{0,1\}^n$ and they respond by means of YES/NO, i.e. binary 0 or 1. We use binary notation instead of applying decimal numbers – in spite of the fact that they are equivalent – in this section because the former one proves to be more convenient for the mathematical formalism. Furthermore they tell us that one of them answers consequently with either 0 or 1 to all the possible questions and the other one replies with 0 for half of all possible x and 1 for the remaining half. The function $f(x)$ implemented by the former witch is called *constant* in the literature while the latter one *balanced* and we have to guess which of the witches is constant and which is the balanced one.

Classical heroes such as Odysseus or King Arthur would need $2^n/2 + 1 = 2^{n-1} + 1$ questions to carry out such a classification with certainty but for pioneers of quantum computing – Deutsch and Jozsa – it was enough to ask a single question to one of the witches (assuming they are quantum witches). In this section we present a suitable algorithm proposed in its original form by Deutsch and Jozsa and later refined by other scientists (see *Further Reading*) to solve this *good way-bad way* type of problem.

Assuming n-bit long questions we have all together $N = 2^n$ different possibilities for x, and we know that $f(x) : \{0,1\}^n \rightarrow \{0,1\}^1$. It is obvious that quantum parallelism and interference (amplitude amplification) are more efficient tools than the best classical algorithm. Therefore we use the f-controlled CNOT gate (see Fig. 5.2) supplemented on its inputs and outputs according to the architecture in Fig. 5.3. The control input of gate U_f contains all the possible x prepared by means of an N-dimensional Hadamard gate, i.e. we put all the questions together to the witch in one special question. The novelty appears on the data input in the form of a superposition $|D\rangle_{IN} = \frac{|0\rangle - |1\rangle}{\sqrt{2}}$ instead of the basis state $|0\rangle$. Since the initial state of the system is $|\varphi_0\rangle = |0\rangle_N |1\rangle$, the input state of U_f can be described as

$$|\varphi_1\rangle = H^{\otimes(n+1)}|\varphi_0\rangle = \frac{1}{\sqrt{2^n}} \sum_{x \in \{0,1\}^n} |x\rangle \otimes \frac{|0\rangle - |1\rangle}{\sqrt{2}}$$

$$= \frac{1}{\sqrt{2^{(n+1)}}} \sum_{x \in \{0,1\}^n} |x\rangle |0\rangle - \frac{1}{\sqrt{2^{(n+1)}}} \sum_{x \in \{0,1\}^n} |x\rangle |1\rangle. \qquad (5.5)$$

Now the witch processes this input state using master equation (5.3) and remembering the superposition principle which allows her to use (5.3) independently in the two terms of (5.5). Regarding the first term she can rely on (5.4) and concerning

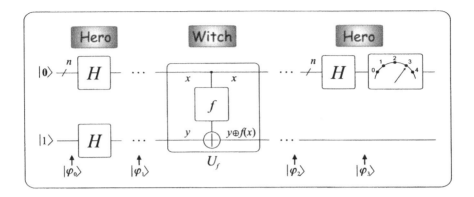

Fig. 5.3 Quantum architecture for solving the Deutsch–Jozsa problem

the second term

$$U_f \frac{1}{\sqrt{2^n}} \sum_{x \in \{0,1\}^n} |x\rangle|1\rangle = \frac{1}{\sqrt{2^n}} \sum_{x \in \{0,1\}^n} |x\rangle|1 \oplus f(x)\rangle. \qquad (5.6)$$

Finally she calculates her answer in the form of the output qregister

$$|\varphi_2\rangle = U_f |\varphi_1\rangle = \frac{1}{\sqrt{2^{(n+1)}}} \sum_{x \in \{0,1\}^n} |x\rangle|f(x)\rangle - \frac{1}{\sqrt{2^{(n+1)}}} \sum_{x \in \{0,1\}^n} |x\rangle|1 \oplus f(x)\rangle$$

$$= \frac{1}{\sqrt{2^n}} \sum_{x \in \{0,1\}^n} |x\rangle \frac{|f(x)\rangle - |1 \oplus f(x)\rangle}{\sqrt{2}}$$

$$= \frac{1}{\sqrt{2^n}} \sum_{x \in \{0,1\}^n} (-1)^{f(x)} |x\rangle \otimes \frac{|0\rangle - |1\rangle}{\sqrt{2}}, \qquad (5.7)$$

where at the last step she utilized the result of **Exercise** 5.2. Interestingly we obtained the same quantum state on the lower output as the corresponding input, thus it seems as if the lower quantum wire were a simple shortcut. This is, however, an 'optical' illusion because only the superposition principle acting inside the gate presented such a special output. In possession of her answer, before performing a suitable measurement, our prince has to amplify the appropriate probability amplitudes. To put this goal into practice we apply a $H^{\otimes n}$ gate to the control output qbits. We know from Section 2.4 that for computational basis vector $|x\rangle$

$$H^{\otimes n}|x\rangle = \frac{1}{\sqrt{2^n}} \sum_{z \in \{0,1\}^n} (-1)^{xz} |z\rangle, \qquad (5.8)$$

where xz refers to the binary scalar product of the two numbers considering them as binary vectors (sum of bitwise products modulo 2). We replace here z by x' in order to highlight the fact that before and after the transformation we use the same computational basis states, only the corresponding probability amplitudes have been modified. Therefore

$$|\varphi_3\rangle = (H^{\otimes n} \otimes I)|\varphi_2\rangle = \frac{1}{\sqrt{2^n}} \sum_{x\in\{0,1\}^n} (-1)^{f(x)} H^{\otimes n}|x\rangle \otimes \frac{|0\rangle - |1\rangle}{\sqrt{2}}$$

$$= \frac{1}{\sqrt{2^n}} \sum_{x\in\{0,1\}^n} (-1)^{f(x)} \frac{1}{\sqrt{2^n}} \sum_{x'\in\{0,1\}^n} (-1)^{xx'}|x'\rangle \otimes \frac{|0\rangle - |1\rangle}{\sqrt{2}}$$

$$= \sum_{x'\in\{0,1\}^n} \underbrace{\left(\frac{1}{2^n} \sum_{x\in\{0,1\}^n} (-1)^{xx'+f(x)} \right)}_{c_{x'}} |x'\rangle \otimes \frac{|0\rangle - |1\rangle}{\sqrt{2}}. \qquad (5.9)$$

Finally we construct a measurement which is able to discriminate between the two possibilities (constant or balanced). In order to carry out this task we examine coefficient c_0. Thus one can observe that

$$c_0 = \frac{1}{2^n} \sum_{x\in\{0,1\}^n} (-1)^{xx'+f(x)} = \frac{1}{2^n} \sum_{x\in\{0,1\}^n} (-1)^{f(x)} \qquad (5.10)$$

since $xx' = x0 \equiv 0$. Now let us investigate (5.10) when $f(x)$ is *constant*, then

$$c_0 = \begin{cases} -1 & \text{if } f(x) \equiv 1 \\ 1 & \text{if } f(x) \equiv 0. \end{cases} \qquad (5.11)$$

When concentrating on $|\varphi_3\rangle$ it is useful to highlight that the state of the data qbit is constant in terms of not depending on x (more precisely we can say that the control and data subsystems are not entangled) hence $c_{x'}$ equals the probability amplitude of corresponding $|x'\rangle$. We would like to emphasize here that in a more general case where entanglement binds together the two subsystems $c_{x'}$ does not represent at all the probability amplitude of $|x'\rangle$ (see Simon algorithm in Section 5.3). Taking into account that c_0 belongs to the partial system comprising the control qbits and it does not depend on the actual status of the data quantum wire, i.e. whether it is measured or not at all, measuring the control qbits in the computational basis states we always get $|0\rangle$ with probability 1, that is probability amplitudes of other basis vectors are expunged. Concerning the *balanced* scenario $c_0 = 0$ since we have the same number of positive (+1) and negative (-1) terms in the sum. Hence one thing is certain, namely the measuring equipment may respond to any of the computational basis states except $|0\rangle$. Keeping in mind these two results the prince[2] is able to decide by means of a single challenge whether the given witch is constant or balanced with sure success.

---

[2]Important hint for princes who are still wet behind the ears: before challenging an unknown witch make sure of her quantum capabilities!

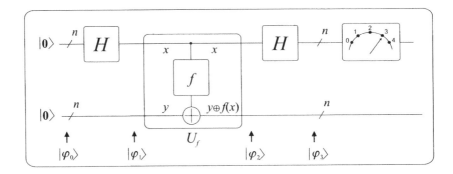

Fig. 5.4   Quantum architecture for solving Simon's problem

Remark: The single-control bit version $(n = 1)$ of the Deutsch–Jozsa algorithm refers to the original Deutsch problem where one has to decide whether $f(x) : \{0, 1\}^1 \to \{0, 1\}^1$ it is constant or varying.

Exercise 5.2. Prove that $|f(x)\rangle - |1 \oplus f(x)\rangle = (-1)^{f(x)}(|0\rangle - |1\rangle)$.

5.3   SIMON ALGORITHM

Let us modify the function f and the related question under discussion in the Deutsch–Jozsa problem in the following way: $f : \{0, 1\}^n \to \{0, 1\}^n$, i.e. Simon's algorithm deals with a binary vector valued function which is constrained by a special condition. f is periodical in terms of $f(x) = f(y)$ if and only if $x = y$ or $x = y \oplus r$, where $r \neq 0$ stands for the binary period of f. There are two obvious questions, namely how and in how many steps (evaluation of f) can r be computed. These questions can answered both classically and quantum computationally but with a major difference. A traditional computer requires an exponential number of queries while Simon's solution is able to find r after $O(n)$ iterations with high probability. To achieve this promising efficiency, master equation (5.3) has to be modified in compliance with f

$$U_f : |x\rangle_N |y\rangle_N \to |x\rangle_N |y \oplus f(x)\rangle_N. \tag{5.12}$$

The required architecture is depicted in Fig. 5.4. As one may recognize we start from $|\varphi_0\rangle = |0\rangle_N |0\rangle_N$, which is the modified version of the Deutsch–Jozsa scenario for multiqbit data output, where $N = 2^n$. Next an N-dimensional Hadamard gate is applied to the control qbits, but as an essential difference, data qbits are left to flow into the U_f gate without any transformation, thus

$$|\varphi_1\rangle = (H^{\otimes n} \otimes I^{\otimes n})|\varphi_0\rangle = \frac{1}{\sqrt{2^n}} \sum_{x \in \{0,1\}^n} |x\rangle |0\rangle_N. \tag{5.13}$$

The output of U_f can be determined easily because quantum parallelism is acting in the gate

$$|\varphi_2\rangle = U_f|\varphi_1\rangle = \frac{1}{\sqrt{2^n}} \sum_{x \in \{0,1\}^n} |x\rangle|f(x)\rangle. \tag{5.14}$$

Since the two-to-one constraint $|f(x)\rangle = |f(x \oplus r)\rangle$ pertaining to f strictly regulates that not only a given value of f originates *exactly* from two different arguments, but a given x may result *exactly* in one f value, the following superposition equals (5.14)

$$|\varphi_2\rangle = \frac{1}{\sqrt{2^n}} \sum_{x \in \{0,1\}^n} |x \oplus r\rangle|f(x \oplus r)\rangle. \tag{5.15}$$

Combining (5.14) with (5.15) and considering $f(x) = f(x \oplus r)$ and if r is a nontrivial period $(r \neq 0)$ of f we get

$$|\varphi_2\rangle = \frac{1}{\sqrt{2^n}} \sum_{x \in \{0,1\}^n} \frac{|x\rangle + |x \oplus r\rangle}{2}|f(x)\rangle, \tag{5.16}$$

where the extra division by factor 2 corrects the fact that every term in the sum is counted twice, i.e. we guaranteed in this way that $|\varphi_2\rangle$ remains a vector of unit length.

We have again the $H^{\otimes n}$ gate at the control output to accomplish constructive interference in order to eliminate probability amplitudes of unwanted computational basis states. According to (5.8) the measurement device is fed with the upper n control qbits of the following superposition

$$|\varphi_3\rangle = (H^{\otimes n} \otimes I^{\otimes n})|\varphi_2\rangle = \frac{1}{\sqrt{2^{(n+2)}}} \sum_{x \in \{0,1\}^n} H^{\otimes n}(|x\rangle + |x \oplus r\rangle) \otimes |f(x)\rangle$$

$$= \sum_{x' \in \{0,1\}^n} \sum_{x \in \{0,1\}^n} \underbrace{\left(\frac{1}{2^{n+1}}[(-1)^{xx'} + (-1)^{(x \oplus r)x'}]\right)}_{c_{x',x}} |x'\rangle \otimes |f(x)\rangle. \tag{5.17}$$

Similarly to the Deutsch–Jozsa algorithm we try to draw conclusions evaluating coefficient $c_{x',x}$ but in this case the control and data subsystems are entangled therefore it represents probability amplitude of $|x'\rangle|f(x)\rangle$. Taking into account that $xx' = (x \oplus r)x' \equiv xx' \oplus rx'$ if and only if $rx' = 0$ else the two terms in $c_{x',x}$ eliminate each other, thus

$$c_{x',x} = \begin{cases} \dfrac{2}{2^{n+1}}(-1)^{xx'} = 2^{-n}(-1)^{xx'} & \text{if } rx' = 0 \\ 0 & \text{if } rx' = 1. \end{cases} \tag{5.18}$$

Obviously $P(x' = z \wedge rz = 1) = 0$. When we are interested in $P(x' = z \wedge rz = 0)$, however, first we realize that $c_{x',x}$ and $c_{x',x \oplus r}$ belong to the same computational basis state $|x'\rangle|f(x)\rangle$ therefore they have to be added together as probability amplitudes. This means that the number of different basis states are exactly half of the number of different x. Moreover at a fixed $x' = z$ we have to sum up the absolute-squared probability amplitudes (probabilities) of all the computational basis states $|x' = z\rangle|f(x)\rangle$. Thus any measurement on the control qbits in the computational basis states will result in $|x' = z\rangle$ such that $rz = 0$ with uniformly distributed probability

$$P(x' = z \wedge rz = 0) = \sum_{x \in \{0,1\}^n} \frac{|c_{z,x} + c_{z,x \oplus r}|^2}{2}$$

$$= \left(\frac{1}{2^n}\right)^2 \sum_{x \in \{0,1\}^n} \underbrace{\frac{1}{2} |2(-1)^{xz}|^2}_{\equiv 2^2}$$

$$= 2\frac{1}{2^{2n}} 2^n = \frac{1}{2^{(n-1)}}. \tag{5.19}$$

The division by 2 is needed because the sum runs over all possible x so without it we would consider two times each basis vector. Performing L times this algorithm we will have a linear equation system in our hand that can be solved by means of Gaussian elimination (see Section 12.2.2)

$$rx'_l = 0, l = 1, 2, \ldots, L, \tag{5.20}$$

where x'_l refers to the result of the lth measurement. If x'_l were different then $L = n$ measurements would be enough to calculate r exactly. Unfortunately the applied quantum measurements select among the computational bases states $|x'\rangle$ probabilistically in each turn, which allows repeated occurrence of a given x'_l. Fortunately it was proven in [52] that the probability that the equation system (5.20) cannot be solved unambiguously after n trials is exponentially small in n. Conversely a classical random search would require trivially $2^{n-1} - 1$ turns in the worst case while on the average $O(\sqrt{2^n})$ function call is required [139].

Finally a natural question may arise since we used a constraint $r \neq 0$ when deriving (5.16) – what happens when we try to trick the Simon algorithm[3] using trivial period $r = 0$? In this case (5.16) becomes

$$|\varphi_2\rangle = \frac{1}{\sqrt{2^n}} \sum_{x \in \{0,1\}^n} |x\rangle|f(x)\rangle, \tag{5.21}$$

---

[3] Or we have no information about r.

because $|x\rangle \equiv |x \oplus r\rangle$. Applying the Hadamard gate for the upper quantum wire we get

$$|\varphi_3\rangle = (H^{\otimes n} \otimes I^{\otimes n})|\varphi_2\rangle = \frac{1}{\sqrt{2^n}} \sum_{x \in \{0,1\}^n} H^{\otimes n}|x\rangle \otimes |f(x)\rangle$$

$$= \sum_{x' \in \{0,1\}^n} \sum_{x \in \{0,1\}^n} \underbrace{\frac{1}{2^n} |x'\rangle \otimes |f(x)\rangle}_{c_{x',x}}$$

$$= \left(\frac{1}{\sqrt{2^n}} \sum_{x' \in \{0,1\}^n} |x'\rangle \right) \otimes \left(\frac{1}{\sqrt{2^n}} \sum_{x \in \{0,1\}^n} |f(x)\rangle \right). \qquad (5.22)$$

The last row highlights the fact that the two qregisters are separable (not entangled). Thus any measurement on the control qbits in the computational basis states will result in any $x' \in \{0,1\}^n$ with uniformly distributed probability and $rx' = 0$ only if $r = 0$ except $x' = 0$

$$P(x' = z) = \sum_{x \in \{0,1\}^n} |c_{z,x}|^2 = (2^{-n})^2 2^n = \frac{1}{2^n}. \qquad (5.23)$$

So we can repeat the algorithm similarly to the $r \neq 0$ case in order to collect a linear equation system which allows computing $r = 0$.

5.4 FURTHER READING

The term *amplitude amplification* was originally used in solving a set separation type problem by Brassard, Hoyer, Mosca and Tapp in [62].

Deutsch raised his problem with a probabilistic answer in [51]. However, the first practical application of quantum parallelism in solving a theoretical problem was introduced by Deutsch and Jozsa [49] in 1992. The original probabilistic solution was refined in [124] and extended by Constantini and Smeraldi [63] to the case $f : \{0,1\}^n \to \{0,1\}^m$. The algorithm presented in this book is based on [124].

The Deutsch–Jozsa algorithm was generalized for continuous variables by Pati and Braunstein in [11]. The original Deutsch–Jozsa problem – whether a function f is constant or balanced – has been replaced by the decision whether f is constant or evenly distributed in [50]. An infocom related application of the Deutsch–Jozsa algorithm in handling the so-called *Guessing secrets problem* (arising in context with the Internet) will be explained in Part III, Chapter 11.

Regarding implementation issues of the Deutsch–Jozsa algorithm many proposals were made during the last decade, e.g. using Josephson charge qbits in [85], applying NMR in [82] and [18] or an optical solution in [55]. Those readers who are interested in additional techniques and solutions are suggested to look at references in the above citations.

Simon introduced his problem with a probabilistic solution in [140]. We followed a similar way to the original one in this chapter in order to explain the algorithm, however, also its QFT based extension for period finding is presented in Section 6.5.1. An exact quantum polynomial-time algorithm with worst case $O(n)$ steps instead of expected $O(n)$ was proposed by Brassard and Hoyer for Simon's problem in [60]. Biham *et al.* presented an alternative technique to solve the Deutsch–Jozsa and Simon problem without entanglement but in a more efficient way than the best classical one in [52].

6

Quantum Fourier Transform and its Applications

When Fourier published his most famous work *Théorie analitique de la chaleur* in 1822 he had not the slightest idea that his transform – which was originally applied in thermodynamics – would run such a widespread course in many different areas of signal/information processing from spectroscopy to telecommunications where this transform constitutes the bridge between signal representations in time and frequency domains. The extraordinary success of the Fourier transform is due to its discrete version the so-called discrete Fourier transform (DFT), which has a computationally very efficient implementation in the form of the fast Fourier transform (FFT).

The quantum version of the Fourier transform lies at the core of many quantum computing algorithms. The quantum Fourier transform (QFT) is analogous to the classical FFT, and by exploiting the advantages of quantum parallelism, can be computed exponentially faster. However, as we will explain in this chapter this advantage cannot be used to enhance the speed of data processing directly, since all the individual Fourier coefficients (probability amplitudes) cannot be accessed by a measurement, similar to the fact we experienced with quantum parallelism. Instead QFT can be regarded as a building block of complex quantum algorithms.

First classical Fourier transform and its quantum counterpart will be introduced in Section 6.1 which is followed in Section 6.2 by its very useful application called quantum phase estimation that serves also as an important element of several efficient quantum algorithms (e.g. the Grover searching algorithm, see Chapter 7). Another important and interesting application of QFT investigated within this chapter is order finding, which forms the basis of efficient quantum factorization algorithms and is explained in Section 6.3. We stop for a while to build bridges between Chapter 6

Quantum Computing and Communications   S. Imre, F. Balázs
© 2004 John Wiley & Sons, Ltd   ISBN 0-470-86902-X (HB)

and 5 in Section 6.4. As a generalization of order finding, period finding and discrete logarithm algorithms are discussed in Section 6.5. In order to exploit advantages of QFT, related infocommunication problems are discussed in Part III. This chapter requires some basic knowledge of number theory which has been summarized in Section 12.3.

6.1 QUANTUM FOURIER TRANSFORM

In order to illuminate the similarities and differences between classical DFT and quantum QFT first traditional DFT is summarized. Let us assume a vector $\mathbf{x} = [x_0, x_1, \ldots, x_{N-1}]^T$ with complex coordinates $x_i \in \mathbb{C}$. The discrete Fourier transform of $\mathbf{x}$ is denoted by $\mathbf{y} = \text{DFT}\{\mathbf{x}\}$ where the Fourier coefficients of $\mathbf{y}$ are defined as[1]

$$y_k \triangleq \frac{1}{\sqrt{N}} \sum_{i=0}^{N-1} x_i e^{j\frac{2\pi}{N}ik}. \tag{6.1}$$

DFT determines a transformation which creates a connection between two vectors. As we know from the postulates of quantum mechanics closed physical systems are also represented by complex vectors called superpositions using the 'ket' $|.\rangle$ notation, where coordinates stand for the probability amplitudes of related computational basis vectors. So let us define a transformation called QFT and denoted by F in an analogous way to the classical DFT in the following manner. We start from a superposition $|\varphi\rangle$ in the space of computational basis vectors $|i\rangle, i = 0 \ldots N - 1$

$$|\varphi\rangle = \sum_{i=0}^{N-1} \varphi_i |i\rangle$$

and transform it to $|\psi\rangle = F|\varphi\rangle$ in compliance with the following rule (cf. (6.1))

$$\psi_k \triangleq \frac{1}{\sqrt{N}} \sum_{i=0}^{N-1} \varphi_i e^{j\frac{2\pi}{N}ik}, \tag{6.2}$$

which results in a superposition

$$|\psi\rangle = \sum_{k=0}^{N-1} \psi_k |k\rangle = \frac{1}{\sqrt{N}} \sum_{k=0}^{N-1} \sum_{i=0}^{N-1} \varphi_i e^{j\frac{2\pi}{N}ik} |k\rangle. \tag{6.3}$$

We mention here that applying QFT to computational basis state $|i\rangle$ produces

$$F|i\rangle = \frac{1}{\sqrt{N}} \sum_{k=0}^{N-1} e^{j\frac{2\pi}{N}ik} |k\rangle. \tag{6.4}$$

---

[1] $\frac{2\pi}{N}$ is often referred to as ω_0 in electrical engineering practice.

Finally it is worth defining the inverse of the quantum Fourier transform since it is often used as a building block in more sophisticated algorithms

$$\varphi_i \triangleq \frac{1}{\sqrt{N}} \sum_{k=0}^{N-1} \psi_k e^{-j\frac{2\pi}{N}ik}, \qquad (6.5)$$

and for computational basis states

$$F^\dagger |k\rangle = \frac{1}{\sqrt{N}} \sum_{i=0}^{N-1} e^{-j\frac{2\pi}{N}ik} |i\rangle. \qquad (6.6)$$

Because the operator of QFT is unitary (see **Exercise** 6.1), we refer to the operator of IQFT as $F^\dagger$.

Although QFT is exponentially faster in some sense than its classical counterpart as we will see later in this chapter, the task that they perform is quite different. QFT does not explicitly produce any of the Fourier coefficients. Intuitively, the difference between performing DFT and QFT can be regarded as computing all the probabilities of a probability distribution or sampling this distribution.

Having defined the quantum Fourier transform and before applying it as a building block of a more complex algorithm the following natural question may arise, namely how to implement QFT by means of elementary quantum gates. Of course we cannot avoid answering questions pertaining to computational complexity, either. Fortunately two talented teams – Griffiths, Niu and Cleve, Ekert, Macciavello, Mosca – found a way to trace back QFT to its tensor product decomposition. This was a stroke of a genius since by having the terms of decomposition in our hands we can associate one quantum wire with one-qbit gates to each term! In the remaining part of this section we reach step by step the quantum circuit implementing QFT efficiently.

An integer number $k \in \{0, 1, \ldots, 2^n - 1\}$ can be represented in the binary form of $(k_1, k_2, \ldots, k_n) = k_1 2^{n-1} + k_2 2^{n-2} + \cdots + k_n 2^0$, where $k_l \in \{0, 1\}$. Let us introduce moreover for $h \geq 0$ the binary notation of

$$0.k_l k_{l+1} \ldots k_{l+h} \triangleq \frac{k_l}{2^1} + \frac{k_{l+1}}{2^2} + \cdots + \frac{k_{l+h}}{2^{h+1}}; k_m \in \{0, 1\}. \qquad (6.7)$$

Taking into account the superposition principle it is enough to design a quantum circuit which carries out the transformation of a computational basis state $|k\rangle$ in compliance with (6.4) because this circuit will work for arbitrary superposition $|\varphi\rangle$ as well. So we start from (6.4) using a binary form of integer numbers and replacing N by 2^n

$$F|i\rangle = \frac{1}{\sqrt{N}} \sum_{k=0}^{N-1} e^{j\frac{2\pi}{N}ik} |k\rangle = \frac{1}{\sqrt{2^n}} \sum_{k=0}^{2^n-1} e^{j2\pi i \sum_{l=1}^{n} k_l \frac{2^{n-l}}{2^n}} |k\rangle.$$

Recognizing that $\frac{2^{n-l}}{2^n} = 2^{-l}$ and exploiting that $|k\rangle = |k_1, k_2, \ldots, k_n\rangle = |k_1\rangle \otimes |k_2\rangle \otimes \cdots \otimes |k_n\rangle$ and $e^{\alpha+\beta} \equiv e^\alpha e^\beta$

$$F|i\rangle = \frac{1}{\sqrt{2^n}} \sum_{k=0}^{2^n-1} \prod_{l=1}^{n} e^{j2\pi i k_l 2^{-l}} \bigotimes_{l=1}^{n} |k_l\rangle = \frac{1}{\sqrt{2^n}} \sum_{k=0}^{2^n-1} \bigotimes_{l=1}^{n} e^{j2\pi i k_l 2^{-l}} |k_l\rangle.$$

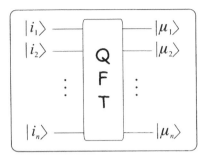

Fig. 6.1   Sketch of QFT circuit

Considering that $k_l \in \{0,1\}$ we collect the factors of the tensor product into two groups with respect to $|0\rangle$ and $|1\rangle$

$$F|i\rangle = \frac{1}{\sqrt{2^n}} \bigotimes_{l=1}^{n} \left(e^{j2\pi i(k_l=0)2^{-l}} |0\rangle + e^{j2\pi i(k_l=1)2^{-l}} |1\rangle \right)$$

$$= \frac{1}{\sqrt{2^n}} \bigotimes_{l=1}^{n} \left(|0\rangle + e^{j2\pi i2^{-l}} |1\rangle \right). \tag{6.8}$$

Equation (6.8) clearly highlights the fact that tensor product decomposition exists for any computational basis vectors for any superposition states, moreover it advices us to choose an n-qbit circuit (see Fig. 6.1). For the sake of simplicity we introduce the notation

$$|\mu_l\rangle \triangleq \frac{1}{\sqrt{2}} \left(|0\rangle + e^{j2\pi i2^{-l}} |1\rangle \right). \tag{6.9}$$

Definition (6.9) can be further simplified realizing $i = \sum_{l=1}^{n} i_l 2^{n-l}$ and using definition (6.7), thus $(2\pi i 2^{-l}) \bmod 2\pi = 0.i_{l-n}i_{l-n+1}\dots i_n$ where only $i_h, h \geq 0$ terms count

$$F|i\rangle = \underbrace{\left(\frac{|0\rangle + e^{j2\pi 0.i_n}|1\rangle}{\sqrt{2}} \right)}_{|\mu_1\rangle} \otimes \underbrace{\left(\frac{|0\rangle + e^{j2\pi 0.i_{n-1}i_n}|1\rangle}{\sqrt{2}} \right)}_{|\mu_2\rangle} \otimes \cdots$$

$$\otimes \underbrace{\left(\frac{|0\rangle + e^{j2\pi 0.i_1 i_2 \dots i_n}|1\rangle}{\sqrt{2}} \right)}_{|\mu_n\rangle}. \tag{6.10}$$

Now we show what type of elementary gates in which sequence have to be deployed onto the quantum wires to implement (6.10). First we reverse the order of qbits at the output by means of an n-qbit swap gate so that it is enough to carry out $U_l : |i_l\rangle \rightarrow |\mu_{n-l+1}\rangle$ transformations (see Fig. 6.3). Let us start with the determination of operator U_n. Since $e^{j2\pi 0.i_n} = \pm 1$ having in sight $i_n = 0, 1$

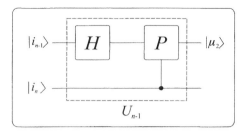

Fig. 6.2   Circuit of U_{n-1}

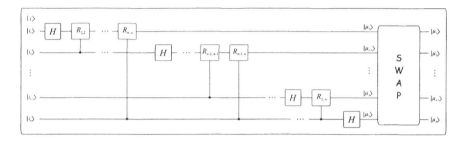

Fig. 6.3   Quantum circuit implementing QFT

therefore

$$|\mu_1\rangle = \begin{cases} \dfrac{|0\rangle + |1\rangle}{\sqrt{2}} & \text{if } i_n = 0 \\[2mm] \dfrac{|0\rangle - |1\rangle}{\sqrt{2}} & \text{if } i_n = 1, \end{cases}$$

which trivially characterizes the operation of a Hadamard gate i.e. $U_n = H$. Next we turn to $U_{n-1} : |i_{n-1}\rangle \rightarrow |\mu_2\rangle$ and rewrite $|\mu_2\rangle$ bearing in mind (6.10) and the knowledge about U_n

$$|\mu_2\rangle = \frac{1}{\sqrt{2}} \left[|0\rangle + e^{j2\pi 0.i_{n-1}} \cdot \left\{ \begin{array}{ll} P\left(2\pi \dfrac{1}{2^2}\right)|1\rangle & \text{if } i_n = 1 \\[2mm] 1|1\rangle & \text{if } i_n = 0 \end{array} \right\} \right],$$

where $P(\cdot)$ refers to a phase gate and factor $\frac{1}{2^2}$ in the argument of the phase gate follows from the fact that i_n represents the value of the second bit. $|\mu_2\rangle$ shows some similarities with $|\mu_1\rangle$, however, it seems to be a Hadamard gate if $i_n = 0$ and a combination of Hadamard and phase gates otherwise. The difference can be concentrated into i_n that controls the operation of the phase gate. The circuit implementing operator U_{n-1} is depicted in Fig. 6.2.

In order to use a more compact notation when describing U_l we introduce a special controlled phase gate characterized by the following operator

$$
R_{h,p} \triangleq \begin{cases} P\left(2\pi\dfrac{1}{2^h}\right) & \text{if } i_p = 1 \\ 1 & \text{if } i_p = 0. \end{cases} \tag{6.11}
$$

Now it is time to generalize the technique applied for U_n and U_{n-1}. The quantum circuit that has to be deployed onto the lth quantum wire can be built up using Hadamard and special controlled phase gates as we sketched the circuit performing QFT in Fig. 6.3. This architecture requires $O(n^2)$ elementary gates including the swap gate. However, for advances in the field of QFT implementation the reader is advised to skim through *Further Reading* of this chapter.

Exercise 6.1. Prove that operator F is unitary.

Exercise 6.2. Determine the matrix of QFT.

6.2 QUANTUM PHASE ESTIMATION

Phase estimation is an important building block of several quantum algorithms e.g. quantum counting, factorization of large numbers, etc. and offers excellent possibilities to exploit what we have learned about QFT. Let us assume that we have a unitary operator U with eigenvector $|u\rangle$. We already know that any eigenvalue of a unitary operator has the form of $e^{j\alpha_u}$ with real α_u (see Section 12.2.4). Phase estimation is interested in the phase α_u. From a practical point of view we are searching for the phase ratio $\kappa_u \in [0,1) : \alpha_u = 2\pi\kappa_u$, which is equivalent to the original problem. Furthermore we do not explicitly know the matrix of U but instead we have a device that implements it and allows controlled operation.

6.2.1 Idealistic phase estimation

First we investigate the case when $\kappa_u = i/2^n$ and $i \in \{0, 1, \ldots, 2^n - 1\}$. Now we ask the reader to take a look at (6.4). Considering that $N = 2^n$ if we were able to produce the right-hand side of (6.4) such that $i/2^n = \kappa_u$ it would be enough to perform an IQFT to get back $|i\rangle$ from which κ_u is trivially available. Assuming constraint $i/2^n = \kappa_u$ is fulfilled the definition of $|\mu_l\rangle$ in (6.9) can be reformulated as

$$
|\mu_l\rangle = \frac{1}{\sqrt{2}}\left(|0\rangle + e^{j2\pi 2^{n-l}\kappa_u}|1\rangle\right). \tag{6.12}
$$

Following the technique introduced at the implementation of QFT we try to exploit the tensor product decomposition to design a suitable circuit that produces $|\mu_l\rangle$ wire by wire. We start with $|\mu_n\rangle = \frac{1}{\sqrt{2}}\left(|0\rangle + e^{j2\pi\kappa_u}|1\rangle\right)$. It is similar to the output superposition of a Hadamard gate feeded by $|0\rangle$, but we should smuggle somehow the

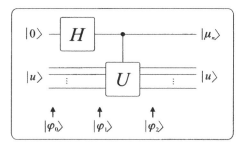

Fig. 6.4   Quantum circuit producing $|\mu_n\rangle$

exponential factor in front to $|1\rangle$. Since for any eigenvector $|u\rangle : U|u\rangle = e^{j2\pi\kappa_u}|u\rangle$ and bearing quantum parallelism in mind as was exploited by Simon in Section 5.3 we propose the circuit depicted in Fig. 6.4 that consists of two qregisters. The upper one contains only a single qbit $|0\rangle$ while the lower one has been initialized with the eigenvector $|u\rangle$ with t qbit of length, so the starting state equals $|\varphi_0\rangle = |0\rangle \otimes |u\rangle$. Let us check the operation of this circuit. Applying the Hadamard gate to the upper qregister

$$|\varphi_1\rangle = (H \otimes I^{\otimes t})|\varphi_0\rangle = \frac{|0\rangle + |1\rangle}{\sqrt{2}}|u\rangle = \frac{|0\rangle|u\rangle + |1\rangle|u\rangle}{\sqrt{2}}.$$

Because we do not have any direct information about the matrix of operator U, in order to compute $|\varphi_2\rangle$ we utilize the superposition principle keeping the control qbit in mind

$$|\varphi_2\rangle = (I \otimes U)|\varphi_1\rangle = \frac{1}{\sqrt{2}}\left(|0\rangle|u\rangle + e^{j2\pi\kappa_u}|1\rangle|u\rangle\right)$$
$$= \frac{1}{\sqrt{2}}\left(|0\rangle + e^{j2\pi 2^0\kappa_u}|1\rangle\right) \otimes |u\rangle,$$

which clearly equals $|\mu_n\rangle$ on the upper (control) wire.

Now we are ready to construct $|\mu_l\rangle$. The only difference arises in the exponent, namely in the generalized case $2^0 = 1$ is replaced by 2^{n-l}. This minor departure can be handled quite easily if we consider the effect of repeated applications of operator U on its eigenvector $|u\rangle$

$$U^h \triangleq \underbrace{UU\ldots U}_{h},$$
$$U^h|u\rangle = \underbrace{e^{j2\pi\kappa_u}e^{j2\pi\kappa_u}\ldots e^{j2\pi\kappa_u}}_{h}|u\rangle = e^{j2\pi h\kappa_u}|u\rangle.$$

Based on this observation when we are designing circuit for $|\mu_l\rangle$, the gate $U = U^{2^0}$ has to be replaced by a gate implementing $U^{2^{n-l}}$. Thus the architecture which aims to

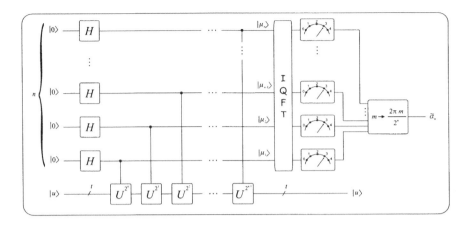

Fig. 6.5   Quantum circuit computing the phase

compute phase α_u in question contains an upper qregister with n qbits and is showed in Fig. 6.5. Furthermore we recall that a measuring equipment after the IQFT gives back an integer number m – which is equal to i in this case – therefore a classical gate is required to calculate $\tilde{\alpha}_u = 2\pi m/2^n = 2\pi i/2^n = \alpha_u$. So we managed to calculate the exact value for the phase due to the fact $m = i$.

Remark: After the measurement the MSB can be found on the bottom wire and the LSB on the topmost one. Thus omitting qbits from the top on one hand classical accuracy of $\tilde{\alpha}_u$ will be reduced while on the other hand less Hadamard and U gates are needed.

Remark: We avoided answering how to initialize the lower quantum register. This problem will be handled in context with the practical solution in the next section.

6.2.2   Phase estimation in practical cases

Unfortunately before celebrating this clever circuit we must mention that our high spirits are dampened by the constraint $\kappa_u = i/2^n$. What is going to happen if we allow arbitrary $\kappa_u \in [0, 1)$? In most of the applications we cannot expect that anybody guarantees a phase ratio with such special property. As a qualitative analysis, we may realize at first sight that the IQFT will work inaccurately in terms of calculating the phase since $i/2^n$ has been replaced by κ_u, i.e. the phase will only be estimated. On the other hand we may expect that the larger the number of qbits n of the upper qregister is the more precise will be the estimation of phase because $i/2^n \rightarrow \kappa_u$. Higher numbers of qbits, however, typically goes together with higher costs, hence the trade off between price and accuracy always lies at the center of engineering practice. Moreover in everyday applications exact solutions are typically not of interest.[2] Therefore it seems to be more important from an engineering point of view to derive the relation between n and the error in phase than calculating the phase without any error. Of course for mathematicians this is not the case, hence for those readers who are interested in exact computation of phase useful hints can be found in *Further Reading*.

When carrying out error analysis it is worth formulating the output state of the IQFT. To do this we determine first the superposition fed to the IQFT

$$|\mu\rangle = \bigotimes_{l=1}^{n} \frac{1}{\sqrt{2}} \left(|0\rangle + e^{j2\pi 2^{n-l}\kappa_u}|1\rangle \right), \tag{6.13}$$

which can be rewritten by exploiting the equivalence of (6.4) and (6.8) in the following way

$$|\mu\rangle = \sum_{k=0}^{2^n-1} \frac{1}{\sqrt{2^n}} e^{j2\pi k\kappa_u}|k\rangle. \tag{6.14}$$

Now we apply the IQFT rule (6.6) to each computational basis state $|k\rangle$ in $|\mu\rangle$ relying on the superposition principle

$$F^\dagger|\mu\rangle = \sum_{k=0}^{2^n-1} \frac{1}{\sqrt{2^n}} e^{j2\pi k\kappa_u} \frac{1}{\sqrt{2^n}} \sum_{i=0}^{2^n-1} e^{-j2\pi \frac{i}{2^n}k}|i\rangle$$

$$= \frac{1}{2^n} \sum_{k=0}^{2^n-1}\sum_{i=0}^{2^n-1} e^{j2\pi k(\kappa_u - \frac{i}{2^n})}|i\rangle = \sum_{i=0}^{2^n-1}\sum_{k=0}^{2^n-1} \frac{1}{2^n} \left(e^{j2\pi(\kappa_u - \frac{i}{2^n})} \right)^k |i\rangle. \tag{6.15}$$

As we mentioned earlier if κ_u were equal to $\frac{i}{2^n}$ then the IQFT would answer exactly $F^\dagger|\mu\rangle = |i\rangle$, but this is a more general scenario. We investigate now the probability amplitude of $|i\rangle$

$$\varphi_i = \frac{1}{2^n} \sum_{k=0}^{2^n-1} \left(e^{j2\pi(\kappa_u - \frac{i}{2^n})} \right)^k, \tag{6.16}$$

which is simply the sum of a geometrical sequence with quotient $q = e^{j2\pi(\kappa_u - \frac{i}{2^n})}$. On one hand if the quotient equals 1 which happens only if κ_u is an integer multiple of $\frac{1}{2^n}$ then $\varphi_{i=\kappa_u 2^n} = 1$ and any other probability amplitudes disappear. On the other hand if $q \neq 1$ then

$$\varphi_i = \frac{1}{2^n} \frac{1-q^{2^n}}{1-q} = \frac{1}{2^n} \frac{1 - e^{j2\pi(2^n\kappa_u - i)}}{1 - e^{j2\pi(\kappa_u - \frac{i}{2^n})}}, \tag{6.17}$$

which gives another good explanation of uncertainty and thus appearing inaccuracy when measuring the output of IQFT. If more than one φ_i differs from zero then

---

[2]Electrical engineers may recall e.g. color TV which is one of the biggest cheats (of eyes) of the 20th century, experts of informatics may remember hash functions in security systems!

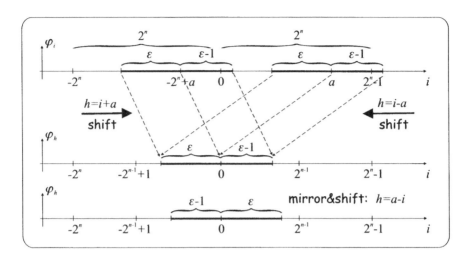

Fig. 6.6 Illustration of probability amplitude regions before measurement with different index transformations

there is a nonzero probability of receiving different phases after the measurement when repeating the algorithm. Let us denote the closest n-bit long integer to $\kappa_u 2^n$ by a. It is easy to see that $0 \le a \le 2^n - 1$, moreover if $\Delta_u \triangleq \kappa_u - a/2^n$ then $|\Delta_u| \le 2^{-(n+1)}$. Assuming that the error ε allowed at the IQFT's output is bounded by ε i.e. $a - \varepsilon \le m < a + \varepsilon$, where m stands for the measured integer value m, then the conditional probability P_ε that we measure value m out of the range ε around a can be defined as

$$P_\varepsilon \triangleq P(m < a - \varepsilon \lor a + \varepsilon \le m | a). \tag{6.18}$$

Thus P_ε can be traced back to those probability amplitudes φ_i which have fallen into the region denoted by thin lines on the horizontal axes in Fig. 6.6, while thick lines represent those amplitudes which lead to success. We can observe that $e^{j2\pi(\kappa_u - \frac{i}{2^n})}$ is periodic in i according to 2^n thus φ_i has the same periodicity. Unfortunately this figure highlights the fact that these regions are typically not contiguous on $[0, 2^n)$, which means taking stock of probability amplitudes.

In order to overcome this problem and to simplify further analysis we define symmetric indices $h \in (-2^{n-1}, 2^{n-1}]$ around a in compliance with Fig. 6.6. We have several alternatives to perform this operation with the common feature that they transform $i = a$ to $h = 0$: either we shift axis i from right to left by using $h = i - a$ or from left to right by $h = i + 2^n - a = i - a$ (exploiting the periodicity of 2^n) and last but not least we can reflect axis i onto its basis $i = 0$ and then applying a shift by a i.e. $h = a - i$ will result in the required index h. These methods do not cause any substantial differences during the analysis therefore we select the last one for historical reason. So the relationship between i and h is simply $h = (a - i)$, which corresponds to the fact that probability amplitude $\varphi_h = \varphi_{i=(a-h) \bmod 2^n}$ and

φ_h belong to the computational basis state $|(a - h) \bmod 2^n\rangle$. Therefore if $\kappa_u = \frac{a}{2^n}$ then $\varphi_{h \neq 0} = 0$ and only $\varphi_0 = 1$ (idealistic scenario). Contrary if $\kappa_u \neq \frac{a}{2^n}$ then

$$\varphi_h = \frac{1}{2^n} \frac{1 - e^{j2\pi(2^n \kappa_u - (a-h))}}{1 - e^{j2\pi(\kappa_u - \frac{a-h}{2^n})}},$$

which can be further simplified keeping in view that $\kappa_u = \Delta_u + a/2^n$

$$\varphi_h = \frac{1}{2^n} \frac{1 - e^{j2\pi(2^n \Delta_u + h)}}{1 - e^{j2\pi(\Delta_u + \frac{h}{2^n})}}, \quad \Delta_u \neq 0. \tag{6.19}$$

Now we are able to derive the probability P_s of successfully measuring an m within the acceptable region around $i = a$ (equivalently around $h = 0$) by summing up the probabilities of corresponding computational basis states[3]

$$P_s = \sum_{h=-\varepsilon+1}^{\varepsilon} |\varphi_h|^2, \quad \Delta_u \neq 0. \tag{6.20}$$

Using the result of **Exercise** 6.3 i.e. $\left|1 - e^{j\gamma}\right|^2 = 4\sin^2(\frac{\gamma}{2})$ together with (6.19)

$$|\varphi_h|^2 = \frac{1}{2^{2n}} \frac{\sin^2(\pi(2^n \Delta_u + h))}{\sin^2(\pi(\Delta_u + \frac{h}{2^n}))}, \quad \Delta_u \neq 0 \tag{6.21}$$

and substituting it into (6.20) we get

$$P_s = \sum_{h=-\varepsilon+1}^{\varepsilon} \frac{1}{2^{2n}} \frac{\sin^2(\pi(2^n \Delta_u + h))}{\sin^2(\pi(\Delta_u + \frac{h}{2^n}))}, \quad \Delta_u \neq 0. \tag{6.22}$$

Now we have a beautiful result in our hands with a minor flaw, namely parameter ε has no useful meaning from an engineering point of view. We would rather be familiar with the relationship between probability of success P_s (or probability of error $P_\varepsilon = 1 - P_s$), number of applied qbits n in the upper register of the phase estimator device and the required accuracy of phase κ_u originating from the engineering problem, or formulating much precisely the question: how many qbits should be bought (*cost*) and built in to provide accuracy, say 2^{-c} (*demand*), with probability at least P_s (*trade off*)? This requires a little cogitation upon the sources of phase error.

Let us denote the difference between the exact and the measured value of phase $\tilde{\alpha}_u$ by $d_u = |\alpha_u - \tilde{\alpha}_u|$. *First type phase error* is fully classical since it originates from the allowed inaccuracy, i.e. the specification of the technical problem demands that $d_u \leq \check{d}_{\max}$. This can be easily converted into $\check{D}_{\max} = \frac{\check{d}_{\max}}{2\pi} \geq |\Delta_u|$. Clearly speaking this inaccuracy can be regarded as an error only from a theoretical point of

---

[3]We have transformed index $i \in [a - \varepsilon, a + \varepsilon - 1]$ to $h \in [-\varepsilon + 1, \varepsilon]$.

view because from the application side it does not cause any malfunction. Assuming a demand $\check{D}_{\max} = 2^{-c}$ to handle this type of error we would need an $n = (c-1)$-qbit register because $|\Delta_u| \leq 2^{-(n+1)} = 2^{-(c-1+1)} = 2^{-c}$. The source of the *second type error* – called quantum inaccuracy or uncertainty – lies in the quantum world. As we discussed earlier unwanted probability amplitudes may occur because of the IQFT in spite the fact that no classical inaccuracy is allowed. So the upper n-qbit register of the phase estimator has to contain $(c-1)$ qbits for the sake of allowing classical inaccuracy 2^{-c}, but in order to hold quantum inaccuracy below a certain limit $\check{P}_\varepsilon$, another p qbits are required $(n = c - 1 + p)$.

Remark: If $\check{d}_{\max} = 2^{-r}$ is given as an engineering parameter for the phase then $n = r - 1 + p + \lceil \mathrm{ld}(2\pi) \rceil$ qbits are needed because phase estimation deals with phase ratios and only indirectly with phases. Therefore if we are able to provide $2^{-(r+\lceil \mathrm{ld}(2\pi) \rceil)}$ accuracy in the phase ratio then it will result in 2^{-r} accuracy of the phase.

Remark: The additional p qbits are deployed to amplify the amount of probability around a and have no influences on classical accuracy, hence measurement can be reduced onto the lower $(c-1)$ qbits of the upper section!

Finally the connection between ε and p can be easily derived bearing in mind that the phase estimation is successful if a has been measured on the lower $(c-1)$ qbits of the upper qregister. If this happens the upper p qbits of the upper section contain one of the possible 2^p different bitstrings. Probability amplitudes belonging to these vectors increase the probability of measuring a hence

$$2\varepsilon = 2^p \Rightarrow \varepsilon = 2^{p-1}. \tag{6.23}$$

Remark: In the case when $p = 0$ has to be handled in a special way since the $(-\varepsilon, \varepsilon]$ region reduces to a single probability amplitude located in $h = 0$:

$$P_s = \frac{1}{2^{2c-2}} \frac{\sin^2(\pi 2^{c-1}\Delta_u)}{\sin^2(\pi \Delta_u)}, \quad \Delta_u \neq 0. \tag{6.24}$$

The only parameter that remains to be expressed by means of design parameters in (6.22) is Δ_u. Since

$$a = \left\lfloor \frac{\alpha_u}{2\pi} 2^n \right\rfloor \Rightarrow \Delta_u = \kappa_u - \frac{\left\lfloor \frac{\alpha_u}{\pi} 2^{n-1} \right\rfloor}{2^n}. \tag{6.25}$$

Exercise 6.3. Prove that $\left| 1 - e^{j\gamma} \right|^2 = 4\sin^2(\frac{\gamma}{2})$.

6.2.3 Quantitative analysis of the phase estimator

Now we are ready to analyze (6.22), which depends only on engineering parameters n, c, p and of course on α_u. Let us assume classically required accuracy $c = 10 \Rightarrow 2^{-c} = \check{D}_{\max} = \frac{1}{1024} \approx 10^{-3}$. Fig. 6.7 presents the probability $P(h)$ of measuring h on a logarithmic scale if $\alpha_u = 0.4 \cdot 2\pi \Rightarrow \kappa_u = 0.4$ and $p = 4$ auxiliary qbits are invested. The curve is rather promising. Despite the logarithmic representation the probabilities are strongly concentrating around $h = 0$ thus providing high probability of measuring $i = a$. During the next investigation in Fig. 6.8 we keep the previous parameters except allowing p the variation between 0 (no redundancy) and 10. Obviously the advantageous shape of $P(h)$ is practically independent from p, only the ranges of h differ.

Beside the probability density function of measuring a given m we are also interested in the probability of achieving $m = a$. Fig. 6.9 presents P_s vs. p when $c = 10$ and $\alpha_u = 0.4 \cdot 2\pi$. The result is a bit surprising because although P_s converges to sure success very fast when we invest more and more auxiliary qbits, the curve is not a strictly monotonously increasing function. Why?

Fig. 6.10 allows us to take a look at the principles working deep inside in quantum phase estimation. One would naturally expect that increasing the number of additional qbits ensures finer resolution of a thus it brings us closer to our estimation to κ_u i.e. $\Delta_u \rightarrow 0$, therefore the probability of success will also be closer to 1 (we know that $\Delta_u = 0$ provides sure success of measuring $\alpha_u = \kappa_u 2^n$). Unlike this reasoning – which is correct, but a little bit coarse – the alteration in Fig. 6.10 points out that increasing p does not necessarily mean smaller Δ_u! This effect is marginalized, however, at large values of p by another not so obvious effect which increases the probability of success. It can be summarized with respect to (6.22): each new auxiliary qbit restructures the probability amplitudes φ_h involving more and more probability into the exponentially increasing $\varepsilon = 2^{p-1}$ range of $h = 0$ (or equivalently $i = a$) while c remains fixed.[4] This reasoning explains the shape of P_s in Fig. 6.9, but does not reassure an engineer about the required number of additional qbits. Maybe the fast convergence of P_s is not typical? To overcome this problem we are going to deliver a useful practical approximation formula in Section 6.2.4.

We illustrated the trade off between classical (c) and quantum (p) accuracy in the case of fixed $n = 10$ in Fig. 6.11. Starting from $p = 0$ we increased p step by step. Since the probability amplitudes depend only on n, they can be regarded as constants during the investigation. Obviously smaller c ensures less accurate estimation of the phase while larger p enables the measuring device to collect probability amplitudes from a wider range (ε) around a (see Fig. 6.6), thus probability of successful measurement also increases.

A previously mentioned salutary special scenario is depicted in Fig. 6.12. We assumed no quantum uncertainty restriction ($p = 0$) and the probability P_s is sketched in the function of c and Δ_u. As the reader would expect if best approximation $a/2^{c-1}$ is equal to κ_u in question (i.e. $\Delta_u = 0$) then sure success ($P_s = 1$) can be provided. The worst case situation occurs if $|\Delta_u|$ reaches its maximum 2^{-c}.

Now let us determine a lower bound for successful measurement when no additional qbits are deployed at all to decrease quantum inaccuracy. Equation (6.24)

---

[4]An astronomer would say that the black hole located in $h = 0$ feeds more and more percentages of the whole matter of pdf until it swallows asymptotically the entire one.

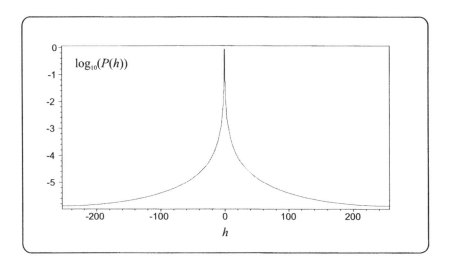

Fig. 6.7 $\log_{10}(P(h))$ in case $c = 10, p = 4$ and $\alpha_u = 0.4\pi$

can be further simplified by substituting the worst case $|\Delta_u| = 2^{-c}$ (because of $\sin^2(\cdot)$ the surface is symmetric onto h and the sign of Δ_u has no importance)

$$P_s = \frac{1}{2^{2c-2}} \frac{\sin^2(\pi 2^{c-1} 2^{-c})}{\sin^2(\pi 2^{-c})} = \frac{4}{2^{2c}} \frac{\sin^2(\pi/2)}{\sin^2(\pi 2^{-c})} = \frac{4}{2^{2c} \sin^2(\pi 2^{-c})}. \qquad (6.26)$$

Computing (6.26) for the smallest reasonable $c = 2$ we get 0.5 in accordance with Fig. 6.12. Studying the figure we can observe that $P_s \approx 0.4$ if c goes to infinity and exact calculations show that

$$\lim_{c \to +\infty} \frac{4}{2^{2c} \sin^2(\pi 2^{-c})} = \frac{4}{2^{2c}(\pi 2^{-c})^2} = \frac{4}{\pi^2}, \qquad (6.27)$$

where we used the well-known relation $\gamma \ll 1 : \sin(\gamma) \cong \gamma$.

6.2.4   Estimating quantum uncertainty

The previous analysis is quite useful to understand the basics of phase estimation but from an engineering point of view it cannot be applied as a rule of thumb because of its time-consuming evaluation and we have no information about the convergence of P_s. Instead we would prefer a less accurate but easily computable relation between engineering parameters n, p, c, P_ε. In order to accomplish this task we try to upper estimate the probability of error. The probability of measuring m which is different from a can be derived by simply summing up the probabilities of

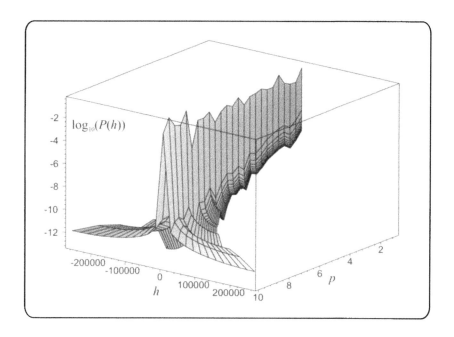

Fig. 6.8 $\log_{10}(P(h))$ in case $c = 10$ and $\alpha_u = 0.4 \cdot 2\pi$ when p varies between 0 and 10

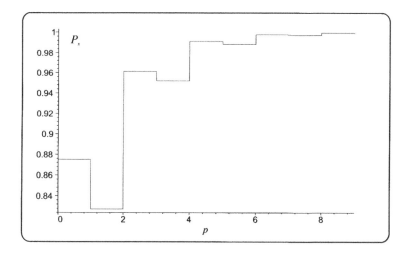

Fig. 6.9 P_s vs. p in case $c = 10$ and $\alpha_u = 0.4 \cdot 2\pi$

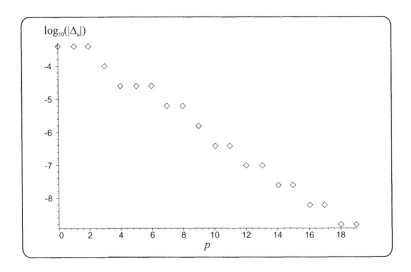

Fig. 6.10 $\log_{10}(|\Delta_u|)$ vs. p in case $c = 10$ and $\alpha_u = 0.4 \cdot 2\pi$

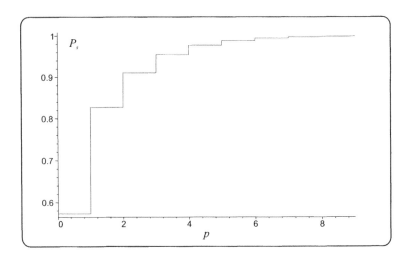

Fig. 6.11 Trade off between c and p at fixed $n = 10$

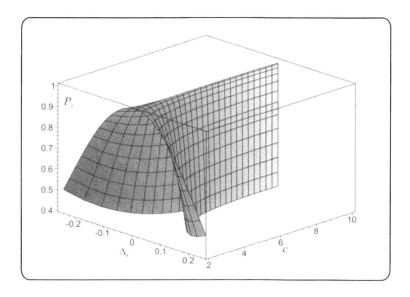

Fig. 6.12 P_s vs. c and Δ_u if $p = 0$

unwanted computational basis states

$$P_\varepsilon = \sum_{h=-2^{n-1}+1}^{-\varepsilon} |\varphi_h|^2 + \sum_{h=\varepsilon+1}^{2^{n-1}} |\varphi_h|^2. \tag{6.28}$$

Substituting (6.19) into (6.28) we get

$$P_\varepsilon = \sum_{h=-2^{n-1}+1}^{-\varepsilon} \frac{1}{2^{2n}} \frac{|1 - e^{j2\pi(2^n\Delta_u+h)}|^2}{|1 - e^{j2\pi(\Delta_u+\frac{h}{2^n})}|^2}$$

$$+ \sum_{h=\varepsilon+1}^{2^{n-1}} \frac{1}{2^{2n}} \frac{|1 - e^{j2\pi(2^n\Delta_u+h)}|^2}{|1 - e^{j2\pi(\Delta_u+\frac{h}{2^n})}|^2}, \Delta_u \neq 0. \tag{6.29}$$

Instead of calculating the exact value of P_ε we attempt to upperbound it. To do this on one hand we upperbound the numerator of (6.19) by means of **Exercise** 6.4 that claims $|1 - e^{j\gamma}| \leq 2$ and on the other hand the denominator of (6.21) is lowerbounded using the result of **Exercise** 6.5 ($|1 - e^{j\gamma}| \geq \frac{2|\gamma|}{\pi}$ if $\gamma \in [-\pi, \pi]$) because $|\gamma| = 2\pi|\Delta_u + \frac{h}{2^n}| \leq \pi$ if $h \in (-2^{n-1}, 2^{n-1})$. Therefore

$$|\varphi_h| \leq \frac{1}{2 \cdot 2^n|\Delta_u + \frac{h}{2^n}|} = \frac{1}{2|2^n\Delta_u + h|}. \tag{6.30}$$

Substituting (6.30) into (6.29) we get a much more treatable upperbound for P_ε

$$P_\varepsilon \leq \frac{1}{4}\left(\sum_{h=-2^{n-1}+1}^{-\varepsilon}\frac{1}{(2^n\Delta_u + h)^2} + \sum_{h=\varepsilon+1}^{2^{n-1}}\frac{1}{(2^n\Delta_u + h)^2}\right). \tag{6.31}$$

Concerning the fact that $2^n\Delta_u \in [-1/2, 1/2]$ therefore

$$P_\varepsilon \leq \frac{1}{4}\left(\sum_{h=-2^{n-1}+1}^{-\varepsilon}\frac{1}{(h+\frac{1}{2})^2} + \sum_{h=\varepsilon+1}^{2^{n-1}}\frac{1}{h^2}\right)$$

$$= \frac{1}{4}\left(\sum_{h=\varepsilon}^{2^{n-1}-1}\frac{1}{(h-\frac{1}{2})^2} + \sum_{h=\varepsilon+1}^{2^{n-1}}\frac{1}{h^2}\right)$$

$$\leq \frac{1}{4}\left(\sum_{h=\varepsilon}^{2^{n-1}-1}\frac{1}{(h-\frac{1}{2})^2} + \sum_{h=\varepsilon+1}^{2^{n-1}}\frac{1}{(h-\frac{1}{2})^2}\right) \leq \frac{1}{2}\sum_{h=\varepsilon}^{2^{n-1}-1}\frac{1}{(h-\frac{1}{2})^2}. \tag{6.32}$$

So we are near to the final solution. Since $\frac{1}{(h-\frac{1}{2})^2}$ is strictly monotonously decreasing if $h \geq$ we can upperestimate the sum by the following integral on $[\varepsilon - 1, 2^{n-1} - 1]$ if $\varepsilon > 1$

$$P_\varepsilon < \frac{1}{2}\int_{\varepsilon-1}^{2^{n-1}-1}\frac{1}{(h-\frac{1}{2})^2}dh < \frac{1}{2\varepsilon - 3}; \quad \varepsilon > 1. \tag{6.33}$$

Let us compute the unconditional error probability related to the event that the estimation fails

$$P_{error} = \sum_a P_\varepsilon P(a), \tag{6.34}$$

where P_ε represents the conditional error probability defined in (6.18). Because we have no information about the statistics of a it is assumed that $P(a)$ is uniformly distributed. The right-hand side of (6.33) does not depend on a, which allows us to replace P_ε with a quantity that is independent from the summation index thus

$$P_{error} < \frac{1}{2\varepsilon - 3} \leq \check{P}_\varepsilon. \tag{6.35}$$

If we have an engineering constraint for P_{error} say $\check{P}_\varepsilon$ then via combining (6.35) with (6.23) we manage to find a rule of thumb between the probability of phase ratio error and the number of used auxiliary qbits p

$$p \geq \mathrm{ld}\left(3 + \frac{1}{\check{P}_\varepsilon}\right). \tag{6.36}$$

Since p should be an integer – but as small as possible – number, our final result for the upper qregister in the phase estimator is

$$n = c - 1 + \left\lceil \mathrm{ld}\left(3 + \frac{1}{\check{P}_\varepsilon}\right)\right\rceil. \tag{6.37}$$

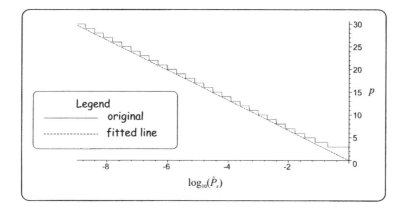

Fig. 6.13   Quantum error probability $\log_{10}(\check{P}_\varepsilon)$ vs. number of required additional qbits p

Remark: If classical accuracy 2^{-c} is related to the phase (d_u) instead of the phase ratio then obviously

$$n = c - 1 + \left\lceil \mathrm{ld}(2\pi) + \mathrm{ld}\left(3 + \frac{1}{\check{P}_\varepsilon}\right) \right\rceil . \tag{6.38}$$

We presented the relationship between 'overhead' p and demand $\check{P}_\varepsilon$ in compliance with (6.36) assuming equality in Fig. 6.13. We emphasize that the curve is fairly rough (it suggests at least two extra qbits) for small p because of the applied approximations during upper estimating P_ε. Conversely advantageously the curve is independent from n, c and the phase itself. A straight line with slope ≈ -3.3 and offset ≈ 0 can be fitted to the curve.[5] Since $\check{P}_\varepsilon$ has been sketched on a logarithmic scale one can deduce as an engineering rule of thumb that each additional qtribit reduces the probability of phase error to one-tenth.

Remark: As a matter of fact we obtained (6.38) after several approximations. Therefore if we get $n < 1$ then obviously n has to be set to 1.

Remark: We were afraid of the convergence speed of P_s in function of p. Fortunately Fig. 6.13 resolves our doubt, e.g. $P_s = 0.999$ can be achieved by means of only 10 extra qbits.

We have determined all the required parameters and their relation to estimating phase α_u of eigenvalue $e^{j2\pi\kappa_u}$, but what if $|u\rangle$ is unknown? We remember that eigenvectors of a unitary operator always form a set of orthonormal basis states. Therefore we initialize the lower qregister of the phase estimator with $|\psi\rangle = \sum_u \psi_u |u\rangle$. Because of the superposition principle we will get back an estimation of phase α_u, where u has been selected according to the probability distribution $|\psi_u|^2$.

[5] $p \simeq -3.3\log_{10}(\check{P}_\varepsilon)$.

As a last step of discussion about phase estimation let us determine how many U, denoted by $T(n)$, are needed to build the phase estimator circuit. Taking a look at Fig. 6.5 it becomes obvious that we have to calculate the sum of a geometric sequence comprising n terms and having quotient 2, thus

$$T(n) = \frac{q^n - 1}{q - 1} = \frac{2^n - 1}{2 - 1} = 2^n - 1. \tag{6.39}$$

However, if we are interested in the number of elementary gates required to implement the sequence of U^{2^l} operators, instead of the total number of U then we need only $O(n^3)$ elementary gates! Furthermore the Hadamard transform requires $O(n)$ elementary gates while for the IQFT we need $O(n^2)$ gates. Thus from the number of elementary gates, point of view we need only $O(n^3)$ gates.

Exercise 6.4. Prove that $|1 - e^{j\gamma}| \leq 2$.

Exercise 6.5. Prove $|1 - e^{j\gamma}| \geq \frac{2|\gamma|}{\pi}$ if $\gamma \in [-\pi, \pi]$.

6.3   ORDER FINDING AND FACTORING – SHOR ALGORITHM

Shor's efficient factoring algorithm consists of a quantum and a classical part. As a matter of fact the former one is a quantum-based solution of the so-called *order-finding* problem. Because this algorithm hides the seminal idea, which allows factoring a large number N in $O(\mathrm{ld}^3(N))$ steps (gates) instead of the best-known classical method requiring asymptotically $O(\exp[c \cdot \mathrm{ld}^{\frac{1}{3}}(N)\mathrm{ld}^{\frac{2}{3}}(\mathrm{ld}(N))])$ steps (i.e. it is exponential in $\mathrm{ld}^{\frac{1}{3}}(N)$) with some constant c [10], we show first how to trace classically factoring to find the order of an integer x and the quantum-based order-finding algorithm will be introduced afterwards.

6.3.1   Connection between factoring and order finding

Let us assume two positive integers $x < N$ that are co-primes, i.e. $\gcd(x, N) = 1$. The *order* of x in modulo N sense is defined as the least natural number r such that

$$x^r \bmod N = 1 \tag{6.40}$$

and it is easy to see that $1 < r < N$, too. The order of x is in close connection with the period of the function $f(z) = x^z \bmod N$ since

$$f(z + r) = x^{z+r} \bmod N = ((x^z \bmod N) \cdot \underbrace{(x^r \bmod N)}_{\equiv 1}) \bmod N = f(z). \tag{6.41}$$

Now in possession of the above definition we go ahead to find prime factors of A. First if A is even then one can divide A by 2 repeatedly until it becomes an odd B. Next we select randomly $x < B$. If $\gcd(x, B) = b$ and $b \neq 1$ then b is a common factor of x and B hence B can be divided by b. This step can be repeated until $b = 1$ resulting in N. Therefore it is sufficient to investigate the case when $0 < x < N$ and composite odd N are relative primes. When N is a power of a prime number then there exists an efficient classical algorithm to recognize this fact and to find that prime. If N comprises different prime factors then let us assume that order r of x modulo N is even thus we can define variable y as

$$y \triangleq x^{\frac{r}{2}}.$$

It follows from (6.40) that

$$y^2 \bmod N = 1. \tag{6.42}$$

Equation (6.42) can be rearranged by subtracting 1 from both sides as

$$(y^2 - 1) \bmod N = 0 \Rightarrow ((y+1)(y-1)) \bmod N = 0, \tag{6.43}$$

which corresponds to the fact that N divides $(y + 1)(y - 1)$ without any remainder. Equation (6.43) can be reformulated using the associative property of modular arithmetic

$$(\underbrace{[(y+1) \bmod N]}_{b_{+1}} \underbrace{[(y-1) \bmod N]}_{b_{-1}}) \bmod N = 0, \tag{6.44}$$

where obviously $0 \le b_{+1}, b_{-1} < N$. Calculating $c_{+1} = \gcd(b_{+1}, N)$ and $c_{-1} = \gcd(b_{-1}, N)$ we have the following possibilities[6] to ensure the equality to zero in (6.44)

- either $b_{+1} = 0$ then $c_{+1} = N$ and $b_{-1} = N - 2$, since neighboring odd numbers are co-primes therefore $c_{-1} = 1$,

- or $b_{-1} = 0$ then $c_{-1} = N$ and $b_{+1} = 2$, because N is odd hence $c_{+1} = 1$,

- finally $b_{+1}b_{-1} = kN, 0 < k < N \Rightarrow 0 < b_{-1} < b_{+1} < N$ therefore N divides into neither b_{+1} nor b_{-1}, thus to fulfil expectation in (6.44) $b_{+1}b_{-1}$ must have common factor(s) with N, i.e. c_{+1} and c_{-1} represent nontrivial factor(s) of N.

If x does not satisfy $0 < c_{-1}, c_{+1} < N$ (it would result in trivial factors of N) or N has further nontrivial factors then a new x has to be selected (in a random way) and corresponding greatest common divisors have to be calculated until we have all the prime factors of N in our hands. We emphasize here, that computing c_{+1} and c_{-1} requires the knowledge of r.

There are two important questions remaining:

1. We had an initial assumption on r and the algorithm itself proved to be probabilistic. Is it reasonable to use this algorithm, i.e. is the probability of finding a prime factor in one turn high enough?

---

[6]The first two scenarios are often summarized in the literature as $y \bmod N \ne \pm 1$.

2. We have efficient classical solutions for all the above listed steps of the factorization algorithm except for finding the order of x. Maybe quantum computing can assist us in this problem?

The first question was answered by Shor in [137]. He proved that for an odd natural number N and for a random integer x uniformly selected from $[1, N)$ that satisfy $\gcd(x, N) = 1$ the probability being order r even and $x^{\frac{r}{2}} \bmod N \neq \pm 1$ is greater or equal to $1 - 2^{1-l}$, where l stands for the number of prime factors of N. For instance in the worst case when $l = 2$ the probability of finding nontrivial factors is at least 0.5. The second question proves to be, however, more challenging therefore the next section is dedicated to constructing an efficient quantum-based order-finding algorithm.

Exercise 6.6. Factorize $A = 66$! To find the order use exhaustive search.

6.3.2 Quantum-based order finding

In order to design a polynomial-time quantum order-finding algorithm we turn to the well-tried and successful technique already used plenty of times in this book, namely to quantum parallelism combined with constructive interference. It seems to be reasonable to compute and store all the possible $x^k \bmod N$ for $0 \leq k < N$ in a quantum register $t = \lceil \mathrm{ld}(N) \rceil$ qbit of size and related k values in another entangled qregister with the same size. Next we try to increase the probability amplitude of $|x^k \bmod N = 1\rangle$ in the first qregister as close to 1 as possible, then a measurement on the second qregister will return the requested order r with high probability. This idea seems to be very simple, however, to turn it into cash a slightly longer discussion is needed and the reader can follow the design of the corresponding quantum circuit in Fig. 6.14.

First of all the system is initialized with computational basis (classical) states $|\varphi_0\rangle = |\gamma_0\rangle |\psi_0\rangle$, where $\gamma_0, \psi_0 \in [0, 2^t - 1)$. Next we fill the upper qregister with potential values k of the order r providing uniform probability amplitudes. This can be done using an n-qbit Hadamard gate for $|\gamma_0\rangle = |0\rangle$. At this stage of the discussion we assume $n = t$ and it will be corrected later when designing considerations imply this, thus

$$|\varphi_1\rangle = \frac{1}{\sqrt{2^n}} \sum_{k=0}^{2^n-1} |k\rangle \otimes |\psi_0\rangle. \tag{6.45}$$

Now we have to construct a gate V which consists of a lower part producing $x^k \bmod N$ and an upper section with a qregister containing all the possible values of k while controlling the lower part. So we expect that $V|\varphi_1\rangle = |\varphi_2\rangle$, where

$$|\varphi_2\rangle = \frac{1}{\sqrt{2^n}} \sum_{k=0}^{2^n-1} |k\rangle |x^k \bmod N\rangle. \tag{6.46}$$

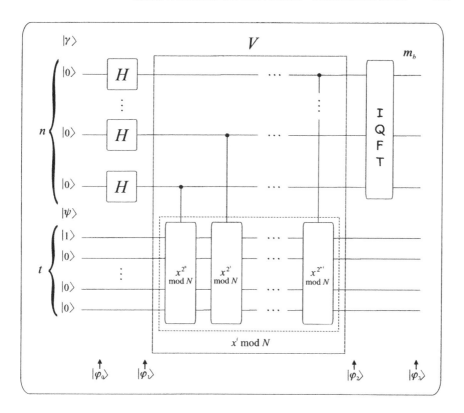

Fig. 6.14 Quantum circuit implementing order finding

We invoke modular exponentiation from Section 12.3.1 which has the form in our case

$$x^k \bmod N = \prod_{l=1}^{2^n} \left(x^{k_l 2^{n-l}} \bmod N \right)$$

$$= \left(x^{k_1 2^{n-1}} \bmod N \right) \left(x^{k_2 2^{n-2}} \bmod N \right) \dots \left(x^{k_n 2^0} \bmod N \right), \quad (6.47)$$

where $k = k_1 2^{n-1} + k_2 2^{n-2} + \dots + k_n 2^0$ and $k_l \in \{0, 1\}$. Equation (6.47) can be interpreted as a set of consecutive gates with the following properties: the $(n - l)^{\text{th}}$ gate implements $f(l) = x^{2^{n-l}}$ and it is controlled by the lth wire of the upper section of the circuit due to k_l in the exponent. This structure is nothing more than the first stage of the phase estimator circuit (cf. Fig. 6.5) with a special operator U that simply multiplies its input q by x (of course in modulo N sense) instead of an arbitrary one

$$U : |q\rangle \rightarrow |(qx) \bmod N\rangle. \quad (6.48)$$

Remark: Wide-awake readers may pose this question. We rounded up N to 2^t since we can buy qregisters comprising only integer numbers of qbits. However, this operation introduces extra values of $k = N \dots 2^t - 1$ which should be chosen to keep unitarity of U. In order to avoid this problem we extend the $N \times N$ matrix to $2^t \times 2^t$ by means of rows/columns such that they become orthogonal to the original ones. The simplest way to do this if we put 1s into the main diagonal positions using $|k\rangle \rightarrow |k\rangle$ if $k = N \dots 2^t - 1$ (see **Exercise** 6.7).

Remark: It is interesting to show that if the order-finding circuit is initialized with $|\varphi_0\rangle = |0\rangle|0\rangle$ and V is replaced by $V' : |k\rangle|q\rangle \rightarrow |k\rangle|(q + x^k) \bmod N\rangle$ then it produces $|\varphi_2\rangle$ according to (6.46) (see **Exercise** 6.8).

We now return to order finding and remember that if we used an IQFT for the upper section then in accordance with the operation of the phase estimator circuit we would get the eigenvalues of U. Now let us stop for a while and check whether it is worth applying IQFT. One way to find eigenvalues and eigenvectors is if we follow the traditional method summarized in Section 12.2.4. Unfortunately solving characteristic equations seems to be quite hard for arbitrary x and N therefore we propose to utilize our knowledge about the phase estimator. Let us denote the state of the phase estimator at checkpoint 2 by $|\varphi_{P2}\rangle$ in Fig. 6.5 to distinguish it from the state (6.46) of the order-finding circuit at the same checkpoint. We make an attempt to derive corresponding eigenvalues and eigenvectors by comparing the two states and ensuring that $|\varphi_2\rangle$ is a given solution of the general case $|\varphi_{P2}\rangle$.

First we reformulate (6.46) with respect to the fact that function $x^k \bmod N$ is periodic in r (see (6.41)) and thus there are only r different values of $x^k \bmod N$

$$|\varphi_2\rangle = \frac{1}{\sqrt{2^n}} \sum_{k=0}^{r-1} \left(\sum_{z=0}^{Z_k} |zr + k\rangle \right) |x^k \bmod N\rangle, \qquad (6.49)$$

where we concentrated the states of the upper section belonging to a given $|x^k \bmod N\rangle$, $k = 0 \dots r - 1$ into a superposition. When calculating Z_k one has to bear in mind that $0 \leq zr + k \leq 2^n - 1$ and z is integer, which results in $0 \leq z \leq \lfloor \frac{2^n - 1 - k}{r} \rfloor = Z_k$.

On the other hand $|\varphi_{P2}\rangle$ can be formulated in accordance with (6.14) as

$$|\varphi_{P2}\rangle = \sum_{k=0}^{2^n - 1} \frac{1}{\sqrt{2^n}} e^{j2\pi k \kappa_u} |k\rangle|u\rangle. \qquad (6.50)$$

Equation (6.50) is valid only for the case if $|\psi_0\rangle$ had been initialized by known eigenvector $|u\rangle$, however, we have no information yet about $|\psi_0\rangle$, only the output $|x^k \bmod N\rangle$ of the lower section is known. Hence recalling the life-belt from this awkward situation $|\psi_0\rangle$ is set to an equal superposition of eigenvectors

$$|\psi_0\rangle = \sum_{b=0}^{B-1} \frac{1}{\sqrt{B}} |u_b\rangle, \qquad (6.51)$$

where B refers to the number of involved eigenvectors, whose exact value should be determined during the analysis. Now, using the superposition principle the output of the phase estimator can be described by applying (6.50) for $|\psi_0\rangle$

$$|\varphi_{P2}\rangle = \frac{1}{\sqrt{2^n}} \sum_{k=0}^{2^n-1} \sum_{b=0}^{B-1} \frac{e^{j2\pi k\kappa_b}}{\sqrt{B}} |k\rangle |u_b\rangle = \frac{1}{\sqrt{2^n}} \sum_{k=0}^{2^n-1} |k\rangle \sum_{b=0}^{B-1} \frac{e^{j2\pi k\kappa_b}}{\sqrt{B}} |u_b\rangle,$$
(6.52)

where κ_b stands for the phase ratio belonging to eigenvector $|u_b\rangle$. Remembering that we plan to derive a common form for $|\varphi_{P2}\rangle$ and $|\varphi_2\rangle$ it seems to be reasonable to perform the same index transformation on k

$$|\varphi_{P2}\rangle = \frac{1}{\sqrt{2^n}} \sum_{k=0}^{r-1} \sum_{z=0}^{Z_k} |zr+k\rangle \sum_{b=0}^{B-1} \frac{e^{j2\pi k\kappa_b}}{\sqrt{B}} |u_b\rangle.$$
(6.53)

Comparing (6.49) and (6.53) one can deduce that the equivalence of $|\varphi_{P2}\rangle$ and $|\varphi_2\rangle$ requires

$$|x^k \bmod N\rangle = \sum_{b=0}^{B-1} \frac{e^{j2\pi k\kappa_b}}{\sqrt{B}} |u_b\rangle, k = 0 \dots r-1.$$
(6.54)

To find suitable parameters for the right-hand side that provides the equality in (6.54) we start to form the left-hand side. Using the well-known relation

$$\sum_{b=0}^{B-1} \frac{e^{-j2\pi \frac{b}{B}s}}{B} = \sum_{b=0}^{B-1} \frac{e^{+j2\pi \frac{b}{B}s}}{B} = \delta(s-B) = \begin{cases} 1, & \text{if } s \text{ is a multiple of } B \\ 0, & \text{else,} \end{cases}$$
(6.55)

we can write

$$|x^k \bmod N\rangle = \sum_{s=0}^{B-1} \underbrace{\sum_{b=0}^{B-1} \frac{e^{-j2\pi \frac{b}{B}s}}{B}}_{\delta(s-0)} |x^k \bmod N\rangle.$$

Because k runs from 0 up to $r-1$ it is reasonable to set $B = r$ and to involve $|x^k \bmod N\rangle$ in the summation

$$|x^k \bmod N\rangle = \sum_{s=0}^{r-1} \underbrace{\sum_{b=0}^{r-1} \frac{e^{-j2\pi \frac{b}{r}(s-k)}}{r}}_{\delta(s-k)} |x^s \bmod N\rangle.$$

Applying some algebraic steps we reach the final form

$$|x^k \bmod N\rangle = \sum_{b=0}^{r-1} \frac{e^{j2\pi \frac{k}{r}b}}{\sqrt{r}} \sum_{s=0}^{r-1} \frac{e^{-j2\pi \frac{b}{r}s}}{\sqrt{r}} |x^s \bmod N\rangle.$$
(6.56)

If we compare the right-hand side of (6.54) with this result we can conclude that for $k = 1 \dots r-1$

$$\kappa_b = \frac{b}{r}, \quad |u_b\rangle = \sum_{s=0}^{r-1} \frac{e^{-j2\pi \frac{b}{r}s}}{\sqrt{r}} |x^s \bmod N\rangle.$$
(6.57)

We ask the reader to check whether $|u_b\rangle$ are eigenvectors of U in **Exercise** 6.9.

Remark: It has to be emphasized that in spite of the fact that here we used only r eigenvectors of operator U it has 2^t orthonormal eigenvectors because of its unitary nature.

Now we have reached a very promising point. The phase ratios, which are the results of an IQFT on the upper section, contain the order r! Before designing an appropriate technique to obtain r from κ_b we have to find a suitable initialization vector for $|\psi_0\rangle$. Since neither of the eigenvectors can be implemented trivially (all of them requires the knowledge of r) we turn back to the superposition of eigenvectors and compute (6.51) with $B = r$

$$|\psi_0\rangle = \sum_{b=0}^{r-1} \frac{1}{\sqrt{r}} |u_b\rangle = \sum_{b=0}^{r-1} \frac{1}{\sqrt{r}} \sum_{s=0}^{r-1} \frac{e^{-j2\pi \frac{b}{r} s}}{\sqrt{r}} |x^s \bmod N\rangle$$

$$= \frac{1}{r} \sum_{s=0}^{r-1} \underbrace{\left(\sum_{b=0}^{r-1} e^{-j2\pi \frac{b}{r} s} \right)}_{r\delta(s-0)} |x^s \bmod N\rangle = |x^0 \bmod N\rangle = |1\rangle_{2^t}. \quad (6.58)$$

So it is enough to put a classical state $|1\rangle_{2^t}$ to the lower input of the phase estimator.

Remark: We would like to call the attention of the reader to an important aspect. We did not require explicit knowledge about the transformation rule of U to derive its eigenvalues, eigenvectors and $|\psi_0\rangle$. Instead we used the indirect information related to U hidden in $|\varphi_1\rangle$ and $|\varphi_2\rangle$. This technique will be referred to in Section 6.5.1 when we are trying to find the period of function f.

Being professional in phase estimation we expect that a measurement on the IQFT output (see Fig. 6.14) gives back an estimation m_b for $\kappa_b \approx m_b/2^n$ where κ_b has been selected in accordance with uniform distribution on $b \in [0 \ldots r)$. Next we show how to determine r in possession of $m_b/2^n$. Theorem 12.1 provides the key to the solution.

In order to fulfil the condition in the theorem

$$\left| \frac{b}{r} - \frac{m_b}{2^n} \right| \leq \frac{1}{2r^2} \quad (6.59)$$

we recall the error analysis of the phase estimator in Section 6.2.2. We concluded there that if $m_b/2^n$ is the closest estimation[7] to b/r then $|\Delta_b| = |\kappa_b - \tilde{\kappa}_b| = \left| \frac{b}{r} - \frac{m_b}{2^n} \right| \leq 2^{-(n+1)}$. Thus we need

$$\frac{1}{2^{(n+1)}} \leq \frac{1}{2r^2} \Rightarrow r^2 \leq 2^n \underbrace{\Rightarrow}_{r<N} N^2 \leq 2^n \Rightarrow n = \lceil \mathrm{ld}(N^2) \rceil. \quad (6.60)$$

However, we have also learned that IQFT may introduce a quantum error – if $m_b/2^n$ does not exactly equal s/b – with probability P_ε, which advises us to buy $n = \lceil \mathrm{ld}(N^2) \rceil + p$ qbits for the upper section of the order-finding device.

---

[7]Assuming m_b is a natural number and no auxiliary qbits are involved to lower quantum uncertainty i.e. $n = c - 1$.

Having designed all the important blocks of the equipment from the required number of qbits up to unitary gates, we are now ready to perform the continued fraction algorithm in compliance with Section 12.3.4 to derive the convergents of $m_b/2^n$. Because we have chosen 2^n such that it is greater or equal to N^2 and $r < N$ hence there is only a single b which fulfils (6.59). Let us assume the convergent has the form of b'/r', i.e. we have to search for the closest convergent with denominator $r' < N$. Calculating $x^{r'} \bmod N$ either we get 1 which proves that $r' = r$ is the order of x or we receive any other value, which points out that r is a multiple of r' (this occurs if m_b and r have common factor(s)). In the latter case we have to repeat the algorithm to obtain a different r'. Fortunately from the probability of being r and r' relative primes $P(\gcd(r, r') = 1) = \frac{1}{O(\text{ld}(\text{ld}(N)))}$ and by repeating the steps of the algorithm $O(\text{ld}(\text{ld}(N)))$ times we may expect an appropriate r' with high probability.

This section began by emphasizing the efficiency of Shor's algorithm over the best (equal) classical one. We do not discuss this topic in detail, interested users are advised to read [139] or [149]. Here we lay stress upon the essence of this topic. It was previously mentioned that the required $O(\text{ld}^3(N))$ gates can be further reduced to $O(\text{ld}^2(N) \cdot \text{ld}(\text{ld}(N)) \cdot \text{ld}(\text{ld}(\text{ld}(N))))$ for moderately large N if the grade school multiplication algorithm is replaced by Schönhage–Strassen [20] fast integer multiplication during the modular exponentiation. However, both results are basically influenced by $O(\text{ld}^2(N))$ originating from the IQFT implementation.

Exercise 6.7. Derive the matrix of operator $U : |q\rangle \rightarrow |(qx) \bmod N\rangle$.

Exercise 6.8. Prove that if the order-finding circuit initialized with $|\varphi_0\rangle = |0\rangle|0\rangle$ and its gate V is replaced by $V' : |k\rangle|q\rangle \rightarrow |k\rangle|(q + x^k) \bmod N\rangle$ then it produces $|\varphi_2\rangle = \frac{1}{\sqrt{2^n}} \sum_{k=0}^{2^n - 1} |k\rangle|x^k \bmod N\rangle$, too.

Exercise 6.9. Prove that $|u_b\rangle = \sum_{s=0}^{r-1} \frac{e^{-j2\pi \frac{b}{r} s}}{\sqrt{r}} |x^s \bmod N\rangle$, $b = 0 \ldots r - 1$ are eigenvectors of $U : |q\rangle \rightarrow |(qx) \bmod N\rangle$.

6.3.3 Error analysis and a numerical example

There is only one point in the previous subsection which remained open, namely we alluded that m_b/r may be a rough estimation of b/r instead of being the best one. This follows from the operation of the phase estimator. Next we calculate the probability of measuring $i = m_b$ at the output of the IQFT. Afterwards we use this result in numerical examples to illuminate the most important steps in order finding and to summarize the algorithm. To compute pdf $P(i)$ one has two choices. Either the results obtained at phase estimation can be exploited or we calculate $|\varphi_3\rangle$ in Fig. 6.14. We decided for the latter one to give a comprehensive discussion of the order-finding circuit, however, we ask the reader to also follow the former way.

$|\varphi_3\rangle$ can be determined simply by using IQFT (see (6.6)) on the upper n qbits of $|\varphi_2\rangle$ (see (6.49))

$$|\varphi_3\rangle = (F^{\dagger} \otimes I^{\otimes t})|\varphi_2\rangle = \frac{1}{\sqrt{2^n}} \sum_{k=0}^{r-1} \sum_{z=0}^{Z_k} \frac{1}{\sqrt{2^n}} \sum_{i=0}^{2^n-1} e^{-j\frac{2\pi}{2^n}i(zr+k)}|i\rangle|x^k \bmod N\rangle$$

$$= \sum_{i=0}^{2^n-1} \sum_{k=0}^{r-1} \underbrace{\left(\sum_{z=0}^{Z_k} \frac{e^{-j\frac{2\pi}{2^n}i(zr+k)}}{2^n} \right)}_{\varphi_{ik}} |i\rangle|x^k \bmod N\rangle. \tag{6.61}$$

Coefficient $|\varphi_{ik}|^2$ represents the probability of measuring $|i\rangle|x^k \bmod N\rangle$ at the output of the circuit. The summation within the parenthesis demonstrates the constructive interference which was mentioned as a required technique beside quantum parallelism at the very beginning of the previous subsection. The probability amplitudes may cancel each other while increasing the probability of measuring a suitable state as we will see later. Basic probability theory ensures that

$$P(i) = \sum_{k=0}^{r-1} |\varphi_{ik}|^2 = \sum_{k=0}^{r-1} \left| \sum_{z=0}^{Z_k} \frac{e^{-j\frac{2\pi}{2^n}i(zr+k)}}{2^n} \right|^2$$

$$= \sum_{k=0}^{r-1} \underbrace{\left| e^{-j\frac{2\pi}{2^n}ik} \right|^2}_{\equiv 1} \left| \frac{1}{2^n} \sum_{z=0}^{Z_k} \left(e^{-j\frac{2\pi}{2^n}ir} \right)^z \right|^2, \tag{6.62}$$

which can be further simplified realizing that a sum of geometrical sequence can be found within the argument of the absolute value operator with quotient $q = e^{-j\frac{2\pi}{2^n}ir}$ and starting value $1/2^{2n}$. If $q = 1 \Rightarrow \frac{ir}{2^n} \in \mathbb{Z}$ then

$$P(i) = \sum_{k=0}^{r-1} \left(\frac{Z_k+1}{2^n} \right)^2, \tag{6.63}$$

else

$$P(i) = \sum_{k=0}^{r-1} \frac{1}{2^{2n}} \left| \frac{1-q^{Z_k+1}}{1-q} \right|^2 = \sum_{k=0}^{r-1} \frac{1}{2^{2n}} \left| \frac{1-e^{-j\frac{2\pi}{2^n}ir(Z_k+1)}}{1-e^{-j\frac{2\pi}{2^n}ir}} \right|^2$$

$$= \sum_{k=0}^{r-1} \frac{1}{2^{2n}} \frac{\sin^2\left(\frac{\pi ir(Z_k+1)}{2^n}\right)}{\sin^2\left(\frac{\pi ir}{2^n}\right)}, \quad \text{if } q \neq 1, \tag{6.64}$$

where we used the result of **Exercise** 6.3 in the last step. Trivially (6.63) belongs to the idealistic case when $\frac{b}{r} = \frac{m_b}{2^n}$ and (6.64) to the practical one. The pdf of random variable i has been depicted for $n = 11, N = 33, x = 5, r = 10$ in Fig. 6.15. According to the expectations the reader may observe peaks near to $\frac{2^n}{r}b$ since the ideal case would be $\frac{b}{r} = \frac{m_b}{2^n}$. The figure highlights the fact that probabilities are concentrating around the wanted phase ratios thus quantum inaccuracy has marginal influence on successful order finding. Furthermore we emphasize that if 2^n is a multiple of r then the peaks move exactly to $\frac{2^n}{r} b$ and what is more interesting is that the quantum uncertainty also disappears (see **Exercise** 6.10). Unfortunately we do not know r in advance hence suitable n cannot be chosen. However, as we discussed in connection with the phase estimation this quantum inaccuracy can be handled by means of some overhead p qbits deployed in the upper qregister.

As an example and illustration of quantum-based order finding we continue the factorization example introduced in **Exercise** 6.6 and replace the exhaustive search for the order. Remember that we have to find the order r of $x = 5$ modulo $N = 33$. First one should define the initialization parameters of the order-finding device. We set $n = \lceil \mathrm{ld}(33^2) \rceil = 11$ and $t = \lceil \mathrm{ld}(33) \rceil = 6$, therefore the circuit is initialized with $|\varphi_0\rangle = |0\rangle_{2^{11}} |1\rangle_{2^6}$, which is followed by a $H^{\otimes 11}$ gate on the upper qregister resulting $|\varphi_1\rangle$ according to (6.45)

$$|\varphi_1\rangle = \frac{1}{\sqrt{2048}} \sum_{k=0}^{2047} |k\rangle \otimes |1\rangle_{2^6}.$$

Now we let gate V operate on both qregister in compliance with (6.46)

$$|\varphi_2\rangle = \frac{1}{\sqrt{2048}} \sum_{k=0}^{2047} |k\rangle |x^k \bmod 33\rangle,$$

which has the following more illustrative form

$$
\begin{aligned}
|\varphi_2\rangle = \frac{1}{\sqrt{2048}} \big(& |0\rangle|1\rangle + |1\rangle|5\rangle + |2\rangle|25\rangle + |3\rangle|26\rangle + |4\rangle|31\rangle + |5\rangle|23\rangle \\
& + |6\rangle|16\rangle + |7\rangle|14\rangle + |8\rangle|4\rangle + |9\rangle|20\rangle + |10\rangle|1\rangle + |11\rangle|5\rangle \\
& + |12\rangle|25\rangle + |13\rangle|26\rangle + \cdots \big).
\end{aligned}
$$

It is obvious that $x^k \bmod 33$ has a period $r = 10$ as we determined earlier by exhaustive search. Terms of $|\varphi_2\rangle$ can be regrouped as was advised in (6.49) according to the computational basis states stored in the second qregister (1,5,25,26,31,23,16, 14,4,20)

$$|\varphi_2\rangle = \sum_{k=0}^{9} \underbrace{\left(\frac{1}{\sqrt{2048}} \sum_{z=0}^{Z_k} |10z + k\rangle \right)}_{|\varphi_{2k}\rangle} |x^k \bmod 33\rangle$$

$$
\begin{aligned}
= & \frac{1}{\sqrt{2048}} (|0\rangle + |10\rangle + |20\rangle + \cdots + |2030\rangle + |2040\rangle)|1\rangle \\
& + \frac{1}{\sqrt{2048}} (|1\rangle + |11\rangle + |21\rangle + \cdots + |2031\rangle + |2041\rangle)|5\rangle \\
& + \frac{1}{\sqrt{2048}} (|2\rangle + |12\rangle + |22\rangle + \cdots + |2032\rangle + |2042\rangle)|25\rangle
\end{aligned}
$$

$$+ \frac{1}{\sqrt{2048}}(|3\rangle + |13\rangle + |23\rangle + \cdots + |2033\rangle + |2043\rangle)|26\rangle$$

$$+ \frac{1}{\sqrt{2048}}(|4\rangle + |14\rangle + |24\rangle + \cdots + |2034\rangle + |2044\rangle)|31\rangle$$

$$+ \frac{1}{\sqrt{2048}}(|5\rangle + |15\rangle + |25\rangle + \cdots + |2036\rangle + |2045\rangle)|23\rangle$$

$$+ \frac{1}{\sqrt{2048}}(|6\rangle + |16\rangle + |26\rangle + \cdots + |2036\rangle + |2046\rangle)|16\rangle$$

$$+ \frac{1}{\sqrt{2048}}(|7\rangle + |17\rangle + |27\rangle + \cdots + |2037\rangle + |2047\rangle)|14\rangle$$

$$+ \frac{1}{\sqrt{2048}}(|8\rangle + |18\rangle + |28\rangle + \cdots + |2038\rangle)|4\rangle$$

$$+ \frac{1}{\sqrt{2048}}(|9\rangle + |19\rangle + |29\rangle + \cdots + |2039\rangle)|20\rangle.$$

The reader may recognize that not all the $|\varphi_{2k}\rangle$ contain the same number of computational basis states because of Z_k, however, as we concluded in **Exercise** 6.10 if r divided 2^n without reminder Z_k values would lose their dependence on k and all the superpositions $|\varphi_{2k}\rangle$ would comprise equal numbers of basis vectors. We will point out soon that quantum inaccuracy when finding the order can be traced back to this anomaly.

As the last step before measurement an IQFT is performed on the upper section bearing in mind (6.61). The superposition principle allows this operator to act one by one on each $|\varphi_{2k}\rangle$ thus

$$|\varphi_3\rangle = (F^\dagger \otimes I^{\otimes 6})|\varphi_2\rangle = \sum_{k=0}^{9}(F^\dagger \otimes I^{\otimes 6})|\varphi_{2k}\rangle|x^k \bmod 33\rangle$$

$$= \sum_{k=0}^{9}\sum_{i=0}^{2047}\overbrace{\sum_{z=0}^{Z_k}\frac{1}{2048}e^{-j\frac{2\pi}{2048}i(10z+k)}}^{\varphi_{ik}}|i\rangle \underbrace{\qquad\qquad}_{|\varphi_{3k}\rangle}|x^k \bmod 33\rangle$$

$$= \sum_{k=0}^{9}\underbrace{(\varphi_{0k}|0\rangle + \varphi_{1k}|1\rangle + \cdots + \varphi_{ik}|i\rangle + \cdots + \varphi_{2047k}|2047\rangle)}_{|\varphi_{3k}\rangle}|x^k \bmod 33\rangle.$$

Finally the measurement randomly selects a computational basis vector $|i\rangle$. Since all possible $|i\rangle$ occur in all $|\varphi_{3k}\rangle$ therefore the probability of measuring i is

$$P(i) = \sum_{k=0}^{9}|\varphi_{ik}|^2 = \begin{cases} \sum_{k=0}^{9}\left(\frac{Z_k+1}{2048}\right)^2 & \text{if } \frac{10i}{2048} \in \mathbb{Z} \\[2ex] \sum_{k=0}^{9}\frac{1}{2048^2}\frac{\sin^2(\frac{\pi 10i(Z_k+1)}{2048})}{\sin^2(\frac{\pi 10i}{2048})} & \text{else,} \end{cases}$$

where we used the results of (6.63) and (6.64). Fig. 6.15 depicts $P(i)$. Peaks can be observed at $0, 205, 410, 614, 819, 1024, 1229, 1434, 1638, 1843$ which are the closest integers to $b2^n/r$ with periodicity $\approx 2^n/r = 205$. Related peak probability values are $0.1, 0.0875, 0.0573, 0.0573, 0.08753, 0.1, 0.08753, 0.0573, 0.0573, 0.08753$. The probability of measuring one of them is 0.779. Because we set $n = \lceil \mathrm{ld}(N^2) \rceil$, if we measured one of the peaks then they are close enough to $b\frac{2^n}{r}$ to perform continued fraction algorithms to extract r from m_b. Let us assume $m_b = 614$. The corresponding convergents are: $\frac{1}{3}, \frac{2}{7}, \frac{3}{10}, \frac{152}{507}, \frac{307}{1024}$. Among them $\frac{3}{10}$ is the closest one to $\frac{614}{2048}$ with denominator less than N. Therefore we check 5^{10} mod 33 which equals 1 thus we managed to find r. However, if m_b were measured to 819 then convergents would be: $\frac{1}{2}, \frac{1}{3}, \frac{2}{5}, \frac{819}{2048}$. According to the selection rules we should take $\frac{2}{5}$, but when testing it 5^5 mod $33 = 23$, which implies that $r' = 5$ is a factor of r and not r itself. Unlike the ideal case (see **Exercise** 6.10) when 2^n is a multiple of r – or equivalently $\frac{m_b}{2^n} = \frac{b}{r}$ – in our realistic scenario values of peaks are not uniformly equal to $1/r$ and probabilities are not concentrated exactly into special values $b\frac{2^n}{r}$. Applying logarithmic scale emphasizes this fact in Fig. 6.16. Since we are not aware of r in advance and therefore an appropriate value cannot be set to n the only chance of reducing the probability of error P_ε is if we increase the size of the upper qregister by p additional qbits according to (6.36)

$$ n = c - 1 + p = \left\lceil \mathrm{ld}(N^2) + \mathrm{ld}\left(3 + \frac{1}{\breve{P}_\varepsilon}\right) \right\rceil, \tag{6.65} $$

where the term $\mathrm{ld}(2\pi)$ was removed because order finding is related to the accuracy of phase ratio $\kappa_b = b/r$ instead of the phase $\alpha_b = 2\pi b/r$ itself.

Finally we remind the reader the basic concept of designing the quantum order-finding circuit, which corresponds to a general cooking recipe. First quantum parallelism was exploited in order to produce all the $|k\rangle|x^k \bmod N\rangle$ states. Next instead of performing an immediate measurement promising an equiprobable result for all $x^k \bmod N$ we used constructive interference to amplify those probability amplitudes which were closely related to the r in question. In this case an IQFT gate was responsible for this interference. Finally some classical postprocessing steps were utilized to obtain r from the measurement result.

Exercise 6.10. Assuming 2^n is a multiple of r (r is a power of 2) prove that quantum inaccuracy disappears from $|\varphi_3\rangle$.

6.4 QFT AS GENERALIZED HADAMARD TRANSFORM

Now, it is time to stop for a while in order to build bridges between this chapter and other parts of this book. First let us reconsider the transformation rule of Hadamard

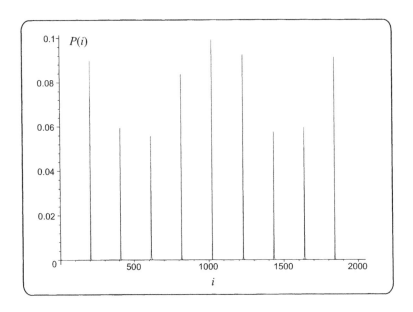

Fig. 6.15 $P(i)$ assuming $n = 11, N = 33, x = 5, r = 10$

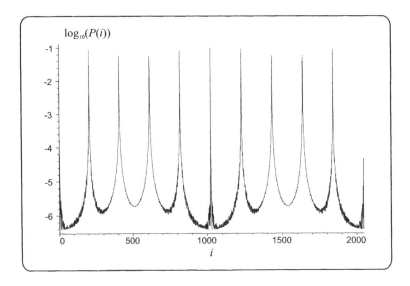

Fig. 6.16 $\log_{10}(P(i))$ assuming $n = 11, N = 33, x = 5, r = 10$

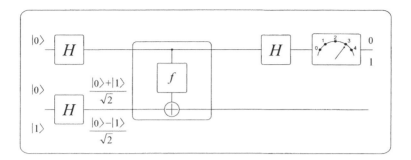

Fig. 6.17   Deutsch–Jozsa circuit as a decision maker whether f is constant or varying

gates: $H|0\rangle = (|0\rangle + |1\rangle)/\sqrt{2}$, $H|1\rangle = (|0\rangle - |1\rangle)/\sqrt{2}$. Using $n = 1$ in (2.9)

$$H^{\otimes 1}|i\rangle = \frac{1}{\sqrt{2^1}} \sum_{k \in \{0,1\}^1} (-1)^{ik}|k\rangle = \frac{1}{\sqrt{2}} \sum_{k=0}^{1} (-1)^{ik}|k\rangle, \qquad (6.66)$$

where $i \in \{0, 1\}$. Recalling that $-1 = e^{j2\pi \frac{1}{2}}$ (6.66) can be rewritten as

$$H|i\rangle = \frac{1}{\sqrt{2}} \sum_{k=0}^{1} e^{j2\pi \frac{ik}{2}}|k\rangle. \qquad (6.67)$$

If the reader compares (6.67) with (6.4) he/she can conclude that $H|i\rangle$ is nothing more than the QFT of $|i\rangle$ i.e. the one-qbit Hadamard gate corresponds to the QFT over $\mathbb{Z}_{N=2}$. Based on this fact it is reasonable to point out that $H^{\otimes n}$ is the equivalent of QFT over $(\mathbb{Z}_2)^n$. As we discussed in Section 6.1 QFT over $(\mathbb{Z}_2)^n = \mathbb{Z}_{N=2^n}$ (i.e. $H^{\otimes n}$) can be extended to $\mathbb{Z}_N$ with arbitrary nonnegative integer N by means of controlled phase gates $R_{h,p}$ (see Fig. 6.3). For further extensions of QFT over more general groups see *Further Reading*.

As a next step we build the connection between the Deutsch–Jozsa algorithm (see Section 5.2) and QFT. In Fig. 6.17 we presented the $n = 1$ qbit version of the circuit depicted in Fig. 5.3, which is often referred to as the Deutsch circuit. Let us moreover select $f(x) : f(0) = 0$, $f(1) = 1$ that results in a $U_f = \text{CNOT}$ gate in the middle. If the lower (data) input has been fed by $|0\rangle$ the measuring equipment answers with $|0\rangle$ since f is a balanced function. In the opposite case when we initialize data input to $|1\rangle$ the output will be $|1\rangle$.[8]

Now let us assume the role of a phase estimation expert! Suddenly the CNOT gate turns into a controlled X gate and the H gate at the output has been changed to an IQFT in accordance with the above observation on the relationship between the QFT and Hadamard gate[9] (see Fig. 6.18). Leaning on the results of **Exercise** 6.11 we

---

[8]One may remark that we managed to realize a quantum-assisted classical shortcut, but fortunately this circuit has more important lessons.

[9]Do not forget that H is a Hermitian operator (and therefore also unitary), hence $H^{-1} = H$.

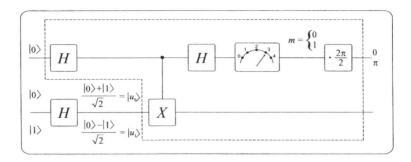

Fig. 6.18   Deutsch–Jozsa circuit as a simple phase estimator

know that operator X has eigenvalues $e^{j\alpha_0} = 1$ and $e^{j\alpha_1} = -1$ ($\alpha_0 = 0$, $\alpha_1 = \pi$) with eigenvectors $|u_0\rangle = (|0\rangle + |1\rangle)/\sqrt{2}$ and $|u_1\rangle = (|0\rangle - |1\rangle)/\sqrt{2}$ respectively. It is clear from the above analysis that the Deutsch circuit emits either $m = 0$ which corresponds to $2\pi \frac{m}{2} = 0 = \tilde{\alpha}_0$ or $m = 1$ which reflects to $2\pi \frac{m}{2} = \pi = \tilde{\alpha}_1$, that is $\tilde{\alpha}_0 = \alpha_0$ and $\tilde{\alpha}_1 = \alpha_1$. So we can conclude that the circuit for solving the Deutsch problem can be regarded as a phase estimator device as well.

Finally as an example we investigate the case of unknown eigenvectors. If we are not familiar with the matrix of operator X – it can be regarded as a black box – then we have to send a superposition of eigenvectors into the data input of the phase estimator in Fig. 6.18. However, without any information about eigenvectors how can a superposition be prepared? Since the eigenvectors of any unitary operator form an orthonormal basis, i.e. an arbitrary state $|\psi\rangle$ can be expressed as their linear combination. Let us for instance set $|\psi\rangle = |0\rangle$ and calculate the pdf of the measurement results. The results can be originated either from an $n = 1$ qbit Simon circuit (Fig. 5.4) with $f(x) : f(0) = 0, f(1) = 1$ or by simply computing the effect of Hadamard and CNOT gates as Fig. 6.18 and linear algebra claim. We chose the former solution and let the reader follow the latter one in **Exercise** 6.12. Function f has only a trivial period $r = 0$, therefore probability amplitude $c_{x',x}$ of state $|x'\rangle|f(x)\rangle$ can be calculated easily for $n = 1$ and $x', x \in \{0,1\}$ based on (5.22) bearing in mind that here x' belongs to the upper quantum wire connected to the measuring device and x to the lower qbit, respectively

$$c_{00} = \tfrac{1}{2}, \quad c_{01} = \tfrac{1}{2}, \quad c_{10} = \tfrac{1}{2}, \quad c_{10} = -\tfrac{1}{2},$$

from which by measuring the first qbit we get

$$P_0 = \left(\tfrac{1}{2}\right)^2 + \left(\tfrac{1}{2}\right)^2 = \tfrac{1}{2} \quad \text{and} \quad P_1 = \left(\tfrac{1}{2}\right)^2 + \left(-\tfrac{1}{2}\right)^2 = \tfrac{1}{2}.$$

This result corresponds to the fact that $|\psi\rangle = |0\rangle$ represents an equal superposition of $|u_0\rangle$ and $|u_1\rangle$ thus the observed probabilities at the output are expected to be uniform.

Exercise 6.11. Determine the eigenvectors and eigenvalues of operator X.

Exercise 6.12. Calculate the probabilities (P_0 and P_1) of measuring $m = 0$ and $m = 1$ for the phase estimator circuit in Fig. 6.18 using linear algebraic operations if the eigenvector input has been initialized to $|0\rangle$.

6.5 GENERALIZATIONS OF ORDER FINDING

We have shown an efficient quantum-based solution for an order-finding problem in the context of factorization in Section 6.3.2. However, order finding is only a special case of more general problems. The following subsections introduce two of them, namely period finding for one- and two-dimensional functions with a related application called the discrete logarithm.

6.5.1 Period finding

Simon's algorithm was the most complex and sophisticated basic quantum algorithm introduced in Section 5.3; it was able to find the period r of a function $f : \{0, 1\}^n \to \{0, 1\}^n$. If we compare the master equation (5.12) of gate U_f in Fig. 5.4 with that of V' in the alternative version of the quantum order-finding device explained in **Exercise 6.8** then we can easily recognize the similarities. Based on these observations we design a quantum period-finding equipment on the range $[0, N)$ for $f : \mathbb{Z}_N \to \mathbb{Z}_N$, $f(k) = f(k + r)$ in a similar way as we did for order finding. Our first goal is to produce a superposition containing all the possible $f(k)$ values. Since f is not reversible, we need to store k as well. Therefore our target state should be (see Fig. 6.19)

$$|\varphi_2\rangle = \frac{1}{\sqrt{2^n}} \sum_{k=0}^{2^n-1} |k\rangle |f(k)\rangle. \tag{6.68}$$

To produce this state we have two possibilities. Either we use the first stages of Simon's circuit with $|\varphi_0\rangle = |0\rangle_{2^n} |0\rangle_{2^t}$ (without loss of generality we can assume that $N = 2^t$ and $n \geq 2t$), next a Hadamard gate on the upper qbits results in

$$|\varphi_1\rangle = \frac{1}{\sqrt{2^n}} \sum_{k=0}^{2^n-1} |k\rangle |0\rangle \tag{6.69}$$

and generalizing (5.12) we get

$$U_f : |k\rangle |q\rangle \to |k\rangle |(q + f(k)) \bmod N\rangle. \tag{6.70}$$

Or we approach the problem from the phase estimation point of view. Analogously to order finding $|\varphi_2\rangle$ can be established replacing U_f with V_f comprising controlled U gates and using appropriate $|\psi_0\rangle$. As it was pointed out during the design process eigenvectors, eigenvalues of U and $|\psi_0\rangle$ can be determined in possession of $|\gamma_0\rangle = |0\rangle$ and $|\varphi_2\rangle$. By means of replacing the special case $f(k) = x^k \bmod N$ with $f(k)$

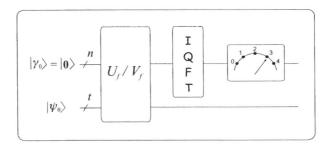

Fig. 6.19   Period-finding quantum circuit over $\mathbb{Z}_N$

itself in equations from (6.49) to 6.56) we obtain

$$\kappa_b = \frac{b}{r}, \quad |u_b\rangle = \sum_{s=0}^{r-1} \frac{e^{-j2\pi \frac{b}{r}s}}{\sqrt{r}} |f(s)\rangle, \tag{6.71}$$

and

$$|\psi_0\rangle = \sum_{b=0}^{r-1} \frac{1}{\sqrt{r}} |u_b\rangle = |f(s=0)\rangle_{2^t}. \tag{6.72}$$

The IQFT gate in Fig. 6.19 is fed with $|\varphi_2\rangle$, but it is not interested in which way $|\varphi_2\rangle$ has been produced since both solutions are equivalent. Of course it is reasonable to choose the first method since it does not require any information about f to prepare initial state $|\varphi_0\rangle$. Fortunately this decision does not prevent us from evaluating the effect of IQFT as if the second method had been applied.[10] According to the discussion of order finding when measuring the output of the IQFT we receive one of the phase ratios $\frac{b}{r}$ with probability P_s if n is set to at least $\lceil \mathrm{ld}(N^2) \rceil$. Finally performing the already known classical steps one can obtain r.

Exercise 6.13. Determine the transformation rule of controlled operator U applied in gate V_f.

6.5.2   Two-dimensional period finding and discrete logarithm

In possession of the period-finding algorithm discussed in the previous subsection we may wonder whether it is possible to generalize this result for two-dimensional periodic functions. More specifically having a function f with the property $f(k_1, k_2) = f(k_1 + r_1, k_2)$ and $f(k_1, k_2) = f(k_1, k_2 + r_2)$ for $k_1, k_2 \in [0, N)$ and N is assumed to be a power of 2 ($N = 2^t$) without loss of generality then we

---

[10] A goblin sitting in the box of IQFT gate takes care only of the input superposition and therefore may imagine that V_f was used with corresponding $|\psi_0\rangle$.

would like to design an efficient quantum algorithm that is able to find both periods r_1 and r_2. Periodicity of f is represented by the (r_1, r_2) pair. The methodology of developing such an algorithm has already been explained several times in this chapter therefore we can follow a well-known track.

First we produce $|\varphi_1\rangle$ in Fig. 6.20 containing all the possible k_1, k_2 values by means of two Hadamard gates acting on the upper two quantum registers[11] n qbit of size each ($n \geq \lceil \mathrm{ld}(N^2) \rceil$) and initialization vector $|\varphi_0\rangle = |0\rangle|0\rangle|0\rangle$ (cf. (6.45))

$$|\varphi_1\rangle = \frac{1}{2^n} \sum_{k_1=0}^{2^n-1} \sum_{k_2=0}^{2^n-1} |k_1\rangle|k_2\rangle \otimes |0\rangle. \tag{6.73}$$

Next we apply $U_f : |k_1\rangle|k_2\rangle|q\rangle \rightarrow |k_1\rangle|k_2\rangle|(q + f(k_1, k_2)) \bmod N\rangle$ exploiting quantum parallelism to evaluate f for all the (k_1, k_2) pairs (see (6.46))

$$|\varphi_2\rangle = \frac{1}{2^n} \sum_{k_1=0}^{2^n-1} \sum_{k_2=0}^{2^n-1} |k_1\rangle|k_2\rangle|f(k_1, k_2)\rangle, \tag{6.74}$$

If the sums of (6.74) are regrouped in the following way

$$|\varphi_2\rangle = \frac{1}{\sqrt{2^n}} \sum_{k_1=0}^{2^n-1} |k_1\rangle \underbrace{\frac{1}{\sqrt{2^n}} \sum_{k_2=0}^{2^n-1} |k_2\rangle|f(k_1, k_2)\rangle}_{|\varphi_2'\rangle}, \tag{6.75}$$

then it becomes obvious that $|\varphi_2'\rangle$ is nothing more than $|\varphi_2\rangle$ in the case of one-dimensional period finding (cf. (6.68)) with fixed k_1, i.e. applying an IQFT gate and a measurement on the qbits belonging to the second qregister in the upper section and some classical processing steps in compliance with order finding will result in r_2. Since exchanging the indices k_1 and k_2 does not influence $|\varphi_2\rangle$ the same method can be used for obtaining r_1. The two measurements do not influence each other since the lower qregister has not been measured at all!

Remark: As **Exercise** 6.14 claims that the two IQFT gates can be combined into a single one.

Remark: The presented technique can be easily extended for finding periods of arbitrary dimensional f.

As a practical example for the above algorithm we bring out the so-called *discrete logarithm* problem, which emerges when breaking certain cryptographic systems (see Chapter 9). The problem can be formulated in the following way: suitable smallest w is requested that satisfies $b = a^w \bmod N$ if $a, b, w \in \mathbb{Z}_N$ where a, b and N are known, i.e. $w = \log_a(b) = ?$ The order-finding modulo N problem is a special case with $w = r$ and $b = 1$!

---

[11]Of course the two n-dimensional Hadamard gates can be replaced by a single $H^{\otimes 2n}$.

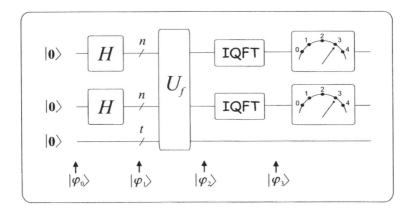

Fig. 6.20 Two-dimensional period-finding quantum circuit

We start with $f(k_1, k_2) = a^{k_1} b^{k_2} \mod N$ which has two periods r_1 and r_2, where r_1 and r_2 are the orders of a and b modulo N respectively (see (6.41)). We have a given relationship between a and b therefore the two periods are not independent, either. In order to derive this connection first we realize that in this special case $f(k_1, k_2) = f(k_1 + r_1, k_2 + r_2)$ because

$$(a^{k_1} b^{k_2}) \mod N = [(a^{k_1 + r_1} \mod N)(b^{k_2 + r_2} \mod N)] \mod N \qquad (6.76)$$

and r_1, r_2 have been defined according to $a^{r_1} \mod N = 1$, $b^{r_2} \mod N = 1$. Next substituting $b = a^w \mod N$ into the definition of $f(k_1, k_2)$ we get

$$f(k_1, k_2) = (a^{k_1} b^{k_2}) \mod N = a^{k_1 + w k_2} \mod N = a^{k_1 + r_1 + w(k_2 + r_2)} \mod N,$$
$$(6.77)$$

where in the last step we utilized (6.76). Applying modular arithmetic the last equality can be further processed

$$a^{k_1 + w k_2} \mod N = [(a^{k_1 + w k_2} \mod N) \underbrace{(a^{r_1} \mod N)(a^{w r_2} \mod N)}_{\equiv 1}] \mod N.$$
$$(6.78)$$

Equality in (6.78) can be maintained only if $w r_2 \equiv l r_1$ (do not forget that r_1 is the smallest integer satisfying $a^{r_1} \mod N = 1$, where l is a positive integer). Now we are almost ready because by deploying an appropriate $U_f : |k_1\rangle |k_2\rangle |q\rangle \to |k_1\rangle |k_2\rangle |(q + a^{k_1} b^{k_2}) \mod N\rangle$ we can receive r_1 and r_2 at the output of the circuit, which allows calculating lw and thus w itself using a few steps.

Remark: It is obvious that this two-dimensional period-finding algorithm for solving the discrete logarithm problem is equivalent to two independent one-dimensional period finding (order finding) because there is a one-to-one connection between the two periods (orders).

Exercise 6.14. Show that $F^{\otimes n} \otimes F^{\otimes n} \equiv F^{\otimes 2n}$.

6.6 FURTHER READING

The original version of QFT was introduced by Coppersmith [44] and also by Shor [122]. The standard QFT has order 2^n and it is applied to a qregister of n qbits. Similarly to FFT it can be generalized to orders which are a power of a small prime and more generally to so-called smooth numbers, i.e. integers which have only small prime factors [42]. Kitaev [91] gave an approximate implementation for arbitrary order based on eigenvalue estimation. This result was improved by Mosca and Zalka [108] involving amplitude amplification to replace the estimation by an exact solution. Jozsa described the quantum algorithms of Deutsch, Simon and Shor in a way which highlights their dependence on the Fourier transform in [89].

Besides outlining the milestones it is worth discussing implementation-related questions and solutions of QFT, dividing them into circuit and physical level approaches.

Classical FFT, which was proposed by Cooley and Tukey in [86], computes the DFT with $O(N\mathrm{ld}(N))$ elementary arithmetic operations compared to the trivial $O(N^2)$ steps. As for the classical case for special values of N there are quite efficient QFT algorithms available. This fact was firstly recognized by Shor [122], providing a polynomial solution which requires $O(\mathrm{ld}^2(N))$ quantum gates assuming the particular case when modulus $N = 2^n$. The product state decomposition of QFT explained here in this chapter was published independently in [123] and [124].

Another fundamental endeavor can be observed concerning computation of QFT, namely since physical implementation of quantum gates and circuits always suffers from noise and consequently from some amount of inaccuracy, it seems to be a very reasonable approach to allow some imperfections when designing QFT algorithms in exchange for faster computation, i.e. unitary transforms have to be designed whose difference from the original QFT operator is limited in terms of e.g. Euclidean distance-based operator norm. Coppersmith proposed the first approximation of QFT with error bounded by P_ε in [44]. His proposal required $O(n\log(n/P_\varepsilon))$ gates assuming modulus $N = 2^n$. As we mentioned above Kitaev presented an algorithm to calculate QFT for an arbitrary modulus N and showed that it needs $O(\log(N/P_\varepsilon))$ gates in [91]. Cleve and Watrous gave new bounds on the circuit complexity of QFT in [125]. They provided an upper bound of $O(\log(n)+\log(\log(1/P_\varepsilon)))$ on the circuit depth for computing an approximation of the QFT in case of $N = 2^n$ and error smaller than P_ε. Thus, even for exponentially small error, QFT circuits have depth $O(\log(n))$. The best previous depth bound was $O(n)$, even for approximations with constant error. Moreover, their circuits contain $O(n\log(n/P_\varepsilon))$ elementary gates. They also proved an upper bound of $O(n(\log(n))^2 \log(\log(n)))$ on the circuit size in the case of the exact QFT modulo 2^n, for which the best previous bound was $O(n^2)$. As an application of their depth bound, Cleve and Watrous showed that Shor's factoring algorithm may be based on quantum circuits with depth only $O(\log(n))$ and polynomial size, *in combination* with classical polynomial-time pre- and post-processing. A sophisticated survey of different extensions of original QFT can be found in [100].

Because of its important role in quantum computing implementation of QFT has been widely discussed in the literature. Therefore here we make an attempt to collect several typical references that more or less cover this area but we suggest the interested reader follow their reference lists. A three-qbit NMR processor has been considered for QFT in [156]. Various quantum computing schemes implementing the QFT on a spin-based two-qbit NMR quantum information processor were compared by Dorai and Suter [90] from a time-costs and accuracy point of view, and for bulk spin resonance computer and spin resonance transistor by Saito *et al.* in [19]. A. Muthukrishnan and Stroud proposed an implementation of the QFT in an entangled system of multilevel atoms in [16].

Phase estimation was the first application of QFT in quantum computing introduced by Kitaev [91] and further refined in [124]. Discussion of phase estimation especially the error analysis is based on this latter excellent work, however, the design method of the phase estimating circuit was replaced by a constructive one instead of the original analytic solution. Moreover Kitaev [91] generalized Shor's algorithm, showing how a quantum computer can generate an eigenvalue of an arbitrary unitary operator (with the limit of a large number of qbits, and not necessarily efficiently). Travaglione and Milburn presented in [25] how to use the phase estimation algorithm for generation of eigenvalues associated with an operator and how to implement this method on a small-scale ion trap quantum computer. Later they showed with Ralph the connection between phase estimation and non-demolition measurements in [26]. Wei and Nori discussed the problem of coherent phase errors produced by the time delays between sequential operations in [95]. They presented that in the framework of quantum phase estimation these coherent phase errors can be avoided efficiently by setting up the delay times to satisfy certain matching conditions.

The efficient quantum algorithm for calculation of the discrete logarithm was born together with factorization in [122].

Peter Shor's spectacular application of the Fourier transform has led to the discovery of an efficient quantum factoring algorithm [122] and in a more mature and extended version [137], [138] and [124]. Zalka proposed a technique parallelizing the individual addition steps in order to provide a better space-time tradeoff in [158]. An interesting attempt to replace QFT with a simpler operator in the Shor algorithm was presented by Lev in [94]. Wei and his colleagues enhanced their phase-matching approach on QFT [95] to the Shor algorithm in order to eliminate the dynamic phase error in [96]. Lomonaco and Kauffman introduced the continuous variable analog of Shor's quantum factoring algorithm in [134].

Shor's factorization algorithm is arguably the driving force behind much experimental quantum computer research. Therefore it is crucial to investigate whether realistic quantum computers can successfully run Shor's algorithm on integers of commercially interesting length. The Shor algorithm has been verified experimentally in a liquid-state NMR system with a few qbits using pentafluoro-butadienyl cyclopentadienyldicarbonyliron complex (molecule) by Vandersypen *et al.* in [98] and [97]. Fowler and Hollenberg investigated in [6] in detail the effect of imposing a rotation control limit of $2\pi/2^{d_{\max}}$. They found that integers thousands of bits long can be factorized provided rotation gates of magnitude $\pi/64$ can be implemented.

A more general formulation of the order-finding problem as well as the discrete logarithm [137] problem, and the Abelian stabiliser problem is the hidden subgroup problem or the unknown sub-group problem. A good overview can be found in [107].

For those readers who are interested in the discrete cosine transform (DCT) its quantum equivalent is discussed in [12].

Part III

Quantum-assisted Solutions of Infocom Problems

7

Searching in an Unsorted Database

In order to survive from day to day in a very hostile and dangerous environment prehistoric men spent most of their time seeking for such resources as food, fresh water, suitable stones for tools, etc. The world around us was nothing more than a large *unsorted database*. Efficiency of the two basic methods, namely random and exhaustive search, proved to be rather poor. The only way to achieve some improvement was the involvement of more people (*parallel processing*). The first breakthrough in this field can be connected to the first settlements and the appearance of agriculture which brought along the intention to make and keep order in the world.[1] A field of wheat or a vegetable garden compared to a meadow embodied the order which increased the probability of successful searching almost up to 1. Therefore our ancestors were balancing during the last 10 thousand years between the resource requirement of making order and seeking for a requested thing. However, at the dawn of the third millennium our dreams seem to become true due to quantum computing. Grover's database search algorithm enables a dramatic reduction in the computational complexity of seeking in an unsorted database. The change is tremendous, the classically required $O(N)$ database queries when we have N different entries has been replaced by $O(\sqrt{N})$ steps using quantum computers.

We follow the evolution of quantum-based searching from the basic idea to the most sophisticated general solution in this chapter which is organized as follows: Section 7.1 introduces the original Grover algorithm explaining the related architecture and error analysis as well. Afterwards phase estimation based quantum

---

[1] Ancient Greeks referred to this change as the birth of cosmos ($\kappa o\sigma\mu o\sigma$ = order) from chaos ($\chi\alpha o\sigma$ = disorder). So to use cosmos as a synonym of universe is not unintentional.

Quantum Computing and Communications   S. Imre, F. Balázs
© 2004 John Wiley & Sons, Ltd   ISBN 0-470-86902-X (HB)

counting is discussed in Section 7.2, which can be used both as a standalone algorithm or enables minimizing the error probability when searching for a given entry in the database. A special and often used case of counting is when we are interested in whether a database contains a certain entry at all. The solution to this problem originates from phase estimation. It is called existence testing and it is explained in Section 7.3. We show how to use quantum existence testing when one is interested in the largest or smallest entry of an unsorted database in Section 7.4. Finally Section 7.5 focuses on the generalization of the basic algorithm providing sure success measurements and enabling an arbitrary initial state of the algorithm, which can be quite useful when deploying the searching circuit within a larger quantum network.

7.1 THE BASIC GROVER ALGORITHM

First of all let us define more precisely the problem: Considering a database DB with N different entries (e.g. names of fruits) indexed by $x \in [0, N-1]$ we are looking for that index x_0 which points to the requested entry $DB[x_0] = apple$.

Before buckling down to the design of a suitable quantum algorithm for database searching it is worth looking at the already known quantum algorithms and check whether we can exploit some parts of them. All of them started with quantum parallelism in order to prepare all the potential results with uniform probability amplitudes in a qregister. Remember the prince who put all his questions to the witch in a single but quantum question (see the introduction of Deutsch–Jozsa problem in Section 5.2). This first stage is followed typically by a unitary operator (often referred as U_f) being responsible for processing all the computational basis states according to the given problem. U_f always requires an auxiliary (lower) qregister that provides reversible operation of the gate. Finally we use a Hadamard or IQFT gate in order to have quantum interference to act on the upper qregister and the algorithm is finished by measuring this qregister. According to these lessons quantum searching operator G consists of two regular stages (see Fig. 7.1) preceded by an initialization phase.

7.1.1 Initialization – quantum parallelism

As we did several times during the design of basic quantum algorithms we prepare two quantum registers. The upper one contains n qbits with respect to the size $N = 2^n$ of the database[2] and it is initialized with $|\gamma_0\rangle = |0\rangle$. We feed an n-dimensional Hadamard gate with this qregister while the lower qregister is connected to an unknown gate T producing

$$|\varphi_1\rangle = (H^{\otimes n} \otimes T^{\otimes t})(|\gamma_0\rangle \otimes |\psi_0\rangle) = \frac{1}{\sqrt{N}} \sum_{x=0}^{N-1} |x\rangle \otimes T|\psi_0\rangle, \qquad (7.1)$$

[2]If N is not a power of 2 we extend the database with several dummy entries to fulfil this requirement.

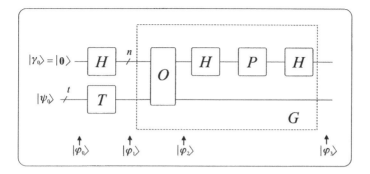

Fig. 7.1   Circuit implementing the Grover operator

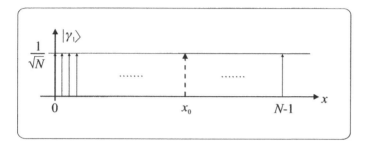

Fig. 7.2   Probability amplitude distribution of the index register at $|\varphi_1\rangle$

where $|\psi_1\rangle = T|\psi_0\rangle$ stands for the state of the lower auxiliary qregister t bit of size and

$$|\gamma_1\rangle = \frac{1}{\sqrt{N}} \sum_{x=0}^{N-1} |x\rangle. \tag{7.2}$$

The exact value of $|\psi_0\rangle$ and T will be determined later according to the considerations originating from the following stage. In order to make it easier to follow the operation of different stages we present the probability amplitude distribution of the index register at the end of each stage. Fig.7.2 depicts these probability amplitudes at $|\varphi_1\rangle$, where x_0 stands for the index of the requested entry.

Remark: Entries, which are solutions of the search problem, are called *marked* states according to the literature and ones which do not lead to a solution are referred as *unmarked* states.

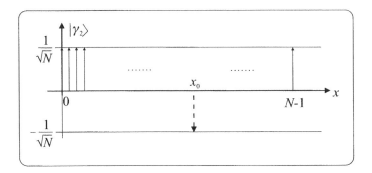

Fig. 7.3 Content of qregister $|\gamma_2\rangle$ after invoking the Oracle

7.1.2 First stage of G – the Oracle

In the second stage a special gate, the so-called Oracle,[3] is used to distinguish between the marked and unmarked states. The Oracle multiplies the probability amplitude of the requested item by -1 and leaves any other amplitudes unchanged. This functionality is presented in Fig. 7.3 and can be summarized as

$$O : |x\rangle|y\rangle \rightarrow (-1)^{f(x)}|x\rangle|y\rangle, \tag{7.3}$$

where

$$f(x) = \begin{cases} 1 & \text{if } x = x_0 \text{ (i.e. DB}[x_0] \text{ matches the searched item),} \\ 0 & \text{otherwise.} \end{cases} \tag{7.4}$$

Function $f(x)$ seems to be a bit contradictory because it has to know whether a given x leads to the solution of the searching problem or not. If we know the solution in advance we do not need searching, but to know the solution we always have to perform searching. The only way to escape from this vicious circle is to decide that $x = x_0$ does not require any *a priori* knowledge about x_0, it can be evaluated real time using a simple comparison.

Without loss of generality we assumed that N is an integer power of 2. If not we extend N to the nearest 2^n sticking entries with $f(x) = 0$.

The next naturally arising question is related to the implementation of O. Before the reader begins to look for a suitable answer we remember an intermediate result (5.5) from the analysis of the Deutsch–Jozsa algorithm (see Section 5.2). Applying what we have learned there we use a single qbit ($t = 1$) lower qregister initialized with $|\psi_0\rangle = |1\rangle$ and T is set to a Hadamard gate hence

$$|\varphi_1\rangle = \frac{1}{\sqrt{N}} \sum_{x=0}^{N-1} |x\rangle \otimes \frac{|0\rangle - |1\rangle}{\sqrt{2}}. \tag{7.5}$$

---

[3]Unlike oracles in the ancient Egypt, Greece or Roman Empire our quantum oracle proves to be a quite deterministic one.

If we select the Oracle according to U_f (the witch) in Fig. 5.3

$$O : |x\rangle|y\rangle \to |x\rangle|y \oplus f(x)\rangle, \tag{7.6}$$

then the status of the lower qbit remains unchanged and

$$|\varphi_2\rangle = \frac{1}{\sqrt{N}} \sum_{x=0}^{N-1} (-1)^{f(x)} |x\rangle \otimes \frac{|0\rangle - |1\rangle}{\sqrt{2}} = |\gamma_2\rangle \otimes \frac{|0\rangle - |1\rangle}{\sqrt{2}}. \tag{7.7}$$

in compliance with (5.7).

Finally the Oracle can be represented using operator formalism in compliance with **Exercise** 7.1 in the following manner

$$O = I - 2|x_0\rangle\langle x_0|. \tag{7.8}$$

Exercise 7.1. Show that the transformation of the Oracle can be represented as $O = I - 2|x_0\rangle\langle x_0|$.

Exercise 7.2. Determine the matrix of the Oracle in the case of an $N = 4$ database assuming $x_0 = 2$.

7.1.3   Second stage of G – inversion about the average

As we discussed earlier the second stage is responsible for amplifying the probability amplitude of $|x_0\rangle$ while suppressing any other probability amplitudes. The only limiting restriction which has to be kept in mind is the unitary nature of the chosen transformation. Furthermore this transform cannot distinguish between computational basis states according to their marked or unmarked status, hence we need such a gate which applies the same rule for all the basis vectors. Therefore we can exploit the only difference, namely the sign of the probability amplitudes. This aim can be achieved by means of a clever mathematical tool called *inversion about the average*. First we show how it operates on the probability amplitudes, the exact mathematical formulation will be provided afterwards.

Let us assume that we are able to calculate the average $\bar{a}$ of the probability amplitudes in $|\gamma_2\rangle$

$$\bar{a} = \frac{1}{N} \sum_{x=0}^{N-1} \gamma_{2x}, \tag{7.9}$$

where γ_{2x} refers to the probability amplitude of computational basis state $|x\rangle$ in $|\gamma_2\rangle$. If we reflect each amplitude onto $\bar{a}$ then the amplitude of the marked state becomes greater than $\bar{a}$ since a negative number was subtracted from a positive one. Any other amplitudes will then be decreased (see Fig. 7.4). Thus x_0 appears with an amplified amplitude in $|\gamma_3\rangle$. Moreover with respect to our expectations this transform seems to be reversible and because the probability amplitude of x_0 has been increased at the expense of other probability amplitudes we may expect that $|\gamma_3\rangle$ has unit length, too. So both requirements of unitary operators may be accomplished.

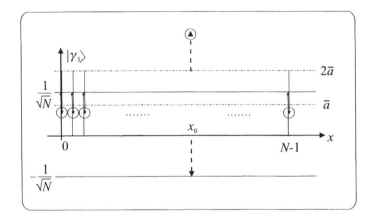

Fig. 7.4 Effect of inversion about the average $\bar{a}$

Now to validate the previous qualitative analysis and to design the Grover circuit we have to find unitary gate(s) implementing this transform. However, in order to be more general because of later considerations we assume that very special $|\gamma_1\rangle$ is replaced by an almost arbitrary superposition $|\gamma_1^\spadesuit\rangle$, which contains uniform probability amplitudes for unmarked states. Observing Fig. 7.4 one can infer the following transformation rule

$$\gamma_{3x} = 2\bar{a} - \gamma_{2x}, \tag{7.10}$$

where $|\gamma_2\rangle$ refers to $O|\gamma_1^\spadesuit\rangle$ from which

$$|\gamma_3\rangle = \sum_{x=0}^{N-1}(2\bar{a} - \gamma_{2x})|x\rangle = 2\sum_{x=0}^{N-1}\bar{a}|x\rangle - \sum_{x=0}^{N-1}\gamma_{2x}|x\rangle. \tag{7.11}$$

Obviously the second sum in (7.11) is nothing more than $|\gamma_2\rangle$ while the first one can be expressed using (7.9) as $2|\gamma_1\rangle\langle\gamma_1||\gamma_2\rangle$ – where $|\gamma_1\rangle$ is according to (7.2) – because

$$\langle\gamma_1|\gamma_2\rangle = \frac{1}{\sqrt{N}}\sum_{x=0}^{N-1}\gamma_{2x} = \sqrt{N}\bar{a},$$

hence $|\gamma_3\rangle$ can be expressed as

$$|\gamma_3\rangle = 2|\gamma_1\rangle\langle\gamma_1||\gamma_2\rangle - |\gamma_2\rangle.$$

Therefore to produce $|\gamma_3\rangle$ from $|\gamma_2\rangle$ we need an operator

$$U_\gamma = 2|\gamma_1\rangle\langle\gamma_1| - I \tag{7.12}$$

with matrix

$$
\mathbf{U}_\gamma =
\begin{bmatrix}
\frac{1}{\sqrt{N}} \\
\frac{1}{\sqrt{N}} \\
\frac{1}{\sqrt{N}} \\
\vdots \\
\frac{1}{\sqrt{N}}
\end{bmatrix}
\begin{bmatrix}
\frac{1}{\sqrt{N}} & \frac{1}{\sqrt{N}} & \cdots & \frac{1}{\sqrt{N}}
\end{bmatrix}
-I =
\begin{bmatrix}
\frac{1}{N} & \frac{1}{N} & \cdots & \frac{1}{N} \\
\frac{1}{N} & \frac{1}{N} & \cdots & \frac{1}{N} \\
\vdots & & \ddots & \vdots \\
\frac{1}{N} & \cdots & \cdots & \frac{1}{N}
\end{bmatrix}
-I =
\begin{bmatrix}
\frac{2}{N}-1 & \frac{2}{N} & \cdots & \frac{2}{N} \\
\frac{2}{N} & \frac{2}{N}-1 & \cdots & \frac{2}{N} \\
\vdots & & \ddots & \vdots \\
\frac{2}{N} & \cdots & \frac{2}{N} & \frac{2}{N}-1
\end{bmatrix}.
$$
(7.13)

Taking into account that $|\gamma_1\rangle = H|0\rangle$, $H = H^\dagger$ and $HIH \equiv I$, (7.12) can be further refined

$$U_\gamma = 2H|0\rangle\langle0|H - HIH = H(2|0\rangle\langle0| - I)H. \tag{7.14}$$

Equation (7.14) provides the key to the realization of the inversion about the average. We require two Hadamard gates and a *controlled phase shifter* gate P in the middle (see Fig. 7.1). The transformation rule of P is quite simple: it leaves all the probability amplitudes unchanged except that of $|0\rangle$ whose sign is inverted.

Remark: Since P consists of unitary operators inversion about the average is also unitary!

Now we are ready to derive the Grover operator G itself

$$G = HPHO = (2H|0\rangle\langle0|H - I)O = (2|\gamma_1\rangle\langle\gamma_1| - I)(I - 2|x_0\rangle\langle x_0|). \tag{7.15}$$

Bearing in mind (7.10) we can state that after a single operation of G for $\bar{a} > 0$

$$
\gamma_{3x}
\begin{cases}
> \gamma_{1x}^{\spadesuit} & \text{if } x = x_0 \\
< \gamma_{1x}^{\spadesuit} & \text{otherwise.}
\end{cases}
\tag{7.16}
$$

Amplitude amplification aims to increase γ_{3x_0} as close to 1 as possible, which implies that other probability amplitudes go to zero since $\sum_x |\gamma_{3x}|^2 = 1$. Obviously a single run of G will achieve this goal only in very special cases (see **Exercise** 7.3). Fortunately the status of the auxiliary qbit does not change between the input and output therefore we can loop back the output of G to its input or equivalently invoke G several times successively.

Remark: The function f in (7.3) can have the value 1 either at a single or multiple (say M) indices, depending on how many identical searched entries exist in a particular database. The above-discussed technique is trivially not sensitive to this modification at all. The only difference appearing due to this fact is that the value of probability belonging to the marked states is divided uniformly among them.

Remark: The major difference and novelty which can be observed if one makes a comparison between the operation of previous algorithms such as Deutsch–Jozsa, Simon or Shor and Grover's database search is the repeated application of quantum interference (so-called amplitude amplification) instead of a single Hadamard or IQFT gate. Thus the Grover algorithm itself can be regarded as a sequence of the same Grover operator.

Remark: Obviously in case of multiple marked entries in the database (say M) all of these states have uniform probability amplitudes since the Grover algorithm does not make any difference among them.

Exercise 7.3. Show an example scenario when a single application of G ensures sure success for measuring $|x_0\rangle$.

7.1.4 Required number of iterations

The next question we have to answer is obvious. How many Grover gates have to be applied – how many times shall we turn to the database – in order to get γ_{3x_0} as close to 1 as possible? Or from an economical point of view: does there exist an optimal number of iterations or do we have to buy as many G as our budget allows? To find a satisfactory answer to these questions we introduce a very spectacular geometrical interpretation of the Grover algorithm. For the sake of being more general we are considering multiple marked entries ($M \geq 1$).

First we form two sets from the indices, one S for the marked ($f(x) = 1$) and another $\overline{S}$ for the unmarked ($f(x) = 0$) ones, i.e. we build two superpositions comprising uniformly distributed computational basis states

$$|\alpha\rangle \triangleq \frac{1}{\sqrt{N - M}} \sum_{x \in \overline{S}} |x\rangle, \tag{7.17}$$

$$|\beta\rangle \triangleq \frac{1}{\sqrt{M}} \sum_{x \in S} |x\rangle, \tag{7.18}$$

where $|\alpha\rangle$ and $|\beta\rangle$ form an orthonormal basis of a two-dimensional Hilbert space which is depicted in Fig. 7.5. The original input state $|\gamma_1\rangle$ of G can be expressed in this space in the following way

$$|\gamma_1\rangle = \frac{1}{\sqrt{N}} \sum_{x \in \overline{S}} |x\rangle + \frac{1}{\sqrt{N}} \sum_{x \in S} |x\rangle,$$

$$= \sqrt{\frac{N - M}{N}} |\alpha\rangle + \sqrt{\frac{M}{N}} |\beta\rangle. \tag{7.19}$$

Remark: There are two special cases. If all the entries are marked then we have only vector $|\beta\rangle$ and a measurement before the search will provide sure success or if the database does not contain the requested item at all then only vector $|\alpha\rangle$ exists. Both scenarios can be recognized and excluded using quantum counting (see later in Section 7.2) prior to the search. Therefore in the forthcoming analysis we assume that both vectors exist, i.e. neither of the two sets are empty.

Coordinates of $|\gamma_1\rangle$ are strictly related to the angle between $|\gamma_1\rangle$ and $|\alpha\rangle$ denoted by $\frac{\Omega_\gamma}{2}$ in Fig. 7.5. Using basic trigonometry we can calculate the projection of $|\gamma_1\rangle$

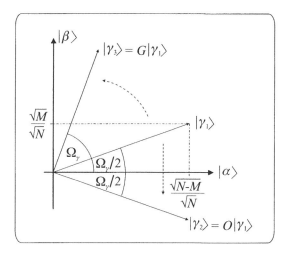

Fig. 7.5 Geometrical interpretation of the Grover operator

onto the axes

$$\cos\left(\frac{\Omega_\gamma}{2}\right) = \frac{\sqrt{\frac{N-M}{N}}}{1},$$

$$\sin\left(\frac{\Omega_\gamma}{2}\right) = \frac{\sqrt{\frac{M}{N}}}{1} \Rightarrow \Omega_\gamma = 2\arcsin\left(\sqrt{\frac{M}{N}}\right), \qquad (7.20)$$

where denominators in (7.20) correspond to the fact that vector $|\gamma_1\rangle$ has unit length.

As it was described earlier in this section the basic Grover operator consists of two transformations on the index register. First the Oracle flips all the probability amplitudes of the marked states, which can be regarded as a reflection about axis $|\alpha\rangle$ because these indices are contained only by $|\beta\rangle$ (see Fig. 7.5), that is

$$O(a|\alpha\rangle + b|\beta\rangle) = a|\alpha\rangle - b|\beta\rangle.$$

Of course in the case of multiple marked states the Oracle has to be defined in the following manner

$$O = I - 2\sum_{x \in S} |x\rangle\langle x|. \qquad (7.21)$$

The inversion about the average HPH transformation reflects its input state $|\gamma_2\rangle$ about $|\gamma_1\rangle$ as the reader may prove in **Exercise** 7.4. These two reflections together form a rotation by angle Ω_γ starting from $|\gamma_1\rangle$ towards $|\beta\rangle$. Within the frames of this geometrical interpretation our goal simplifies to rotating the index qregister as close to $|\beta\rangle$ as possible. Performing a projective measurement in the computational basis vectors afterwards will return one of the marked states with high probability.

Remark: This interpretation highlights the very important fact that applying less rotations than the optimal is as bad as applying greater rotations.

The effect of rotating the initial state $|\gamma_1\rangle$ to the desired state $|\beta\rangle$ after l evaluations of the Grover operator can be summarized as

$$
\begin{aligned}
G^l|\gamma_1\rangle &= \cos\left(l\Omega_\gamma + \frac{\Omega_\gamma}{2}\right)|\alpha\rangle + \sin\left(l\Omega_\gamma + \frac{\Omega_\gamma}{2}\right)|\beta\rangle \\
&= \cos\left(\frac{2l+1}{2}\Omega_\gamma\right)|\alpha\rangle + \sin\left(\frac{2l+1}{2}\Omega_\gamma\right)|\beta\rangle. \quad (7.22)
\end{aligned}
$$

It is worth performing a measurement if $G^l|\gamma_1\rangle$ is equal to the basis vector $|\beta\rangle$, or equivalently if $G^l|\gamma_1\rangle$ is orthogonal to the basis vector $|\alpha\rangle$ i.e

$$
\langle\alpha|G^l|\gamma_1\rangle = \cos\left(\frac{2l+1}{2}\Omega_\gamma\right) = 0,
$$

which can be transformed to

$$
\frac{2l+1}{2}\cdot\Omega_\gamma = \frac{\pi}{2} + i\pi,
$$

where $i = 0, 1, \ldots$. Thus the optimal number of iterations is simply

$$
l_{opt_i} = \frac{\frac{\pi}{2} + i\pi - \frac{\Omega_\gamma}{2}}{\Omega_\gamma}. \quad (7.23)
$$

Equation (7.23) corresponds to the geometrical approach (see Fig. 7.5) because the numerator represents the angle between the initial state $|\gamma_1\rangle$ and the final state $|\beta\rangle$ while the denominator substitutes the rotation step, respectively. Trivially we are forced to employ as few iterations as possible, therefore $\min_i l_{opt_i} = l_{opt_0}$. Furthermore, one can apply only integer numbers of iterations, L_{opt_0}, in a quantum circuit which has to be calculated as

$$
L_{opt_0} = \lfloor l_{opt_0}\rceil = \left\lceil \frac{\frac{\pi}{2} - \frac{\Omega_\gamma}{2}}{\Omega_\gamma} \right\rceil. \quad (7.24)
$$

This selects the vector that results in the smaller angle between Θ_1 and Θ_2 in compliance with Fig. 7.6 since the probability of measuring one of the marked states is in unambiguous connection with the projection of the final state to $|\beta\rangle$.

Remark: According to our expectations the optimal number of iterations depends on the initial angle $\frac{\Omega_\gamma}{2}$ and indirectly (see (7.20)) on the size (N) of the database and the number of the marked entries M, i.e. a larger database requires more iterations to find a given entry while replicated items increase the chance of finding one of them.

In the case of practical applications the size of the database is typically significantly larger than the occurrences of the searched entry, that is $M \ll N$ (i.e. $\Omega_\gamma \ll 1$) therefore

$$
\frac{\Omega_\gamma}{2} \simeq \sin\left(\frac{\Omega_\gamma}{2}\right) = \sqrt{\frac{M}{N}}, \quad (7.25)
$$

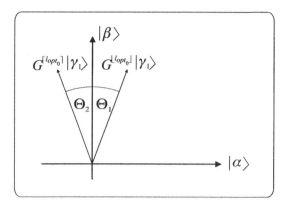

Fig. 7.6 Explanation of the decision about the number of iterations

yielding from (7.20). Substituting (7.25) into (7.24) one achieves an important and surprising result related to the optimal number of evaluations

$$L_{opt_0} = \left\lceil \frac{\pi}{4} \sqrt{\frac{N}{M}} - 1 \right\rceil \simeq \frac{\pi}{4} \sqrt{\frac{N}{M}}. \tag{7.26}$$

Now, we have reached the surprising result $L_{opt_0} = O\left(\sqrt{\frac{N}{M}}\right)$, which points out the tremendous possibilities hidden in quantum computing. Although it is straightforward to expect that finding a needle in a haystack comprising more needles than hay is a much simpler job then looking for a single one, classically the improvement is in proportion to the number of needles M while quantum mechanically only a reduction by $\sqrt{M}$ can be achieved. Fortunately the influence of N on the number of required Oracle calls (database queries) proves to be much stronger than that of M thus the classical and quantum solutions have the same performance only in the trivial case $N = M$.

Exercise 7.4. Prove that inversion about the average is equivalent to a reflection about $|\gamma_1\rangle$ in the two-dimensional geometrical interpretation.

7.1.5 Error analysis

If l_{opt_0} proves to be a non-integer number then $G^l|\gamma_1\rangle$ is angular to $|\beta\rangle$ thus the probability of error resulting from basic Grover's search algorithm is calculated as

$$P_\varepsilon = |\langle \alpha | G^{L_{opt_0}} | \gamma_1 \rangle|^2 = \cos^2 \left(\frac{(2L_{opt_0} + 1)\Omega_\gamma}{2} \right), \tag{7.27}$$

and the probability of success

$$P_s = 1 - P_\varepsilon = \sin^2\left(\frac{(2L_{opt_0} + 1)\,\Omega_\gamma}{2}\right). \tag{7.28}$$

Since $\Theta_1, \Theta_2 \leq \frac{\Omega_\gamma}{2}$ therefore

$$P_\varepsilon \leq \sin^2\left(\frac{\Omega_\gamma}{2}\right). \tag{7.29}$$

Substituting Ω_γ according to (7.20),

$$P_\varepsilon \leq \frac{M}{N} = \tilde{P}_\varepsilon = 1 - \tilde{P}_s. \tag{7.30}$$

Considering L_{opt_0} and P_s one may reach a surprising conclusion. The efficiency (number of iteration steps) and the quantum accuracy depend only on the ratio of M and N. Therefore let us examine $\frac{M}{N}$.

- It is clear that $\frac{M}{N}$ must be less than or equal to 1, otherwise it would stand for more marked states than the entire number of entries in the database. A trivial solution occurs when $\frac{M}{N} = 1$, which means an initial angle $\frac{\Omega_\gamma}{2} = \frac{\pi}{2}$ implying no need for any rotation. Immediate measurement produces the correct solution, however, this case has no practical importance. We mentioned it only because it highlights the consistency of the classical and quantum interpretation of our world.

- Keeping in mind the geometrical interpretation (see Fig. 7.5) the reader may wonder what happens if $\frac{\Omega_\gamma}{2} > \frac{\pi}{4} \Rightarrow$ the rotation angle is $\Omega_\gamma > \frac{\pi}{2} \Rightarrow \frac{M}{N} > \frac{1}{2}$? The algorithm seems to fail. Fortunately we can avoid this difficulty by doubling the index space of the database (and not the database itself) and setting $f(x) = 0$ for $N \leq x < 2N$. Thus $M \leq \frac{N}{2}$ always holds. Another rather pragmatic solution if we realize from (7.30) that the probability of success is $P_s \geq \frac{M}{N} > \frac{1}{2}$ in this case, therefore repeating the algorithm several times we will measure a marked state with high probability.

We depicted the probability of successful measurement and corresponding P_ε in Fig. 7.7 in function of $\frac{M}{N}$ assuming an optimal number of iterations. First we can observe that the straight line of $\tilde{P}_\varepsilon$ really upperbounds the error probability. Furthermore P_ε has local minimum and maximum points in accordance with the cases where l_{opt_0} is an integer number or $P_\varepsilon = \tilde{P}_\varepsilon = \frac{M}{N}$, respectively. The exact locations of the minimums ($P_\varepsilon = 0 \Rightarrow P_s = 1$) can be derived from (7.23) substituting $i = 0$ and having in mind (7.20)

$$\frac{M}{N} = \sin^2\left(\frac{\pi}{4(l_{opt_0} + \frac{1}{2})}\right), \tag{7.31}$$

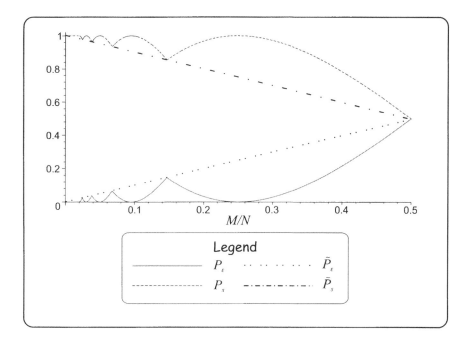

Fig. 7.7 $P_\varepsilon, P_s, \tilde{P}_\varepsilon$ and $\tilde{P}_s$ vs. $\frac{M}{N}$

where we know that $l_{opt_0} \in \mathbb{Z}^+$. On the other hand maximums can be determined using $P_\varepsilon = \frac{M}{N}$ in (7.27) but we can achieve our goal much faster if we realize that maximum points are connected to $l_{opt_0} = 0.5, 1.5, 2.5, \ldots$ because they result in $\Theta_i = \frac{\Omega_\gamma}{2}$. Therefore we can utilize (7.31) again.

Finally, we have to mention an important aspect. The decision for $i = 0$ in (7.24) was inspired by the principle that efficiency is playing a more important role than quantum accuracy. So we were interested in the least number of iterations. However, there are practical applications where the requirements are reversed. Clearly speaking i allows a tradeoff between P_ε and L_{opt_i}, because l_{opt_0} can be regarded only as a local minimum of the number of iterations. For instance $-|\beta\rangle$ could also be an appropriate target state of the repeated rotation while the increase in the number of iterations remains marginal because of the square root operator.

Another approach which provides tradeoff between uncertainty (P_ε) and efficiency (number of iterations) is if we extend the database with dummy entries, i.e. with $f(x) = 0$. The increased size of the database will cause smaller Ω_γ thus less uncertainty at a price of more iteration steps. Doubling the size of the database will halve the probability of error (7.30) while the number of rotations has to be multiplied only by $\sqrt{2}$, see (7.26).

Unlike performing more and more iterations there is another alternative, namely if we are able to adjust (or replace) the elementary gates forming operator G we can guarantee sure success using about L_{opt_0} iterations (see Section 7.5). However, if we are restricted to buying the original Grover circuit at the grocer's it may be worth seeking for the global optimum.

Remark: We would like to strongly emphasize that the database does not need to exist at all in the form of a memory! To implement the Grover operator one requires only a function $f(x)$ whose only job is to compare the requested item to another value which may originate either from a database (DB[x]) or for instance from another function $g(x)$. This kind of freedom allows the usage of Grover algorithm in a wide range of engineering problems since $g(x)$ cannot be sorted typically in advance.

Exercise 7.5. – single marked state case – Assuming $N = 4$, $M = 1$ and $x_0 = 2$ determine the matrices of O, U_f and G, the optimal number of iterations and the probability of error.

Exercise 7.6. – multiple marked state case – Assuming $N = 8$, $M = 3$ and marked states $x = 1, 4, 7$ determine the matrices of O, U_f and G, the optimal number of iterations and the probability of error.

7.2 QUANTUM COUNTING

Readers having followed carefully the previous analysis of Grover algorithm may hit on an important shortcoming. Namely in order to determine the optimal number of iterations L_{opt_0} in (7.24) we require indirectly exact knowledge about the order of multiplicity M. One may imagine engineering problems where it is available, but this is typically not the case. It looks like we have fallen into a very serious trap which may call the conduciveness of all the already achieved results into question. Fortunately quantum computing drops a rope to escape from this serious problem because it provides us with an algorithm capable of computing M efficiently.

7.2.1 Quantum counting based on phase estimation

First we utilize the result of **Exercise** 7.7 which claims that the matrix of the Grover operator can be expressed in the basis of $|\alpha\rangle$ and $|\beta\rangle$ as

$$\mathbf{G} = \begin{bmatrix} \cos(\Omega_\gamma) & -\sin(\Omega_\gamma) \\ \sin(\Omega_\gamma) & \cos(\Omega_\gamma) \end{bmatrix}.$$

Solving **Exercise** 7.8 the reader will realize that G has two eigenvalues namely $e^{\pm j\Omega_\gamma}$. Recalling phase estimation from Section 6.2, which aimed to determine the phase belonging to a given eigenvalue of an operator, we are out of the trap. A phase estimation applying $U = G$ and using appropriate parameters and initialization will return a good estimation of Ω_γ with high probability, which is in direct connection with M via (7.20). We depicted the quantum counting circuit in Fig. 7.8 keeping in mind Fig. 6.5.

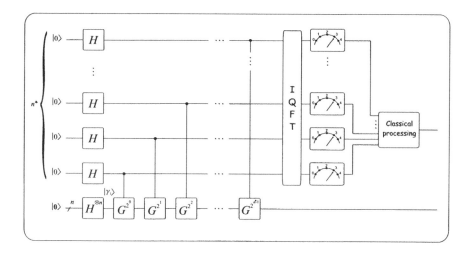

Fig. 7.8 Quantum counting circuit

Before celebrating our clever 'discovery', however, we have to set some parameters for the circuit of Fig. 6.5. As we have learned at the phase estimation we need a lower section comprising n qbits and initialized by the eigenvectors of the expected eigenvalue. **Exercise** 7.8 provides the corresponding eigenvectors

$$|g_1\rangle = \frac{e^{j\xi}}{\sqrt{2}}\begin{bmatrix} j \\ 1 \end{bmatrix}, \quad |g_2\rangle = \frac{e^{j\xi}}{\sqrt{2}}\begin{bmatrix} -j \\ 1 \end{bmatrix}, \quad \xi \in \mathbb{R},$$

but unfortunately we are not able to feed the circuit either with $|g_1\rangle$ or $|g_2\rangle$ because it would require $|\alpha\rangle$ or $|\beta\rangle$, i.e. the complete knowledge about the marked and unmarked sets. Thus another trap is seeming to crop up but we have all the required capabilities to avoid it. We know that by using a superposition of the eigenvectors as the lower input we get one of the eigenvalues after the measurement at the upper output. Luckily we have only two and easily distinguishable phases Ω_γ and $-\Omega_\gamma = 2\pi - \Omega_\gamma$ in our very special case since $\Omega_\gamma \leq \frac{\pi}{4}$. Therefore without being familiar in advance with Ω_γ we are able to compute it from the measurement result. For the sake of simplicity we use $|\gamma_1\rangle$ for this purpose, which is trivially a superposition of $|\alpha\rangle$ and $|\beta\rangle$. Because $|g_1\rangle$ and $|g_2\rangle$ form an orthonormal basis of the space spanned by $|\alpha\rangle$ and $|\beta\rangle$, $|\gamma_1\rangle$ can be expressed as a linear combination of $|g_1\rangle$ and $|g_2\rangle$.

Finally we have to set up the size of the upper quantum register. In order to avoid the confusion of using notation n in two different meanings, the number of qbits in the upper section of the counting circuit will be denoted by $n^\clubsuit$. As we saw in Section 6.2.4 practical setting of $n^\clubsuit$ depends on both classical accuracy 2^{-c} of Ω_γ and allowed quantum uncertainty $\check{P}_{\varepsilon P}$ of the phase estimation in the following manner

$$n^{\clubsuit} = c - 1 + \left\lceil \operatorname{ld}(2\pi) + \operatorname{ld}\left(3 + \frac{1}{\check{P}_{\varepsilon P}}\right) \right\rceil. \tag{7.32}$$

Exercise 7.7. Determine the matrix of the Grover operator in the basis of $|\alpha\rangle$ and $|\beta\rangle$.

Exercise 7.8. Determine the eigenvalues and corresponding eigenvectors of the Grover operator in the basis of $|\alpha\rangle$ and $|\beta\rangle$.

7.2.2   Error analysis

In the case of quantum counting we have a demand on accuracy 2^q of M that upperbounds the maximum difference between the real value of M and the measured value $\tilde{M}$, i.e $\Delta_M \triangleq \tilde{M} - M \Rightarrow |\Delta_M| \leq 2^q$. For the sake of simplifying the forthcoming analysis we assume that the size of the database has been doubled using unmarked entries thus $M \leq N/2$. In order to use (7.32) the relation between c and q has to be analyzed. We know that $0 \leq M \leq N/2$ and therefore $2^q \leq N/2$. Furthermore we have to bear in mind during the forthcoming analysis that $0 \leq \tilde{M} \leq N^4$ thus $\max\{M - 2^q, 0\} \leq \tilde{M} \leq \min\{M + 2^q, N\}$. M and Ω_γ are linked together by (7.20) and we depicted

$$\Omega_\gamma(M) = 2\arcsin\left(\sqrt{\frac{M}{N}}\right), \quad \Omega_{\gamma\pm}(M,q) = 2\arcsin\left(\sqrt{\frac{M \pm 2^q}{N}}\right), \tag{7.33}$$

in Fig. 7.9. It is easy to recognize that increasing q enables exponentially more and more deviation in Ω_γ and $\Omega_{\gamma\pm}(M,q)$ has a cut off because $0 \leq \tilde{M} \leq N$. When determining the required $c(M,q)$ in the phase estimator we consider the worst-case scenario

$$|\tilde{\Omega}_\gamma - \Omega_\gamma| \leq 2^{-c(M,q)} \leq \min_\pm\{|\Omega_{\gamma\pm}(M,q) - \Omega_\gamma(M)|\} = \Omega_{\gamma+}(M,q) - \Omega_\gamma(M), \tag{7.34}$$

where we exploited the strictly monotonously increasing nature of $\arcsin(\cdot)$ in the last step. Taking the logarithm to base 2 of both sides

$$c(M,q) \geq \lceil -\operatorname{ld}(\Omega_{\gamma+}(M,q) - \Omega_\gamma(M)) \rceil. \tag{7.35}$$

The points of $c(M,q)$ in the case of different $M = 1, 4, 64, 2048$ – from $M \ll N$ to $M \approx N/2$ – are presented in Fig. 7.10. All of the curves are crossing axis q at 11 because $N/2 = 2048 = 2^{11}$. A straight line can be fitted to each curve in the range $q \in [0, \operatorname{ld}(N/2)]$ with slope from $\approx -1/2$ to 1 at $q = \operatorname{ld}(N/2)$ (where $c(M,q)$ crosses the horizontal axis), that is each bit increase in accuracy of M requires from half to one additional qbit in the upper qregister depending on the ratio of M and N.

---

[4]Of course if the phase estimator gives back an $\tilde{M} > N/2$ we may be suspicious about the result. If such situation happens obviously one should replace $\tilde{M}$ with $N/2$.

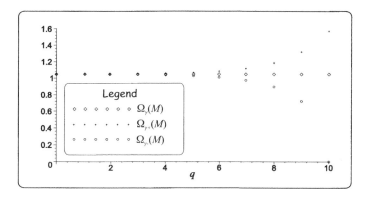

Fig. 7.9 $\Omega_\gamma(M), \Omega_{\gamma+}(M), \Omega_{\gamma-}(M)$ vs. q if $M = 1024$ and $N = 4096$

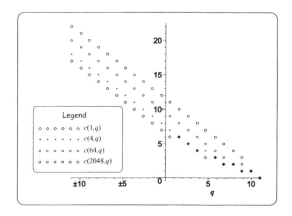

Fig. 7.10 $c(M, q)$ (assuming equality in the definition) vs. q if $M = 1, 4, 64, 2048$ and $N = 4096$

Or taking into account that we need $\mathrm{ld}(N/2)$ qbits to represent M exactly, if we are satisfied with $\mathrm{ld}(N/2) - q$ MSB bits of the closest integer to M to describe M, then we have to install $c(M, q) - 1$ qbits in the phase estimator. At $q = 0$, which can be regarded as reasonable setup, small Ms require about half the amount of qbits than large M values. Furthermore in the latter case $c(M, q = 0) \approx \mathrm{ld}(\max \tilde{M}) = \mathrm{ld}(N)$. The reader may wonder whether this observation can be generalized or is it valid for this special parameter setup only?

To answer this question we investigate $c(M, q)$ in $M \ll N$ and $M = N/2$ cases at $q = 0$. Substituting (7.20) into (7.35) and assuming equality as the most pragmatic case we get

$$c(M, q) = \left\lceil -\mathrm{ld}\left(2 \arcsin\left(\sqrt{\frac{M + 2^q}{N}}\right) - 2 \arcsin\left(\sqrt{\frac{M}{N}}\right)\right) \right\rceil, \qquad (7.36)$$

from which using $q = 0$

$$c(M,0) = \left\lceil -\mathrm{ld}\left(2\arcsin\left(\sqrt{\frac{M+1}{N}}\right) - 2\arcsin\left(\sqrt{\frac{M}{N}}\right)\right)\right\rceil. \qquad (7.37)$$

If $M \ll N$, i.e. extreme value $M = 1$ is assumed then

$$c(1,0) = \left\lceil -\mathrm{ld}\left(2\arcsin\left(\sqrt{\frac{2}{N}}\right) - 2\arcsin\left(\sqrt{\frac{1}{N}}\right)\right)\right\rceil.$$

Considering that $1/N \ll 1$ and $\arcsin(x) \approx x$ if $x \ll 1$

$$c(1,0) \approx \left\lceil -\mathrm{ld}\left(2\sqrt{\frac{2}{N}} - 2\sqrt{\frac{1}{N}}\right)\right\rceil$$

$$= \left\lceil -\mathrm{ld}(2\sqrt{2} - 2) + \frac{1}{2}\mathrm{ld}(N)\right\rceil = \frac{1}{2}\mathrm{ld}(N) + 1, \qquad (7.38)$$

where we remember that N is assumed to be an integer power of 2.

Concentrating on the case of $M = N/2$ (7.37) becomes

$$c(N/2,0) = \left\lceil -\mathrm{ld}\left(2\arcsin\left(\sqrt{\frac{N+2}{2N}}\right) - 2\arcsin\left(\sqrt{\frac{1}{2}}\right)\right)\right\rceil.$$

Applying $\arcsin(x) - \arcsin(y) = \arcsin(x\sqrt{1-y^2} - y\sqrt{1-x^2})$ if $x^2 + y^2 \le 1$
we get

$$c(N/2,0) \approx \left\lceil -\mathrm{ld}\left(2\arcsin\left(\sqrt{\frac{1}{4N}}(\sqrt{N+2} - \sqrt{N-2})\right)\right)\right\rceil.$$

Approximating $(\sqrt{N+2} - \sqrt{N-2})$ with $\sqrt{4/N}$ and using again $\arcsin(x) \approx x$ if $x \ll 1$

$$c(N/2,0) \approx \left\lceil -\mathrm{ld}\left(2\arcsin\left(\sqrt{\frac{1}{4N}}\sqrt{\frac{4}{N}}\right)\right)\right\rceil = \mathrm{ld}(N) + 1, \qquad (7.39)$$

which is in full harmony with our expectations.

Remark: Obviously q can be lowerbounded by -1 because we can perform only integer number of rotations (Grover operators) thus if $|M - \tilde{M}| < \frac{1}{2}$ then we have to choose the closest integer to $\tilde{M}$ to get the correct value of M.

As an extreme scenario of $q = -1$ from which follows that the probability of counting error, i.e. determining another value for M than the exact one, $P_{\varepsilon C} = P_{\varepsilon P}$. If $M = N/2$ then classically we have to check all the N entries to determine M exactly. The corresponding quantum solution calls the Oracle $T(n^\clubsuit) = O(N)$ times in compliance with (6.39) so no significant difference can be found between the two approaches. However, if $M = 1$ then $T(n^{\clubsuit}) = O(2^{c(1,-1)}) = O(\sqrt{N})$ (see (7.38)) while classically $O(N)$ database queries are still required. Furthermore if we used classically only $\sqrt{N}$ queries it would result in a probability of counting error $P_{\varepsilon C} = 1 - \frac{1}{\sqrt{N}}$ (see **Exercise** 7.9), which is greater than $\frac{1}{2}$ if $N > 4$.

What happens if $q \geq -1$ is allowed in the engineering problem when applying quantum counting, that is we are investigating the effect of varying q? Since quantum counting inherits quantum based uncertainty $\check{P}_{\varepsilon P}$ from the phase estimation (7.32), which can be controlled fortunately very efficiently using a small, constant[5] number of additional qbits in the upper register, we have here nothing to do about the error probability. However, (7.36) and Fig. 7.10 emphasize that the number of required Grover gates $T(n^{\clubsuit}) = O(2^{c(M,q)})$ will be reduced! Therefore the reference classical algorithm will require less queries to the database to achieve the same probability of error or the same number of queries results in a smaller error probability.

This line of thought can be summarized/rephrased much practically in the following way: a tiny M allows large q. Because the required resource $c(M,q)$ in the upper section of the quantum counting circuit (7.32) is in inverse proportion to q (7.36), small Ms require less qbits assuming given $\check{P}_{\varepsilon}$. Therefore if one has *a priori* information about the order of M then significant amount of qbits can be saved.

Remark: Of course if we select a $c(M,q)$ curve at a given q it will work as a worst-case scenario for all $M' \leq M$ from an accuracy point of view.

However, if we have no information about M then the worst of the worst-case scenarios has to be considered, that is the curve belonging to $M = N/2$ must be selected at a given q to determine the required $c(M = N/2, q)$. This fact implies not only economical considerations but also it is fundamental from a computational complexity point of view since $c(M,q)$ strongly influences the number of Grover gates $T(n^{\clubsuit})$ to be deployed within the quantum counting device (6.39) and thus the running time. Classically if we have no information about the database entries we can only check step by step – selecting randomly or deterministically – the items belonging to the database whether they match the marked state or not. Hence classically M can be obtained via counting the number of matching indexes.

Selecting $c(M = N/2, q)$ is equivalent to choosing the greatest q belonging to different Ms (i.e drawing a horizontal line across $c(M = N/2, q)$) in Fig. 7.10. Therefore when measuring $\tilde{M}$ the accuracy (the projection of the intersection of the horizontal line and a given curve $c(M,q)$ onto the horizontal axis) depends on M. Of course we cannot exploit this fact directly because M is unknown and therefore we cannot assume a lower $2^{q'}$ than 2^q, but there are applications such as finding an extreme value in a database where this hidden information can be utilized.

If one would like to use quantum counting as a block in unsorted database searching which allows determining M – and thus the optimal number of iterations – for the Grover algorithm then demand for the accuracy 2^q of M originates from the maximum allowed error probability $\check{P}_{\varepsilon}$. Here we assume that $P_{\varepsilon P}$ is negligible or can be made negligible compared with P_{ε}. We know from (7.29) that an error 2^q

---

[5] It does not depend on q, N, M.

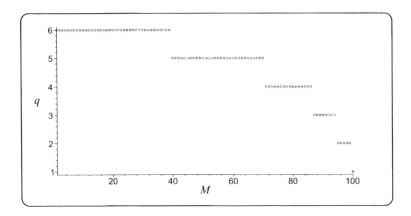

Fig. 7.11   Connection between M and q assuming system parameters $\check{P}_\varepsilon = 0.1$ and $2N = 4096$

in M will cause that the probability of measuring a false index during the Grover algorithm is

$$P_\varepsilon \leq \sin^2 \left(\frac{\Omega_\gamma(M + 2^q)}{2} \right) \leq \check{P}_\varepsilon, \qquad (7.40)$$

from which with respect to (7.33) if we have a constraint that the probability of error must be less than $\check{P}_\varepsilon$

$$q \leq \left\lfloor \mathrm{ld} \left(N \sin^2 \left(\arcsin \left(\sqrt{\check{P}_\varepsilon} \right) \right) - M \right) \right\rfloor, \qquad (7.41)$$

where obviously the argument of $\mathrm{ld}(\cdot)$ has to be chosen such that the argument remains positive because we cannot guarantee smaller error probability than that one belonging to the optimal number of iterations. Of course q depends on $\Omega_\gamma(M)$ which is influenced by the actual value of M. Therefore we depicted the relationship between M and allowed inaccuracy q in the case of demand $\check{P}_\varepsilon = 0.1$ in a database $N = 4096$ of size in Fig. 7.11.

According to our expectations a small M – which is related to small $\Omega_\gamma(M)$ thus small P_ε (see (7.40)) – allows larger deviation in M still remaining under $\check{P}_\varepsilon$. Contrary if M is big then by performing optimal number of iterations we cannot rotate $|\gamma_1\rangle$ close to $|\beta\rangle$ hence only a small error in M can be allowed.

The results we have already achieved in this chapter are summarized in Fig. 7.12. First we run a quantum counting $(Q\#)$ procedure to find the number of repeated occurrences of M in the database DB. In possession of M we are able to calculate the optimal number of Grover iterations (L_{opt_0}) and initialize a classical counter $(C\#)$, which loops back the output of G to its input until we managed to rotate $|\gamma_1\rangle$ as close to $|\beta\rangle$ as possible. Finally a projective measurement in the computational basis states provides one of the marked entries with high probability or in certain cases with sure success.

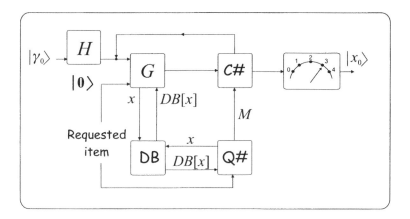

Fig. 7.12 Quantum circuit for searching in an unsorted database

Remark: What happens if the database does not contains the requested item at all? In this case $|\gamma_1\rangle = |\alpha\rangle \Rightarrow \Omega_\gamma = 0$ thus the phase estimator returns $M = 0$.

Remark: It is important to emphasize that concerning the scenario when the database is virtual (e.g. a given function defines it and we do not need to build special hardware to access the database) we are interested rather in the number of elementary gates implementing the counting than in the number of applied Grover operators. As we learned at the end of Section 6.2.4 the complexity can be expressed with $O((n^\clubsuit)^3) = O(\mathrm{ld}^3(N))$ gates, which is a significantly favorable metrics for complexity!

Remark: Obviously determining M for computing the number of iterations in the Grover algorithm is only one potential application of quantum counting. We show as an example a telecommunications related problem where quantum counting is used in Chapter 8.

Exercise 7.9. Prove that the probability of failing in seeking for the marked entry ($M = 1$) after putting L queries to the database classically is $P_{\varepsilon C}(L) = \frac{N-L}{N}$.

7.2.3 Replacing quantum counting with indirect estimation on M

Boyer and his colleagues proposed an ingenious alternative solution in [104], which may replace quantum counting if one needs M to determine the optimal number of rotations L_{opt_0} in the Grover algorithm. Instead of wasting time with quantum counting we try to estimate M indirectly. We know from (7.28) that the probability of measuring a marked state after l iterations is

$$P_s(l, M) = \sin^2 \left(\frac{(2l+1)\,\Omega_\gamma(M)}{2} \right), \tag{7.42}$$

provided there are M marked states in the database. Therefore we decide to repeat several times – we call one turn a cycle – the Grover algorithm (and not the Grover operator!) with l rotations. After each cycle we check whether the measured index leads to a marked state or not. In the latter case we run the Grover algorithm again and again g times until we get a marked entry when finishing the cycle. The expected number of cycles $\mathbb{E}(g|M \wedge l)$ which is needed before successfully finding a marked state can be calculated as the inverse of $P_s(l, M)$. Thus the expected value of the total number z of Grover operators $\mathbb{E}(z|M \wedge l)$ can be expressed as the product of the number of cycles and the number of Grover calls in each cycle (we have increased l by 1 because to check the result requires an extra query to the database at the end of each Grover algorithm)

$$\mathbb{E}(z|M \wedge l) = (l+1)\frac{1}{P_s(l, M)} = \frac{l+1}{\sin^2\left(\frac{(2l+1)\Omega_\gamma(M)}{2}\right)}. \tag{7.43}$$

In the case of $l = 0$ where although we do not use any rotations at all, measurements cannot be omitted in harmony with classical probability theory

$$\mathbb{E}(z|M \wedge 0) = \frac{1}{P_s(0, M)} = \frac{N}{M}.$$

If we were in possession of M then $\mathbb{E}(z|M \wedge l)$ could be minimized on l by setting its first derivative to zero

$$\frac{d\mathbb{E}(z|M \wedge l)}{dl} = 0 \Rightarrow \tan\left(\frac{(2l+1)\,\Omega_\gamma(M)}{2}\right) = 2(l+1)\Omega_\gamma(M). \tag{7.44}$$

In spite of the fact that M is unknown in our case it is worth making a detour to investigate this idea in **Exercise** 7.10.

What shall we do if we have only partial information about M or we have no guess for M at all. Let us assume that at least one marked item exists and we can upperbound M with $M_{\max}$. Here $M_{\max} = N/2$ can be considered as a worst-case scenario with totally unknown M. If $M_{\max}$ is assumed and the Grover search is repeated a large amount of times with potentially different Ms then the best strategy we can follow is to handle M as a uniform random variable on $[1, M_{\max}]$, i.e. $P(M) = \frac{1}{M_{\max}}$. Now, we can easily calculate the total number of required Grover calls in the following way

$$\mathbb{E}(z|l) = \sum_{M=1}^{M_{\max}} \mathbb{E}(z|M \wedge l) \cdot P(M)$$

$$= \frac{1}{M_{\max}} \sum_{M=1}^{M_{\max}} \frac{l+1}{\sin^2\left(\frac{(2l+1)\Omega_\gamma(M)}{2}\right)}. \tag{7.45}$$

Concerning the $l = 0$ scenario we get

$$\mathbb{E}(z|0) = \frac{1}{M_{\max}} \sum_{M=1}^{M_{\max}} \frac{N}{M}.$$

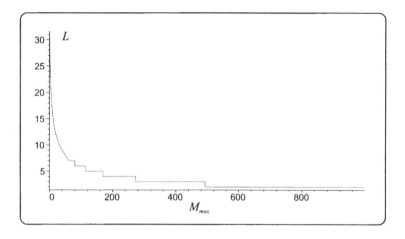

Fig. 7.13 Optimal number of rotations L vs. $M_{\max}$ if $N = 4096$

We have optimized $\mathbb{E}(z|l)$ in function of l at different $M_{\max} \in [1, N/2]$ and the corresponding optimal L and minimal $\mathbb{E}(z|L)$ values are depicted in Fig. 7.13 and Fig. 7.14, respectively. Obviously when optimizing z we try to find a good trade off between the number of cycles and the number of applied Grover operators l in a given cycle. Increasing l in the case of small M values will enhance significantly the probability of successful measurements and thus less cycles are required. Conversely if we let large Ms dominate (i.e. $M_{\max} \to N/2$) then the probability of success becomes big enough to provide a marked state after a few rotations, hence small l can be optimal (cf. Fig. 7.13). Fig. 7.14 contains not only $\mathbb{E}(z|L)$ but we presented $\sqrt{N}$ and $\sqrt{N/M_{\max}}$ as references. As the reader may recognize the original and the expected value based approach have almost the same performance. Of course with the major difference being that the latter one requires typically less or more Grover gates than the former one.

Exercise 7.10. Let us consider a database with $N = 2^{20}$ and $M = 8$. Calculate the optimal number of rotations L which minimizes the expected number of required Grover gates $\mathbb{E}(z|M \wedge l)$ when using the cycle repetition based searching. Compare the optimal number of Grover operators in case of the original Grover algorithm to $\mathbb{E}(z|M \wedge L)$.

7.3 QUANTUM EXISTENCE TESTING

A special case of quantum counting is if one is interested in whether a given entry exists in the database at all instead of the number M of occurrences. Clearly speaking our goal is to determine whether the initial vector of the index qregister is parallel or angular to basis state $|\alpha\rangle$ in the two-dimensional rotation based picture of the

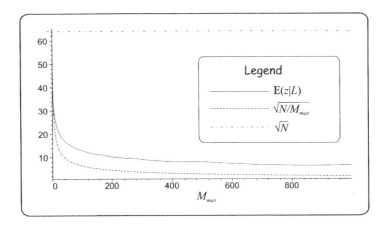

Fig. 7.14 Optimized expected total number of Grover operators $\mathbb{E}(z|L)$ vs. $M_{\max}$ if $N = 4096$ with $\sqrt{N}$ and $\sqrt{N/M_{\max}}$ as references

Grover operator, that is we would like to distinguish the case $\frac{\Omega_\gamma}{2} = 0 \Rightarrow \Omega_\gamma = 0$ from $\frac{\Omega_\gamma}{2} \neq 0$. Trivially we can use quantum counting to solve this problem, namely if we yield $M \neq 0$ then the database contains the requested entry else it does not. However, quantum counting involves some amount of overhead information because from an existence point of view the accurate value of M is indifferent. Hence it is worth discussing the required number of qbits for the upper section (based on (7.32)) and suitable error analysis.

Concerning this question let us deal first with classical accuracy. If $M = 0$ then the output of the IQFT should be unambiguously $|0\rangle$ while provided $M \neq 0$ we can accept any other computational basis states except $|0\rangle$. So we do not need the precise value of M in the latter case instead classically less accurate results are as appropriate as the exact one. Thus the worst-case scenario occurs when $\frac{\Omega_\gamma}{2}$ is the smallest, that is we have the smallest angle between $|\gamma_1\rangle$ and $|\alpha\rangle$. Hence the classical accuracy c should be chosen such that in the case $M = 1$ the measured output of the IQFT contains at least one nonzero bit which allows distinguishing it from $|0\rangle$. Let us assume again without loss of generality that we have a database $N = 2^n$ entry of size, therefore using (7.20) we need

$$\min(\Omega_\gamma) = 2 \arcsin\left(\sqrt{\frac{1}{N}}\right) \simeq 2\sqrt{\frac{1}{N}} = 2^{(-n/2+1)} \geq 2^{-c} \tag{7.46}$$

where we applied the well-known relation $\arcsin(y) = y$ if $y \ll 1$, from which we get

$$c = \left\lceil \frac{n}{2} \right\rceil - 1.$$

Of course we have to take care of quantum uncertainty of phase estimation as well, hence we need all together

$$n^{\clubsuit} = \left\lceil \frac{n}{2} + \mathrm{ld}(2\pi) + \mathrm{ld}\left(3 + \frac{1}{\check{P}_{\varepsilon P}}\right) \right\rceil - 2$$

qbits, where $\check{P}_{\varepsilon P}$ stands for the allowed maximum quantum uncertainty and correction $\mathrm{ld}(2\pi)$ is required because c refers to the accuracy of the estimated phase instead of the phase ratio itself. Since the -2 term has marginal influence on the complexity we omit it during the further discussion, that is

$$n^{\clubsuit} = \left\lceil \frac{n}{2} + \mathrm{ld}(2\pi) + \mathrm{ld}\left(3 + \frac{1}{\check{P}_{\varepsilon P}}\right) \right\rceil. \tag{7.47}$$

Moreover if one gets $n^{\clubsuit} < 1$ then $n^{\clubsuit}$ has to be set to 1.

7.3.1 Error analysis

Formula (7.47) gives a rule of thumb when roughly estimating the required qbits in the upper section of the phase estimator. However, as we have seen in the previous subsection the interpretation of classical accuracy was a bit different in the case of counting and existence testing (in the latter case we have a softer constraint). Thus we expect that a similar effect will emerge when investigating quantum inaccuracy. Therefore let us derive the required number p of additional qbits in the upper section of the device if we have a constraint $\check{P}_{\varepsilon}$ of quantum uncertainty.

It is easy to see that if $M = 0$ then $\Omega_\gamma = 0$ is measured *always* with certainty since the phase ratio $\kappa = \Omega_\gamma/2\pi$ is also equal to zero, which corresponds to the idealistic phase estimation discussed in Section 6.2.1. Hence only the case $\Omega_\gamma \neq 0$ should be taken into consideration from a quantum error point of view when seeking the relationship between the required number of additional qbits and $P_{\varepsilon E}$, where subscript E refers to *existence testing*. For the sake of controlling precisely this $P_{\varepsilon E}$ one needs p additional qbits to $\frac{n}{2} + \mathrm{ld}(2\pi)$ qbits in the upper qregister to guarantee classical accuracy 2^{-c}. An error occurs if $\tilde{\Omega}_\gamma = 0$ is measured although $\Omega_\gamma \neq 0$ which is equivalent to the case when we get a computational basis state having zero bits on the $n^{\clubsuit} - p$ MSB positions that is

$$P_{\varepsilon E} = \underbrace{P(\tilde{\Omega}_\gamma \neq 0|\Omega_\gamma = 0)}_{\equiv 0} P(\Omega_\gamma = 0) + \sum_{\Omega_\gamma \neq 0} P(\tilde{\Omega}_\gamma = 0|\Omega_\gamma)P(\Omega_\gamma). \tag{7.48}$$

On one hand the conditional error probability can be calculated in the following way

$$P(\tilde{\Omega}_\gamma = 0|\Omega_\gamma) = \sum_{i=0}^{2^p - 1} \left|\varphi_i(n^{\clubsuit}, \Omega_\gamma)\right|^2 \tag{7.49}$$

where $\varphi_i(n^{\clubsuit}, \Omega_\gamma)$ is an adapted version of (6.17) and $i \in [0, 2^n)$

$$\varphi_i(n^{\clubsuit}, \Omega_\gamma) = \frac{1}{2^{n^{\clubsuit}}} \frac{1 - e^{j2\pi(2^{n^{\clubsuit}} \frac{\Omega_\gamma}{2\pi} - i)}}{1 - e^{j2\pi(\frac{\Omega_\gamma}{2\pi} - \frac{i}{2^{n^{\clubsuit}}})}}. \tag{7.50}$$

On the other hand we assume that $P(M)$ is uniformly distributed as a worst-case approach. Furthermore since $M \in [0, N-1]$ and M is connected to Ω_γ via a reversible function (7.20) therefore $P(\Omega_\gamma) = \frac{1}{N}$.

Unlike (7.48) in order to build a useful connection between $P_{\varepsilon E}$ and overhead p it is worth searching for an appropriate upperbound P_{upper} for $P(\tilde{\Omega}_\gamma = 0|\Omega_\gamma)$, which is independent from Ω_γ

$$P_{\varepsilon E} = \sum_{\Omega_\gamma \neq 0} P(\tilde{\Omega}_\gamma = 0|\Omega_\gamma) P(\Omega_\gamma) \leq P_{upper} \frac{N-1}{N}. \tag{7.51}$$

In order to majorize $|\varphi_i(n^\clubsuit, \Omega_\gamma)|^2$ we upperbound its numerator and lowerbound its denominator applying the same inequalities $|1 - e^\alpha| \leq 2$ and $|1 - e^\alpha| \geq \frac{2|\alpha|}{\pi}$ as we used for the phase estimation, respectively. Thus we get

$$|\varphi_i(n^\clubsuit, \Omega_\gamma)|^2 \leq \frac{1}{4} \frac{1}{2^{n^\clubsuit} \left(\frac{\Omega_\gamma}{2\pi} - \frac{i}{2^{n^\clubsuit}} \right)^2},$$

which can be further majorized exploiting $\min(\Omega_\gamma)$ from (7.46)

$$|\varphi_i(n^\clubsuit, \Omega_\gamma)|^2 \leq \frac{1}{4} \frac{1}{\left(\frac{2^{n^\clubsuit}}{\pi\sqrt{N}} - i \right)^2}. \tag{7.52}$$

Considering that $\sqrt{N} = 2^{\frac{n}{2}}$ and $n^\clubsuit = \frac{n}{2} + \mathrm{ld}(2\pi) + p$ the right-hand side of (7.52) simplifies to

$$|\varphi_i(n^\clubsuit, \Omega_\gamma)|^2 \leq \frac{1}{4} \frac{1}{(2^{p+1} - i)^2}.$$

Now we are able to derive a suitable P_{upper}

$$P(\tilde{\Omega}_\gamma = 0|\Omega_\gamma) \leq \sum_{k=0}^{2^p - 1} \frac{1}{4} \frac{1}{(2^{p+1} - k)^2}. \tag{7.53}$$

If $(2^{p+1} - k)^2$ were strictly monotonously increasing in $[0, 2^p]$ then the sum in (7.53) could be upperbounded by the corresponding integral i.e.

$$\sum_{k=0}^{2^p - 1} \frac{1}{4} \frac{1}{(2^{p+1} - k)^2} \leq \int_0^{2^p} \frac{1}{4} \frac{1}{(2^{p+1} - k)^2} dk.$$

This requires that $2^{p+1} - k \geq 0 \Rightarrow 2^{p+1} \geq 2^p$ which is trivially satisfied. Evaluating the above integral one obtains

$$P(\tilde{\Omega}_\gamma = 0|\Omega_\gamma) \leq \int_0^{2^p} \frac{1}{4} \frac{1}{(2^{p+1} - k)^2} dk = \frac{1}{4} \left(\frac{1}{2^{p+1} - 2^p} - \frac{1}{2^{p+1}} \right)$$

$$= \frac{1}{8} \frac{1}{2^p} = P_{upper}, \tag{7.54}$$

which allows upperbounding $P_{\varepsilon E}$ itself based on (7.51)

$$P_{\varepsilon E} \leq \frac{1}{8} \frac{1}{2^p} \frac{2^n - 1}{2^n}.$$
(7.55)

Provided we have an engineering constraint $\check{P}_\varepsilon \geq P_{\varepsilon E}$ one needs

$$p = \mathrm{ld}\left(\frac{2^n - 1}{8 \cdot 2^n \check{P}_\varepsilon}\right) \leq \mathrm{ld}\left(\frac{1}{8\check{P}_\varepsilon}\right),$$
(7.56)

qbits to fulfil it and the total number of required qbits in the upper section is

$$n^{\clubsuit} = \left\lceil \frac{n}{2} + \mathrm{ld}(2\pi) + \mathrm{ld}\left(\frac{1}{8\check{P}_\varepsilon}\right) \right\rceil.$$
(7.57)

Using the above derived existence tester, in order to separate the two outcome categories, it is enough to check whether the output of the device contains at least one nonzero bit or not. If yes then the database comprises the requested item else it is not in. Furthermore we emphasize that this method does not suffer from any classical errors!

Concerning the computational complexity we can state that the quantum existence tester saves $n/2$ qbits and 3 qbits in classical accuracy and quantum uncertainty compared to the quantum counting circuit, which can be significant if $N \gg 1$.

7.4 FINDING EXTREME VALUES IN AN UNSORTED DATABASE

Many computing and engineering problems can be traced back to an optimization process which aims to find the extreme value (minimum or maximum point) of a so-called cost function or a database. We list here only several well-known cases of these types of problems. For instance global infocom networks needing to find the optimum route between two terminals located on different continents in terms of the shortest path or optimal signal detection on the air interfaces of state-of-the art mobile networks need to perform maximum likelihood hypothesis testing based on finding the largest conditional probability density function (pdf) among say 10^{30} pdfs. Unfortunately because of their huge computational complexity these problems are typically answered by means of suboptimal solutions. From this point on we use notions *database* and *function* as synonyms.

From a quantum computing point of view we should consider the Grover algorithm as the most promising candidate. Unfortunately as we summarize in the corresponding *Further Reading* the proposed Grover-based solutions are efficient only in terms of expected number of database queries. In order to overcome this major shortcoming we decided to use the quantum existence testing algorithm as a core function. This is because our special problem does not require quantum counting on the whole, that is we do not need to determine the number of occurrences of a certain entry in the database rather we are interested in whether the database contains it at all.

Having introduced the quantum existence testing algorithm in Section 7.3 we are ready to turn to extreme value searching. We will embed our special core function into a classical logarithmic search (see e.g. [143, 92]). Let us assume that we have a function $y = g[x]$ which has integer input $x \in [0, N-1]$ and integer output $y \in [G_{\min 0}, G_{\max 0}]$, that is we have a rough estimation about the range of y (e.g. we know that y is non-negative thus $G_{\min 0} = 0$ proves to be a suitable lower bound). Using these notations the problem can be formulated as follows. We are interested in y_{opt} such that $\min_x(g[x]) = g[x_{opt}] = y_{opt}$. We emphasize that although a minimum value search is considered here, the suggested technique can be trivially transformed to find the maximal entry of a database. The best classical solutions require N queries to the database to find x_{opt} hence our aim is to design a more efficient algorithm based on quantum computing.

To solve the above-mentioned problem we combine the well-known logarithmic (often referred as binary) search algorithm – which is originally intended for searching a given item in a *sorted* database – with quantum existence testing. Hereby we produce an algorithm which keeps the efficiency of binary search while processing an *unsorted* database. It operates in a recursive way where in the sth step we halve the actual searching region splitting it into two subregions. Let $G_{\text{med } s}$ denote that y value which separates the subregions. Next we launch the quantum existence testing algorithm – represented here by function $QET(z)$ – to check whether there is a $y < z$ marked state in the lower subregion or not. If the answer is YES then we use the lower subregion as the input of the next searching step else the upper one has to be chosen. In order to be more precise the proposed algorithm is now given in detail:

1. We start with $s = 0$: $G_{\min 1} = G_{\min 0}$, $G_{\max 1} = G_{\max 0}$ and $\Delta G = G_{\max 0} - G_{\min 0}$

2. $s = s + 1$

3. $G_{\text{med } s} = G_{\min s} + \left\lceil \frac{G_{\max s} - G_{\min s}}{2} \right\rceil$

4. $flag = QET(G_{\text{med } s})$

   - if $flag = YES$ then $G_{\max s+1} = G_{\text{med } s}$, $G_{\min s+1} = G_{\min s}$
   - else $G_{\max s+1} = G_{\max s}$, $G_{\min s+1} = G_{\text{med } s}$

5. if $s < \text{ld}(\Delta G)$ then go to (2) else stop and $y_{opt} = G_{\text{med } s}$.

We have two additional remarks about this algorithm. First it can be used obviously in the case of multiple minimum values, too. Next if one is interested in the corresponding $x_{opt} = g^{-1}[y_{opt}]$ then a single quantum counting followed by a single Grover search has to be performed resulting in the number of different x values belonging to y_{opt} and obtaining one of them according to a uniform distribution.

Finally computational complexity should be considered. Obviously for the best classical strategy the exhaustive search needs $O(N)$ steps to find y_{opt} with sure success. Already available quantum computing based solutions require $O(\sqrt{N} +$

$\mathrm{ld}^2(N))$ [32, 1] iterations (i.e. Grover operators) for an *expected value*. Conversely the proposed new approach obtains y_{opt} using $O(\mathrm{ld}(\Delta G)\mathrm{ld}^3(\sqrt{N}))$ elementary steps originating from the computational complexity of the phase estimation, which means a fairly huge difference if $N \gg 1$. The initial searching range influences the complexity as well, but in many practical applications one has enough pieces of basic information about $G_{\min 0}$ and $G_{\max 0}$, without causing difficulties thanks to the $\mathrm{ld}(\cdot)$ function.

7.5 THE GENERALIZED GROVER ALGORITHM

During the previous analysis of the basic Grover algorithm we aspired to find a suitable trade off between computational complexity (number of rotations or more precisely number of database queries l) and uncertainty (probability of error P_ε). We tried to use as few iterations as possible meanwhile ensuring as high probability of success as achievable. Moreover we have some limitations that may prevent the application of our clever quantum-searching algorithm in many practical cases.

- Unfortunately sure success cannot be guaranteed merely in exchange of increased number of rotations in the basic Grover algorithm. We have proposed some techniques (e.g. extended database with 'dummy' entries) at the end of Section 7.1.5 which provides sure success asymptotically but require $O(N)$ rotations to achieve this. However, there are technical problems where we are not permitted to exceed a given $\check{P}_\varepsilon$ while the number of Grover operators also has to be upperbounded.

- According to the potential applications of Grover's database search algorithm in practice, larger quantum systems should be taken into account where the input index register of the algorithm is given as an arbitrary output state of a former circuit and the output of the algorithm can feed another circuit without any measurement. Therefore we need a modified Grover algorithm which allows an arbitrary initial state instead of the original $H|0\rangle$.

In order to minimize the above listed problems the original Grover algorithm will be generalized and discussed in the next subsections.

7.5.1 Generalization of the basic Grover database search algorithm

Before investigating the possibilities of how to introduce some freedom into the Grover algorithm to enable its generalization let us summarize our knowledge about the Grover operator (7.15) which was originally defined in Section 7.1.3 as

$$G \triangleq HPHO,$$

where

$$P \triangleq 2|0\rangle\langle 0| - I,$$

$$O \triangleq I - 2 \sum_{x \in S} |x\rangle\langle x|.$$

These definitions were motivated by considerations emerging during the design of the searching algorithm. Furthermore we learned in Section 6.4 that the Hadamard transform is nothing more than a special QFT. Therefore it seems to be reasonable to replace the original operators with more general ones. New parameters can be involved in this way, which could be the base of a more efficient solution.

1. We allow an arbitrary unitary gate U instead of the Hadamard gate H.

2. We let the Oracle rotate the probability amplitudes of the marked items in the index register with angle ϕ in lieu of π (the original setup), where $\phi \in [-\pi, \pi]$. Thus (7.21) is altered to

$$O \rightarrow I_\beta \triangleq I + \left(e^{j\phi} - 1\right) \sum_{x \in S} |x\rangle\langle x|, \tag{7.58}$$

   where subscript β refers to the fact that the Oracle modifies the probability amplitudes of the computational basis states forming $|\beta\rangle$. The matrix of I_β is a modified identity matrix with diagonal elements $I_{\beta_{xx}} = e^{j\phi}$ if $x \in S$.

3. Analogously to the Oracle above, the controlled phase gate P, which was working originally on state $|0\rangle$, should be based on an arbitrary basis state $|\eta\rangle$ resulting in a multiplication by $e^{j\theta}$ instead of -1, where $\theta \in [-\pi, \pi]$. In more exact mathematical formalism

$$P \rightarrow I_\eta \triangleq I + \left(e^{j\theta} - 1\right) |\eta\rangle\langle\eta|. \tag{7.59}$$

   The matrix of I_η is a modified identity matrix with diagonal element $I_{\beta_{xx}} = e^{j\theta}$ if $x = \eta$.

4. Finally the initial state of the index register at the input of the first Grover gate is considered as

$$|\gamma_1\rangle \triangleq \sum_{x=0}^{N-1} \gamma_{1x}|x\rangle, \tag{7.60}$$

   where $\sum_{x=0}^{(N-1)} |\gamma_{1x}|^2 = 1$ as appropriate.

Next the two basis vectors $|\alpha\rangle$ and $|\beta\rangle$ comprising the indexes leading to unmarked items (set $\overline{S}$) and that ending in a marked entry (set S) should be redefined, which were originally set in (7.17) and (7.18), respectively

$$|\alpha\rangle = \frac{1}{\sqrt{\sum_{x \in \overline{S}} |\gamma_{1x}|^2}} \sum_{x \in \overline{S}} \gamma_{1x}|x\rangle, \tag{7.61}$$

$$|\beta\rangle = \frac{1}{\sqrt{\sum_{x \in S} |\gamma_{1x}|^2}} \sum_{x \in S} \gamma_{1x}|x\rangle. \tag{7.62}$$

Observing the new basis vectors $|\alpha\rangle$ and $|\beta\rangle$ orthogonality is still given between them, $\langle\alpha|\beta\rangle = 0$, since during the pairwise multiplication within the inner product one of the probability aplitudes is always zero.

Remark: In order to avoid the division by zero in (7.61) and (7.62) we require that at least one nonzero probability amplitude exists for the marked and unmarked indices. If all the entries are marked then we have only vector $|\beta\rangle$ and a measurement before the search will result in a marked state with certainty. Conversely if the database does not contain the requested item at all then only vector $|\alpha\rangle$ exists. As we will discuss later at the end of Section 7.5.3 both scenarios can be recognized by means of a phase estimation. Therefore in the forthcoming analysis we assume that both vectors exist, that is neither of the two sets are empty.

Now it is time to construct the generalized Grover operator Q from previously defined gates $(G \rightarrow Q)$

$$
\begin{aligned}
Q \triangleq -U I_\eta U^\dagger I_\beta &= -U \left(I + \left(e^{j\theta} - 1 \right) |\eta\rangle\langle\eta| \right) U^\dagger I_\beta \\
&= - \left(U I U^{-1} + \left(e^{j\theta} - 1 \right) U |\eta\rangle\langle\eta| U^\dagger \right) I_\beta \\
&= - \left(I + \left(e^{j\theta} - 1 \right) |\mu\rangle\langle\mu| \right) I_\beta,
\end{aligned}
\tag{7.63}
$$

where

$$
|\mu\rangle \triangleq U|\eta\rangle
\tag{7.64}
$$

and relation $U^\dagger = U^{-1}$ is exploited in consequence of the unitary property.

In possession of N-dimensional Q first we have to prove that its output vector always remains in the two-dimensional space of $|\alpha\rangle$ and $|\beta\rangle$, which helps us to preserve our rotation-based visualization. This requires the proof of the following theorem:

If the state vectors $|\alpha\rangle$ and $|\beta\rangle$ are defined according to (7.61) and (7.62) and both of them contain at least one nonzero probability amplitude, as well as the unitary operator U and an arbitrary state $|\eta\rangle$ are taken in such a way that $U|\eta\rangle$ lies within the vector space V spanned by the state vectors $|\alpha\rangle$ and $|\beta\rangle$, then the generalized Grover operator Q preserves this two-dimensional vector space. In other words for any $|v\rangle \in V$, $Q|v\rangle \in V$ is true.

Proof. Following the geometrical definition of the inner product, the projection of $U|\eta\rangle$ on vector $|\beta\rangle$ can be calculated as $\langle\beta|U|\eta\rangle \cdot |\beta\rangle$. Since $U|\eta\rangle$ is defined in the vector space V and it has unit length, vector $U|\eta\rangle - \langle\beta|U|\eta\rangle|\beta\rangle$ is parallel to $|\alpha\rangle$ and it can be computed in the following way

$$
U|\eta\rangle - \langle\beta|U|\eta\rangle|\beta\rangle = \sqrt{1 - |\langle\beta|U|\eta\rangle|^2}|\alpha\rangle,
$$

from which $|\alpha\rangle$ can be expressed in the nontrivial case, i.e. if $|\langle\beta|U|\eta\rangle| \neq 1$ as

$$
|\alpha\rangle = \frac{1}{\sqrt{1 - |\langle\beta|U|\eta\rangle|^2}} \left(U|\eta\rangle - \langle\beta|U|\eta\rangle|\beta\rangle \right).
$$

Vector $|\mu\rangle$ is considered as an arbitrary unit vector in V

$$|\mu\rangle_2 = \cos{(\Omega)}\,|\alpha\rangle + \sin{(\Omega)}\,e^{j\Lambda}|\beta\rangle, \tag{7.65}$$

where $\Omega, \Lambda \in [-\pi, \pi]$ and the subscript 2 refers to the two-dimensional representation of originally N-dimensional $|\mu\rangle$. The global phase was omitted in (7.65) since it does not influence the operation and the final result.

In order to reach the well-tried rotation-based picture of searching, the generalized Grover operator should be determined in V where the required two-dimensional Grover matrix is searched in the form of

$$\mathbf{Q_2} = \begin{bmatrix} Q_{11} & Q_{12} \\ Q_{21} & Q_{22} \end{bmatrix}. \tag{7.66}$$

Now we are able to compute the effect of Q on the basis vectors $|\alpha\rangle$ and $|\beta\rangle$. Provided the resulting vectors remain in V then this property will be valid for their arbitrary linear combination (superposition) $|v\rangle = a|\alpha\rangle + b|\beta\rangle$ because of the superposition principle. Therefore we apply Q for basis vector $|\beta\rangle$ first

$$Q|\beta\rangle = -\left(I + \left(e^{j\theta} - 1\right)|\mu\rangle\langle\mu|\right)I_\beta|\beta\rangle. \tag{7.67}$$

As I_β multiplies[6] every index leading to a marked entry by $e^{j\phi}$, i.e. $|\beta\rangle$ is an eigenvector of I_β with eigenvalue $e^{j\phi}$ thus

$$I_\beta|\beta\rangle = e^{j\phi}|\beta\rangle. \tag{7.68}$$

Substituting (7.68) into (7.67) we get

$$Q|\beta\rangle = -e^{j\phi}\left(\left(e^{j\theta} - 1\right)\langle\mu|\beta\rangle|\mu\rangle + |\beta\rangle\right). \tag{7.69}$$

Applying (7.65) and relation $\langle\mu|\beta\rangle = \langle\beta|\mu\rangle^* = \sin{(\Omega)}\,e^{-j\Lambda}$

$$
\begin{aligned}
Q|\beta\rangle &= -e^{j\phi}\left(e^{j\theta} - 1\right)\sin{(\Omega)}\,e^{-j\Lambda}\left(\cos{(\Omega)}\,|\alpha\rangle + \sin{(\Omega)}\,e^{j\Lambda}|\beta\rangle\right) - e^{j\phi}|\beta\rangle \\
&= \underbrace{-e^{j\phi}\left(e^{j\theta} - 1\right)\sin{(\Omega)}\cos{(\Omega)}\,e^{-j\Lambda}}_{Q_{21}}|\alpha\rangle
\end{aligned}
$$

$$+ \underbrace{-e^{j\phi}\left[\left(e^{j\theta} - 1\right)\sin^2{(\Omega)} + 1\right]}_{Q_{22}}|\beta\rangle. \tag{7.70}$$

Moreover, the other two entries in $\mathbf{Q}$ can be determined by feeding Q with $|\alpha\rangle$

$$Q|\alpha\rangle = -\left(I + \left(e^{j\theta} - 1\right)|\mu\rangle\langle\mu|\right)I_\beta|\alpha\rangle, \tag{7.71}$$

where $I_\beta|\alpha\rangle = |\alpha\rangle$, because only those indices belonging to solutions of the searching problem are rotated by I_β others are left unchanged.[7] Exploiting the

---

[6]The Oracle O did the same using multiplication factor -1.
[7]Thus $|\alpha\rangle$ and 1 are the eigenvector and eigenvalue of I_β respectively.

relation

$$\langle\mu|\alpha\rangle = \langle\alpha|\mu\rangle^* = \cos(\Omega) \tag{7.72}$$

we get the missing two elements

$$Q|\alpha\rangle = \underbrace{-\left[1 + \left(e^{j\theta} - 1\right)\cos^2(\Omega)\right]|\alpha\rangle}_{Q_{11}} + \underbrace{-\left[\left(e^{j\theta} - 1\right)\cos(\Omega)\sin(\Omega)e^{j\Lambda}\right]|\beta\rangle}_{Q_{12}}.$$

$$\tag{7.73}$$

Now, the reader may conclude from (7.70) and (7.73) that $Q|\alpha\rangle$ and $Q|\beta\rangle$ did not leave vector space V, therefore all their linear superpositions $|v\rangle = a|\alpha\rangle + b|\beta\rangle$ transformed by Q still remain in V.

Based on equations (7.70) and (7.73) we have matrix $\mathbf{Q_2}$ in a suitable two-dimensional form

$$\mathbf{Q_2} = -\begin{bmatrix} 1 + \left(e^{j\theta} - 1\right)\cos^2(\Omega) & e^{j\phi}\left(e^{j\theta} - 1\right)\sin(\Omega)\cos(\Omega)e^{j\Lambda} \\ \left(e^{j\theta} - 1\right)\cos(\Omega)\sin(\Omega)e^{-j\Lambda} & e^{j\phi}\left[1 + \left(e^{j\theta} - 1\right)\sin^2(\Omega)\right] \end{bmatrix}$$

$$= -\begin{bmatrix} e^{j\theta}\cos^2(\Omega) + \sin^2(\Omega) & e^{j\phi}e^{-j\Lambda}\left(e^{j\theta} - 1\right)\frac{\sin(2\Omega)}{2} \\ \left(e^{j\theta} - 1\right)e^{j\Lambda}\frac{\sin(2\Omega)}{2} & e^{j\phi}\left[e^{j\theta}\sin^2(\Omega) + \cos^2(\Omega)\right] \end{bmatrix}.$$

From this point forward $\mathbf{Q}$ always refers to the two-dimensional Grover matrix, if not indicated otherwise.

7.5.2 Required number of iterations in the generalized Grover algorithm

Having obtained the two-dimensional generalized Grover operator Q, we try to follow the rotation-based representation of the search. Therefore the optimal number of iterations (Grover gates) l_s required to find a marked item with sure success should be derived. Starting from initial state $|\gamma_1\rangle$ sure success can be provided if

$$\langle\alpha|Q^{l_s}|\gamma_1\rangle = 0, \tag{7.74}$$

which stands for having an index register orthogonal to the vector including all the indices which do not lead to a solution. Because $|\alpha\rangle$ and $|\beta\rangle$ are orthogonal and $|\gamma_1\rangle \in V$, this assumption can be interpreted as $Q^{l_s}|\gamma_1\rangle$ is parallel to $|\beta\rangle$, i.e. $Q^{l_s}|\gamma_1\rangle = e^{j\delta}|\beta\rangle$. In this case sure success can be reached after a single measurement. Since Q is unitary and therefore it is a normal operator too, it has a spectral decomposition

$$Q = q_1|\psi_1\rangle\langle\psi_1| + q_2|\psi_2\rangle\langle\psi_2|, \tag{7.75}$$

where $q_{1,2}$ denote the eigenvalues of Q and $|\psi_{1,2}\rangle$ stand for the corresponding eigenvectors, respectively. Thus the following equalities hold

$$Q|\psi_{1,2}\rangle = q_{1,2}|\psi_{1,2}\rangle, \tag{7.76}$$

where $\langle \psi_1 | \psi_2 \rangle = 0$, because of the orthogonality property of the eigenvectors of any normal operators. The eigenvalues which can be determined from the characteristic equation $\det (\mathbf{Q} - q\mathbf{I}) = 0$ are

$$q_{1,2} = -e^{j\left(\frac{\theta + \phi}{2} \pm \Upsilon\right)}. \tag{7.77}$$

In addition we claim the following restriction on angle Υ

$$\cos(\Upsilon) = \cos\left(\frac{\theta - \phi}{2}\right) + \sin^2(\Omega) \left(\cos\left(\frac{\theta + \phi}{2}\right) - \cos\left(\frac{\theta - \phi}{2}\right)\right). \tag{7.78}$$

In possession of the eigenvalues the next step towards the optimal number of iterations is the determination of the normalized eigenvectors $|\psi_{1,2}\rangle$, which are

$$|\psi_1\rangle = \cos(z)\, e^{j\left(\frac{\phi}{2} - \Lambda\right)} |\alpha\rangle + \sin(z)\, |\beta\rangle, \tag{7.79}$$

$$|\psi_2\rangle = -\sin(z)\, e^{j\left(\frac{\phi}{2} - \Lambda\right)} |\alpha\rangle + \cos(z)\, |\beta\rangle, \tag{7.80}$$

where

$$\sin^2(z) = \frac{\sin^2(2\Omega) \sin^2\left(\frac{\theta}{2}\right)}{2\left(1 - \cos\left(\frac{\theta}{2}\right) \cos\left(\frac{\phi}{2} - \Upsilon\right) - 2\cos(2\Omega) \sin\left(\frac{\theta}{2}\right) \sin\left(\frac{\phi}{2} - \Upsilon\right)\right)}.$$

The detailed derivation of the eigenvectors and eigenvalues can be found in Appendices 13.1 and 13.2.

Having the required elements of the spectral decomposition of Q we are able to calculate the operator representing the l-times repetition of Q

$$Q^l = q_1^l |\psi_1\rangle\langle\psi_1| + q_2^l |\psi_2\rangle\langle\psi_2| = (-1)^l\, e^{j \cdot l\left(\frac{\theta + \phi}{2}\right)}$$

$$\cdot \begin{bmatrix} e^{j2\left(\frac{\phi}{2} - \Lambda\right)} \left(e^{jl\Upsilon} \cos^2(z) + e^{-jl\Upsilon} \sin^2(z)\right) & j \sin(l\Upsilon) \sin(2z)\, e^{j\left(\frac{\phi}{2} - \Lambda\right)} \\ j \sin(l\Upsilon) \sin(2z)\, e^{-j\left(\frac{\phi}{2} - \Lambda\right)} & e^{jl\Upsilon} \sin^2(z) + e^{-jl\Upsilon} \cos^2(z) \end{bmatrix}, \tag{7.81}$$

where we exploited the fact that $\langle\psi_1|\psi_2\rangle = \langle\psi_2|\psi_1\rangle = 0$. Based on (7.81) the optimal l_s enabling sure success can be derived using (7.74) which is fulfilled if both – the real and the imaginary – parts of $\langle\alpha|Q^{l_s}|\gamma_1\rangle$ are equal to zero.

Let $|\gamma_1\rangle$ be defined as an arbitrary unit vector in V standing for the initial state of the index qregister

$$|\gamma_1\rangle = \cos\left(\frac{\Omega_\gamma}{2}\right) |\alpha\rangle + \sin\left(\frac{\Omega_\gamma}{2}\right) e^{j\Lambda_\gamma} |\beta\rangle. \tag{7.82}$$

Thus (7.74) becomes

$$\langle\alpha|Q^{l_s}|\gamma_1\rangle = \cos\left(\frac{\Omega_\gamma}{2}\right) Q_{11}^{l_s} + \sin\left(\frac{\Omega_\gamma}{2}\right) e^{j\Lambda_\gamma} Q_{12}^{l_s}$$

$$= \cos\left(\frac{\Omega_\gamma}{2}\right) \left[e^{jl_s\Upsilon} \cos^2(z) + e^{-jl_s\Upsilon} \sin^2(z)\right]$$

$$+ je^{j\left(\frac{\phi}{2} - \Lambda + \Lambda_\gamma\right)} \sin(l_s\Upsilon) \sin(2z) \sin\left(\frac{\Omega_\gamma}{2}\right) = 0. \tag{7.83}$$

First we calculate the real part of (7.83)

$$\Re\left\{\langle\alpha|Q^{l_s}|\gamma_1\rangle\right\} = \cos\left(\frac{\Omega_\gamma}{2}\right)\underbrace{\left[\cos\left(l_s\Upsilon\right)\cos^2\left(z\right) + \cos\left(l_s\Upsilon\right)\sin^2\left(z\right)\right]}_{\cos(l_s\Upsilon)}$$

$$-\sin\left(\Lambda_\gamma - \Lambda + \frac{\phi}{2}\right)\sin\left(l_s\Upsilon\right)\sin\left(2z\right)\sin\left(\frac{\Omega_\gamma}{2}\right)$$

$$= \cos\left(\frac{\Omega_\gamma}{2}\right)\cos\left(l_s\Upsilon\right)$$

$$-\sin\left(\frac{\Omega_\gamma}{2}\right)\sin\left(l_s\Upsilon\right)\sin\left(2z\right)\sin\left(\Lambda_\gamma - \Lambda + \frac{\phi}{2}\right) = 0,$$

$$(7.84)$$

which is followed by the imaginary part

$$\Im\left\{\langle\alpha|Q^{l_s}|\gamma_1\rangle\right\} = \cos\left(\frac{\Omega_\gamma}{2}\right)\underbrace{\left[\sin\left(l_s\Upsilon\right)\cos^2\left(z\right) - \sin\left(l_s\Upsilon\right)\sin^2\left(z\right)\right]}_{\sin(l_s\Upsilon)\cos(2z)}$$

$$+ \cos\left(\Lambda_\gamma - \Lambda + \frac{\phi}{2}\right)\sin\left(l_s\Upsilon\right)\sin\left(2z\right)\sin\left(\frac{\Omega_\gamma}{2}\right) = 0.$$

$$(7.85)$$

Let us first consider that $\sin\left(l_s\Upsilon\right) = 0 \Rightarrow \cos\left(l_s\Upsilon\right) = 1$. In this case the real part of (7.84) is simplified to

$$\cos\left(\frac{\Omega_\gamma}{2}\right)\cos\left(l_s\Upsilon\right) = \cos\left(\frac{\Omega_\gamma}{2}\right) = 0 \Rightarrow \Omega_\gamma = 0 \pm k\pi,$$

while the imaginary part equals constantly 0. Therefore this scenario represents the situation where all the entries are unmarked. Conversely if $\sin\left(l_s\Upsilon\right) \neq 0$ then

$$\frac{\Im\left\{\langle\alpha|Q^{l_s}|\gamma_1\rangle\right\}}{\sin\left(l_s\Upsilon\right)} = \cos\left(\Lambda_\gamma - \Lambda + \frac{\phi}{2}\right)\sin\left(2z\right)\sin\left(\frac{\Omega_\gamma}{2}\right)$$

$$+ \cos\left(\frac{\Omega_\gamma}{2}\right)\cos\left(2z\right) = 0. \qquad (7.86)$$

Equation (7.86) does not depend on l_s, which makes it suitable to determine the so-called 'matching condition' (MC), the relationship between θ and ϕ

$$\cos\left(\Lambda_\gamma - \Lambda + \frac{\phi}{2}\right) = -\cot\left(2z\right)\cot\left(\frac{\Omega_\gamma}{2}\right),$$

and thus

$$\tan\left(\frac{\phi}{2}\right) = \frac{\cos\left(2\Omega\right) + \sin\left(2\Omega\right)\cdot\tan\left(\frac{\Omega_\gamma}{2}\right)\cos\left(\Lambda - \Lambda_\gamma\right)}{\cot\left(\frac{\theta}{2}\right) - \tan\left(\frac{\Omega_\gamma}{2}\right)\sin\left(2\Omega\right)\sin\left(\Lambda - \Lambda_\gamma\right)}. \qquad (7.87)$$

It is worth emphasizing that according to (7.78) Υ seems to be 4π periodical in function of θ, which implies 4π periodicity for ϕ as well when determining ϕ from θ because Υ also depends on ϕ. This seems to be inconsistent with the fact that eigenvalues $q_{1,2}$ should be 2π periodical in θ and ϕ, see (7.77). This problem can be resolved if $\phi(\theta)$ is calculated for the range $[-2\pi, 2\pi]$ in function of $\theta \in [-2\pi, 2\pi]$. Practically $\pm 2\pi$ should be added to ϕ if it has a cut-off at certain θs. The points where $\phi(\theta)$ has cut-offs within the range of $[-2\pi, 2\pi]$ can be determined easily in the following manner

$$\phi = \pm \pi \Rightarrow \tan\left(\frac{\phi}{2}\right) = \pm \infty.$$

Since the numerator of the matching condition in (7.87) is constant in θ, the denominator has to be zero to achieve the condition $\phi = \pm \infty$. The cut-off angles $\theta_{co_{1,2}}$ can be derived from the denominator of (7.87) as follows

$$\cot\left(\frac{\theta}{2}\right) = \tan\left(\frac{\Omega_\gamma}{2}\right) \sin(2\Omega) \sin(\Lambda - \Lambda_\gamma)$$

thus the cut-off angles in $[-2\pi, 2\pi]$ are

$$\theta_{co_1} = 2\operatorname{arccot}\left(\tan\left(\frac{\Omega_\gamma}{2}\right) \sin(2\Omega) \sin(\Lambda - \Lambda_\gamma)\right), \tag{7.88}$$

$$\theta_{co_2} = \theta_{co_1} \pm 2\pi. \tag{7.89}$$

We depicted $\phi(\theta)$ with and without the $\pm 2\pi$ correction in Fig. 7.15. The cut-off points are in this case $\theta = \pm \pi$. By means of this correction 2π periodicity of Υ is achieved, hence the eigenvalues and eigenvectors of Q; even Q itself can boast a 2π periodicity in θ.

Now, the way is open to determine l_s from (7.84) supporting a final measurement with $P_s = 1$. The matching condition (7.87) should also be considered leading to

$$\cos\left(l_s \Upsilon + \arcsin\left(\sin\left(\frac{\phi}{2} - \Lambda + \Lambda_\gamma\right) \sin\left(\frac{\Omega_\gamma}{2}\right)\right)\right) = 0,$$

which is equivalent to

$$l_s \Upsilon = \pm \frac{\pi}{2} \pm i\pi - \arcsin\left(\sin\left(\frac{\phi}{2} - \Lambda + \Lambda_\gamma\right) \sin\left(\frac{\Omega_\gamma}{2}\right)\right), \tag{7.90}$$

where $\pm i\pi, i > 1$ can be omitted from the right-hand side, because it would result in a bigger l_s than absolutely necessary. Unlike the basic algorithm where $i > 0$ could result in a more accurate measurement – in exchange of increased number of rotations – in the case of the generalized algorithm $i = 0, 1$ can provide $P_\varepsilon = 0$. Expression (7.90) can be interpreted in the following way. The generalized Grover operator (Q) rotates the new initial state $|\gamma_1\rangle'$ having the initial angle

$$\frac{\Omega_\gamma'}{2} = \arcsin\left(\sin\left(\frac{\phi}{2} - \Lambda + \Lambda_\gamma\right) \sin\left(\frac{\Omega_\gamma}{2}\right)\right) \tag{7.91}$$

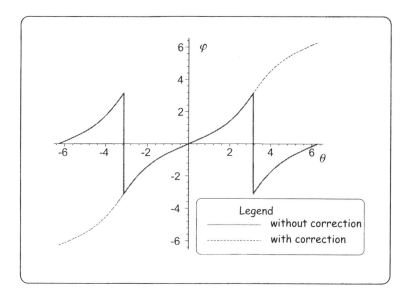

Fig. 7.15 The matching condition between ϕ and θ with and without correction assuming $\Omega = 0.5$, $\frac{\Omega_\gamma}{2} = 0.0001$, $\Lambda_\gamma = 0.004$, $\Lambda = 0.004$

in a plane V' spanned by the basis vectors $|\alpha\rangle'$ and $|\beta\rangle'$ with a rotation angle Υ towards $|\beta\rangle'$ as it is depicted in Fig. 7.16. It has to be remarked that $|\alpha\rangle'$ and $|\beta\rangle'$ are real valued axes while $|\alpha\rangle$ and $|\beta\rangle$ are complex valued. Because of the arbitrary sign of $\sin\left(\frac{\phi}{2} - \Lambda + \Lambda_\gamma\right)$, $\frac{\Omega'_\gamma}{2}$ can take different values depending on

$$\nu = \arcsin\left(\sin\left(\frac{\phi}{2} - \Lambda + \Lambda_\gamma\right)\sin\left(\frac{\Omega_\gamma}{2}\right)\right), \tag{7.92}$$

where $\arcsin(\cdot)$ is defined as

$$|\arcsin(\cdot)| \leq \frac{\pi}{2}.$$

If ν is positive the initial angle $\frac{\Omega'_\gamma}{2}$ could be $(\pi - \nu)$ or (ν), in the other case the possible values are $(-\pi+\nu)$ or $(-\nu)$ (see Fig. 7.17). Substituting matching condition into (7.78) it becomes obvious that

$$\Upsilon \in \begin{cases} \left[0, \dfrac{\pi}{2}\right] & \text{if } \dfrac{\Omega'_\gamma}{2} \in \text{I. or III. quadrant} \\[3mm] \left[-\dfrac{\pi}{2}, 0\right) & \text{if } \dfrac{\Omega'_\gamma}{2} \in \text{II. or IV. quadrant} \end{cases}$$

and because $+|\beta\rangle'$ is as appropriate for the final state as $-|\beta\rangle'$ therefore $\pm|\beta\rangle'$ can be reached from any interpretation of $\frac{\Omega'_\gamma}{2}$ by means of an overall rotation smaller

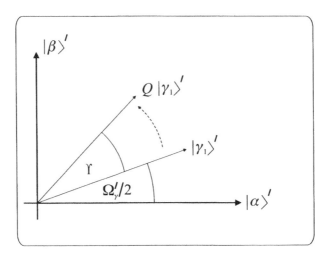

Fig. 7.16   Geometrical interpretation of the generalized Grover iteration

than $\frac{\pi}{2}$ (see Fig. 7.17). Υ can be seen in function of θ in Fig. 7.18. The number of iterations l_s ensuring sure success can be expressed from (7.90) as

$$l_s = \frac{\frac{\pi}{2} - \left| \arcsin\left(\sin\left(\frac{\phi(\theta)}{2} - \Lambda + \Lambda_\gamma\right)\sin\left(\frac{\Omega_\gamma}{2}\right)\right)\right|}{\Upsilon}, \tag{7.93}$$

where the absolute value operator is omitted in the denominator because

$$0 \leq \arccos\left(\cdot\right) \leq \pi$$

has been assumed.

However, we need an integer number of rotations in practice, moreover it is worth investigating the effect of different variables determining l_s especially ϕ which is restricted by the matching condition, therefore the next subsection is dedicated to these questions.

7.5.3   Design considerations of the generalized Grover operator

In order to build the generalized Grover operator one has to define θ, ϕ and $|\mu\rangle$. On one hand the first two parameters have fixed relation via the matching condition, on the other hand Q provides sure success, therefore the design process of Q can be traced back to minimizing l_s in function of θ and $|\mu\rangle$. To achieve this goal we investigate several scenarios differing in the amount of available information.

The basic Grover algorithm
As the first scenario we analyze the original Grover algorithm (see Section 7.1) as a special case of the generalized one. Thus we have the following setup: $\theta = \phi = \pi$,

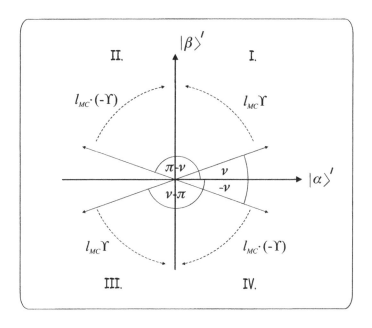

Fig. 7.17   Different possible interpretations of $|\gamma_1\rangle'$

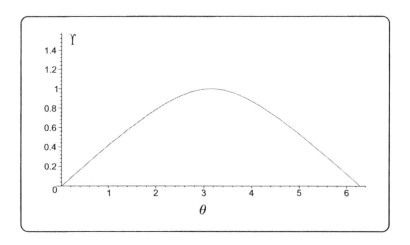

Fig. 7.18 Υ vs. θ assuming $\Omega = 0.5$, $\frac{\Omega_\gamma}{2} = 0.0001$, $\Lambda_\gamma = 0.004$, $\Lambda = 0.004$

$U = H$, $|\eta\rangle = |0\rangle$. Furthermore we know that input state $|\gamma_1\rangle$ equals the axis of the inversion about average $|\mu\rangle$ that is $\Lambda = \Lambda_\gamma = 0$ as well as $\Omega = \frac{\Omega_\gamma}{2} =$ arcsin $\left(\sqrt{M/N} \right)$.

In possession of this information let us calculate the corresponding Υ using (7.78)

$$\cos(\Upsilon) = \cos \overbrace{\left(\frac{\theta - \phi}{2} \right)}^{=1} + \sin^2 (\Omega) \cdot \left(\overbrace{\cos \left(\frac{\theta + \phi}{2} \right)}^{=-1} - \overbrace{\cos \left(\frac{\theta - \phi}{2} \right)}^{=1} \right)$$

$$= \cos^2 \left(2 \frac{\Omega_\gamma}{2} \right) - \sin^2 \left(2 \frac{\Omega_\gamma}{2} \right) = \cos \left(\Omega_\gamma \right), \tag{7.94}$$

from which $\Upsilon = \Omega_\gamma$ and thus the optimal number of iterations from (7.93)

$$l_{opt} = \frac{\frac{\pi}{2} - \left| \arcsin \left(\sin \left(\frac{\phi}{2} - \Lambda + \Lambda_\gamma \right) \sin \left(\frac{\Omega_\gamma}{2} \right) \right) \right|}{\Upsilon} = \frac{\frac{\pi}{2} - \frac{\Omega_\gamma}{2}}{\Omega_\gamma},$$

which is nothing more than the required number of rotations l_{opt_0} (7.23) in the basic Grover algorithm. Unfortunately choosing the predefined fixed relation $\theta = \phi = \pi$ does not guarantee sure success by all means, because the matching condition may be violated.

Providing sure success by modifying the basic Grover algorithm
Now we try to measure one of the marked entries with $P_s = 1$. To achieve this we keep all the previous parameters, except θ and ϕ are adjusted according to the matching condition, i.e. $\phi(\theta)$ becomes a function of θ. Remember that Ω_γ is available from performing a quantum counting (see Section 7.2.1) with $\theta = \phi = \pi$. The optimal θ_{opt} which minimizes l_s can be computed solving

$$\frac{dl_s(\phi(\theta), \theta)}{d\theta} = \frac{\partial l_s(\phi(\theta), \theta)}{\partial \phi(\theta)} \cdot \frac{d\phi(\theta)}{d\theta} + \frac{\partial l_s(\phi(\theta), \theta)}{\partial \theta} = 0,$$

i.e. we determine the minimum point of l_s in Fig. 7.19. In order to be able to substitute $\phi(\theta)$ into (7.78) and (7.93) one has to evaluate the matching condition (7.87) assuming the given parameter setup

$$\tan \left(\frac{\phi}{2} \right) = \frac{\cos \left(2 \frac{\Omega_\gamma}{2} \right) + \sin \left(2 \frac{\Omega_\gamma}{2} \right) \cdot \tan \left(\frac{\Omega_\gamma}{2} \right) \overbrace{\cos \left(\Lambda - \Lambda_\gamma \right)}^{=1}}{\cot \left(\frac{\theta}{2} \right) - \tan \left(\frac{\Omega_\gamma}{2} \right) \sin \left(2 \frac{\Omega_\gamma}{2} \right) \underbrace{\sin \left(\Lambda - \Lambda_\gamma \right)}_{=0}}$$

$$= \tan \left(\frac{\theta}{2} \right) \cdot \left(\cos(\Omega_\gamma) + \sin(\Omega_\gamma) \tan \left(\frac{\Omega_\gamma}{2} \right) \right)$$

$$= \tan \left(\frac{\theta}{2} \right) \cdot (\cos(\Omega_\gamma) + 1 - \cos(\Omega_\gamma)) = \tan \left(\frac{\theta}{2} \right),$$

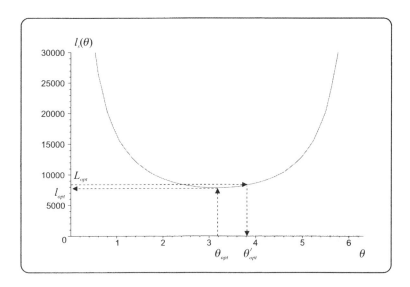

Fig. 7.19 Number of iterations l_s vs. θ assuming the matching condition is fulfilled and $\Omega = 0.0001$, $\frac{\Omega_\gamma}{2} = 0.0001$, $\Lambda_\gamma = \Lambda = 0$

where we exploited basic trigonometric relation $\tan\left(\frac{x}{2}\right) \equiv \frac{1-\cos(x)}{\sin(x)}$. We reached an important result, namely to provide sure success we need $\theta = \phi$. Substituting this special matching condition into (7.78)

$$\cos(\Upsilon) = \cos\left(\frac{\phi-\phi}{2}\right) + \sin^2\left(\frac{\Omega_\gamma}{2}\right) \cdot \left(\cos\left(\frac{\phi+\phi}{2}\right) - \cos\left(\frac{\phi-\phi}{2}\right)\right)$$

$$= \cos(\phi)\sin^2\left(\frac{\Omega_\gamma}{2}\right) + \cos^2\left(\frac{\Omega_\gamma}{2}\right).$$

Now we can turn to minimize l_s in θ

$$l_s(\theta) = \frac{\frac{\pi}{2} - \left|\arcsin\left(\sin\left(\frac{\phi}{2}\right)\sin\left(\frac{\Omega_\gamma}{2}\right)\right)\right|}{\arccos\left(\cos(\phi)\sin^2\left(\frac{\Omega_\gamma}{2}\right) + \cos^2\left(\frac{\Omega_\gamma}{2}\right)\right)}.$$

However, instead of beginning long-lasting derivations the reader may realize that the denominator has a maximum if $\cos(\phi) = 1 \Rightarrow \phi = \pi$ and the numerator has a minimum if $\sin\left(\frac{\phi}{2}\right) = 1 \Rightarrow \phi = \pi$ therefore $\theta_{opt} = \phi_{opt} = \pi$, which is the original setup of the basic Grover algorithm. *Thus the basic Grover algorithm proves to be optimal in terms of the number of database queries if we have no a priori information about the database, i.e. it is really unsorted.*

We depicted $l_s(\theta)$ in Fig. 7.19. Since $l_{opt} = l_s(\theta_{opt})$ is not an integer, the nearest superior integer L_{opt} has to be taken into account. In consequence of this deferral, the matching condition is affected, which requires the calibration of angle θ and ϕ. In possession of L_{opt} we can calculate ϕ'_{opt} from (7.93) and substituting it into (7.87) we get θ'_{opt}. Obviously there are two such values for θ but we present only one of them in Fig. 7.19.

Finally we would like to emphasize that to achieve a sure success searching algorithm we did not need to increase the number of database queries compared to the basic algorithm, instead the Oracle and the phase gate were modified!

Starting from an arbitrary initial state
The initial state of the index qreqister was set to $|\gamma_1\rangle = H|0\rangle$ in the case of the basic Grover algorithm since we had no information about the structure of the database, i.e. it was considered as being unsorted. However, as we mentioned in the introduction of this subsection there are practical problems when we have some *a priori* information about the database. Based on this information one can preprocess the index qregister amplifying the probability amplitudes of the marked states – even not uniformly – producing an arbitrary $|\gamma_1\rangle$, see (7.60). Is it possible to exploit this fact by means of the generalized Grover algorithm or shall we lose this advantage when returning to the uniformly distributed initial probability amplitudes of the index qregister of the basic algorithm? To answer this question we have to determine θ, ϕ and $|\mu\rangle$ in possession of $|\gamma_1\rangle$.

Obviously if we were familiar with which states are marked and unmarked then we are able to calculate $|\mu\rangle$ in such a way that a single rotation would provide sure success. As an example let us consider the basic Grover algorithm. Provided the axis of the inversion about the average is chosen to $\Omega = \frac{\frac{\pi}{2}+\frac{\Omega_\gamma}{2}}{2}$ then the reflection about $|\mu\rangle$ after applying the Oracle (reflecting $|\gamma_1\rangle$ onto $|\alpha\rangle$) will result in $|\beta\rangle$ (see Fig. 7.5).

Unfortunately when searching is needed this information is not available. Therefore the best we can do is to set $|\mu\rangle = |\gamma_1\rangle$, that is $\Omega = \frac{\Omega_\gamma}{2}$ and $\Lambda = \Lambda_\gamma$. Since the matching condition and thus l_{opt} depend only on the difference between Λ and Λ_γ their actual values do not influence the design of Q, i.e. $\Lambda - \Lambda_\gamma \equiv 0$. Since $|\gamma_1\rangle$ is known, $|\mu\rangle$ can be easily produced using an appropriate U. In order to minimize l_s in θ the only missing parameter is Ω. We showed in (7.77) that the eigenvalues of Q have the following form $q_{1,2} = -e^{j\left(\frac{\theta+\phi}{2}\pm\Upsilon\right)}$. Hence using a phase estimation with $\theta = \phi = \pi$ it returns Υ unambiguously from which Ω can be computed exploiting (7.78) and bearing in mind the actual values of θ and ϕ, namely $\Omega = \frac{\Upsilon(\theta=\pi,\phi=\pi)}{2}$ (see (7.94)). Next the same technique can be applied as for the enhanced basic Grover algorithm to determine ϕ'_{opt}, θ'_{opt} and the corresponding L_{opt}.

7.6 FURTHER READING

L. K. Grover published his fast database searching algorithm first in [70] and [68] using the diffusion matrix approach to illustrate the effect of the Grover operator, that took $\mathcal{O}(\sqrt{N})$ iterations to carry out the search, which is the optimal solution, as it was proved in [160]. Boyer, Brassard, Hoyer and Tapp [104] enhanced the original algorithm for more than one marked entry in the database and introduced upper bounds for the required number of evaluations.

After a short debate, Bennett, Bernstein, Brassard and Vazirani gave the first poof of the optimality of Grover's algorithm in [33]. The proof was refined by Zalka in [160] and [159].

Later the rotation in a two-dimensional state space (with the bases of separately superpositioned marked and unmarked states) the SU(2) approach was introduced by Boyer *et al.* in [104]. Within this book we followed this representation according to its popularity in the literature.

During the above-mentioned evolution of the Grover algorithm a new quest started to formulate the building blocks of the algorithm as generally as possible. The motivations for putting so much effort into this direction were on one hand to get a much deeper insight into the heart of the algorithm and on the other hand to overcome the main shortcoming of the algorithm, namely the sure success of finding a marked state cannot be guaranteed. In [69] the authors replaced the Hadamard transformation with an arbitrary unitary one. The next step was the introduction of arbitrary phase rotations in the Oracle and in the phase shifter instead of π in [67]. To provide sure success at the final measurement Brassard *et al.* [62] ran the original Grover algorithm, but for the final turn a special Grover operator with a smaller step was applied. Hoyer *et al.* [74] gave another ingenious solution of the problem. They modified the original Grover algorithm and the initial distribution.

To give another viewpoint Long *et al.* introduced the three-dimensional SO(3) picture in the description of Grover operator in [65]. The achievements were summarized and extended by Long [99] and an exact matching condition was derived for multiple marked states in [66]. Unfortunately the SO(3) picture is less picturesque and it misses the global phase factor before the measurement. In normal cases it does not cause any difficulty because measurement results are immune to it. However, if it is planned (we plan) to reuse the final state of the index register without measurement as the input of a further algorithm (operator), it is crucial to deal with the global phase. Therefore, Hsieh and Li [87] returned to the traditional two-dimensional SU(2) formulation and derived the same matching condition for one marked element as Long achieved but they saved the final global phase factor. One important part of these solutions, however, was missing. Namely, they required that the initial state should fit into the two-dimensional state space defined by the marked and unmarked states with uniform probability amplitudes. This gives large freedom for designers but encumbers the application of the generalized Grover algorithm as a building block of a larger quantum system.

Therefore another very important question within this topic proved to be the analysis of the evolution of the basic Grover algorithm when it is started from an arbitrary initial state, i.e. the amplitudes are either real or complex and follow any arbitrary distribution. In this case sure success cannot be guaranteed, but the probability of success can be maximized. Biham and his team first gave the analysis of the original Grover algorithm in [46] and [53]. In [54] the analysis was extended to the generalized Grover algorithm with arbitrary unitary transformation and phase rotations.

Within this book we combined and enhanced the results for the generalized Grover searching algorithm in terms of arbitrary initial distribution, arbitrary unitary transformation, arbitrary phase rotations and arbitrary number of marked items to construct an unsorted database search algorithm which can be included inside a quantum computing system. Because of its constructive nature this algorithm is capable of any amplitude distribution at its input, provides sure success in case of measurement and allows connecting its output to another algorithm if no measurement is performed. Of course, this approach assumes that the initial distribution is given and it determines all the other parameters according to the construction rules. However, readers who are interested in applying a predefined unitary transformation as the fixed parameter should settle for a restricted set of initial states and it is suggested that they look at [87].

Grover's database search algorithm assumes the knowledge of the number of marked states, but it is typical that we do not have this information in advance. Brassard *et al.* [61] gave the first valuable idea of how to estimate the missing number of marked states, which was enhanced in [62] and traced back to a phase estimation of the Grover operator.

A rather useful extension of the Grover algorithm is finding the minimum/maximum point of a cost function. Dürr and Hoyer suggested the first statistical method and bound to solve the problem in [32]. Later, based on this result, Ahuya and Kapoor improved the bounds in [1]. Both papers exploit the estimation of the expected number of iterations introduced in [104]. Unfortunately all these algorithms provide the extreme value efficiently in terms of expected value thus no reasonable upper bound for the number of required elementary steps can be given. This fact strongly restricts the usage of such solutions in real applications. Therefore we introduced another approach based on quantum existence testing.

Recently Grover emphasized in [71] that the number of elementary unitary operations can be reduced which launched a new quest for the most effective Grover structure in terms of the number of basic operations.

The Grover algorithm has been verified first experimentally in a liquid-state NMR system [81] and [88] with a few qbits. Bhattacharya and his colleagues reported the implementation of the quantum search algorithm using classical Fourier optics in [112].

8

Quantum-based Multi-user Detection

Every telecommunication system designed to provide services for more than one subscriber has to cope with the problem of medium access control (MAC), which regulates how to share the common medium (channel) among the users. Unlike traditional solutions where subscribers are separated in time, frequency or space, state of the art third/fourth generation mobile systems differentiate the users based on special individual codes assigned to each customer. Unfortunately performing optimal detection proves to be a hard task classically, therefore suitable suboptimal solutions are the focus of international research. However, quantum computing offers a direct way to the optimal solution because of its parallel processing capabilities.

Hence we introduce a mobile telecommunication oriented application based on quantum counting in this chapter: Section 8.1 explains the theoretical background of code division multiple access systems, highlights the related detection problem and gives the most trivial answer to it. Optimal detection criteria and their complexity are summarized and classical optimum detectors are discussed in Section 8.2. Finally we trace the optimal detection to quantum counting in Section 8.3.

8.1 INTRODUCTION TO CODE DIVISION MULTIPLE ACCESS AND CLASSICAL MULTI-USER DETECTION

Traditional telecommunication systems share the channel among the users in different ways:

TDMA Time Division Multiple Access ensures separation by assigning time slots to the users. The time axis consists of so-called frames which are repeated

Quantum Computing and Communications   S. Imre, F. Balázs
© 2004 John Wiley & Sons, Ltd   ISBN 0-470-86902-X (HB)

periodically. Each frame is subdivided into slots (channels) representing transmission opportunities for the customers.

FDMA Frequency Division Multiple Access supports distinction among subscribers by frequency. The available frequency spectrum is divided into frequency bands (channels). Signals which are limited within a certain band theoretically do not disturb signals of other users in different bands.

SDMA Space Division Multiple Access exploits the trivial fact that if radiations from directed antennas do not cross one another then users can be separated reliably.

Of course arbitrary combinations of the above approaches are allowed. For instance in the case of GSM 200 kHz bands are used with eight time slots in each.

Remark: While multiple access refers to the notion that information from sources placed on distributed locations are collected together (e.g. mobile terminals transmit to the same base station from different positions). The reverse process, when several pieces of information are collected together at a given point and then distributed among the subscribers, is called multiplexing and corresponding techniques are denoted by TDM, FDM and SDM respectively.

The above solutions have several advantages e.g. call admission control (CAC) becomes very simple since a new call can be accepted until we run out of channels, or by assigning time slots with different length we can easily adjust the network resources to various traffic demands. Unfortunately there are also some disadvantages. The most common and important one can be summarized in the following way. Although theoretically all the above-mentioned techniques ensure perfect separation of the users, this is not actually the case in practice. Since we are not able to build switches working infinitely fast or filters with infinite slope, or antennas with square-shaped lobes thus we need to apply guard slots, bands between adjacent channels to avoid mixed signals. However, these guard channels mean overhead, which decreases the spectral efficiency[1] of the system.

The ultimate idea to handle this problem was discovered during World War II when members of the resistance tried to prevent German eavesdropper teams intercepting radio messages and locating their positions via periodically changing the transmission frequency. If the sender and receiver have the same code table containing the sequences of frequency bands then they can listen to each other otherwise the eavesdropper can only guess the currently used frequency. Clearly speaking this approach enables users to be distinguished by means of non-overlapping (in the literature: *orthogonal*) code (frequency) sequences. Thus this technique is called *code division multiple access* (CDMA). As the reader may realize all the users use the same band, time slot and spatial region at the same time

---

[1] Spectral efficiency is one of the most important descriptors of a telecom system. It defines how many bits can be transmitted reliably in each second projected onto one Hz of bandwidth. Since network providers buy frequency bands typically at enormously high rates spectral efficiency strongly influences their returns.

without involving guard resources! The codes in this example hop among frequencies therefore it is referred to as *frequency hopping* (FH) CDMA. Beside enabling secure communications CDMA has another tremendous advantage. The fast changes in the signal because of the hopping produces high frequency components in the spectrum of the signal, that is the bandwidth of an FH-CDMA signal is much wider than that of the original narrowband one. This phenomenon is cited in the literature as spectrum spreading and related systems are known as *spread spectrum* (SS) systems. Therefore anybody who wants to blanket the radio transmission with a narrowband source will fail. This capability can be utilized against non-intentional interferers as well thus the reader may understand why CDMA based solutions are so popular in 3G/4G wireless systems.

Remark: The previous explanation concluded that combining spectrum spreading and code division multiple access has many advantages. However, in certain systems such as wireless local area networks (WLANs), where no central entity exists, which is responsible for distributing the codes among users, SS is used alone to combat the hostile nature of the radio channel while MAC is e.g. TDMA based.

8.1.1 DS-CDMA in theory

The most popular public land mobile networks (UMTS, IS-95, cdma2000, W-CDMA) apply another way to implement SS-CDMA. The reader can follow the operation of the system with Alice as sender and Bob as the receiver in Fig. 8.1. Alice has a sequence of symbols to transmit. For the sake of simplicity we assume that each symbol corresponds to one bit of the message. For practical reasons Alice produces +1 and -1 according to the logical value of the actual bit (0 or 1) with a certain transmission rate, say some kbps. Instead of feeding her antenna with these symbols directly she sends a binary chip sequence into the channel in place of each symbol. A symbol representing a certain chip can have a value +1 or -1 similar to the symbols substituting bits. The only difference is that the chip rate is much faster than the bit rate, say some Mbps. Keeping in view that we use ± 1 instead of 0/1 this procedure can be modelled as a multiplication of the two sequences in compliance with Fig. 8.2. Since the transmitted signal has fast variations the spectrum of the original signal becomes fairly wide after the multiplication. For example third-generation mobile systems use 5 MHz bandwidth compared to the GSM's 200 kHz. Roughly speaking this is the reason why these types of CDMA systems are called wideband CDMA or WCDMA. Equivalently T_c, representing the time duration of one chip, is significantly smaller than T_s, standing for the symbol's length.

Detection at the receiver side is very easy. Bob multiplies the received sequence chip by chip with the same chip sequence as Alice used previously and sums the products, i.e. he computes the inner product of the two sequences. He obtains $\pm PG$ if ± 1 has been sent, respectively, where PG – the so-called processing gain – denotes the length of the chip sequence. Thus a simple comparator is able to decide the original value of Alice's bit symbol.

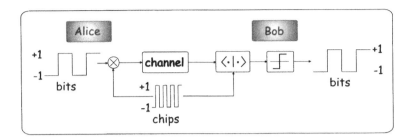

Fig. 8.1 Idealistic DS-CDMA architecture

So Alice and Bob can protect themselves from narrowband interferers, but how can they share the channel with Eve? The answer is fairly simple. An individual chip sequence has to be assigned to each user with the property that the sequences are orthogonal, that is their pairwise inner product equals zero. Thus as Fig. 8.3 explains Bob is able to detect a signal from Alice using Alice's chip sequence because the inner product operation suppresses the component from Eve in the received signal. Similarly Bob uses Eve's chip code when detecting her message. This pragmatic approach using spectrum spreading is called direct sequence CDMA (DS-CDMA).

In our example Alice is holding a mobile phone and her intention is to send signals to Bob. These signals are received by a special access point of the system the so-called base station (BS) (see Fig. 8.4). The BSs are connected to one another via the access and core networks in cellular mobile systems. Thus Alice's signal is received first at the closest base station to Alice, than it is delivered across the access-core-access networks (they are typically wired and use their own transmission schemes) to the base station whose range Bob is located in. Finally this latter base station sends Alice's bits applying DS-CDMA again to Bob's mobile. Now let us concentrate on the air interface of the above system. Alice is assumed to be the sender and Bob is playing the role of a base station's receiver. This set up is referred to as the *uplink* scenario, which describes the case when mobile terminals are transmitting and the base station is receiving the signals[2] (see Fig. 8.4).

8.1.2   DS-CDMA in practice

DS-CDMA works very well, in theory, where signals from different users remain orthogonal at the receiver. In practice, however, the radio channel proves to be much more hostile. It has deterministic modifications and e.g. random variations in signal strength and delay. Deterministic channel attenuation originates from the fact that mobile terminals are typically at different distances from the base station. We can fight against this effect using power control, that is the base station instructs the

---

[2]The opposite direction is called *downlink*.

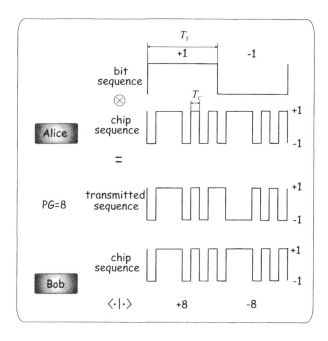

Fig. 8.2 Sequences, modulation and detection in DS-CDMA

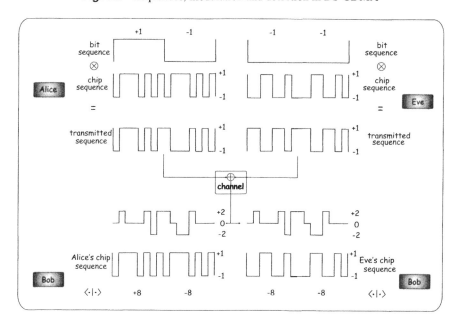

Fig. 8.3 Separation in the detector

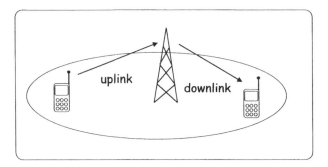

Fig. 8.4 Mobile access directions

mobiles to adjust their transmission powers so that all the signals are received with almost the same signal strength at the base station. Since the speed of light and thus that of electromagnetic radiation is constant, terminal positions with different distances around the base station cause differences in delays as well. This effect is further complicated if one considers that a transmitted signal may travel in different tracks with different lengths at the same time. This latter effect is referred to as *multi-path propagation*. Hence Bob does not know exactly when he has to start the inner product operation (detection). If he is late or in a hurry then orthogonality may be upset. We show a simple example for this effect in Fig. 8.5. While orthogonal code families can be produced easily by the reader as well, such code families whose members are orthogonal to any shifted versions of other members prove to be a really hard task even for experts. The suggested remedy to this problem is the so-called Rake receiver which applies the inner product operation with different shifted versions of the corresponding chip sequence at the same time and combines the results. Roughly speaking it can be regarded as a kind of synchronization.

Remark: We can conclude that orthogonality means the common basis of different medium access schemes. They achieve this property in different ways using frequency bands, time slots, spatial regions or codes. The difference lies in the important fact that the first three approaches have *hard limits* regarding the admitted users in the network, that is if we run out of e.g. form time slots then no subscriber can be accepted until somebody leaves the system. On the other hand a new user entering a CDMA system only decreases the orthogonality in the receivers, which produces more errors as a consequence but the number of acceptable users is only asymptotically limited, i.e. the more users we have the less transmission rates can be offered. Thus CDMA networks are much more flexible from this point of view, and we call them *soft limited* systems.

Random effects, however, are more dangerous. Random attenuation and delay may cause different weighting and shift of the individual signals in the received signal, which is advantageous for certain signals and disadvantageous for others in the detector when the inner product operation is performed. In order to describe these phenomena we derive the received signal $r(t)$ at the base station using

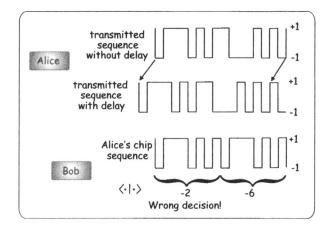

Fig. 8.5 Detection in the case of delayed signal

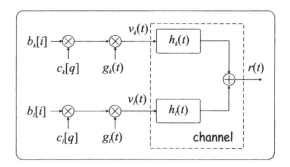

Fig. 8.6 DS-CDMA transmitter and channel

appropriate mathematical formalism. Similar to radio broadcasting each wireless system uses a different frequency band, which complicates the discussion because carrier frequencies have to be involved into the description. Clearly speaking we are interested in the baseband signals and carriers represent the unavoidable necessary evil element of the formalism. Fortunately a complex baseband-equivalent description allows omitting carriers and using complex valued functions instead of real ones, e.g. $r_{ekv}(t)$ instead of $r(t)$. Readers unfamiliar with this useful technique can find a brief summary in Section 14. From this point we consider complex baseband-equivalent signals and symbols therefore we omit the subscript *eqv*. We suggest following the steps of producing $r(t)$ in Fig. 8.6 which depicts the block diagram of the transmitter and the channel.

As we mentioned earlier an uplink DS-DCDMA system is investigated. The ith symbol of the kth $(k = 1, 2, \ldots, K)$ user is denoted by $b_k[i] \in \{+1, -1\}$. This assumption corresponds to the simplest scenario where symbols remain real-valued although we use the complex equivalent description. We call this type of modulation binary phase shift keying (BPSK). Its alphabet consists of only two elements. Of course higher level modulations with a larger symbol alphabet such as 16 quadrature amplitude modulation can be applied in practice, but from our point of view this fact would not influence the theoretical background of the detection therefore we use BPSK for the sake of simplicity.

In DS-CDMA systems an information-bearing bit is encoded by means of a user-specific chip code having the length of the processing gain (PG). Let $c_k[q]$ refer to the qth chip of the code word of subscriber k, and we chose again the simplest alphabet $c_k[q] \in \{+1, -1\}$. Since only continuous electromagnetic waveforms can be transmitted in the radio channel in practice each chip has to be multiplied with the so-called chip elementary waveform denoted by $g_k(t)$. Thus the analog version of the chip sequence is referred to as the user continuous *signature waveform*

$$s_k(t) = \sum_{q=0}^{PG-1} c_k[q]g_k(t - qT_c), \tag{8.1}$$

where T_c stands for the time duration of one chip. Obviously members of $\{s_k(t)\}$ are orthogonal concerning the symbol length T_s i.e.

$$\int_0^{T_s} s_k(t)s_l(t)dt \equiv 0, \quad \forall k \neq l, \tag{8.2}$$

and normalized

$$\int_0^{T_s} \Re^2(s_k(t))dt + \int_0^{T_s} \Im^2(s_k(t))dt = 1.$$

Thus the output signal of the kth user related to the ith symbol, denoted by $v_k(t)$, is given as

$$v_k(i, t) = b_k[i]s_k(t). \tag{8.3}$$

Alice sends strings of consecutive symbols called bursts. Let us assume that each burst consist of $R + 1$ symbols. Therefore we introduce vector $\mathbf{b}_k = [b_k[0], \ldots, b_k[R]]^T$ denoting the data symbols of the kth user in a certain burst. Thus the kth user's signal during this burst can be expressed as

$$v_k(t) = \sum_{i=0}^{R} b_k[i]s_k(t - iT_s). \tag{8.4}$$

Now, Alice's signal is sent out to the air. We apply here a widely used channel model and remark that of course other, more sophisticated models are also available in the literature (see *Further Reading*). However, the selected model contains the most important impacts and does not require us to be lost in details. The channel distortion from the kth user point of view is modelled via an impulse response function as if the channel were a filter

$$h_k(i, t) = a_k[i]\delta(t - \tau_k),$$

where $a_k[i] = A_k[i]e^{j\alpha_k[i]}$ with real $A_k[i]$ and $\alpha_k[i]$. $a_k[i]$ comprises phenomena causing the random nature of the channel and it is called *fading*. $A_k[i]$, $\alpha_k[i]$ and τ_k are typically independent random variables while let us suppose as the worst case that they are uniformly distributed about the following regions:

$$A_k[i] \in [-A, A]; \quad \alpha_k[i] \in [0, 2\pi]; \quad \tau_k \in [0, T_s].$$

Deterministic attenuation is omitted since it can be handled using power control. Similarly we do not consider Gaussian noise because CDMA systems are strongly interference limited thus Gaussian noise has marginal influence on detection. Finally we assume that τ_k remains constant during each burst while $a_k[i]$ varies from symbol to symbol. The channel not only delays and distorts Alice's transmitted signal but also adds together all the signals originating from other users, hence we are able to describe the received signal at the base station via convolving the channel input with its impulse response in the following manner

$$r(t) = \sum_{k=1}^{K}\sum_{i=0}^{R} h_k(i, t) * v_k(i, t) = \sum_{k=1}^{K}\sum_{i=0}^{R} a_k[i]b_k[i]s_k(t - iT_S - \tau_k). \quad (8.5)$$

8.2   OPTIMAL MULTI-USER DETECTION

Now, having received $r(t)$ at the base station Bob would like to extract (demodulate) Alice's signal. Let us assume that $\tau_k = 0$ and $a_k = 1$ deterministically (equivalently the channel is regarded as a shortcut or an identity transformation). In this case the received signal becomes

$$r(i, t) = \sum_{k=1}^{K} b_k[i]s_k(t), \quad (8.6)$$

considering the interval belonging to the ith symbol.

Bob tries to obtain a fairly good estimation $\tilde{b}_k[i]$ using the orthogonality of signature waveforms according to (8.2). This requires multiplication with Alice's waveform $s_k(t)$ and integration on $[0, T_s]$ (see Fig. 8.7). This operation is nothing more than the calculation of the inner product for continuous variables. Bearing in mind the often used notion for this operation in the literature we call it a *matched filter*. Let us denote the output of the matched filter in case of the ith symbol

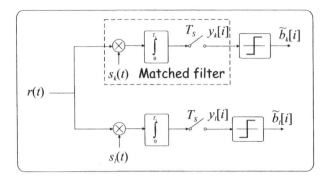

Fig. 8.7   Single-user DS-CDMA detector with matched filter, idealistic case

with $y_k[i]$

$$
y_k[i] = \int_0^{T_s} r(i,t)s_k(t)dt
$$

$$
= \int_0^{T_s} b_k[i]s_k(t)s_k(t)dt + \int_0^{T_s} \sum_{l=1,l\neq k}^{K} b_l[i]s_l(t)s_k(t)dt = b_k[i]. \qquad (8.7)
$$

Thus theoretically the output of the matched filter contains information only about $b_k[i]$ and its sign can be used to decide which symbol has been sent by applying a comparator. Therefore Bob can use $y_k[i]$ directly to determine $\tilde{b}_k[i] = \mathrm{sgn}(y_k[i])$.

As we discussed earlier orthogonality may be violated because of the random delays in the channel. In a realistic scenario the above introduced detector may fail with certain probability. Optimal solutions minimize this probability by possessing additional information. If we insist on using only Alice's signature waveform to detect symbols originating from Alice then this technique is referred to as *single-user detection*. This approach can be appropriate when the detector is located in a mobile terminal whose computational power is moderated. However, sitting at a base station's receiver module we are allowed to be more pragmatic. Since all the signals arriving from different users must be detected all the signature waveforms are available! Why not exploit this possibility? Thus those schemes performing combined detection are called *multi-user detectors* (MUD) .

Before explaining how the optimal MUD operates it is worth classifying our scenario. Since different τ_k delays are considered the channel is *asynchronous*. Furthermore $a_k[i]$ is assumed to be completely unknown in the receiver hence we have to solve a *non-coherent* detection problem.

In possession of the concept of the single-user DS-CDMA detectors and being familiar with the effects of the radio channel waiting for naive subscribers we are ready to design an optimal detector architecture.

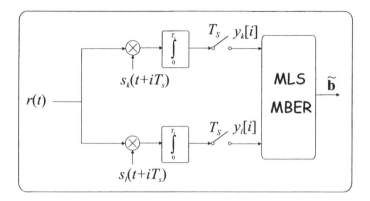

Fig. 8.8 Multi-user DS-CDMA detector

First of all we have to realize that in the case of random delays to detect the ith symbol it is not enough to take into account the incoming signal during the corresponding symbol period. Instead we need to consider the whole burst. Therefore we concentrate on vector $\mathbf{b}_k$ representing the data symbols of the kth user's burst under detection.

Next we require a suitable definition for optimality. Two extreme answers and many intermediate criteria can be found in the literature. The most popular definition is based on the *maximum likelihood sequence* (MLS) decision principle – often referred to as the *jointly optimum decision* – while the other end ensures *minimum bit error rate* (MBER) and is cited as the *individually optimum decision*.

In order to formulate more precisely these two decision techniques and explain the origin of their names let us introduce the following matrix

$$\mathbf{B} = [\mathbf{b}_1, \mathbf{b}_2, \ldots, \mathbf{b}_K] \Rightarrow B_{ik} = b_k[i], \quad k = 1, \ldots, K; \ i = 0, \ldots, R. \quad (8.8)$$

Furthermore Bob collects the outputs of the matched filters

$$y_k[i] = \int_{iT_s}^{(i+1)T_s} r(t)s_k(t - iT_s)dt \quad (8.9)$$

into $\mathbf{Y}$ such that

$$\mathbf{Y} = [\mathbf{y}_1, \mathbf{y}_2, \ldots, \mathbf{y}_K] \Rightarrow Y_{ik} = y_k[i], \quad k = 1, \ldots, K; \ i = 0, \ldots, R. \quad (8.10)$$

In the case of an MLS decision we have $2^{K(R+1)}$ different hypotheses according to the different $\mathbf{B}_m$ vectors

$$
\begin{aligned}
H_1 &: \mathbf{Y} = w(\mathbf{B}_1) \\
H_2 &: \mathbf{Y} = w(\mathbf{B}_2) \\
&\vdots \\
H_{2^{K(R+1)}} &: \mathbf{Y} = w(\mathbf{B}_{2^{K(R+1)}})
\end{aligned}
\quad (8.11)
$$

where $w(\mathbf{B}_m)$ denotes a matrix-matrix function producing the matrix of the matched filters' outputs provided $\mathbf{B}_m$ contains the symbols sent by all the users during the burst in question and related to the mth hypothesis ($m = 1, \ldots, 2^{K(R+1)}$). The corresponding architecture is depicted in Fig. 8.8. It does not matter whether we use MLS or MBER detectors. The difference lies in the decision boxes. Obviously $w(\cdot)$ depends not only on the transmitted symbols but on random channel parameters too. Moreover $w(\cdot)$ is not reversible. Therefore Bob is not able to compute unambiguously that $\mathbf{B}$ leads to $\mathbf{Y}$. Instead he invokes decision theory (see Section 12.1.2). The optimal decision in an MLS sense 'simply' requires us to find that hypothesis with maximal conditional probability density function i.e.

$$\tilde{\mathbf{B}}_{MLS} : \max_m f(\mathbf{Y}|\mathbf{B}_m). \tag{8.12}$$

Let us suppose that we quantize the random variables characterizing the radio channel into sufficiently small pieces from the detector point of view. Say N_A, N_α and N_τ represent the number of different values of $A_k[i], \alpha_k[i]$ and τ_k respectively. Furthermore we collect the supposed values of these parameters during the detected burst into the following matrices and vector

$$\mathbf{A} : A_{ik} = A_k[i]; \quad \mathbf{C} : C_{ik} = \alpha_k[i]; \quad \mathbf{d} : d_k = \tau_k.$$

Next we form a single matrix in the following manner

$$\mathbf{Z} = [\mathbf{A}, \mathbf{C}, \mathbf{d}].$$

Bearing in mind that all the random variables are uniformly distributed, in order to calculate the conditional density functions in (8.12) one has to count those $\mathbf{Z}$ matrices which lead to $\mathbf{Y}$ i.e.

$$f(\mathbf{Y}|\mathbf{B}_m) = \frac{\#(\mathbf{Z} : \mathbf{Y} = u(\mathbf{B}_m, \mathbf{Z}))}{\#(\mathbf{Z})}, \tag{8.13}$$

where $w(\mathbf{B}_m, \mathbf{Z})$ represents a matrix-matrix function computing the matrix of the matched filters' outputs if $\mathbf{B}_m$ and $\mathbf{Z}$ are assumed.

While an MLS detector tries to estimate all the symbols jointly during a given burst in the case of MBER detectors we decide for $b_k[i]$ from symbol to symbol. Thus we have to perform $K(R + 1)$ decisions each of which selects one of the following two hypotheses

$$H_1 : y_k[i] = w'(b_k[i] = 1)$$
$$H_2 : y_k[i] = w'(b_k[i] = -1)$$

where function $w'(b_k[i])$ calculates the output of the kth user's matched filter after the ith symbol interval. This hypothesis testing requires maximizing the following conditional pdfs

$$\tilde{b}_k[i] : \max_{b_k[i]=\pm 1} f(y_k[i]|b_k[i]) \tag{8.14}$$

and $\tilde{\mathbf{B}}_{MBER} = [\tilde{b}_k[i]]$. In order to express conditional pdfs in (8.14) we introduce

$$Z_{\pm 1} = [\mathbf{B}_{\pm 1}, \mathbf{A}, \mathbf{C}, \mathbf{d}],$$

where matrices $\mathbf{B}_{\pm 1}$ consist of possible values for $b_l[c]$ ($l \neq k$ and $c \neq i$ at the same time) while $b_k[i]$ is set either $+1$ or -1. Since each $b_l[c]$ can be assumed as an independent equiprobable random variable

$$f(y_k[i]|b_k[i] = \pm 1) = \frac{\#(Z_{\pm 1} : y_k[i] = u'(Z_{\pm 1}))}{\#(Z_{\pm 1})}, \qquad (8.15)$$

where $u'(Z_{\pm 1})$ calculates the outcome of the corresponding matched filter.

Unfortunately both MUD techniques are rather time consuming. In the case of MLS approach one needs to test $2^{K(R+1)}$ different hypotheses, which grows exponentially with the number of active users. On the other hand MBER detection requires $2K(R+1)$ evaluation of the conditional pdfs. Furthermore the evaluations of the conditional pdfs are rather hard tasks especially in the latter case. Therefore they cannot be used in practice and suboptimal approximations are the focus of research and used in practical applications such as single-user, interference cancelling, decorrelating detectors (see *Further Reading*).

8.3 QUANTUM-BASED MULTI-USER DETECTION

Although MLS-based optimal multi-user detectors are more popular than the MBER based ones because of their less computational complexity, both approaches are far from practical implementations. However, quantum assisted computing exploiting quantum parallelism may help us to attack the optimum MUD problem directly.

Let us discuss the MBER problem and concentrate on the detection of the $b_k[i]$ symbol. As we deduced in (8.14) Bob needs to evaluate two conditional pdfs. We derived some hints about how to perform this in (8.15). Since we are interested only in the larger pdf the denominators can be omitted. Both numerators require solving a special counting problem. Because all the channel parameters and other symbols are independent and uniformly distributed Bob has to decide whether the number of Z_{+1} or Z_{-1} leading to $y_k[i]$ is bigger, which is equivalent to the question whether $b_k[i] = +1$ or $b_k[i] = -1$ have the larger probability of being the originator of $y_k[i]$?

We have already discussed the counting problem related to the search in an unstructured database in Section 7.2, where a fairly efficient quantum-based solution was proposed, which uses phase estimation on the Grover operator. Concerning our special multi-user detection scenario we have a virtual database encoded into function $u'(\cdot)$ instead of a real one.

In possession of a promising idea and with knowledge about quantum counting next we determine the architecture and initialization parameters of the quantum-based MUD (QMUD) detector. We apply the top-down design principle thus we depict the system concept in Fig. 8.9. We define two counting circuits according to the two hypotheses, one that assumes $b_k[i] = +1$ and another for $b_k[i] = -1$. Their outputs representing the numerators in (8.15) are denoted by

$$e_{\pm 1} = \#(\mathbf{Z}_{\pm 1} : y_k[i] = u'(\mathbf{Z}_{\pm 1})). \tag{8.16}$$

Each quantum counter is fed with the outcome $y_k[i]$ of the matched filter, the corresponding hypothesis $b_k[i] = \pm 1$ and the set $S = \{s_k(t)\}$ of individual signature waveforms of all the active users. Next the outputs $e_{\pm 1}$ are compared and the result determines Bob's estimation $\tilde{b}_k[i] = \arg \max_{\pm 1}\{e_{\pm 1}\}$.

Following the top-down concept we have to examine the design of the Grover operator. Without harming generality we use the basic Grover box introduced in Section 7.1. First of all it requires an index register input denoted by $|\gamma\rangle$. As Fig. 8.10 shows we form each computational basis state $|x\rangle$ of $|\gamma\rangle$ from consecutive blocks. Each block is responsible for the storage of different parameters. First we use all the $K(R+1) - 1$ qbits to represent different $b_l[c]$ symbols $l = 1, \ldots, K; c = 0, \ldots, R$, only $b_k[i]$ is omitted because there is an individual input defined for it directly to the Oracle. This is followed by three other blocks consisting of $K(R+1)n_A, K(R+1)n_\alpha$ and Kn_τ qbits and comprising values for $A_k[i], \alpha_k[i]$ and τ_k respectively, where

$$n_A = \lceil \mathrm{ld}(N_A) \rceil; \quad n_\alpha = \lceil \mathrm{ld}(N_\alpha) \rceil N_\alpha; \quad n_\tau = \lceil \mathrm{ld}(N_\tau) \rceil.$$

Therefore Bob requires

$$n = K(R+1)(n_A + n_\alpha + 1) + Kn_\tau - 1$$

qbits to describe a given configuration. Having defined the size of the index register we turn to the Oracle. Originally it calls the database and compares DB[x] with the requested item in compliance with (7.4). Now, we use $u''(b_k[i], x)$ as a 'database' which computes the matched filter output as if $b_k[i] = \pm 1$ and x were given to it and the Oracle compares the result with $y_k[i]$ in the following way

$$f(x) = \begin{cases} 1 & \text{if } y_k[i] = u''(b_k[i], x), \\ 0 & \text{otherwise.} \end{cases} \tag{8.17}$$

As the last design step we remember that phase estimation and thus quantum counting includes quantum uncertainty, which can be controlled by means of additional qbits in the upper section of the phase estimator according to (7.32). Considering the worst-case scenario i.e. (7.39), this means in our case

$$n^{\clubsuit} = n + \left\lceil \mathrm{ld}(2\pi) + \mathrm{ld}\left(3 + \frac{1}{\check{P}_\varepsilon}\right) \right\rceil,$$

where $\check{P}_\varepsilon$ stands for the maximum allowed quantum uncertainty. Taking a look at Fig. 6.13 the reader can conclude that a fairly good quantum uncertainty from the air interface point of view, say less than 10^{-8}, can be achieved by using about 25 extra qbits which is negligible compared to n.

Finally the computational complexity of the QMUD algorithm can be easily determined if the reader recalls our remarks from the end of Section 7.2.2, namely we need $O(n^3)$ elementary gates, where 2^n represents the size of the database.

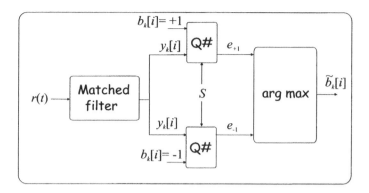

Fig. 8.9 System concept of quantum counting-based multi-user DS-CDMA detector

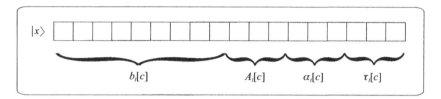

Fig. 8.10 The structure of the index register

Remark: The above method can be trivially extended to that case when we use multi-level symbols instead of binary ones. If M-level symbols are applied then Bob needs to run M quantum counters in parallel or sequentially.

8.4 FURTHER READING

Subscribers of the next generation wireless systems will communicate simultaneously, sharing the same frequency band. All around the world 3G mobile systems apply DS-CDMA because of its high capacity and inherent resistance to interference, hence it comes into the limelight in many communication systems. Nevertheless due to the hostile property of the channel, in the case of CDMA communication the orthogonality between user codes at the receiver is lost, which leads to performance degradation in a multi-user environment. A good overview of wireless channel models can be found in [118, 45] while state-of-the-art mobile systems such as GSM, IS-95, cdma2000, UMTS, W-CDMA, etc. are surveyed in [73, 101, 144].

Single-user detectors were overtaxed and showed rather poor performance even in multi-path environments [146]. To overcome this problem, in recent years multi-user detection has received considerable attention and has become one of the most important signal-processing tasks in wireless communication.

Verdu [146] has proved that the optimal solution is an *NP*-hard problem as the number of users grows, which causes significant limitations in practical applications. Many authors proposed suboptimal linear and nonlinear solutions such as decorrelating detector, MMSE (minimum mean square error) detector, recurrent and Hoppfield neural network based detectors, multi-stage detector [24, 109, 146, 5], and the references therein. One can find a comparison of the performance of the above-mentioned algorithms in [64].

The unwanted effects of the radio channel can be compensated by means of channel equalization [3, 129, 7]. The most conventional method for channel equalization employs training sequences of known data. However, such a scheme requires more bandwidth to transmit the some amount of payload. Furthermore, in multi-user CDMA systems the coordination of users is a difficult task. Consequently, there is a tremendous interest in blind detection schemes for multi-user systems, where no training sequences are needed. Our quantum-based MUD proposal belongs to this latter group because it does not require any information about the channel. The basic idea which traces MUD to set separation was published in [130, 131] and analyzed [133, 132]. This chapter introduces a refined version which extends (deterministic) set separation to (probabilistic) hypothesis testing.

9

Quantum-based Code Breaking

Damocles's sword is hanging over our widespread classical public key cryptosystems because their security is based on the belief that computing certain mathematical functions are hard tasks. However, due to the advent of quantum computing the long desired wish of code-breakers has been fulfilled.

Section 9.1 summarizes the basic terminology of cryptology. Next we introduce two fundamental cryptosystems based on symmetric key and asymmetric key architectures in Section 9.2 and Section 9.3, respectively. Both sections contain a practical example, the RSA algorithm for the former and the ElGamal algorithm for the latter. Well-tried security techniques such as public key cryptography seem to become obsolete at the dawn of the third millennium while new quantum-based solutions are emerging. We explain in Section 9.4 how to exploit quantum algorithms introduced in previous chapters of this book to break public key cryptosystems.

Fortunately defense against such quantum-assisted attacks is available by also using quantum principles. We explain them in Chapter 10.

9.1 INTRODUCTION TO CRYPTOLOGY

Keeping information secret played/plays/will always play an important role the history. Battles, wars or the destiny of whole nations depended often on broken codes e.g. the fact that the Allies were in possession of the German ciphering system called ENIGMA proved to be decisive in World War II.

Quantum Computing and Communications   S. Imre, F. Balázs
© 2004 John Wiley & Sons, Ltd   ISBN 0-470-86902-X (HB)

The science dealing with secret information is called *cryptology*.[1] It consists of two major areas:

- *Cryptography* covers all the efforts to produce secure transmission of information implementing different aspects such as confidentiality, data integrity, authentication and non-repudiation.

- *Cryptoanalysis* gathers all the techniques aiming to break encrypted messages.

Instead of introducing all the above functionalities in detail we concentrate only on those items which are playing certain roles in this book.[2]

We assume in our model that Alice would like to send messages to Bob in a secure way i.e.

- preventing Eve from accessing the original information (no eavesdropping) and

- preventing Eve from being able to send messages to Bob as if she were Alice (no impersonation).

Therefore Alice performs *encryption* (*ciphering*) to produce secret messages from plain ones

$$E = e_A(P), \tag{9.1}$$

where P represents the plain message, $e_B(\cdot)$ stands for Alice's ciphering function when communicating with Bob and E denotes the encrypted message. Roughly speaking encryption is responsible for *code making*, while cryptoanalysis for *code breaking*, respectively. Bob receives E from the communication channel and by applying corresponding decryption function $d_B(\cdot)$ obtains the original message that is

$$P = d_B(E). \tag{9.2}$$

In order to provide safe information transfer $e_B(\cdot)$ and $d_B(\cdot)$ must be kept secret. Unfortunately this approach is not practical enough because it requires a large amount of different function pairs according to the typical number of users in an infocom system, moreover hardware/software implementation of various functions is not efficient. As a trivial example the reader may think of the following scenario. Alice writes her message onto a sheet of paper and puts it into a box equipped with a special lock. She has to buy different boxes for sending messages to each partner. A more straightforward and cost-effective solution is if she uses uniform boxes with individual keys. In this way security is concentrated into the keys which are cheap, small and therefore it is easy to hide them. Similar to this concept we use symbol

---

[1] The word *cryptology* originates from the Greek *cryptos = hidden* and *logos = word*.
[2] *Further Reading* of this chapter contains appropriate hints for those readers interested in a wider overview of this topic.

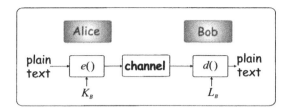

Fig. 9.1 Basic concept of secure information transfer

sequences called keys in cryptography. Thus (9.1) and (9.2) becomes

$$E = e(P, K_B),$$
$$P = d(E, L_B), \tag{9.3}$$

where the ciphering and deciphering functions have encryption key and decryption key inputs K_B and L_B and the functions do not depend on the parties. We allow different keys here for the sake of generality. Later we will see that it proves to be rather useful in certain cases. The basic architecture of secure message transfer can be seen in Fig. 9.1.

9.2   SYMMETRIC KEY CRYPTOGRAPHY

In the case of a secret key or symmetric key cryptographic system the communicating parties use the same key for ciphering the plain message and deciphering the encrypted one i.e. $K_B \equiv L_B$. After several preliminaries Gilbert Vernam proposed the so-called one-time pad or Vernam cipher – the state-of-the-art solid base of symmetric key cryptographic systems. Its tremendous advantage was proved by Shannon, namely *if the plain text and the key have the same length and the key is really random then the cryptosystem is secure* i.e. while the keys are kept secret there is no systematic algorithm which is able to decrypt the plain text from observed encrypted messages. Clearly speaking until now this is the only known provably secure solution!

In order to explain the basic operation let us assume that Alice and Bob would like to perform a conversation via a secure channel. Therefore first they meet and agree a common pair of identical secret keys. Furthermore a common alphabet comprising N different symbols is considered. Next the architecture proposed in Fig. 9.2 is used. Alice adds together the symbols (bits) of the plain message and the symbols of the secret key in modulo N sense producing the encrypted message

$$E[k] = e(P[k], K_B) = (P[k] + K_B[k]) \bmod N, \tag{9.4}$$

where $E[k]$ stands for the kth symbol of the encrypted message, $P[k]$ and $K_B[k]$ for the plain text and the secret key, respectively. It is important to emphasize

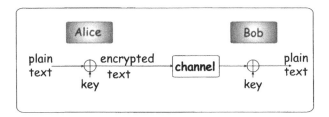

Fig. 9.2 Basic concept of symmetric key cryptosystems

that the ciphering operation is quite simple which is fundamental in reducing the overhead during the communication introduced by the security system. Having received the encrypted message from the channel Bob applies the inverse[3] (modulo N subtraction) operation as Alice used that is he subtracts the symbols of the same key from the incoming symbols recovering the original plain text

$$P[k] = d(E[k], L_B) = (E[k] - K_B[k]) \bmod N. \tag{9.5}$$

The reader may challenge his/her ciphering skills in **Exercise** 9.1 by encrypting the words *quantum computing*.

Because the keys used for encryption and decryption are kept secret our expectations defined in the introductory section are trivially fulfilled. In spite of being a simple and brilliant idea the one-time pad suffers some problems which might lead to serious difficulties. Let us summarize them next with the offered solutions.

9.2.1 Large number of users

The parties must meet first to agree the common keys. In the case of a few number of users this does not cause serious difficulties. However, if we consider a large amount of customers, for instance via the Internet or in a digital cellular mobile network (e.g. GSM, UMTS, IS95), it is unimaginable to organize such key exchanges. There are several solutions to handle this problem.

Either we use several, preprogrammed static keys as typical WLANs do. Of course the number of such keys are rather limited thus really secure transmission cannot be provided.

Or we apply the so-called public key ciphering concept which will be explained in detail in Section 9.3. This technique allows Alice to publicly announce a special key which can be used to encrypt messages intended for her. Unfortunately this solution suffers from the lack of theoretically proven secureness.

---

[3]In the binary case, that is $N = 2$, the two operations are the same i.e. $e(\cdot) = d(\cdot)$!

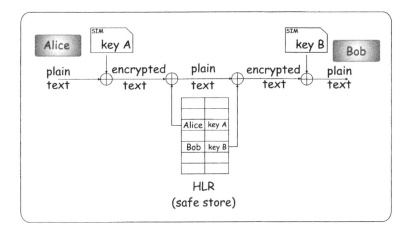

Fig. 9.3 Symmetric key cryptosystem in a public mobile network

Finally we use the GSM[4] network to explain the most practical approach widely used in the telecom world. Each user is provided with a secret key together with his/her subscription. This key is stored on the SIM card – a special smart card located inside the mobile phone – therefore the key is available each time the user initiates a new call. A perfect copy of this key is safely stored in the Home Location Register (HLR) at the operator. When Alice and Bob are communicating with each other the channel between them is split into two parts from a security point of view. Each section is encrypted between the user and the system using the corresponding symmetric key pairs as depicted in Fig. 9.3.

Although this solution passed the test of time two shortcomings should be revealed. First we remark that obviously there are certain point(s) inside the network where the messages appear deciphered or the information travels without ciphering between them. Secondly we have to maintain a network with a strongly centralized infrastructure which takes the weight of key registration and management off customers' shoulders.

Exercise 9.1. Encrypt and decrypt the following message *'QUANTUM COMPUT-ING'* using the following alphabet: space, A, B, C, D, E, F, G, H, I, J, K, L, M, N, O, P, Q, R, S, T, U, V, W, X, Y, Z.

9.2.2 Length of the key and its randomness

Alice and Bob need random keys having the same length as the plain text. Randomness can be easily provided since fairly good random number generators

---

[4]Here we apply a strongly simplified model of the GSM security system, for references see *Further Reading*.

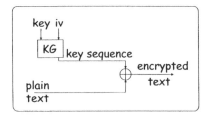

Fig. 9.4 Encryption with key generator

were developed within the frames of information theory. However, the latter constraint seems to be much more challenging because it requires either enormously large memories to store the keys or Alice and Bob must meet very often to agree the new keys. Fortunately a simple circuit, e.g. a feedback shiftregister (or convolutional encoder), can be used as a key generator (KG) because it requires only a short initialization string – in our case the secret key – and it emits a pseudorandom sequence of symbols – used as the key for encryption – with very long periodicity (see Fig. 9.4). Therefore from this point on we assume that $e(\cdot)$ and $d(\cdot)$ contain the key generators.

Because the key sequence is not fully random we violate Shannon's requirement. Fortunately this deviation is marginal and it can be further suppressed if another, time-varying initialization vector (IV) is used each time a new call is established.

9.3 PUBLIC KEY CRYPTOGRAPHY

Unlike centralized networks applying symmetric keys there are distributed systems such as the well-known Internet where no standardized entity is available which is responsible for assigning a secret key for each joining user and for maintaining the database of these keys. Therefore with public key cryptography, often called asymmetric cryptography, our two players Alice and Bob use different keys for encryption and decryption, respectively. More precisely Bob defines its secret key L_B for deciphering messages arriving from Alice and publicly announce another one K_B which can be used by Alice to encrypt the messages, that is

$$d(e(P, K_B), L_B) = P. \tag{9.6}$$

Furthermore when exchanging the keys the following connection also has to be fulfilled

$$d(e(P, L_B), K_B) = P \tag{9.7}$$

i.e. the keys are inverses of each other.

However, the public key allows Eve to send messages to Bob instead of Alice. Therefore before sending encrypted messages we have to extend the new concept in the following way. Alice copies Bob in key preparation, which results in another

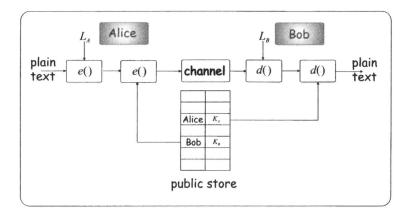

Fig. 9.5   Architecture implementing the Diffie–Hellman concept

pair of keys K_A and L_A. Next Alice produces the ciphered text using a two-step procedure, first she uses her own private key, which is followed by an encryption with Bob's public key

$$E = e(e(P, L_A), K_B). \tag{9.8}$$

To obtain the original message Bob applies

$$d(d(E, L_B), K_A) = d(d(e(e(P, L_A), K_B), L_B), K_A) = d(e(P, L_A), K_A) = P, \tag{9.9}$$

where we exploited (9.6) and (9.7) subsequently. This excellent idea was invented by Diffie and Hellman thus the algorithm bears their names.

Remark: We ask the reader to notice that Alice uses her secret key to authenticate the message, thus she prevents Eve from being able to send messages as if she were Alice. This technique will be exploited in a related field called digital signatures in Section 9.3.2.

On the first sight this approach seems to be very vulnerable since the relation (function) binding the two keys together must be deterministic (*and therefore reversible*), thus with possession of the public key and the ciphering/deciphering functions the secret key can be unravelled theoretically. In practice, however, Bob may select such a function for key generation which allows easy computation of the public key from the secret one but the reverse operation proves to be a computationally complex problem. These type of functions are called one-way functions in cryptography (see Section 12.3.2). As a simple example we consider an English–Hungarian dictionary. If we asked the reader to look up the Hungarian counterpart of the English word *home* she/he would find it within seconds because of the alphabetical sorting of the words. Contrary if the task were to find the Hungarian word *otthon* in the same dictionary then hours could be spent without success.

9.3.1 The RSA algorithm

The most widely used realization of the above principle is the RSA algorithm which exploits the multiplication as a one-way function. Multiplication of two integers belongs to the syllabus of any primary school, however, finding factors of a large number there is no known efficient classical algorithm. First let us summarize how to produce the secret and public key pairs in RSA.

1. Bob selects randomly two large prime numbers p and q such that $p \neq q$.

2. He calculates $N = p \cdot q$.

3. Bob selects randomly a small odd number a such that $\gcd(\varphi(N), a) = 1$, where $\varphi(N)$ denotes the corresponding Euler function (see Section 12.3.2). Since N is a product of two prime numbers we can utilize Theorem 12.2 resulting in $\varphi(N) = (p - 1) \cdot (q - 1)$.

4. Next he calculates the multiplicative inverse (see Section 12.3.2) of a in modulo $\varphi(N)$ sense using Euclid's algorithm (see Section 12.3.3) and denotes it with b: $(a \cdot b) \bmod \varphi(N) = 1$. Moreover he knows that b always exists because of Theorem 12.3.

5. Bob announces the public key $K_B = (a, N)$ and

6. keeps secret the private key $L_B = (b, N)$.

Encryption and decryption are performed by means of the following special functions

$$E = e(P, K_B) = (P^a) \bmod N,$$
$$P = d(E, L_B) = (E^b) \bmod N. \tag{9.10}$$

Now we prove that by applying these functions Bob receives Alice's message. Based on (9.9) it is enough to realize that $d(e(P, L_A), K_A) = P$. Substituting the RSA keys we reach
$$d(e(P, L_A), K_A) = (P^{ba}) \bmod N.$$

Since a and b are multiplicative inverses modulo $\varphi(N) = (p - 1) \cdot (q - 1)$ there is an appropriate integer k for which

$$ab = 1 + k\varphi(N).$$

If $P \bmod q \neq 0$ then

$$P^{ba} \equiv P(P^{q-1})^{k(p-1)} \pmod{q},$$

where exploiting Fermat's little theorem (see Theorem 12.4) we get

$$P^{ba} \equiv P(1)^{k(p-1)} \pmod{q} = P \pmod{q}.$$

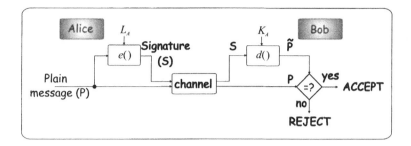

Fig. 9.6 Architecture implementing the digital signature concept

Obviously $P^{ba} \equiv P \pmod{q}$ is fulfilled trivially if $P \bmod q \equiv 0$ thus for all possible P

$$P^{ba} \equiv P \pmod{q}$$

and similarly

$$P^{ba} \equiv P \pmod{p}.$$

Therefore the Chinese remainder theorem (see Theorem 12.6) ensures that

$$P^{ba} \equiv P \pmod{N}, \forall P.$$

9.3.2 Digital signatures

As we discussed earlier with the Diffie–Hellman algorithm the two-stage encoding by Alice was motivated on one hand to prevent Eve from understanding Alice's message and on the other hand to avoid impersonation of Alice by Eve. Alice achieved this latter functionality via using her own secret key originally intended to decipher messages from Bob. In practice we are not restricted to apply these two coding steps together. If a person uses the public key cryptography to authenticate messages or to sign documents electronically then we call that person the user of the digital signature.

The architecture related to digital signatures (without ciphering) is depicted in Fig. 9.6. Alice produces her signature S using the encryption function and her secret key L_A

$$S = e(P, L_A).$$

She amends the original message P with this personal signature and sends it to Bob who obtains Alice's public key from an open server. Next he performs the inverse function on S calculating the assumed plain text

$$\tilde{P} = d(S, K_A).$$

Finally Bob compares $\tilde{P}$ and P to decide whether to accept the message or reject.

In order to highlight that cryptography can be regarded as a really colorful scientific area we present here a discrete logarithm based on the digital signature scheme invented by ElGamal. The keys are generated according to the following steps

1. Alice selects randomly a large prime p and a generator a of the multiplicative group $\mathbb{Z}_p^*$ (see Section 12.3.2).

2. Next she selects a random integer b, $1 \leq b \leq p - 2$.

3. Alice computes $y = a^b \bmod p$ and

4. announces public key $K_B = (p, a, y)$ while keeping $L_B = b$ secret.

In possession of the keys Alice generates the signature in the following way.

1. Alice randomly selects an integer $1 \leq l \leq p - 2$ such that l and $(p - 1)$ are co-prime, $\gcd(l, p - 1) = 1$.

2. Than she calculates $r = a^l \bmod p$ and

3. the multiplicative inverse k of l in modulo $(p-1)$ sense, $(l \cdot k) \bmod (p-1) = 1$.

4. Alice computes $s = [k \cdot (h(P) - b \cdot r)] \bmod (p - 1)$, where $h(\cdot)$ is the so-called hash function, which is used typically to perform a many-to-one transformation from the set of plain messages to $\mathbb{Z}_p$.

5. As the last step Alice's signature for message P is $S = (r, s)$.

In order to check whether the sender of the received message was Alice, Bob should perform the following procedure.

1. Bob obtains Alice's public key $K_B = (p, a, y)$ from a free database.

2. He verifies that $1 \leq r = a^l \bmod p \leq p - 1$, if not he rejects the message else.

3. Bob calculates $q_1 = (y^r r^s) \bmod p$ and

4. $h(P)$ and $q_2 = a^{h(P)} \bmod p$.

5. Finally he accepts the signature if $q_1 = q_2$.

Let us verify the discussed algorithm. We know that during the signature generation Alice produces

$$s = [k \cdot (h(P) - b \cdot r)] \bmod (p - 1).$$

Multiplying both sides by the inverse of k we get

$$l \cdot s \equiv l \cdot k \cdot (h(P) - b \cdot r) \ (\bmod \ p - 1).$$

Since $(l \cdot k) \bmod (p - 1) = 1$ restructuring the congruence

$$h(P) \equiv br + ls \ (\bmod \ p - 1)$$

from which we can conclude that

$$q_2 = a^{h(P)} \equiv a^{br+ls} \equiv (a^b)^r \ (\bmod \ p) = q_1.$$

9.4 QUANTUM-BASED SOLUTIONS FOR BREAKING PUBLIC KEY CRYPTOSYSTEMS

First of all we would like to point out that symmetric key cryptography was proven information-theoretically secure by Shannon as we have already discussed in Section 9.2, hence we put our effort to breaking asymmetric key architectures. The more so since the safety of the latter approach is based on the hope that the applied one-way function is really 'one-way', i.e. the inverse operation has really high complexity from a computational point of view. Unfortunately this property strongly depends on the available computing power and algorithms. This is the point where we have good chances to find a security gap enabling access to the heart of the cryptosystem.

In Part II we introduced and explained such quantum algorithms which proved to be much more efficient than their classical alternatives. We set ourself the target in this section to utilize these algorithms for solving a rather practical engineering problem. RSA is widely used in today's Internet, therefore being able to crack it has great significance.

9.4.1 Using Grover's database search algorithm to break RSA

The Grover algorithm offers two approaches to finding the secret key L_B. We remember that N is a product of two prime numbers and it is enough to find one of its factors to deduce the private key via repeating the steps described in Section 9.3.1.

- The *brute force method* exploits the fact that it is enough to test integer numbers x from 2 up to $\lfloor \sqrt{N} \rfloor$ whether they divide N without reminder or not to find the smaller one among p and q. In order to launch the Grover search we have to define on one hand the function $f(x)$ controlling the Oracle and on the other hand the optimal number of iterations. The first question can be answered based in (7.4)

$$f(x) = \left\{ \begin{array}{ll} 1 & \text{if } N/x = \lfloor N/x \rfloor, \\ 0 & \text{otherwise,} \end{array} \right.$$

  while the second one requires (see 7.26) knowledge of the size of the database and the repeated occurrence M of the searched entry, which equals in our case trivially $\sqrt{N}$ and 1 respectively. Hence we reach the following very promising result

$$L_{opt_0} \simeq \frac{\pi}{4} \sqrt{\sqrt{N}} = O(N^{\frac{1}{4}}).$$

- Another Grover algorithm based solution can be constructed if we use a database search directly for factorization. More precisely we plan to find the prime factors of N according to the combined classical–quantum procedure introduced in Section 6.3.1, however, the phase estimation based order finding Shor algorithm is replaced with a Grover search based one. Assigning the following function to the Oracle

$$f(x) = \begin{cases} 1 & \text{if } a^x \bmod N = 1, \\ 0 & \text{otherwise,} \end{cases}$$

the measurement at the output will give back m which is equal to order r or its integer multiple with high probability. Since x refers here to the computational basis states stored in the index qregister, a plays the role of the random number denoted by x when we were discussing factorization in Section 6.3.1. Of course we need to perform quantum counting to obtain M and thus the optimal number of iterations. In possession of M and m we are able to determine r. Although the resource requirement of this method is obviously larger than the previous one because of the additional classical steps and the quantum counting we mentioned it to emphasize the wide variety of potential solutions emerging from the quantum world.

9.4.2   Using Shor's order finding algorithm to break RSA

Shor's solution for finding the order allows breaking RSA much more efficiently than the Grover algorithm does. Evidently the most trivial solution is if we seek for the prime factors of N using combined classical–quantum algorithms as it was described in Section 6.3. However, another brilliant alternative exists which follows an indirect way to decipher the encoded message $E = (P^a) \bmod N$.

Eve – our evil character in this story – downloads Bob's public key $K_B = (a, N)$ from the free database and launches the following process:

1. First she calculates the order of E in modulo N sense using the Shor algorithm and denotes it with r that is $((P^a)^r) \bmod N = 1$. This step requires that E and N are relative primes. If not Eve can apply Euclid's algorithm (see Section 12.3.3) to eliminate the common factors, which provides p and q.

2. Next she computes the modulo r multiplicative inverse of a. The existence of this inverse $b^\sharp$ requires that a is co-prime to r. Since $(E^r) \bmod N = 1$ and Euler's theorem (see Section 12.5) states that $(E^{\varphi(N)}) \bmod N = 1$ thus $\varphi(N) = k \cdot r$ for certain integer k, that is prime factors of r form a subset of those of $\varphi(N)$. Keeping in view that $\gcd(\varphi(N), a) = 1$, a and $\varphi(N)$ are relative primes, because of the operation of RSA algorithm, we can conclude that a is co-prime to r, too.

3. Furthermore Eve recalls from the RSA algorithm that $(a \cdot b) \bmod \varphi(N) = 1$ while she obtained in Point 2 that $(a \cdot b^\sharp) \bmod r = 1$ and $\varphi(N) = k \cdot r$ hence $b^\sharp = b + k \cdot r$.

4. Now, in possession of $b^\sharp$ Eve replaces in her decipher the unknown b with it. Hence

$$\left((P^a)^{b^\sharp}\right) \bmod N = \left(P^{ab+akr}\right) \bmod N = \left(P^{ab} \cdot (P^{ar})^k\right) \bmod N = P,$$

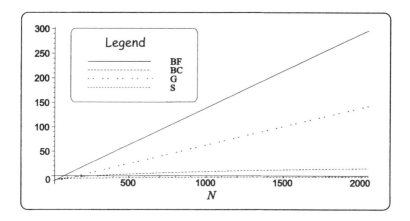

Fig. 9.7 $\log_{10}(\cdot)$ of required time in seconds to break the RSA with different methods

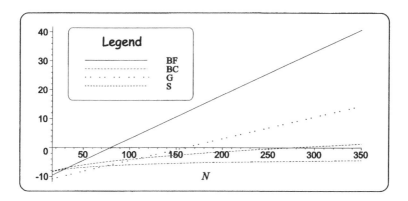

Fig. 9.8 $\log_{10}(\cdot)$ of required time in seconds to break the RSA with different methods (enlarged)

where Eve reveals that the first term modulo N equals P while because of the definition of r (see Point 1) the second term becomes 1. Thus Eve managed to access the plain message without any knowledge about b. Clearly speaking she utilized the special connection between b and $b^\sharp$.

In order to compare the different solutions according to the elapsed time before breaking the code we defined the following scenario. As a reference let us consider a classical and a quantum computer being able to perform 10^{12} steps (evaluations) a second. We varied $n = \mathrm{ld}(N)$ – the length of N – from 16 bits up to 1024 and for the following methods:

Table 9.1   Code-breaking methods and related complexity

Method	$n = 128$	$n = 128$	$n = 1024$	$n = 1024$	1s barrier
BF	$1.8 \cdot 10^7$ s	0.58 year	$1.3 \cdot 10^{142}$ s	$4 \cdot 10^{134}$ year	80 bit
BC	$6 \cdot 10^{-4}$ s	$1.9 \cdot 10^{-11}$ year	$3.5 \cdot 10^8$ s	11.29 year	273 bit
G	$4 \cdot 10^{-3}$ s	$1.3 \cdot 10^{-10}$ year	$1.1 \cdot 10^{65}$ s	$3.7 \cdot 10^{57}$ year	159 bit
S	$2 \cdot 10^{-5}$ s	$6.6 \cdot 10^{-14}$ year	**0.01** s	$3.4 \cdot 10^{-11}$ year	**10000** bit

- BF: *brute force* classical method which scans the integer numbers from 2 to $\lceil \sqrt{N} \rceil$ with complexity $O(\sqrt{N})$,

- BC: *best classical* method requiring $O(\exp[c \cdot \mathrm{ld}^{\frac{1}{3}}(N)\mathrm{ld}^{\frac{2}{3}}(\mathrm{ld}(N))])$ steps,

- G: *Grover* search based scheme with $O(N^{\frac{1}{4}})$,

- S: *Shor* factorization with $O(\mathrm{ld}(N)^3)$.

Fig. 9.7 presents the four curves on a logarithmic scale. As we expected Shor's algorithm proves to be the most efficient while the Grover based solution and the best classical one share second and third place. In order to give a quantitative comparison we enlarged the $n = 16 \ldots 350$ region in Fig. 9.8 and summarized some important points of the curves in Table 9.1. The reader may conclude that Shor's proposal will make RSA-type public key cryptography obsolete once its reliable physical implementation becomes available on the market. Fortunately the panic this fact may evoke can be moderated significantly due to the new ideas explained in Chapter 10.

Finally we would like to point out that discrete logarithms (see Section 6.5.2) based public key cryptosystems (e.g. digital signature scheme introduced in Section 9.3.2) are also very vulnerable because the discrete logarithm problem can be traced back to period finding, which is common in order finding using factorization.

9.5 FURTHER READING

Basic terminology of cryptology was summarized within this chapter using the excellent *Handbook of Applied Cryptography* authored by Menezes, van Oorschot and Vanstone [8]. Readers interested in this specific area are strongly recommended to turn to this book, it is accessible via the Internet, too.

We used a simplified description of the security system of GSM networks in this chapter. In reality it is much more complex. For example the keys used for ciphering are actually derived from the symmetric secret keys each time that a new call is established, or encryption covers only the air-interface sections of the whole connection.

Gilbert Vernam published the so-called one-time pad in [148] in 1926. Shannon proved its secureness in [136] in 1949.

The basic idea of asymmetric cryptography was proposed by two experts from Standford University, Diffie and Hellman [127] in 1976. The most successful implementation – the RSA – algorithm was invented[5] by Rivest, Shamir and Adlemann [128] at the Massachusetts Institute of Technology in 1978. A good survey of public and secret key cryptographic algorithms can be found in [143]. ElGamal's digital signature scheme was introduced in [57].

Concerning our short introduction to cryptography we would like to strongly emphasize that only basic principles and the most popular algorithms were summarized. The related literature covers various versions of these techniques as well as solutions based on different ideas.

---

[5]In accordance with the British Government, an RSA-like public key cryptography algorithm was invented at the Government Communications Headquarters in Cheltenham as early as in 1973 [58], [43].

10

Quantum-based Key Distribution

Quantum key distribution is one of the most discussed topics of quantum computing. The motivation behind this can be traced back to implementation issues. Namely while construction of a quantum computer is fairly difficult at this moment because we are not able to isolate sufficiently the system from the environment, optical fibers or even the open air proved to be appropriate channels for distribution of cryptographic keys if photons are exploited as quantum bits.

As we have discussed in Chapter 9.1 when we were introducing cryptography in connection with code breaking, secure communications between parties can be provided in two essentially different ways. Both are common in using so-called keys to encrypt plain text messages. Symmetric key cryptography (see Section 9.2) applies the same keys at both communication edges. This approach is theoretically secure. From a practical point of view all the technical problems can be solved efficiently (see Sections 9.2.1 and 9.2.2) only sharing the common key represents a real challenge. Either we design a strongly centralized[1] network architecture, e.g. cellular mobile systems, or the parties have to meet regularly to exchange the keys. Public key cryptography (see Section 9.3) is advantageous in a distributed environment because it applies different keys making key exchange obsolete. Unfortunately we have to face the issue that its secureness has never been proven; only a belief shores up our hope that calculation of the secret key from the public one is a really computationally complex problem. This hope is, however, fading due to quantum computing and especially Shor's factorization algorithm. Now, what shall we do in order to provide secure communications in a distributed network if it is endangered by quantum

---

[1] The terms *centralized* and *distributed* characterize here the system only from a security point of view!

Quantum Computing and Communications   S. Imre, F. Balázs
© 2004 John Wiley & Sons, Ltd   ISBN 0-470-86902-X (HB)

computers? The answer is similar to the case when scientists were confronted with quantum mechanical effects reaching the atomic scale due to Moore's law. If we are affected by these strange effects why not benefit from them?

Surprisingly quantum computing proved to be much more efficient in averting eavesdroppers than in supporting agents/criminals hunting for secret information. If we were able to distribute keys in a secure manner based on quantum mechanics then the problem could be traced back to symmetric key cryptography. Thus quantum computing offers the answer to a crucial technical problem.

This chapter summarizes the basic ideas establishing quantum key distribution. We introduce the first successful protocol called BB84 in Section 10.1, which is followed by its simplified version in Section 10.2. The security of both protocols is based on the *no cloning theorem*. Finally we explain the operation of another type of protocols exploiting entanglement and the Bell inequality in Section 10.3.

10.1   THE BB84 PROTOCOL

In the same way as a director of a costume drama we have to assign the roles. We ask Alice and Bob to act the two lovers who are intending to exchange messages while Eve is playing the evil eavesdropper. In order to highlight all the important details of the BB84 protocol we explain first how the parties Alice and Bob are communicating in an idealistic scenario, that is we assume that the communication channel is free of errors and Eve is away on holiday. Next we ask Eve to return unexpectedly and to make an attempt to capture the secret key via observing the channel. Finally we consider a realistic channel with its consequences.

10.1.1   Idealistic scenario

Obviously Alice and Bob have to chose such an idea as the basis of the new key distribution protocol which is rooted in the quantum world since no classical method is known for the problem. We have already met with such phenomena e.g. *no cloning theorem* (see Section 2.7) or *entanglement* (see Section 2.6). The BB84 protocol exploits the former one.

The reader may follow the handshaking steps of the protocol in Fig. 10.1:

1. Since Alice has already learned that perfect secureness requires random keys, she produces first a binary sequence s_A using a random number generator.[2] For the sake of simplicity let us assume the following eight-bit length series [01100101]. Alice is familiar with the rule that non-orthogonal states cannot been copied successfully. Therefore she buys two different modulators in the nearest QAS.[3] One of them polarizes photons horizontally if it has logical 0 input and vertically if it is fed with 1, that is it produces states $|0\rangle$

---

[2]Which can be a quantum-based one as well!

[3]Quantum Accessories Shop.

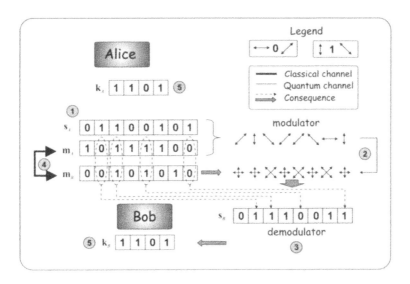

Fig. 10.1 Steps of BB84 protocol if no eavesdropper is present and the channel is idealistic

and $|1\rangle$, respectively. The other device establishes $\pm\frac{\pi}{4}$ polarization to logical 0 and 1 values or equivalently $\frac{|0\rangle\pm|1\rangle}{\sqrt{2}}$ states. Next she produces another binary sequence m_A with the same length, whose 0 bits advise Alice to use modulator No. 0 to polarize the actual photon from s_A before transmission while bits with value 1 suggest using modulator No. 1. Hereby logical 0 and 1 will be encoded into non-orthogonal states.

2. Provided $m_A = [10111100]$ Fig. 10.1 presents the transmitted photon (qbit) series over the quantum channel (e.g. an optical fiber).

3. Obviously if Bob were in possession of m_A he would be able to restore s_A without any error by applying two measurement devices: one of which measures in the $|0\rangle$, $|1\rangle$ basis while the other one in the $\frac{|0\rangle\pm|1\rangle}{\sqrt{2}}$. Unfortunately m_A is unknown to him therefore he tries to guess it using his own random series $m_B = [00101010]$. This sequence has identical and non-agreeing bits compared to m_A. Since about half of the bits are identical the corresponding bits in s_A will be detected correctly in the demodulator output s_B with sure success. Furthermore in the case of the bits belonging to the remaining half the measurement will result in correct answers on average for every second bit. Hence Bob can expect a BER of 25%.

4. However, in order to understand Alice's messages Bob needs to use the same key, i.e. $k_A = k_B$. To fulfil this requirement they have to perform some kind of 'error correction'. Therefore Alice and Bob announce m_A and m_B on a public classical channel.

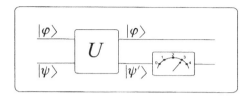

Fig. 10.2 Eve's eavesdropping equipment

5. Finally they discuss which bits are the same in the two sequences. Selecting the related bits from s_A and s_B they obtain two identical series k_A and k_B having on average half of the length compared to s_A.

10.1.2 Eve appears on the scene

Now, Eve returns and attempts to obtain $k_A = k_B$ by placing an eavesdropping device into the quantum channel. Her instrument is depicted in Fig. 10.2 which implements the following general strategy. Eve feeds its equipment on one hand with qbit $|\varphi\rangle$ captured in the channel and on the other hand with a predefined qregister $|\psi\rangle$. Next an arbitrary unitary transform U is executed on the inputs which has to produce $|\varphi\rangle$ and a modified version of $|\psi\rangle$ say $|\psi'\rangle$. If Eve manages to produce different $|\psi'\rangle$s from different $|\varphi\rangle$s then the former deviation can be exploited to differentiate the qbits traveling over the channel.

Clearly speaking Eve would like to build a special quantum copy machine. As we have already learned in connection with the *no cloning theorem* this endeavor will fail unless the states are orthogonal. This fact can be shown using several simple steps. Let us assume that $|\varphi\rangle$ and $|\varphi'\rangle$ are non-orthogonal and non-identical vectors that is

$$\langle\varphi'|\varphi\rangle \neq 0, \quad \langle\varphi'|\varphi\rangle \neq 1, \tag{10.1}$$

then Eve expects that

$$U(|\varphi\rangle \otimes |\psi\rangle) = |\varphi\rangle \otimes |\psi'\rangle$$
$$U(|\varphi'\rangle \otimes |\psi\rangle) = |\varphi'\rangle \otimes |\psi''\rangle,$$

where

$$\langle\psi'|\psi''\rangle \neq 1.$$

Because U is unitary it saves the inner product (see Section 12.2.5), namely the inner product at its input must equal the one computed to its output

$$\langle\varphi|\varphi'\rangle \underbrace{\langle\psi|\psi\rangle}_{\equiv 1} = \langle\varphi|\varphi'\rangle\langle\psi'|\psi''\rangle.$$

Since $\langle\varphi'|\varphi\rangle \neq 0$ because of (10.1) we can divide both sides with $\langle\varphi'|\varphi\rangle$ yielding

$$1 = \langle\psi'|\psi''\rangle, \tag{10.2}$$

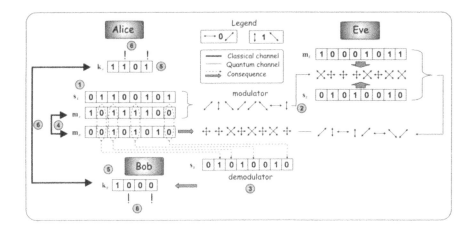

Fig. 10.3   Steps of BB84 protocol if Eve is present and the channel is idealistic

which can be satisfied if and only if $|\psi'\rangle$ and $|\psi''\rangle$ are identical, i.e. Eve can access no information about the captured qbits. The most that she can do is to follow Bob's method as if she were Bob (see Fig. 10.3). So Eve produces $m_E = [10001011]$ and measures the captured photons in compliance with this sequence. Thus she obtains an $s_E = 01010010$ series, but in order to avoid the exposure by Bob she has to send photons towards Bob. Because Eve does not know Alice's m_A she can use only m_E together with s_E instead. Statistically m_A and m_E agree in half of the positions (bits) and the belonging bits in s_A will be detected correctly. These bits can be retransmitted to Bob without revealing the fact of eavesdropping. However, in the case of the other half Eve applies the wrong modulator, which causes errors at Bob. Approximately half of this half i.e. overall 25% of the received bits will fail. Therefore if Alice and Bob introduce a sixth step into the protocol devoted to comparing sufficiently long parts of k_A and k_B – which should be identical – they will find errors (different bits) at certain positions. These errors mean the tragic end for Eve in the drama (or not?).

Remark: This protocol assumes that Eve is not able to perform a so-called man in the middle attack, that is she has no possibility to play for Alice as she were Bob and for Bob as she were Alice in each step of the protocol. In the case of the BB84 protocol this fact can be easily recognized.

10.1.3   When the channel introduces errors

Having been defeated in the first act Eve still does not give up hope of tricking Alice and Bob. At the beginning of the second act the main conclusion of Eve's eavesdropping action can be summarized in a very simple way. She introduces errors into the communication while observing the channel. Wait! By replacing idealistic channels with practical ones Bob will observe errors even if Eve is on holiday.

Therefore the next important question to answer is how to distinguish the two types of errors? Obviously BER values for practical channels are typically known. For instance an optical fiber introduces about 10^{-9} BER. Thus if the experienced BER is significantly higher than the acceptable value for the given channel this fact reveals Eve's attempt.

An interesting idea may be conceived in Eve's mind. As we inferred at the end of the previous subsection obtaining 50% of information at Eve causes 25% BER for Alice and Bob. What if Eve intercepts only one-tenth of the photons in the channel? This strategy would cause only 2.5% BER which is not significant compared to errors introduced by the channel. Of course Eve must pay the price for it, namely she obtains only 5% information about the key. Unfortunately to achieve the magnitude of an optical BER Eve has to give up almost all the information related to the secret key. On the other hand an open air connection is less reliable thus Eve still has some business here. Furthermore Eve can reveal another security gap.

Alice and Bob need the same secret key bit by bit. In order to eliminate the errors caused by the channel (or partly by Eve) they have to perform a classical error correction procedure over the public classical channel which can be accessed by Eve as well. Observing these classical bits Eve may increase mutual information between $\mathbf{k}_A$ and $\mathbf{k}_E$. Hence Alice and Bob must perform another classical algorithm called *privacy amplification* to decrease this unwanted correlation. This technique further reduces the length of the key but the mutual information is made less than a predefined engineering value. For details related to privacy amplification see *Further Reading*.

10.2   THE B92 ALGORITHM

The reader may find that the BB84 protocol is a bit complex in terms of protocol steps. Bennett developed further the BB84 protocol and he published a simple two-state protocol called B92 while still exploiting the *no cloning theorem*. We explain here the basic operation of this protocol because it managed to catch the essence of non-distinguishable quantum states in the simplest way. On the other hand we emphasize that although this algorithm is secure in theory, from the practical point of view it has some shortcomings (see *Further Reading*). Now, the communication steps between Alice and Bob can be followed in Fig. 10.4:

1. First Alice generates a random binary sequence $\mathbf{m}_A = [10111100]$ as she did with the BB84 protocol and modulates *directly*[4] the photons according to a simple rule

$$|\varphi\rangle = \begin{cases} |0\rangle & \text{if } \mathbf{m}_A[i] = 0 \\ \dfrac{|0\rangle + |1\rangle}{\sqrt{2}} & \text{if } \mathbf{m}_A[i] = 1, \end{cases}$$

----

[4]i.e. no $\mathbf{s}_A$ is required!

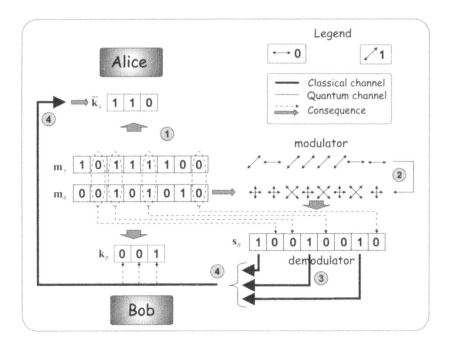

Fig. 10.4   Steps of B92 protocol if Eve is not present and the channel is idealistic

that is she uses non-orthogonal polarizations again. Index i refers to the ith bit of a series.

2. Next Alice sends the ith qbit over the quantum channel to Bob.

3. Bob receives this qbit and because he has no idea about Alice's m_A he generates another random sequence $m_B = [00101010]$ and uses its corresponding bit to determine which of the previously defined two measurement devices should be applied. He stores the measurement results in $s_B = [10010010]$, where Bob gets 0 with sure success in all those positions where $m_A[i] = m_B[i]$. Other bits prove to be 0 or 1 with the same probability.

4. It follows from the previous point that Bob yields $s_B[i] = 1$ only if $m_A[i] \neq m_B[i]$. Therefore he announces s_B and Alice and Bob keep those bits from m_A and m_B as the secret key for which $s_B[i] = 1$. Obviously one of them must invert his/her own key bits.

To avoid eavesdropping Alice and Bob use the same techniques as the BB84 protocol.

Remark: It is easy to see that unlike the BB84 protocol this method can be performed bit by bit.

10.3   EPR PARADOX BASED KEY DISTRIBUTION

Unlike the previous two protocols which exploited the possibilities concealed in the *no cloning theorem* there is another special quantum phenomenon available called *entanglement* for potential application within this topic. However, in order to establish a seamless transition from the BB84 protocol to the new one we ask Eve to play a friend of Alice and Bob in this new scene. Now, Eve generates random sequences s_E and m_E and uses the latter one to determine which of the two bases (modulator) to use for the bits of the former bit series. She makes a copy of the actual qbit[5] and sends half of the pair to Alice and the other half to Bob. They use their own random sequences m_A and m_B to measure the received qbits (similar to Bob's operation in the BB84 protocol). Next Eve announces her m_E, which allows Alice and Bob to filter those qbits which were measured in the same bases. These bits will be identical and can be used as the secret key (of course after classical error correction, etc.). Obviously while Eve remains correct this new protocol and the original BB84 are functionally equivalent as it is depicted in Fig. 10.5.

Unfortunately this protocol is very fragile in Eve's hand because Alice and Bob can never be sure about Eve. Therefore we have to further modify the three-party algorithm asking Eve to send entangled pairs of qbits, e.g. Bell states $|\beta_{00}\rangle = \frac{|00\rangle + |11\rangle}{\sqrt{2}}$. From Alice and Bob's point of view there are only minor changes in the protocol. Since the measured bits are identical at both parties if they used the same measurement bases, Alice and Bob have to exchange their m_A and m_B series over a public classical channel to obtain the key bits. Only one question remains, namely how can they reveal whether $|\beta_{00}\rangle$ has been modified due to an intentional attempt to access the information? The answer is based on the Bell inequality, which is in close connection to the EPR paradox (see Section 2.6.5). Violation of the Bell inequality can be tested by Alice and Bob by devoting several received qbits.

It is interesting to highlight the fact that in the case of the EPR based protocol no predefined key exists! Instead Alice and Bob generate the secret key indirectly when measuring their own halves of the Bell pairs.

Remark: Of course the entangled pairs can be produced not only by a third party but Alice can prepare and send them to Bob or they can share a couple of pairs in advance.

10.4   TELEPORTATION AS A USEFUL ELEMENT IN QUANTUM CRYPTOGRAPHY

This chapter is devoted to secure classical information transfer. As we observed the theoretically secure one-time pad implementing symmetric key cryptography often cannot be applied due to practical reasons in a classical environment. In order to

---

[5] Recall that *known* non-orthogonal states can be copied without any difficulties.

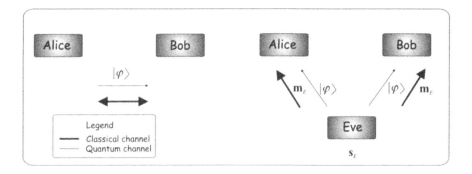

Fig. 10.5 Equivalence of two- and three-party version of BB84 protocol

trace these scenarios to the Vernam cipher previous sections introduced quantum-assisted solutions establishing secure secret key distribution. All of these efforts were devoted to delivering *classical* information from Alice to Bob. However, readers with open minds to this area may put the natural question: what if we would like to send quantum information (a message encoded into a sequence of one-qbit quantum states) between the edges of a larger quantum system in a secure way?

The answer is much simpler than one would expect. We ask the reader to recall quantum teleportation explained in detail in Section 4.2. Using this algorithm Alice was able to transfer an arbitrary qbit $|\varphi\rangle$ to Bob involving an entangled $|\beta_{00}\rangle$ Bell state. As we discussed earlier the two classical bits carry only relative information between $|\varphi\rangle$ and the half of $|\beta_{00}\rangle$ thus intercepting these bits in itself does not allow Eve reproducing $|\varphi\rangle$. Eavesdropping here and cloning in **Exercise** 4.2 have the same fundamental barrier.

10.5 FURTHER READING

The first workable quantum key distribution protocol was invented by Bennett and Brassard [35, 36]. The earliest discussion of privacy amplification can be found in [39]. Later it was extended in [34, 37]. Bennett reduced the number of handshaking of the BB84 protocol in [30] in 1992; this solution is often referred as the B92 protocol. Although this protocol proves to be safe theoretically because non-orthogonal states cannot be copied without perturbation, unfortunately it has some drawbacks in practice. This lies in the fact that in exchange of some losses the states can be distinguished unambiguously [119]. To realize these losses Alice and Bob have to monitor the attenuation of the channel, however, if Eve is able to influence this property of the channel then she can trick our lovers.

We discussed in this chapter the two-state B92 and four-state BB84 protocols. An obvious step ahead is if one considers a two-state protocol for instance as Bruss [31] in 1998 or Bechmann and Gisin [72] did in 1999. The applied six states belong to three different basis. This causes on one hand that the probability of using the same basis by Alice and Bob reduces to $\frac{1}{3}$, on the other hand the bit error ratio originating from Eve's action increases to 33% instead of 25% experienced at the BB84 protocol.

The EPR-paradox based key distribution protocol was published by Ekert [56] in 1991.

We have summarized only the basic ideas behind quantum-based key distribution and some well-known protocols highlighting the applications of these concepts. However, this topic is much more popular and fully discussed in the literature thus interested readers are suggested to follow the links in Chapter 15.

Concerning the implementation of quantum key distribution algorithms there are several problems to solve. First we have to select a suitable physical representation of qbits. A self-evident solution is offered by photons which are the fastest information-carrying alternative. Furthermore as an important advantage light is widely used in classical communications both in wired (optical) or in wireless (infrared) environments, thus large amounts of theoretical knowledge and practical devices are available. Of course in the case of quantum key distribution we are planning to use these channels in different ways. Therefore some extra requirements must be satisfied.

First of all we need appropriate photon sources (so-called photon guns) that are able to fire single photons. On the receiving side we should use single photon detectors. Implementation of both devices seem to be very challenging tasks which can be solved hopefully in the near future. Fortunately we do not have to wait until they are available on the market because faint laser pulses can replace them in the experiments.

Cryptography independently of its classical or quantum origin requires sophisticated random number generators. As a matter of fact the quantum behavior of nature at a small (nano) scale offers a perfect solution. As we learned earlier measuring state $\frac{|0\rangle + |1\rangle}{\sqrt{2}}$ in the $|0\rangle$, $|1\rangle$ basis can be regarded as a perfect coin tossing without hidden variables. Thus quantum-based random number generators are entering a fairly promising arena [21, 76].

As the last but not least barrier repeaters have to be considered. Long-distance communication cannot be maintained without deploying repeaters within certain ranges in order to compensate for the attenuation of the physical medium. Unlike classical optical communications where we use orthogonal (i.e. classical) states to represent information, making copies of the incoming bits does not cause any technical difficulties, however, in the case of quantum information transfer the *no cloning theorem* prevents us from building perfect repeaters.

The first successful experiment [34] related to quantum key distribution was carried out at IBM by in 1989. Bennett and his team managed to transfer keys over a short link 30 cm of length. Muller and his colleagues [15] at University of Geneva, Switzerland increased this distance first to 1100 m in 1993, which was extended [13, 14] to 23 km in 1995. They implemented the BB84 protocol over a traditional optical fiber under Lake Geneva, which was the first experiment outside a laboratory.

In the meantime Huttner and his colleagues [27] (1996) and Clarke *et al.* [105] (2000) have demonstrated how to eavesdrop the B92 protocol in practice.

Jacobs and Franson [28] were the first who managed to demonstrate outdoor free space key distribution over 75 m in 1996. Hughes and his colleagues [150] exceeded the 1 km free space barrier in 1998. Atmospheric key distribution has already been tested by John Rarity [75] over a 2 km link in 2001 while Hughes and his colleagues [126] reached the 10 km distance in 2002.

As the most dynamically developing area in quantum computing quantum key distribution has already reached the commercialization phase, see e.g. [78, 77].

Since the topic is so wide and popular listing both the theoretical and practical results in the field of quantum key distribution is outside the scope of this book therefore interested readers can find a fairly good summary of different realization techniques and results in [113].

11

Surfing the WEB on Quantum Basis

11.1 INTRODUCTION TO WEB SURFING

The number of hosts and the generated traffic on the Internet grows exponentially day by day. The Internet Protocol (IP) which was originally designed for data transfer among academic institutes slowly but surely enmeshes our globe. At the same time the original aim of this network and protocol passed through significant changes. This means not only the appearance of Internet access in each household but state-of-the-art infocom systems use or start using IP as their networking layer protocol. The new, so-called *ALL-IP concept* is depicted in Fig. 11.1. The global infocom network consists of an IP-based backbone and various kinds of access networks, which can be both wired or wireless, and of course it is connected to the Internet as well. Thus users and customers can exploit end-to-end IP connectivity.

The World Wide Web (WWW or simply WEB) is sitting on the Internet and enables users to access WEB content placed anywhere. The spectrum of such contents is quite broad from weather forecasts and stock exchange data through to submarine images about the sea-bottom to movie/music trailers. From a technical point of view Internet content is delivered in IP packets which provide a datagram-type bearer service. This means that the wanted content is segmented into smaller parts and these parts are put into packets. For the sake of simplicity a connection between two points on the Internet are connected together in the IP layer in a fairly straightforward way. There is no call set up phase to reserve resources in advance instead the packets are launched simply into the network and they have to find their destinations. In order to make this job easier useful payload is extended by a so-called header which contains hints for the packet, e.g. the address of the destination

Quantum Computing and Communications   S. Imre, F. Balázs
© 2004 John Wiley & Sons, Ltd   ISBN 0-470-86902-X (HB)

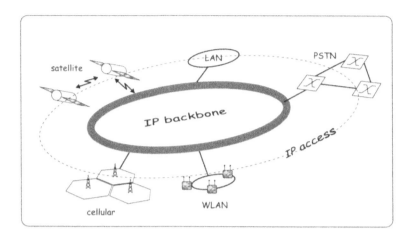

Fig. 11.1 The 'All-IP' concept

and the sender. Furthermore special entities are deployed all around the Internet, we call them routers. They are similar to police officers in a busy metropolis to whom we can turn if we feel lost. Routers have routing tables advising the packet to travel further in a proper direction towards the destination. In order to make this addressing mechanism more sophisticated IP addresses are unique 32- or 128-bit strings[1] and are distributed among hosts on a geographic basis i.e. a 32-bit address is divided into four one-byte fields introducing hierarchical levels into routing e.g. 65.246.255.51 refers to the address of Internet Engineering Task Force (IETF) responsible for the coordination of 'standardization' of the Internet.

Although the hierarchy makes the routing really efficient it has some drawbacks as well. For instance mobile terminals which are continuously changing their access points to the network get into serious trouble. Either they should change their IP addresses at each access point change or the routing tables should be updated. This problem leads far away hence interested users are advised to look for 'IP mobility' (even using a WEB browser). However, hierarchical location-based addressing lies in the heart of this chapter as well. To understand it we shortly summarize how a certain WEB content can be downloaded from a distant server to our host computer.

Memorizing 32-bit binary numbers even in decimal form is not for an everyday human brain therefore nicknames (Uniform Resource Locators, URL) are applied to identify hosts (more precisely hosts and contents), e.g. for IETF we use www.ietf.org. On the other hand we should provide mapping between names and numerical IP addresses. This functionality is provided by Domain Name Servers (DNS). When we launch a request from a WEB browser this request is directed first to a name server

---

[1]In the case of IPv4 we use 32 bits to address a certain host uniquely while IPv6 applies 128 bits for this purpose.

which searches its table and based on the result passes the request to the wanted content server. This strategy works fine until the requests dedicated to a given server exceed a certain amount. Popular WEB sites can become easily overloaded, hence the applied technique needs to be enhanced. Nowadays replicating the WEB content on different servers means a promising breakthrough. If these servers are distributed in a proper way throughout the world then it is enough to direct the request to the nearest server. However, this 'enough' proves to be quite a hard task because it has to be implemented in a totally compatible way. Therefore a special system is realized [121] over the name servers. Thus the name server first obtains a request and forwards this query to the overlay system (called Akamai), which answers with the numerical IP address of the nearest content server storing the requested content. To do this the overlay system needs to know the location of the user. Unfortunately protocols used on the Internet do not allow handling the name server's address and that of its client it is currently serving at the same time. Therefore for compatibility reasons the overlay system only has information about the location of the name server, which might be fairly unreliable. Fortunately the overlay system can start a 'Twenty Questions' or 'Barkohba'[2] like game to guess the user's numerical IP address. If the client has only one single IP address then it is enough to ask for each digit of its address question by question by the overlay system similar to the *Twenty Questions* game where one of the players (we call him/her 'Adversary') selects a secret from a large set e.g. dog from animals, and the other one (let's call him/her 'Seeker') has to guess this secret putting questions to the adversary who answers with *yes* or *no*.

The problem becomes more interesting if the user has more than one address either for security or other reasons. Several important questions arise in this context. How much information can we obtain about the secrets (IP addresses) using yes/no type questions? Is it possible to access completely the secrets with an arbitrary large number of questions? The problem has been tackled from mathematicians' point of view in [59].

Chung, Graham and Leighton investigated this 'Guessing Secret' problem using classical computing tools and listed several strategies and analyzed their computational complexity. Later similarities between the Guessing Secrets problem and list decoding were discovered. This latter problem is related to error correction. When we are transmitting digital information over a noisy channel errors may occur. If the number of erroneous bits are moderated suitably chosen overhead (error-correcting codes) can help to recover the original data. However, in a fairly hostile radio channel this effort could be not enough hence we are not able to decode unambiguously the transmitted information. In this hopeless scenario, however, one can isolate a small set (*list*) of potential messages which contain the original message

---

[2]Bar Kohba ('son of the star') originally Simon bar (ben) Kosiba was the commander of the Jewish troops during the second Jewish War (132–135 B.C.) against Rome [147]. After some success he and his troops became encircled in a mountain fort. Due to betrayal they were captured and executed in 135 B.C. According to a legend Bar Kohba's tongue was cut out. Hence he was able to answer only *yes* or *no* by shaking his head during his imprisonment.

as well. The computational complexity of the best-known classical strategy for the Guessing Secrets problem [111] is $O(\log(L) + \log^3(L))$ whose $\log(L)$ term refers to the number of questions and $\log^3(L)$ refers to the evaluation process of the answers.

11.2 QUANTUM-BASED SOLUTION OF THE GUESSING SECRET PROBLEM

Before invoking quantum computing to handle this challenging problem and prove its superiority over classical approaches let us first give the precise mathematical formulation. We denote the set of potential secrets by Λ containing L different elements. Moreover only the two-secret case ($k = 2$) is considered for the sake of plausible explanation. Interested readers will find references to the generalized ($k \geq 2$) case at the end of this chapter. The two secrets are referred as $s_1, s_2 \in \Lambda$ coded into $l = \operatorname{ld}(L)$-bit binary numbers and the Seeker strives to recover one of them. The Adversary's *yes/no* answers can be modeled via functions $f_q(s_i) : \{0, 1\}^l \to \{0, 1\}$ where $q \in \{0, 1\}^l$ stands for the binary identifier of a certain question. The adversary is assumed *malicious* but *truthful*. The former attribute refers to the fact that he/she may respond a given question q by $f_q(s_1)$ or $f_q(s_2)$ even randomly while the latter ensures us that $f_q(s_i)$ is deterministic. For the sake of better understanding the Guessing Secrets problem can be visualized by means of graphs consisting of vertices representing the secrets and edges showing logical connections between them. A simple four-secret example is depicted in Fig. 11.2. At the beginning of the game the graph (*phase A*) is full meshed and each question eliminates one or more vertices. As Chung and his colleagues noted in [59] the minimal number of questions is $O(\operatorname{ld}(L))$ in compliance with our heuristic expectation (cf. the Twenty Questions as the simplest case). If we manage to reach *phase B* – which comprises two disjoint pairs of vertices (s_1, s_2) and (s_3, s_4) – thanks to our wise questions then the Seeker can hit the jackpot via asking such that $f_q(s_1) = f_q(s_2) \neq f_q(s_3) = f_q(s_4)$. Contrary *phase C* and *D* show two topologies where the Adversary can trick the Seeker. In case of a star centered on s_1 (*phase C*) giving answers related always to s_2 the Seeker is able to deduce only s_2 because it has no common property with other non-selected elements of Λ, but s_1 remains uncovered. Moreover in a triangle-type scenario (*phase D*) independently from the Seeker's questions the Adversary can prevent him from deciding which of the two remaining three elements are the secrets. So our goal is to gain as much information about the secrets as possible using as few questions as possible.

The quantum computing based solution of the Guessing Secrets problem was discussed first by Michael Nathanson [114] in 2003. We will follow his line of thought with minor modifications when explaining how to trace this problem to our previous results.

If the readers make a short inventory of the already discussed algorithms and techniques they can easily recognize the similarities between the Deutsch–Jozsa algorithm presented in Section 5.2 and our actual challenge. As the major difference

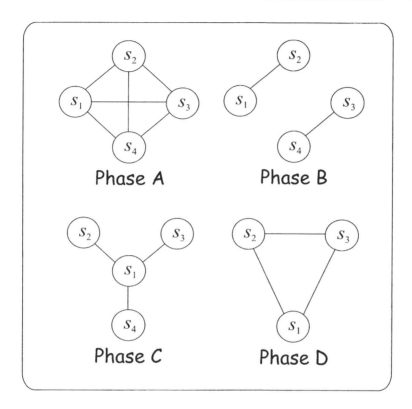

Fig. 11.2 Graph representation of the Guessing Secrets problem

we note that the roles were exchanged, namely we (the hero) had to guess q that is whether $f_q(s_i)$ was constant or balanced using arbitrary inputs s_i. Now, we have freedom to choose any function (questions) and a reduced set of $\{s_1, s_2\} \subset \Lambda$ should be deduced.

As a straightforward approach – often used in the literature – we define the answers as a binary inner product (modulo 2 sum of bitwise products) of index q and question s that is $f_q(s) = qs$. Therefore a similar architecture can be applied as we used in the Deutsch–Jozsa problem in Fig. 5.3 with a bit-modified f-controlled CNOT gate. The original master equation (5.3) has to be replaced by

$$U_f : |q\rangle_L |y\rangle \rightarrow |q\rangle_L |y \oplus f_q(s_i)\rangle, \tag{11.1}$$

and obviously the Adversary selects that gate which belongs to the chosen secret s_i. Furthermore the upper qregister contained after the Hadamard gate an equal superposition of all possible arguments x of $f(x)$ while now we feed the f-controlled CNOT gate with the equal superposition of all possible questions q.

Next, let us investigate the probability amplitudes at the output of the upper qregister similarly to the princess but from the Guessing Secrets problem point of view. Equation (5.9) helps us to derive the amplitude $c_{x'}(s_i)$ belonging to computational basis state $|x'\rangle : x' \in \Lambda$

$$|\varphi_3\rangle = \sum_{x' \in \{0,1\}^n} \underbrace{\left(\frac{1}{L} \sum_{q \in \{0,1\}^n} (-1)^{qx' + f_q(s_i)}\right)}_{c_{x'}(s_i)} |x'\rangle \otimes \frac{|0\rangle - |1\rangle}{\sqrt{2}}. \qquad (11.2)$$

Obviously we are interested in the probability of measuring the secrets $x' = s_1$ or $x' = s_2$. In order to obtain the corresponding probability amplitudes let us interpret $c_{x'}(s_i)$ in the following way

$$c_{x'}(s_i) = \frac{1}{L} \sum_{q \in \{0,1\}^n} (-1)^{qx' + f_q(s_i)},$$

and the sum contains $+1$ and -1 terms according to $qx' + f_q(s_i)$ and is even or odd, that is $qx' = f_q(s_i)$ or not. Therefore $c_{x'}(s_i)$ can be rewritten as

$$c_{x'}(s_i) = \frac{1}{L}[\#(q : qx' = f_q(s_i)) - \#(q : qx' \neq f_q(s_i))] \qquad (11.3)$$

and explained in the following manner: it counts – up to a constant factor $\frac{1}{L}$ – for a certain potential secret x' how many times (for how many different questions) it happens that $f_q(x') = f_q(s_i)$ or $f_q(x') \neq f_q(s_i)$ where s_i depends on the decision of the Adversary.

Since $f_q(s_i)$ equals either qs_1 or qs_2 thus concerning $c_{x'}(s_i)$ there are three different types of questions:

- Type A: $f_q(s_i) = qs_1 = qs_2$

- Type B: $f_q(s_i) = qs_1$ and $qs_1 \neq qs_2$

- Type C: $f_q(s_i) = qs_2$ and $qs_1 \neq qs_2$.

It is easy to see that for fixed $s_1, s_2 \in \Lambda$ exactly half of the questions fall into the first category, i.e. $\#(\text{TypeA}) = \frac{L}{2}$, furthermore

$$c_{x'}(s_1) = \frac{1}{L}[\#(\text{TypeA}) + \#(\text{TypeB}) - \#(\text{TypeC})],$$

while

$$c_{x'}(s_2) = \frac{1}{L}[\#(\text{TypeA}) + \#(\text{TypeC}) - \#(\text{TypeB})].$$

The probability of measuring $|s_1\rangle$ or $|s_2\rangle$ can be obtained by adding together classical probabilities

$$P(s_1 \lor s_2) = |c_{x'}(s_1)|^2 + |c_{x'}(s_2)|^2,$$

which always upperbounds

$$\frac{(c_{x'}(s_1) + c_{x'}(s_2))^2}{2} = \frac{1}{2}\left(\frac{2 \cdot \#(\text{TypeA})}{L}\right)^2 = \frac{1}{2}$$

because of the real coefficients and thanks to **Exercise** 11.1:

$$P(s_1 \vee s_2) \geq \tfrac{1}{2}.$$

Since $c_{x'}(s_1) + c_{x'}(s_2) \equiv 1$ the equality can be achieved if $c_{x'}(s_1) = c_{x'}(s_2)$ which is equivalent to $\#(\text{TypeB}) = \#(\text{TypeC})$. This points out the most efficient strategy of a malicious Adversary. He/she should choose s_1, s_2 when calculating the answers such that this special relation will be achieved. Contrary the Seeker may use this assumption as a worst-case scenario therefore if his/her strategy enables efficient access to the secret(s) even in such an evil-minded case then he/she can always be satisfied. Let us investigate the $P(s_1 \vee s_2) = \tfrac{1}{2}$ case. Obviously the probability of failure is also $P_f = 0.5$. If the Seeker repeats the proposed quantum guessing algorithm then the probability of being unsuccessful after the nth attempt equals $P_F = 0.5^n$, which tends to zero very rapidly as n grows. Returning to our infocom example the list-decoding technique requires $O(l + l^3)$ complexity with $l = 32$ or 128, i.e ~ 32800 or 2097280 elementary operations while enabling the Seeker to use the quantum algorithm l times he/she needs only ~ 1056 or 16512 operations with corresponding failure probability $2^{-32} \approx 10^{-9}$. Moreover the Seeker has the freedom to reduce further the required number of elementary operations in price of less strict probability of fiasco, which means that the computational complexity of the evaluation process of the answers is $O(1)$ while a classical Seeker cannot avoid $O(l^3)$.

Next we assume a well-meaning Adversary. If he/she insists on using the same secret say s_1 for all the questions then $\#(\text{TypeC})$ becomes 0 thus $c_{x'}(s_1) = 1$, therefore a measurement on the upper qregister will yield $|s_1\rangle$ with probability one. To achieve this the Seeker needs only one single but quantum question compared to the known most efficient classical counterpart which scans s_1 bit by bit by means of l questions.

The $k > 2$ case has several surprises in store which are outside the scope of this book. Here we would like only to give some motivation to the interested readers to continue the exploration of the problem. If we have more than two secrets the possibilities for the Adversary begin to flourish. Receiving a certain question he/she can select the secret to compute the answer randomly or can make a majority decision based on the evaluation with all the secrets, etc. Nathanson also investigated this more sophisticated problem in [114] but enough questions have been left open for talented readers.

Finally it is worth emphasizing that the technical problem can add individual colors to the problem. For instance the Internet content hunting may assume a conscious Adversary which could be well-minded or hostile. On the other hand in the case of list decoding the channel behaves rather like a puckish goblin playing dice.

Exercise 11.1. Show that $(a + b)^2 \leq 2(a^2 + b^2)$!

Part IV

Appendices

12

Mathematical Background

Proofs that odd numbers are prime:

- Mathematician: 1 is prime, 3 is prime, 5 is prime, 7 is prime, therefore, by induction, all odd numbers are prime.

- Physicist: 1 is prime, 3 is prime, 5 is prime, 7 is prime, 9 is a bad data point, 11 is prime, 13 is prime...

- Engineer: 1 is prime, 3 is prime, 5 is prime, 7 is prime, 9 is approximately prime, 11 is prime, 13 is prime...

- Computer scientist:[1] 1 is prime, 1 is prime, 1 is prime, 1 is prime...

12.1 BASIC PROBABILITY THEORY

12.1.1 Characterization of random events

Let A and B denote two random events. If the corresponding probabilities are represented by $P(A)$ and $P(B)$ then we have several important relations:

- *OR connection:* $P(A \vee B) = P(A) + P(B) - P(A \wedge B)$. If $P(A \wedge B) = 0$ then $P(A \vee B) = P(A) + P(B)$.

---

[1] working with 0s and 1s.

Quantum Computing and Communications   S. Imre, F. Balázs
© 2004 John Wiley & Sons, Ltd   ISBN 0-470-86902-X (HB)

- *Conditional probability:* $P(A|B) = \frac{P(A)\cdot P(B)}{P(B)}$.

- *Independent events:* If A and B are independent if and only if $P(A \wedge B) = P(A) \cdot P(B)$ then $P(A|B) = P(A)$.

- *Law of total probability:* $P(A) = \sum_i P(A|B_i)P(B_i)$.

- *Bayes formula:* $P(B_i|A) = \frac{P(A|B_i)P(B_i)}{\sum_j P(A|B_j)P(B_j)}$.

A group of mutually excluding probabilistic events $\{a\}$ belonging to the same observable is represented by means of *random variables* in probability theory. If variable A stands for a certain random event then the probability of obtaining $A = a$ is denoted by $P(A = a)$. Random variables are typically categorized according to their discrete or continuous nature. The most typical way to characterize a random variable is when its probability distribution function is given which determines the probability of being the random variable less than a certain value i.e. $F_A(a) \triangleq P(A < a)$. Equivalently the first derivative of the probability distribution $f_A(A)$ – called the probability density function (pdf) – can be used

$$F_A(a) \triangleq \int_{-\infty}^{a} f_A(t)dt,$$

from which

$$P(a \le A < b) = F_A(b) - F_A(a) = \int_a^b f_A(t)dt.$$

Obviously in the case of discrete random variables the integral has to be replaced by a summation, that is

$$F_A(a) \triangleq \sum_{t=-\infty}^{a} P(A = t),$$

where $P(A = a)$ is playing the role of the pdf in question.

Although any random variable can be represented perfectly by means of its moments typically the first two moments are used. These are the *expected value* $\mathbb{E}(A)$ and the *variance* σ_A with the following definitions

$$\mathbb{E}(A) \triangleq \sum_{a=-\infty}^{-\infty} aP(A = a)$$

if A is discrete and

$$\mathbb{E}(A) \triangleq \int_{-\infty}^{\infty} af_A(a)da.$$

Otherwise $\sigma_A^2 \triangleq \mathbb{E}((\mathbb{E}(A) - A)^2) \equiv \mathbb{E}(A^2) - \mathbb{E}^2(A)$.

The above definitions lead to the fact that for independent random variables $f_{A \wedge B}(a, b) = f_A(a) \cdot f_B(b)$ and thus $\mathbb{E}(A \cdot B) = \mathbb{E}(A) \cdot \mathbb{E}(B)$. Moreover it is useful to know that if we are interested in the expected value of a transformed random variable e.g. $B = g(A)$ then we do not need to calculate the pdf of B instead it is enough to know $f_A(a)$ and the following formula should be used

$$\mathbb{E}(B) \triangleq \sum_{a=-\infty}^{-\infty} g(a) P(A = a)$$

if A is discrete otherwise

$$\mathbb{E}(B) \triangleq \int_{-\infty}^{\infty} g(a) f_A(a) da.$$

Furthermore provided one knows $f_{A \wedge B}(a, b)$ and the random variables are not independent (i.e. the product form cannot be applied) then the individual pdfs can be determined as

$$f_A(a) = \int_{-\infty}^{\infty} f_{A \wedge B}(a, b) db,$$

or

$$P(A = a) = \sum_{b=-\infty}^{\infty} P_{A \wedge B}(a, b).$$

Finally we introduce conditional pdfs in the following way

$$f_{A|B=b_0}(a) = \frac{f_{A \wedge B}(a, b = b_0)}{f_B(b = b_0)},$$

which can be further processed to reach the Bayes formula for random variables

$$f_{A|B}(a) = \frac{f_{B|A}(b) f_A(a)}{f_B(b)}.$$

12.1.2 Decision theory

Let us assume that we have a random variable r. Its measured value depends on a selected element x_l from a finite set ($l = 1, \ldots, L$) and a process which can be characterized by means of a conditional pdf $f(r|x_l)$ belonging to the given element. Our task is to decide which x_l was selected if a certain r has been measured. Each guess H_l for x_l can be regarded as a hypothesis. Therefore decision theory is dealing with the design and analysis of suitable rules building connections between the set of observations and hypotheses.

If we are familiar with the unconditional (*a priori*) probabilities $P(x_l)$ then the Bayes formula helps us to compute the conditional (*a posteriori*) probabilities

$P(H_l|r)$ in the following way

$$P(H_l|r) = \frac{f(r|x_l)P(x_l)}{\sum_{i=1}^{L} f(r|x_i)P(x_i)}.$$

Obviously the most pragmatic solution is if one chooses H_l belonging to the largest $P(H_l|r)$. This type of hypothesis testing is called a *maximum a posteriori* (MAP) decision.

If *a priori* probabilities are unknown or x_l is equiprobable then the *maximum likelihood* (ML) decision can be used. It selects H_l resulting in the largest $f(r|x_l)$ when the observed r is substituted in order to minimize the probability of error.

12.2 LINEAR ALGEBRA

12.2.1 Complex numbers

Complex number c can be defined by means of its *real* c_r and *imaginary* c_i parts i.e. $c = c_r + jc_i$, where j stands for $\sqrt{-1}$. c can be interpreted as a vector with two-dimensional Descartes coordinates c_r and c_i. Hence its absolute value (length) C and phase α_c can be computed in the following way

$$C = \sqrt{|c_r|^2 + |c_i|^2}, \quad \alpha_c = \arctan\left(\frac{c_i}{c_r}\right).$$

Furthermore an equivalent representation can be obtained substituting these parameters into the *Euler form* $c = Ce^{j\alpha_c}$.

Addition and substraction of complex numbers c and y can be easily performed based on the vector interpretation

$$x = c \pm y = (c_r \pm y_r) + j(c_i \pm y_i).$$

On the other hand multiplication and division can be achieved much easier by using the exponential form

$$x = c \cdot y = CYe^{j(\alpha_c + \alpha_y)},$$

$$x = \frac{c}{y} = \frac{C}{Y}e^{j(\alpha_c - \alpha_y)}.$$

The *complex conjugate* of a complex number c is denoted by c^* and computed by inverting the imaginary part of c i.e. $c^* \triangleq c_r - jc_i \equiv Ce^{-j\alpha_c}$.

12.2.2 Gaussian elimination

The *Gaussian elimination* algorithm is able to solve systems of linear equations using finite steps in an automated way. Choosing an appropriate arrangement of variables

x_i we can show that a_{11} differs from zero in the following equation system

$$a_{11}x_1 + a_{12}x_2 + \cdots + a_{1n}x_n = b_1,$$
$$a_{21}x_1 + a_{22}x_2 + \cdots + a_{2n}x_n = b_2,$$
$$\vdots$$
$$a_{n1}x_1 + a_{n2}x_2 + \cdots + a_{nn}x_n = b_n,$$

then subtracting the first equation multiplied by a_{k1}/a_{11} from the kth equation for $k = 2, \ldots, n$ we get a new system of $(n-1)$ equations such that it does not contain x_1. Repeating this step at most $(n-1)$ times only a single equation remains with one variable. Solving this equation and substituting its solution back to the former equation systems $x_1, x_2, \ldots, x_n$ will be available.

12.2.3 Vector spaces

V is called an n-dimensional vector space over complex numbers[2] if the following criteria are satisfied:

1. Elements of V called vectors[3] which are n-tuples of complex numbers $|v\rangle = [v_1, v_2, \ldots, v_n]^T, v_i \in \mathbb{C}$.

2. There is an operation called *addition* defined as $|a\rangle = |v\rangle + |b\rangle, a_i = v_i + b_i$. Addition does not lead out from the vector space i.e. $|a\rangle \in V$.

3. Addition is *associative* and *commutative* and a so-called zero vector exists **0** for which $\forall |v\rangle \in V, |v\rangle + \mathbf{0} = |v\rangle$.

4. A so-called *additive inverse* $-|v\rangle$ belongs to each element of V such that $|v\rangle + (-|v\rangle) = \mathbf{0}$.

5. There is another operation called *scalar multiplication* between complex numbers c and vectors, $|a\rangle = c \cdot |v\rangle, a_i = c \cdot v_i$. Multiplication keeps the vector space, it is *associative* and *commutative*, furthermore $1 \cdot |v\rangle = |v\rangle$.

Bases and linear independency:

- $|v_1\rangle, \ldots, |v_m\rangle$ are *spanning vectors* of m-dimensional space V if $\forall |v\rangle \in V, |v\rangle = \sum_i c_i |v_i\rangle, c_i \in \mathbb{C}$. A certain V has several spanning vector sets.

- $|v_1\rangle, \ldots, |v_m\rangle$ are *linearly dependent* if $\exists c_1, \ldots, c_m \in \mathbb{C}, c_i \neq 0$ such that $\sum_i c_i |v_i\rangle = \mathbf{0}$ else $\{|v_i\rangle\}$ are *linearly independent*.

- A spanning set of space V consisting of linearly independent vectors is called a *basis* of this space. The *dimension* of a certain space V equals the number of its basis vectors.

---

[2]Real numbers are regarded in this context as special complex numbers.
[3]Vectors are typically denoted by $\mathbf{x}, \bar{x}$ or $\underline{x}$ by mathematicians but we use here quantum mechanical *'ket'* notation in compliance with the topic of this book.

Basic operations on vectors:

- *Transpose (T)* of vector $|v\rangle$ produces a column vector and vice versa.

- *Complex conjugate (*)* of vector $|v\rangle$ conjugates each coordinate of the vector.

- *Adjoint (†)* of vector $|v\rangle$ is defined as $|v\rangle^{\dagger} \triangleq (|v\rangle^{T})^{*}$ and denoted by $\langle v|$.

- *Scalar product* or *inner product* of two vectors $|v\rangle$ and $|w\rangle$ is a scalar quantity defined as $\langle v|w\rangle \triangleq \sum_{i} v_{i}^{*} \cdot w_{i}$ i.e.

$$\langle v|w\rangle = \begin{bmatrix} v_{1}^{*} & v_{2}^{*} & \cdots & v_{m}^{*} \end{bmatrix} \begin{bmatrix} w_{1} \\ w_{2} \\ \vdots \\ w_{m} \end{bmatrix} \sum_{i} v_{i}^{*} w_{i}.$$

Furthermore in the case of unit vectors $\langle v|w\rangle = 1$ if and only if $|w\rangle \equiv |v\rangle$ and $\langle v|w\rangle = 0$ if and only if $|v\rangle$ and $|w\rangle$ are *orthogonal*. Finally $\langle v|a\rangle \equiv (\langle a|v\rangle)^{*}$.

Norm:

- *Norm* can be interpreted as the generalization of the notion of *absolute value* assigning to each $|v\rangle \in V$ a scalar and it is denoted by $\||v\rangle\|$. Norm has to fulfil the following constraints:

  1. $\||v\rangle\| \geq 0$ and $\||v\rangle\| = 0$ if and only if $|v\rangle = \mathbf{0}$ if $|v\rangle \in V$
  2. $\||v_{1}\rangle + |v_{2}\rangle\| \leq \||v_{1}\rangle\| + \||v_{2}\rangle\|$ if $|v_{1}\rangle, |v_{2}\rangle \in V$
  3. $\|c \cdot |v\rangle\| = |c| \cdot \||v\rangle\|$ if $|v\rangle \in V$ and $c \in \mathbb{C}$.

- A vector space is *normalized* if a certain *norm* is defined for the space.

- A finite dimensional linear vector space is called a *Hilbert space* if its vectors have complex coordinates and the norm is defined as $\||v\rangle\| = \sqrt{\langle v|v\rangle}$. In this case the norm represents the length of the vector.

- A vector $|v\rangle$ is *normalized* or we call it a unit vector if the corresponding norm equals 1.

- Elements of a vector set $\{|v_{i}\rangle\}$ are *orthonormal* if they have unit length and they are mutually orthogonal i.e. $\langle v_{i}|v_{j}\rangle = \delta(i - j)$.

Linear operators:
Let V and W be vector spaces over complex numbers. A transform U is called a *linear operator* if it assigns to $\forall |v\rangle \in V$ a $|w\rangle = U|v\rangle \in W$ such that for arbitrary

scalar $c \in \mathbb{C}$ and vectors $|v\rangle, |v_1\rangle, |v_2\rangle$

$$U(|v_1\rangle + |v_2\rangle) = U|v_1\rangle + U|v_2\rangle,$$
$$U(c \cdot |v\rangle) = c \cdot U|v\rangle.$$

The former constraint is called the *superposition principle* and proves to be very useful when evaluating the operation of a certain quantum circuit. An identity operator I performs the following transformation $\forall |v\rangle \in V$ $I|v\rangle = |v\rangle$ while the zero operator assigns the zero vector to each $|v\rangle \in V$ i.e $O|v\rangle = \mathbf{0}$.

Linear operator U connecting an m-dimensional space to an n-dimensional one is represented by means of its matrix form

$$\mathbf{U}_{nm} = \begin{bmatrix} U_{11} & U_{12} & \cdots & U_{1m} \\ U_{21} & U_{22} & \cdots & U_{2m} \\ \vdots & \vdots & \ddots & \vdots \\ U_{n1} & U_{n2} & \cdots & U_{nm} \end{bmatrix}.$$

The resulting vector $|w\rangle = U|v\rangle$ can be calculated as $w_i = \sum_j U_{ij} v_j$.

Outer product is a special linear operator with the following definition. Let $|v\rangle, |z\rangle \in V$ and $|w\rangle \in W$ be vectors in Hilbert spaces then outer product operator $|w\rangle\langle v|$ connects the two spaces as $|w\rangle\langle v||z\rangle \equiv |w\rangle\langle v|z\rangle = \langle v|z\rangle|w\rangle$. The matrix of $U = |w\rangle\langle v|$ can be computed as $U_{ij} = w_i \cdot v_j^*$ i.e.

$$\mathbf{U} = \begin{bmatrix} w_1 \\ w_2 \\ \vdots \\ w_n \end{bmatrix} \begin{bmatrix} v_1^* & v_2^* & \cdots & v_m^* \end{bmatrix} \begin{bmatrix} w_1 v_1^* & w_1 v_2^* & \cdots & w_1 v_m^* \\ w_2 v_1^* & w_2 v_2^* & \cdots & w_2 v_m^* \\ \vdots & \vdots & \ddots & \vdots \\ w_n v_1^* & w_n v_2^* & \cdots & w_n v_m^* \end{bmatrix}.$$

If $\{|v_i\rangle\}$ forms an orthonormal basis of space V then the following *completeness relation* holds

$$\sum_i |v_i\rangle\langle v_i| \equiv I.$$

Tensor product or *direct product* ($\otimes$) of vectors are used to unify separate vector spaces. If $\{|v_i\rangle \in V\}$ and $\{|w_j\rangle \in W\}$ are orthonormal bases then $\{|v_i\rangle \otimes |w_j\rangle\}$ form an orthonormal basis for vector space $V \otimes W$. Equivalent notations for tensor product are $|v\rangle \otimes |w\rangle, |v\rangle|w\rangle, |vw\rangle$. If operator A acts on space V while operator B acts on space W then $C = A \otimes B$ which operates on $V \otimes W$ and can be calculated as

$$\mathbf{C} = \begin{bmatrix} A_{11}\mathbf{B} & A_{12}\mathbf{B} & \cdots & A_{1m}\mathbf{B} \\ A_{21}\mathbf{B} & A_{22}\mathbf{B} & \cdots & A_{2m}\mathbf{B} \\ \vdots & \vdots & \ddots & \vdots \\ A_{n1}\mathbf{B} & A_{n2}\mathbf{B} & \cdots & A_{nm}\mathbf{B} \end{bmatrix}.$$

12.2.4 Eigenvectors and eigenvalues

Eigenvectors $|u\rangle$ of a linear operator U have the following property

$$U|u\rangle = \omega_u |u\rangle,$$

where $\omega_u \in \mathbb{C}$ represents the *eigenvalues* of U. Eigenvalues can be determined by solving the *characteristic equation system*

$$\det(\mathbf{U} - \omega\mathbf{I}) = 0.$$

If a given eigenvalue belongs to more than one eigenvector then those vectors are called *degenerate*.

Diagonalizable operators have a special – so-called *diagonal* – representation, which is often referred as *spectral/orthogonal decomposition*

$$\mathbf{U}_{N \times N} = \sum_{u=0}^{N-1} \omega_u |u\rangle\langle u| = \begin{bmatrix} \omega_0 & 0 & \cdots & 0 \\ 0 & \omega_1 & \cdots & 0 \\ \vdots & \vdots & \ddots & \vdots \\ 0 & 0 & \cdots & \omega_{N-1} \end{bmatrix},$$

where $\{|u\rangle\}$ form an orthonormal basis vector set in the space U is acting for.

Scalar invariants of the matrix $\mathbf{U}$ belonging to operator U are its determinant and trace

- $\det(\mathbf{U}) = \prod_u \omega_u,$
- $\mathrm{tr}(U) = \sum_i U_{ii} = \sum_u \omega_u.$

12.2.5 Special linear operators

Adjoint
Let us assume a linear operator U acting on a Hilbert space V then the *adjoint* of U is another linear operator which satisfies $\forall |v\rangle, |w\rangle \in V$ with the following equality

$$\langle v|U|w\rangle = \langle w|U^\dagger|v\rangle.$$

As a consequence of this definition the following relations hold:

- $(UT)^\dagger = T^\dagger U^\dagger,$
- $|v\rangle^\dagger = \langle v|,$
- $(U|v\rangle)^\dagger = \langle v|U^\dagger,$
- $((U^\dagger)^\dagger = U.$

Normal operators
Normal operators have the following definition $UU^\dagger \equiv U^\dagger U$. An operator is normal

if and only if it is diagonizable, that is it has spectral decomposition.

Self-adjoint or Hermitian operators
A *self-adjoint* or *Hermitian* operator equals its conjugate transpose i.e. $U \equiv (U^T)^*$ or using adjoint operator notation $U \equiv U^\dagger$. Hermitian operators are normal thus they have special spectral decomposition with real eigenvalues.

Unitary operators
A linear operator is called *unitary* if its adjoint is equal to its inverse $U^\dagger \equiv U^{-1}$. Unitary operators have some very important properties, namely

- they have $n \times n$ matrices,

- they are normal operators $\Rightarrow$ they have spectral decompositions $\Rightarrow$ their eigenvectors always form an orthonormal basis vector set,

- they have eigenvalues in the form of $e^{j\alpha_u}$.

There are three other equivalent definitions for unitarity that may help in certain cases to catch the essence of these very special and in quantum computing very important operators. A linear operator U with an $n \times n$ matrix is unitary if and only if

- the rows (columns) of its matrix form an orthonormal (orthogonal and unit length) vector set or,

- the operator is reversible, i.e. any input vector can be restored in possession of the related output vector and keeps the unit length property of its input vector while producing the output,

- the operator keeps the inner product, i.e. $\langle \varphi | U^\dagger U | \psi \rangle \equiv \langle \varphi | \psi \rangle$.

Operators which are unitary and Hermitian at the same time have eigenvalues ± 1.

Positive definite operators
An operator U is *positive semi-definite* if $\forall |v\rangle \neq \mathbf{0} \in V$ $\langle v|A|v\rangle \geq 0$. If only the inequality is satisfied then U is called *positive definite*. There are several important consequences of this definition:

- Positive semi-definite operators are Hermitian.

- Operators in the form of $|v\rangle\langle v|$ are always positive semi-definite.

- For any U the operator $U^\dagger U$ is positive semi-definite.

Projectors
Projectors form a special group of Hermitian operators. They orthogonally transform ('project') space V to one of its subspaces W. If $\{|v_i\rangle\}$ form an orthonormal basis for V with dimension n then we can select m of them $\{|v_l\rangle\}$ such that this subset represents an orthonormal basis of W having m dimensions. The projector onto W can be computed as $P = \sum_{i=1}^{m} |v_l\rangle\langle v_l|$.

- For projectors $PP = P$.

- Projectors are Hermitian because they are positive semi-definite since $|v\rangle\langle v|$ are positive semi-definite.

12.2.6 Operator functions

Normal operators can be used as an input of any function $f : \mathbb{C} \rightarrow \mathbb{C}$. We call such matrix-fed functions *operator functions* and they can be interpreted in the following way. If U is a normal operator then it has spectral decomposition

$$U = \sum_u \omega_u |u\rangle\langle u|$$

with eigenvalue ω_u and eigenvector $|u\rangle$ and

$$f(U) \equiv U = \sum_u f(\omega_u)|u\rangle\langle u|.$$

As an example $f(X) = e^{j\alpha X}$ can be calculated considering the spectral decomposition of X (see **Exercise** 6.11)

$$X = (+1)\frac{|0\rangle + |1\rangle}{\sqrt{2}}\frac{\langle 0| + \langle 1|}{\sqrt{2}} + (-1)\frac{|0\rangle - |1\rangle}{\sqrt{2}}\frac{\langle 0| - \langle 1|}{\sqrt{2}}$$

$$= (+1)\begin{bmatrix} \frac{1}{2} & \frac{1}{2} \\ \frac{1}{2} & \frac{1}{2} \end{bmatrix} + (-1)\begin{bmatrix} \frac{1}{2} & -\frac{1}{2} \\ -\frac{1}{2} & \frac{1}{2} \end{bmatrix} = \begin{bmatrix} 0 & 1 \\ 1 & 0 \end{bmatrix},$$

hence

$$f(X) = e^{j\alpha}\begin{bmatrix} \frac{1}{2} & \frac{1}{2} \\ \frac{1}{2} & \frac{1}{2} \end{bmatrix} + e^{-j\alpha}\begin{bmatrix} \frac{1}{2} & -\frac{1}{2} \\ -\frac{1}{2} & \frac{1}{2} \end{bmatrix}$$

$$= \begin{bmatrix} \frac{e^{j\alpha}+e^{-j\alpha}}{2} & \frac{e^{j\alpha}-e^{-j\alpha}}{2} \\ \frac{e^{j\alpha}-e^{-j\alpha}}{2} & \frac{e^{j\alpha}+e^{-j\alpha}}{2} \end{bmatrix} = \begin{bmatrix} \cos(\alpha) & j\sin(\alpha) \\ j\sin(\alpha) & \cos(\alpha) \end{bmatrix}.$$

12.3 NUMBER THEORY

12.3.1 Modular arithmetic

Modular arithmetic was introduced by Gauss in his famous work *Disquistiones Arithmeticae* in 1801.

The notation $c = a \bmod b$ refers to the remainder obtained by dividing a by b and results in a number c which is always smaller than a. For instance $5 \bmod 3 = 2$. Numbers a and b are equal in modulo N sense ($b = a \bmod N$) if $a = b + kN$, e.g. $5 \bmod 3 = 10 \bmod 8 = 4 \bmod 2$. This fact can be expressed as 'a is *congruent* to b

modulo N' or 'b is the *residue* of a modulo N'. Modular arithmetic has the following properties

commutative:$(a \pm b) \bmod N = ((a \bmod N) \pm (b \bmod N)) \bmod N$
associative:$(a \cdot b) \bmod N = ((a \bmod N) \cdot (b \bmod N)) \bmod N$
distributive:$(a \cdot (b + c)) \bmod N = (((a \cdot b) \bmod N) + ((a \cdot c) \bmod N)) \bmod N$.

It is useful to highlight that modular addition and multiplication are unitary operators for $x, y, a \in \{0, 1\}^n$

$$|x\rangle \xrightarrow{U_+} |(x + a) \bmod 2^n\rangle = |y\rangle,$$
$$|x\rangle \xrightarrow{U_\times} |(x \times a) \bmod 2^n\rangle = |y\rangle,$$

Since decomposition of modular exponentiation is a very useful tool we summarize it here. Exploiting the binary representation of $a = \sum_{i=1}^{2^n} a_i 2^{n-i}$ and $a_i \in \{0, 1\}$

$$(x^a) \bmod 2^n = \prod_{i=1}^{2^n} \left[\left(x^{a_i 2^{n-i}} \right) \bmod 2^n \right].$$

12.3.2 Definitions

Greatest common divisor: Assuming two positive integers $a, b \in \mathbb{Z}^+$, their greatest common divisor is denoted by $\gcd(a, b)$ and defined as the largest integer number c that divides both a and b. E.g. $\gcd(16, 20) = 5$.

Prime number: an integer $a \geq 2$ is said to be prime if it can be divided only by 1 and a without a remainder.

Relative primes or *co-primes:* Integers a and b are relative primes if $\gcd(a, b) = 1$.

Congruence: equations whose two sides are equal in modulo N sense are called congruences and denoted $a \equiv b \,(\bmod N)$.

Multiplicative inverse: Let a and N be relative primes ($\gcd(a, N) = 1$) and assume that for integer $0 < b \leq N - 1$, $(a \cdot b) \bmod N = 1$ then b is called the multiplicative inverse of a in modulo N sense.

Group: a group $(G, @)$ contains a set G and an operation $@$ fulfilling the following axioms:

1. The group operation is *associative:* $a@(b@c) = (a@b)@c \,\forall\, a, b, c \in G$.

2. *Identity element* $1 \in G$ exists: $a@1 = 1@a = a \,\forall\, a \in G$.

3. *Inverse* of $a \in G$ exists: $a@a^{-1} = a^{-1}@a = 1 \,\forall\, a \in G$.

A group is called *commutative* or *Abelian* if besides these three axioms the following one is also true: $a@b = b@a \ \forall \ a, b \in G$.

Additive group: if the operation @ equals the modulo N addition then the group is called modulo N additive group. Trivially in this case $G = \mathbb{Z}_N$.

Multiplicative group: if the operation @ equals the modulo N multiplication then the group is called modulo N multiplicative group and denoted with

$$G = \mathbb{Z}_N^* = \{a \in \mathbb{Z}_N : \gcd(a, N) = 1\}.$$

For example $\mathbb{Z}_{15}^* = \{1, 2, 4, 7, 8, 11, 13, 14\}$.

Order: Let $x < N$ be two positive integers $x < N$ which are co-primes, i.e. $\gcd(x, N) = 1$. The order of x modulo N is defined as the least natural integer r such that $x^r \bmod N = 1$.

Generator: a group G is called cyclic if there is an element $a \in G$ such that for each $b \in G$ an integer c exists fulfilling $b = a^c$. Moreover a is regarded as the generator of G.

One-way functions: A function $f : x \rightarrow y$ is called a one-way function if computing $f(x)$ for all x can be performed easily (fast) but the opposite direction i.e. calculating x from any $y = f(x)$ proves to be hard.

Euler function: for an arbitrary positive integer N the corresponding Euler function $\varphi(N)$ gives the number of relative primes to N from the range $1, 2, \ldots, N$. E.g. $\varphi(1) = 1, \varphi(10) = 4$.

12.3.3 Euclid's algorithm

Euclid's algorithm aims to find $\gcd(a, b)$ and can be summarized in the following manner.

1. Dividing a by b we get quotient q_1 and nonzero remainder r_1:

$$a = q_1 b + r_1, \quad 0 < r_1 < b.$$

2. b is divided by r_1 i.e. b plays the role of a and r_1 that of b resulting in q_2 and nonzero r_2:
$$b = q_2 r_1 + r_2, \quad 0 < r_2 < r_1.$$

3. We continue the algorithm while the actual remainder remains nonzero:

$$r_k = q_{k+2} r_{k+1} + r_{k+2}, \quad 0 < r_{k+2} < r_{k+1}.$$

4. When the division returns $r_l = 0$ we know that $r_{l-2} = q_l r_{l-1} + 0$ and the algorithm stops with $\gcd(a, b) = r_{l-1}$.

Example: Determine the greatest common divisor of $a = 330$ and $b = 126$!

1. step: $330 = 2 \times 126 + 78$

2. step: $126 = 1 \times 78 + 48$

3. step: $78 = 1 \times 48 + 30$

4. step: $48 = 1 \times 30 + 18$

5. step: $30 = 1 \times 18 + 12$

6. step: $18 = 1 \times 12 + 6$

7. step: $12 = 2 \times \underline{\underline{6}} + 0$

12.3.4   Continued fraction and convergents

If a and b are integers then a/b is called the *rational fraction* or *rational number*. *Continued fraction* representation of a rational fraction can be derived from Euclid's algorithm.

$$a = q_1 b + r_1 \qquad\Rightarrow\qquad \frac{a}{b} = q_1 + \frac{1}{\frac{b}{r_1}}$$

$$b = q_2 r_1 + r_2 \qquad\Rightarrow\qquad \frac{b}{r_1} = q_2 + \frac{1}{\frac{r_1}{r_2}}$$

$$\vdots \qquad\qquad\qquad \Rightarrow \qquad \vdots$$

$$r_k = q_{k+2} r_{k+1} + r_{k+2} \qquad\Rightarrow\qquad \frac{r_k}{r_{k+1}} = q_{k+2} + \frac{1}{\frac{r_{k+1}}{r_{k+2}}}$$

$$\vdots \qquad\qquad\qquad \Rightarrow \qquad \vdots$$

$$r_{l-2} = q_l r_{l-1} \qquad\Rightarrow\qquad \frac{r_{l-2}}{r_{l-1}} = q_l.$$

Thus using the right-hand side equivalences we can describe $\frac{a}{b}$ as

$$\frac{a}{b} = q_1 + \cfrac{1}{q_2 + \cfrac{1}{q_3 + \cdots + \cfrac{1}{q_l}}}.$$

Convergents of rational number $\frac{a}{b}$ are the following rational fractions

$$\zeta_1 = q_1, \quad \zeta_2 = q_1 + \frac{1}{q_2}, \quad \zeta_3 = q_1 + \cfrac{1}{q_2 + \frac{1}{q_3}}, \quad \ldots, \quad \zeta_l = \frac{a}{b}.$$

Example: Determine the continued fraction representation of a/b if $a = 330$ and $b = 126$ and the corresponding convergents.

1. step: $330 = 2 \times 126 + 78 \Rightarrow \dfrac{330}{126} = 2 + \dfrac{1}{\dfrac{126}{78}}$

2. step: $126 = 1 \times 78 + 48 \Rightarrow \dfrac{330}{126} = 2 + \dfrac{1}{1 + \dfrac{1}{\dfrac{78}{48}}}$

3. step: $78 = 1 \times 48 + 30 \Rightarrow \dfrac{330}{126} = 2 + \dfrac{1}{1 + \dfrac{1}{1 + \dfrac{1}{\dfrac{48}{30}}}}$

4. step: $48 = 1 \times 30 + 18 \Rightarrow \dfrac{330}{126} = 2 + \dfrac{1}{1 + \dfrac{1}{1 + \dfrac{1}{1 + \dfrac{1}{\dfrac{30}{18}}}}}$

5. step: $30 = 1 \times 18 + 12 \Rightarrow \dfrac{330}{126} = 2 + \dfrac{1}{1 + \dfrac{1}{1 + \dfrac{1}{1 + \dfrac{1}{1 + \dfrac{1}{\dfrac{18}{12}}}}}}$

6. step: $18 = 1 \times 12 + 6 \Rightarrow \dfrac{330}{126} = 2 + \dfrac{1}{1 + \dfrac{1}{1 + \dfrac{1}{1 + \dfrac{1}{1 + \dfrac{1}{1 + \dfrac{1}{\dfrac{12}{6}}}}}}}$

$$7. \text{step:} 12 = 2 \times 6 + 0 \Rightarrow \frac{330}{126} = 2 + \cfrac{1}{1 + \cfrac{1}{1 + \cfrac{1}{1 + \cfrac{1}{1 + \cfrac{1}{1 + \cfrac{1}{2}}}}}}.$$

The convergents are

$$\zeta_1 = 2; \; \zeta_2 = 2 + \frac{1}{1} = 3; \; \zeta_3 = 2 + \cfrac{1}{1 + \cfrac{1}{1}} = \frac{5}{2} = 2.5;$$

$$\zeta_4 = 2 + \cfrac{1}{1 + \cfrac{1}{1 + \cfrac{1}{1}}} = \frac{8}{3} = 2.6^{\bullet};$$

$$\zeta_5 = 2 + \cfrac{1}{1 + \cfrac{1}{1 + \cfrac{1}{1 + \cfrac{1}{1}}}} = \frac{13}{5} = 2.6;$$

$$\zeta_6 = 2 + \cfrac{1}{1 + \cfrac{1}{1 + \cfrac{1}{1 + \cfrac{1}{1 + \cfrac{1}{1}}}}} = \frac{21}{8} = 2.625;$$

$$\zeta_7 = 2 + \cfrac{1}{1 + \cfrac{1}{1 + \cfrac{1}{1 + \cfrac{1}{1 + \cfrac{1}{1 + \cfrac{1}{2}}}}}} = \frac{55}{21} = \frac{330}{126} = 2.619.$$

12.3.5 Useful theorems

Theorem 12.1. *If $m_b/2^n$ is a rational fraction and b and r are positive integers that satisfy*

$$\left| \frac{b}{r} - \frac{m_b}{2^n} \right| \leq \frac{1}{2r^2}$$

then b/r is a convergent of the continued fraction of $\frac{m_b}{2^n}$.

Theorem 12.2. *The Euler function can be computed for arbitrary positive integer N in the following way*

$$\varphi(N) = N \prod_{p} \left(\frac{p-1}{p} \right)$$

where p runs over all the different prime factors of N including N itself if it is a prime.

Two important consequences: $\varphi(N) = N - 1$ if and only if N is prime. If N is a composite number then $\varphi(N) < N - 1$.

Theorem 12.3. *For arbitrary integer $N > 1$ if $\gcd(N, a) = 1$ then the following congruence $(ax) \bmod N \equiv 1$ has only a single solution in modulo N sense, else no solution exists.*

Theorem 12.4. *Fermat's little theorem: For arbitrary prime N and $a \in \mathbb{Z}_N^*$*

$$(a^{N-1}) \bmod N \equiv 1.$$

This theorem was generalized by Euler in Theorem 12.5.

Theorem 12.5. *Euler's theorem: For arbitrary integer $N > 1$ and $a \in \mathbb{Z}_N^*$*

$$(a^{\varphi(N)}) \bmod N \equiv 1.$$

An important consequence: The Euler function is multiplicative that is $\varphi(a) \cdot \varphi(b) = \varphi(ab)$ whenever $\gcd(a, b) = 1$.

Theorem 12.6. *Chinese remainder theorem: Assume the following system of congruences to different moduli:*

$$x \equiv a_1 \pmod{m_1},$$
$$x \equiv a_2 \pmod{m_2},$$
$$\vdots$$
$$x \equiv a_l \pmod{m_l}.$$

Furthermore it is supposed that m_i and m_k are pairwise co-primes i.e. $\gcd(m_i, m_k) = 1$ if $i \neq k$ then there exists a solution x_0 for all the congruences and any two solutions are congruents to one another in modulo $m = \prod_{i=1}^{l} m_i$ sense.

13

Derivations Related to the Generalized Grover Algorithm

13.1 EIGENVALUES OF THE GENERALIZED GROVER OPERATOR

To find the eigenvalues of Q one should solve the characteristic equation $\det\{Q - qI\} = 0$, which seems to be a fairly hard task

$$(Q_{11} - q)(Q_{22} - q) - Q_{12}Q_{21} = 0,$$

$$q_{1,2} = \frac{Q_{11} + Q_{22} \pm \sqrt{(Q_{11} + Q_{22})^2 - 4(Q_{11}Q_{22} - Q_{12}Q_{21})}}{2}. \tag{13.1}$$

Therefore we follow a more pragmatic way. Applying the basis-independent product of eigenvalues in the form of $\det\{Q\} = q_1 q_2$ as well as exploiting the form of eigenvalues of unitary operators $e^{j\varepsilon}$,

$$\det(Q) = Q_{11}Q_{22} - Q_{12}Q_{21}, \tag{13.2}$$

$$Q_{11}Q_{22} = (-1)(-1)\left[1 + \left(e^{j\theta} - 1\right)\cos^2(\Omega)\right] e^{j\phi}\left[1 + \left(e^{j\theta} - 1\right)\sin^2(\Omega)\right]$$

$$= e^{j\phi}\left[1 + \left(e^{j\theta} - 1\right)\underbrace{\left(\sin^2(\Omega) + \cos^2(\Omega)\right)}_{\equiv 1} + \left(e^{j\theta} - 1\right)^2\sin^2(\Omega)\cos^2(\Omega)\right]$$

$$= e^{j\phi}\left[e^{j\theta} + \left(e^{j\theta} - 1\right)^2\sin^2(\Omega)\cos^2(\Omega)\right]. \tag{13.3}$$

$$Q_{12}Q_{21} = (-1)(-1)e^{j\phi}\left(e^{j\theta} - 1\right)\sin(\Omega)\cos(\Omega)\, e^{j\Lambda}\left(e^{j\theta} - 1\right)\sin(\Omega)\cos(\Omega)\, e^{-j\Lambda}$$

$$= e^{j\phi}\left[\left(e^{j\theta} - 1\right)^2\sin^2(\Omega)\cos^2(\Omega)\right]. \tag{13.4}$$

Quantum Computing and Communications   S. Imre, F. Balázs
© 2004 John Wiley & Sons, Ltd   ISBN 0-470-86902-X (HB)

Substituting (13.3) and (13.4) into (13.2) we get

$$\det(\mathbf{Q}) = e^{j(\theta+\phi)} \tag{13.5}$$

since $q_i = e^{j\varepsilon_i}$, hence the eigenvalues of the generalized Grover operator become

$$q_{1,2} = -e^{j\left(\frac{\theta+\phi}{2}\pm\Upsilon\right)}. \tag{13.6}$$

Furthermore, it is known that the trace of $\mathbf{Q}$ can be expressed as

$$Q_{11} + Q_{22} = q_1 + q_2, \tag{13.7}$$

resulting in

$$Q_{11} + Q_{22} = -\left[1 + \left(e^{j\theta} - 1\right)\cos^2(\Omega) + e^{j\phi}\left[1 + \left(e^{j\theta} - 1\right)\sin^2(\Omega)\right]\right]$$

$$= -\left[\underbrace{1 - \cos^2(\Omega)}_{\sin^2(\Omega)} + e^{j\theta}\underbrace{\cos^2(\Omega)}_{1-\sin^2(\Omega)} + e^{j\phi} + e^{j(\phi+\theta)}\sin^2(\Omega) - e^{j\phi}\sin^2(\Omega)\right]$$

$$= -\left[\sin^2(\Omega) + e^{j\theta} + e^{j\phi} - \sin^2(\Omega)\left(-e^{j\theta} - e^{j\phi} + e^{j(\phi+\theta)}\right)\right], \tag{13.8}$$

where the equality stands if both the real and the imaginary parts of (13.8) holds separately. The imaginary part looks like

$$\Im\{Q_{11} + Q_{22}\}$$
$$= -\left[\sin(\theta) + \sin(\phi) + \sin^2(\Omega)\left(-\sin(\theta) - \sin(\phi) + \sin(\phi+\theta)\right)\right]$$
$$= -\left\{2\sin\left(\frac{\phi+\theta}{2}\right)\cos\left(\frac{\phi-\theta}{2}\right)\right.$$
$$\left. + \sin^2(\Omega)\left[\sin\left(\frac{\phi+\theta}{2}\right)\cos\left(\frac{\phi-\theta}{2}\right) + 2\sin\left(\frac{\phi+\theta}{2}\right)\cos\left(\frac{\phi+\theta}{2}\right)\right]\right\}, \tag{13.9}$$

where the trigonometrical equivalence $\left[\sin x + \sin y = 2\sin\left(\frac{x+y}{2}\right)\cos\left(\frac{x-y}{2}\right)\right]$ is employed. Applying (13.6) on (13.7) and substituting them into (13.8) we get

$$\Im\{q_1 + q_2\} = -\left\{\sin\left(\frac{\theta+\phi}{2} + \Upsilon\right) + \sin\left(\frac{\theta+\phi}{2} - \Upsilon\right)\right\}$$
$$= -2\sin\left(\frac{\theta+\phi}{2}\right)\cos(\Upsilon). \tag{13.10}$$

From (13.9) and (13.10) it follows that

$$
\begin{aligned}
\cos(\Upsilon) &= \cos\left(\frac{\phi - \theta}{2}\right) + \sin^2(\Omega)\left(\cos\left(\frac{\theta + \phi}{2}\right) - \cos\left(\frac{\phi - \theta}{2}\right)\right) \\
&= \cos\left(\frac{\phi - \theta}{2}\right) - 2\sin^2(\Omega)\sin\left(\frac{\phi}{2}\right)\sin\left(\frac{\theta}{2}\right) \\
&= \cos\left(\frac{\phi}{2}\right)\cos\left(\frac{\theta}{2}\right) + \sin\left(\frac{\phi}{2}\right)\sin\left(\frac{\theta}{2}\right)\left[1 - 2\sin^2(\Omega)\right] \\
&= \cos\left(\frac{\phi}{2}\right)\cos\left(\frac{\theta}{2}\right) + \sin\left(\frac{\phi}{2}\right)\sin\left(\frac{\theta}{2}\right)\cos(2\Omega).
\end{aligned}
\tag{13.11}
$$

The derivation of the real part of (13.8) is straightforward, hence

$$
\begin{aligned}
&\Re\left\{Q_{11} + Q_{22}\right\} \\
&= -\left[2\cos\left(\frac{\theta + \phi}{2}\right)\cos\left(\frac{\theta - \phi}{2}\right) + \sin^2(\Omega)\cdot 2\cos^2\left(\frac{\theta + \phi}{2}\right)\right],
\end{aligned}
\tag{13.12}
$$

thus

$$
\Re\left\{q_1 + q_2\right\} = -2\cos\left(\frac{\theta + \phi}{2}\right)\cos(\Upsilon),
\tag{13.13}
$$

whereas we reached the same result as in (13.11)

$$
\cos(\Upsilon) = \cos\left(\frac{\theta - \phi}{2}\right) + \sin^2(\Omega)\left(\cos\left(\frac{\theta + \phi}{2}\right) - \cos\left(\frac{\theta - \phi}{2}\right)\right).
$$

Consequently, only one restriction has to be made, namely $\cos(\Upsilon) = \cos(-\Upsilon)$. At the same time according to the special form of the eigenvalues in (13.6) the two Υ's are equivalent to each other, since both lead to the same eigenvalue pair.

13.2 EIGENVECTORS OF THE GENERALIZED GROVER OPERATOR

In possession of the eigenvalues $q_{1,2}$ derived above in (13.6) we now derive the eigenvectors of **Q**.

Starting from (7.66) and using expression

$$
|\psi_1\rangle = \psi_{1\alpha}|\alpha\rangle + \psi_{1\beta}|\beta\rangle,
\tag{13.14}
$$

a homogeneous linear equation system is obtained

$$
\begin{aligned}
Q_{11}\psi_{1\alpha} + Q_{12}\psi_{1\beta} &= q_1\psi_{1\alpha}, \\
Q_{21}\psi_{1\alpha} + Q_{22}\psi_{1\beta} &= q_2\psi_{1\beta},
\end{aligned}
\tag{13.15}
$$

from which

$$
\frac{\psi_{1\alpha}}{\psi_{1\beta}} = \frac{q_1 - Q_{22}}{Q_{21}},
\tag{13.16}
$$

$$
\frac{\psi_{1\beta}}{\psi_{1\alpha}} = \frac{q_1 - Q_{11}}{Q_{12}}.
\tag{13.17}
$$

Apparently, there are infinite solutions of (13.15), differing only in a scalar factor. For our purposes we only need those ones having unit length in the form

$$|\psi\rangle_{\text{norm}} = \cos(z)e^{jC}|\alpha\rangle + \sin(z)|\beta\rangle. \tag{13.18}$$

According to (13.16) let $\psi_{1\alpha} = q_1 - Q_{22}$ and $\psi_{1\beta} = Q_{22}$. From the possible solutions we focus our attention on those that have unit length, $\||\psi_1\rangle_{\text{norm}}\| = 1$, thus $\left|\cos(z)e^{jC}\right|^2 + |\sin(z)|^2 = 1$, where

$$\sin^2(z) = \frac{|\psi_{1\beta}|^2}{|\psi_{1\alpha}|^2 + |\psi_{1\beta}|^2}, \tag{13.19}$$

$$\cos^2(z) = \frac{|\psi_{1\alpha}|^2}{|\psi_{1\alpha}|^2 + |\psi_{1\beta}|^2}. \tag{13.20}$$

Following our antecedent establishments

$$|\psi_{1\alpha}|^2 = |q_1 - Q_{22}|^2$$

$$= \overbrace{\left(-\cos\left(\frac{\theta+\phi}{2}+\Upsilon\right) + \sin^2(\Omega)\cos\left(\frac{\theta+\phi}{2}\right) + \cos^2(\Omega)\cos(\phi)\right)^2}^{|\Re()|^2}$$

$$+ \underbrace{\left(-\sin\left(\frac{\theta+\phi}{2}+\Upsilon\right) + \sin^2(\Omega)\sin\left(\frac{\theta+\phi}{2}\right) + \cos^2(\Omega)\sin(\phi)\right)^2}_{|\Im()|^2},$$

$$\tag{13.21}$$

and

$$|\psi_{1\alpha}|^2 = \psi_{1\alpha}\psi_{1\alpha}^*, \tag{13.22}$$

$$|\psi_{1\beta}|^2 = \psi_{1\beta}\psi_{1\beta}^*, \tag{13.23}$$

respectively. As the next step let us derive $|\psi_{1\alpha}/\psi_{1\beta}|^2$ as follows

$$\left|\frac{\psi_{1\alpha}}{\psi_{1\beta}}\right|^2 = \frac{-e^{j\left(\frac{\theta+\phi}{2}+\Upsilon\right)} + e^{j\phi}\left[\left(e^{j\theta}-1\right)\sin^2(\Omega) + 1\right]}{-e^{j\phi}\left(e^{j\theta}-1\right)\sin(\Omega)\cos(\Omega)e^{-j\Lambda}}$$

$$\cdot \frac{-e^{-j\left(\frac{\theta+\phi}{2}+\Upsilon\right)} + e^{-j\phi}\left[\left(e^{-j\theta}-1\right)\sin^2(\Omega) + 1\right]}{-e^{-j\phi}\left(e^{-j\theta}-1\right)\sin(\Omega)\cos(\Omega)e^{j\Lambda}}$$

$$= \frac{\left(1 - e^{j\left(\frac{\theta-\phi}{2}+\Upsilon\right)}\right) + \left(e^{j\theta}-1\right)\sin^2(\Omega)}{\left(e^{j\theta}-1\right)\left(e^{-j\theta}-1\right)\sin^2(\Omega)\cos^2(\Omega)}$$

$$\cdot \frac{\left(1 - e^{-j\left(\frac{\theta-\phi}{2}+\Upsilon\right)}\right) + \left(e^{-j\theta}-1\right)\sin^2(\Omega)}{\left(e^{j\theta}-1\right)\left(e^{-j\theta}-1\right)\sin^2(\Omega)\cos^2(\Omega)}$$

$$= \frac{\left[1 - e^{j\left(\frac{\theta - \phi}{2} + \Upsilon\right)} - e^{-j\left(\frac{\theta - \phi}{2} + \Upsilon\right)} + 1\right] + \left[1 - e^{-j\theta} - e^{j\theta} + 1\right]\sin^4(\Omega)}{\sin^2(\Omega)\cos^2(\Omega)\left[1 - e^{-j\theta} - e^{j\theta} + 1\right]}$$

$$+ \frac{\sin^2(\Omega)\left[e^{j\theta} - 1 - e^{j\left(\frac{\theta + \phi}{2} - \Upsilon\right)} + e^{-j\left(\frac{\theta - \phi}{2} + \Upsilon\right)} + e^{-j\theta} - 1 - e^{-j\left(\frac{\theta + \phi}{2} - \Upsilon\right)} + e^{j\left(\frac{\theta - \phi}{2} + \Upsilon\right)}\right]}{\sin^2(\Omega)\cos^2(\Omega)\left[1 - e^{-j\theta} - e^{j\theta} + 1\right]}$$

$$= \frac{2 - 2\cos\left(\frac{\theta - \phi}{2} + \Upsilon\right) - \sin^2(\Omega)\cos^2(\Omega)\left[2 - 2\cos(\theta)\right]}{\sin^2(\Omega)\cos^2(\Omega)\left[2 - 2\cos(\theta)\right]}$$

$$+ \frac{\sin^2(\Omega)\left[2 - 2\cos(\theta) - 2 + 2\cos(\theta) - 2\cos\left(\frac{\theta + \phi}{2} - \Upsilon\right) + 2\cos\left(\frac{\theta - \phi}{2} + \Upsilon\right)\right]}{\sin^2(\Omega)\cos^2(\Omega)\left[2 - 2\cos(\theta)\right]}$$

$$= \frac{2 - 2\cos\left(\frac{\theta - \phi}{2} + \Upsilon\right) - \sin^2(\Omega)\overbrace{\cos^2(\Omega)\, 4\sin^2\left(\frac{\theta}{2}\right)}^{\sin^2(2\Omega)}}{\sin^2(2\Omega)\sin^2\left(\frac{\theta}{2}\right)}$$

$$+ \frac{\sin^2(\Omega)\left[2\cos\left(\frac{\theta - \phi}{2} + \Upsilon\right) - 2\cos\left(\frac{\theta + \phi}{2} - \Upsilon\right)\right]}{\sin^2(2\Omega)\sin^2\left(\frac{\theta}{2}\right)}. \tag{13.24}$$

Keeping in mind expression (13.19) in which $|\psi_{1\alpha}/\psi_{1\beta}|^2$ can be substituted from (13.24),

$$\frac{|\psi_{1\beta}|^2}{|\psi_{1\alpha}|^2 + |\psi_{1\beta}|^2} = \frac{\sin^2(2\Omega)\sin^2\left(\frac{\theta}{2}\right)}{2 - 2\cos\left(\frac{\theta - \phi}{2} + \Upsilon\right)\sin^2(\Omega)\left[2\cos\left(\frac{\theta - \phi}{2} + \Upsilon\right) - 2\cos\left(\frac{\theta + \phi}{2} - \Upsilon\right)\right]}$$

$$= \frac{\sin^2(2\Omega)\sin^2\left(\frac{\theta}{2}\right)}{2 - 2\cos\left(\frac{\theta - \phi}{2} + \Upsilon\right) + 4\sin^2(\Omega)\sin\left(\frac{\theta}{2}\right)\sin\left(\frac{\phi}{2} - \Upsilon\right)}$$

$$= \frac{\sin^2(2\Omega)\sin^2\left(\frac{\theta}{2}\right)}{2 - 2\cos\left(\frac{\theta}{2}\right)\cos\left(\frac{\phi}{2} - \Upsilon\right) - \underbrace{2\sin\left(\frac{\theta}{2}\right)\sin\left(\frac{\phi}{2} - \Upsilon\right) + 4\sin^2(\Omega)\sin\left(\frac{\theta}{2}\right)\sin\left(\frac{\phi}{2} - \Upsilon\right)}_{\underset{-2\cos(2\Omega)}{\sin\left(\frac{\theta}{2}\right)\sin\left(\frac{\phi}{2} - \Upsilon\right)\left(4\sin^2(\Omega) - 2\right)}}}$$

which leads to

$$\sin^2(z) = \frac{\sin^2(2\Omega)\sin^2\left(\frac{\theta}{2}\right)}{2\left(1 - \cos\left(\frac{\theta}{2}\right)\cos\left(\frac{\phi}{2} - \Upsilon\right) - 2\cos(2\Omega)\sin\left(\frac{\theta}{2}\right)\sin\left(\frac{\phi}{2} - \Upsilon\right)\right)} \tag{13.25}$$

and obviously

$$\cos^2(z) = 1 - \sin^2(z).$$

Finally, to determine the eigenvectors $|\psi_{1,2}\rangle$, only the e^{jC} factor is remaining in (13.18). Considering the relation

$$\frac{\psi_{1\alpha}}{\psi_{1\beta}} = \frac{\cos(z)}{\sin(z)}e^{jC_1},$$

and thus

$$\left(\frac{\psi_{1\alpha}}{\psi_{1\beta}}\right)^2 = \cot^2(z)e^{j2C_1} = \frac{Q_{12}}{Q_{21}} \cdot \frac{q_1 - Q_{22}}{q_1 - Q_{11}},$$

where equations (13.16), (13.17) were employed. It can be proven easily that

$$\frac{q_1 - Q_{22}}{q_1 - Q_{11}}$$

is a real number, which implies that

$$\frac{Q_{12}}{Q_{21}} = \frac{e^{-j\Lambda}e^{j\phi}}{e^{-j\Lambda}} = e^{j(\phi - 2\Lambda)},$$

thus

$$\left(e^{jC_1}\right)^2 = \frac{Q_{12}}{Q_{21}} = e^{j(\phi - 2\Lambda)},$$

from which follows

$$e^{jC_1} = \pm e^{j\left(\frac{\phi}{2} - \Lambda\right)}. \tag{13.26}$$

Based on (13.26) the normalized eigenvector is

$$|\psi_1\rangle = \cos(z)\, e^{j\left(\frac{\phi}{2} - \Lambda\right)}|\alpha\rangle + \sin(z)\,|\beta\rangle. \tag{13.27}$$

Eigenvector $|\psi_2\rangle$ has to be calculated in a similar way, where the other eigenvalue q_2 should be taken into account, which results in a simple sign change of Υ. Due to the definition of C_2 in (13.18), it does not depend on the sign of Υ, thus $e^{jC_2} = \pm e^{jC_1}$. To ensure the orthogonality the eigenvectors $|\psi_1\rangle$ and $|\psi_2\rangle$, e^{jC_2} must be equal to $-e^{jC_1}$, whereas the second eigenvector will be

$$|\psi_2\rangle = -\sin(z)\, e^{j\left(\frac{\phi}{2} - \Lambda\right)}|\alpha\rangle + \cos(z)\,|\beta\rangle. \tag{13.28}$$

14

Complex Baseband-equivalent Description of Bandlimited Signals

A bandlimited real-valued signal can be characterized by means of the following formula

$$v(t) = a(t)\cos(\omega_0 t + \phi(t)),$$

where ω_0 stands for the carrier frequency, $a(t)$ represents the amplitude of the signal and $\phi(t)$ denotes the corresponding phase. All of these parameters are real-valued. $v(t)$ can be split into two parts in the following way

$$v(t) = v_I(t)\cos(\omega_0 t) - v_Q(t)\sin(\omega_0 t),$$

where

$$v_I(t) = a(t)\cos(\phi(t)),$$
$$v_Q(t) = a(t)\sin(\phi(t)),$$

are the so called *in-phase* and *quadrature-phase* components, respectively. The two components together are referred to as *quadrature components*.

Since $v_I(t)$ and $v_Q(t)$ are independent from the carrier frequency let us introduce the complex baseband equivalent of $v(t)$

$$v_{eqv}(t) = v_I(t) + jv_Q(t)$$

Quantum Computing and Communications   S. Imre, F. Balázs
© 2004 John Wiley & Sons, Ltd   ISBN 0-470-86902-X (HB)

which is the same as

$$v_{eqv}(t) = a(t)e^{j\phi(t)}.$$

This 'virtual' description can be used between the endpoints without including the carrier and since we are interested in the real signal in the receiver we can apply the following relations

$$a(t) = \sqrt{v_I^2(t) + v_Q^2(t)},$$

$$\phi(t) = \arctan\left(\frac{v_Q(t)}{v_I(t)}\right) \bmod 2\pi,$$

or equivalently

$$v(t) = \Re\left(v_{eqv}(t)e^{j\omega_0 t}\right).$$

The next problem is how to involve the effect of the channel into this description. In reality the channel is characterized by means of its *impulse response function*[1] denoted here by $h(t)$ and in the time domain *convolution* has to be used to compute the output signal $r(t)$

$$r(t) = v(t) * h(t).$$

In our carrier-free world we follow this rule but for equivalent functions

$$r_{ekv}(t) = v_{ekv}(t) * h_{ekv}(t),$$

where

$$h(t) = 2\Re\left(h_{eqv}(t)e^{j\omega_0 t}\right).$$

Therefore the received signal can be expressed as

$$r(t) = \Re\left(r_{eqv}(t)e^{j\omega_0 t}\right) = r_I(t)\cos(\omega_0 t) - r_Q(t)\sin(\omega_0 t).$$

---

[1] If the channel is feeded by a single Dirac pulse it answers with $h(t)$.

15

Useful Links

Leading laboratories and teams

- Center of Quantum Computation, *http://www.qubit.org/*
- Media Lab, Quanta, Massachusetts Institute of Technology, *http://www.media.mit.edu/quanta/*
- Quantum Computing Group, University of Bristol, *http://www.cs.bris.ac.uk/Research/QuantumComputing/index.html*
- Institute for Quantum Information, California Institute of Technology, *http://www.iqi.caltech.edu/index.html*
- IBM Research, *http://www.research.ibm.com/quantuminfo/*
- Institut für Experimentalphysik, Universität Wien, *http://www.quantum.univie.ac.at/*
- Group of Applied Physics at the University of Geneva, *http://www.gap-optique.unige.ch/*
- The Stanford-Berkeley-MIT-IBM NMR Quantum Computation Project, *http://feynman.media.mit.edu/quanta/nmrqc-darpa/index.html*
- Quantum Information Processing and Communications in the 6th Framework European Programme (2003-2006), *http://www.cordis.lu/ist/fet/qipc.htm*
- A good summary of further important links can be found at *http://www.imaph.tu-bs.de/qi/links_html*

Quantum Computing and Communications   S. Imre, F. Balázs
© 2004 John Wiley & Sons, Ltd   ISBN 0-470-86902-X (HB)

Publication and information sources

- http://arxiv.org/archive/quant-ph
- http://quantum.fis.ucm.es/
- http://www.quiprocone.org/
- http://prl.aps.org/

Simulation tools and quantum program languages

- QCL: http://tph.tuwien.ac.at/oemer/qcl.html
- QCE: http://rugth30.phys.rug.nl/compphys0/qce.htm
- QSS: http://strc.herts.ac.uk/tp/info/qucomp/qucompApplet.html

References

1. A. Ahuja, S. Kapoor. A quantum algorithm for finding the maximum. 1999. e-print quant-ph/9911082.

2. A. Aspect, J. Dalibard, G. Roger. Experimental test of Bell's inequalities using time-varying analyzers. *Phys. Rev. Lett.*, 49:1804–1807, 1982.

3. A. Bell, T. J. Sejnowski. An information-maximisation approach to blind separation and blind deconvolution. *Neural Computation*, 7:1129–1159, 1995.

4. B. Podolsky, A. Einstein, N. Rosen. Can quantum-mechanical description of physical reality be considered complete? *Phys. Rev.*, 47:777–780, 1935.

5. A. Engelhart, W. Teich, J. Lindner, G. Jeney, S. Imre, L. Pap. A survey of multiuser/multisubchannel detection schemes based on recurrent neural networks. *Wireless Communications and Mobile Computing*, 2(3):269–284, 2002. Special issue on Advances in 3G Wireless Networks.

6. A. G. Fowler, L. C. L. Hollenberg. Robustness of Shor's algorithm with finite rotation control. 2003. e-print quant-ph/0306018.

7. A. Hyvärinen, J. Karhunen, E. Oja. *Independent Component Analysis*. Adaptive and Learning Systems for Signal Processing, Communication and Control. J. Wiley & Sons, Inc., New York, 2001.

8. A. J. Menezes, P. C. van Oorschot, S. A. Vanstone. *Handbook of Applied Cryptography*. CRC Press, 5th edition, 2001. e-print www.cacr.math.uwaterloo.ca/hac/.

9. A. K. Ekert, P. Hayden, H. Inamori. Basic concepts in quantum computation. *Lectures given at les Houches Summer School on "Coherent Matter Waves"*, July-August 1999. e-print quant-ph/0011013.

10. A. K. Lenstra, H. W. Lenstra, editors. *The Development of the Number Field Sieve*, volume 1554 of *Lecture Notes in Mathematics*. Springer Verlag, Berlin, 1993.

11. A. K. Pati, S. L. Braunstein. Deutsch–Jozsa algorithm for continuous variables. In A. K. Pati, S. L. Braunstein, editors, *Quantum Information with Continuous Variables*. Kluwer, April 2003.

12. A. Klappenecker, M. Rötteler. Discrete cosine transforms on quantum computers. *Proceedings of IEEE of International Symposia on Image and Signal Processing and Analysis (ISPA'01)*, June 19–21, 2001. e-print quant-ph/0111038.

13. A. Muller, H. Zbinden, N. Gisin. Underwater quantum coding. *Nature*, 378:449–449, 1995.

14. A. Muller, H. Zbinden, N. Gisin. Quantum cryptography over 23 km in installed under-lake telecom fibre. *Europhysics Lett.*, 33:335–339, 1996.

15. A. Muller, J. Breguet, N. Gisin. Experimental demonstration of quantum cryptography using polarized photons in optical fiber over more than 1 km. *Europhysics Lett.*, 23:383–388, 1993.

16. A. Muthukrishnan, C. R. Stroud. Quantum fast Fourier transform using multilevel atoms. *J. Mod. Opt.*, 49:2115–2127, 2002. e-print quant-ph/0112017.

17. A. Peres, W. K. Wooters. Optimal detection of quantum information. *Phys. Rev. Lett.*, 66:1119–1122, 1991.

18. A. R. Kessel, N. M. Yakovleva. Schemes of implementation in NMR of quantum processors and Deutsch–Jozsa algorithm by using virtual spin representation. 2002. e-print quant-ph/0206106.

19. A. Saito, K. Kioi, Y. Akagi, N. Hashizume, K. Ohta. Actual computational time-cost of the quantum Fourier transform in a quantum computer using nuclear spins. 2000. e-print quant-ph/0001113.

20. A. Schönhage, V. Strassen. Schnelle multiplication grosser zahlen. *Computing*, 7:281–292, 1971.

21. A. Stefanov, O. Guinnard, L. Guinnard, H. Zbinden, N. Gisin. Optical quantum random number generator. *J. Modern Optics*, 47:595–598, 2000. e-print quant-ph/9907006.

22. A. Zeilinger. Quantum teleportation. *Scientific American*, 285(4):32–41, 2000. e-print *http://www.quantum.univie.ac.at/links/sci_am/teleportation.pdf*.

23. E. S. Abers. *Quantum Mechanics*. Pearson Education Inc., New Jersey, USA, 2004.

24. B. Aazhang, B.-P. Paris, G. C. Orsak. Neural networks for multiuser detection in code-division multiple-access communications. *IEEE Trans. on Communications*, 40(7):1212–1222, July 1992.

25. B. C. Travaglione, G. J. Milburn. Generation of eigenstates using the phase-estimation algorithm. *Phys. Rev. A*, 63(03230), 2001. e-print quant-ph/0008053.

26. B. C. Travaglione, G. J. Milburn, T. C. Ralph. Phase estimation as a quantum nondemolition measurement. 2002. e-print quant-ph/0203130.

27. B. Huttner, J. D. Gautier, A. Muller, H. Zbinden, N. Gisin. Unambiguous quantum measurement of non-orthogonal states. *Phys. Rev. A*, 54:3783–3789, 1996.

28. B. Jakobs, J. Franson. Quantum cryptography in free space. *Rev. Sci. Inst.*, 71:1675–1680, 1996. e-print quant-ph/9912118.

29. J. S. Bell. On the problem of hidden variables in quantum mechanics. *Review of Modern Phys.*, 38:447–452, 1964.

30. C. H. Bennett. Quantum cryptography using any two nonorthogonal states. *Phys. Rev. Lett.*, 68:3121–3124, 1992. e-print http://www.research.ibm.com/people/b/bennetc/qc2nos.pdf.

31. D. Bruss. Optimal eavesdropping in quantum cryptography with six states. *Phys. Rev. A*, 81:3018–3021, 1998. e-print quant-ph/9805019.

32. C. Dürr, P. Hoyer. A quantum algorithm for finding the minimum. 1996. e-print quant-ph/9607014.

33. C. H. Bennett, E. Bernstein, G. Brassard, U. Vazirani. Strengths and weakness of quantum computing. *SIAM Journal on Computing*, 26(5):1510–1523, 1997. e-print quant-ph/9701001.

34. C. H. Bennett, F. Bessette, L. Salvail, J. Smolin. Experimental quantum cryptography. *Journal of Cryptology*, 5:210–229, 1992.

35. C. H. Bennett, G. Brassard. Quantum cryptography: Public key distribution and coin tossing. *Int. conf. Computers, Systems & Signal Processing*, pages 175–179, Bangalore, India, December 10–12 1984. e-print http://www.research.ibm.com/people/b/bennetc/bennettc198469790513.pdf.

36. C. H. Bennett, G. Brassard. Quantum public key distribution system. *IBM Tehnical Disclosure Bulletin*, 28:3153–3163, 1985.

37. C. H. Bennett, G. Brassard , C. Crépeau, U. M. Maurer. Generalized privacy amplification. *IEEE Transaction on Information Theory*, 41:1915–1923, 1995.

38. C. H. Bennett, G. Brassard, A. Ekert. Quantum cryptography. *Scientific American*, 267(4):50–57, 1992.

39. C. H. Bennett, G. Brassard, J.-M. Robert. Privacy amplification by public discussion. *SIAM Journal on Computing*, 17:210–229, 1988.

40. C. H. Bennett, G. Brassard, C. Crépeau, R. Jozsa, A. Peres, W. K. Wootters. Teleporting an unknown quantum state via dual classic and Einstein–Podolsky– Rosen channels. *Phys. Rev. Lett.*, 70:1895–1899, 1993. e-print http://www.research.ibm.com/quantuminfo/teleportation/teleportation.html.

41. C. H. Bennett, S. J. Wiesner. Communication via 1- and 2-particle operators on Einstein–Podolsky–Rosen states. *Phys. Rev. Lett.*, 69:2881–2884, 1992. e-print http://www.research.ibm.com/people/b/bennetc/bennettc19926c731103.pdf.

42. R. Cleve. A note on computing Fourier transforms by quantum programs. Technical report, 1994. e-print http://pages.cpsc.ucalgary.ca/ cleve.papers.html.

43. C. Cocks. Technical report, Communications-Electronics Security Group, 1973.

44. D. Coppersmith. An approximate Fourier transform useful in quantum factoring, IBM research report. Technical Report RC 19642, IBM Research Division T.J. Watson Research Center, December 1994. e-print quant-ph/0201067.

45. L. M. Correia, editor. *Wireless Flexible Personalised Communications.* J. Wiley & Sons, 2001.

46. D. Biron, O. Biham, E. Biham, M. Grassl, D. A. Lidar. *Generalized Grover Search Algorithm for Arbitrary Initial Amplitude Distribution*, volume 1509 of *Lecture Notes in Computer Science*, pages 140–147. Springer, 1998. e-print quant-ph/9801066.

47. D. Bouwmeester, J.-W. Pan, K. Mattle, M. Eibl, H. Weinfurter, A. Zeilinger. Experimental quantum teleportation. *Nature*, (390):575, 1997.

48. D. Deutsch, A. Ekert, R. Lupacchini. Machines, logic and quantum physics. *The Bulletin of Symbolic Logic*, pages 265–283, 2000. e-print http://xxx.lanl.gov/abs/math.HO/9911150.

49. D. Deutsch, R. Jozsa. Rapid solution of problems by quantum computation. *Proc. R. Soc. London, Ser. A*, 439:553–558, 1992.

50. D. P. Chi, J. Kim, S. Lee. Quantum algorithm for generalized Deutsch–Jozsa problem. 2000. e-print quant-ph/0005059.

51. D. Deutsch. Quantum theory, the Church–Turing principle and the universal quantum computer. *Proc. R. Soc., London, Ser. A*, 400:97–117, 1985.

52. E. Biham, G. Brassard, D. Kenigsberg, T. Mor. Quantum computing without entanglement. *Presented at FoCM'02 (Aug 2002), QIP'03 (Dec 2002), Qubit'03 (Apr 2003)*, 2003. e-print quant-ph/0306182.

53. E. Biham, O. Biham, D. Biron , M. Grassl, D. A. Lidar. *Grover's Search Algorithm for an Arbitrary Initial Amplitude Distribution*, volume 60, pages 2742–2745. 1999. e-print quant-ph/9807027.

54. E. Biham, O. Biham, D. Biron , M. Grassl, D. A. Lidar, D. Shapira. Analysis of generalized Grover's search algorithms using recursion equations. *Phys. Rev. A*, 63, 2001. e-print quant-ph/0010077.

55. E. Brainis, L. P. Lamoureux, N. J. Cerf, Ph. Emplit, M. Haelterman and S. Massar. Fiber-optics implementation of Deutsch–Jozsa and Bernstein–Vazirani quantum algorithms with three qbits. *Phys. Rev. Lett.*, 90:157902/1–4, 2003. e-print quant-ph/0212142.

56. A. K. Ekert. Quantum cryptography based on Bell's theorem. *Phys. Rev. Lett.*, (3):661–663, 1991.

57. T. ElGamal. *Cryptography and Logarithms over Finite Fields*. PhD thesis, Stanford University, 1984.

58. J. H. Ellis. Technical report, Communications-Electronics Security Group, 1970.

59. F. Chung, R. Graham, T. Leighton. Guessing secrets. *Electronic Journal of Combinatorics*, 8(R13), 2001. e-print *http://www.combinatorics.org/Volume_8/Abstracts/v8i1213.html*.

60. G. Brassard, P. Hoyer. An exact quantum polynomial-time algorithm for Simon's problem. *Proceedings of the 5th Israeli Symposium on Theory of Computing and Systems (ISTCS)*, July 1997. e-print quant-ph/9704027.

61. G. Brassard, P. Hoyer, A. Tapp. *Quantum Counting*, volume 1443 of *Lecture Notes in Computer Science*, pages 820–831. Springer, July 1998. Proceedings of the 25th International Colloquium on Automata, Languages, and Programming, e-print quant-ph/9805082.

62. G. Brassard, P. Hoyer, M. Mosca, A. Tapp. Quantum amplitude amplification and estimation. *Quantum Computation & Quantum Information Science, AMS Contemporary Math Series*, 2000. e-print quant-ph/0005055.

63. G. Constantini, F. Smeraldi. A generalization of Deutsch's example. 1997. e-print quant-ph/9702020.

64. G. Jeney, S. Imre, L. Pap, A. Engelhart, T. Dogan, W. G. Teich. Comparison of different multiuser detectors based on recurrent neural networks. *COST 262 Workshop on Multiuser Detection in Spread Spectrum Communication, Schloss Reisensburg, Germany*, pages 61–70, January 2001.

65. G. L. Long, C. C. Tu, Y. S. Li, W. L. Zang and L. Niu. A novel so(3) picture for quantum searching. 1999. e-print quant-ph/9911004.

66. G. L. Long, L. Xiao, Y. Sun. General phase matching condition for quantum searching. 2001. e-print quant-ph/0107013.

67. G. L. Long, Y. S. Li, W. L. Zang, L. Niu. Phase matching in quantum searching. *Phys. Lett. A*, 262:27–34, 1999. e-print quant-ph/9906020.

68. L. K. Grover. Quantum mechanics helps in searching for a needle in a haystack. *Phys. Rev. Lett.*, 79(2):325–328, July 1997. e-print quant-ph/9706033.

69. L. K. Grover. Quantum computers can search rapidly by using almost any transformation. *Phys. Rev. Lett*, 80(19):4329–4332, 1998. e-print quant-ph/9712011.

70. L. K. Grover. A fast quantum mechanical algorithm for database search. *Proceedings, 28th Annual ACM Symposium on the Theory of Computing*, pages 212–219, May 1996. e-print quant-ph/9605043.

71. L. K. Grover. Tradeoffs in the quantum search algorithm. 2002. e-print quant-ph/0201152.

72. H. Bechmann-Pasquinucci, N. Gisin. Incoherent and coherent eavesdropping in the 6-state protocol of quantum cryptography. *Phys. Rev. A*, 59:4238–4248, 1999. e-print quant-ph/9807041.

73. F. Hillebrand, editor. *GSM and UMTS: The Creation of Global Mobile Communication*. Wiley & Sons, 2002.

74. P. Hoyer. Arbitrary phases in quantum amplitude amplification. *Phys. Lett. A*, 62(052304), 2000. e-print quant-ph/0006031.

75. http://www.cipherwar.com/news/01/dera_satellites.htm.

76. http://www.gapoptique.unige.ch.

77. http://www.idQuantique.com.

78. http://www.magiqtech.com/products/index.php.

79. http://www.mysteries megasite.com/main/bigsearch/teleportation.html.

80. http://www.qubit.org/library/intros/gmn/gmn.html.

81. I. L. Chuang, N. Gershenfeld, M. Kubinec. Experimental implementation of fast quantum searching. *Phys. Rev. Lett.*, 18(15):3408–3411, 1998. e-print http://feynman.media.mit.edu/ike/homepage/papers/QC-chuang-gershenfeld-kubin ec-nmrqc-grover-alg-prl-13apr98.pdf.

82. J. A. Jones, M. Mosca. Implementation of a quantum algorithm to solve Deutsch's problem on a nuclear magnetic resonance quantum computer. *Journal of Chemical Physics*, 109(5):1648–1653, August 1998. e-print quant-ph/9801027.

83. J. F. Clauser, M. A. Horne, A. Shimony, R. A. Holt. Proposed experiment to test local hidden-variable theories. *Phys. Rev. Lett.*, 23:880–884, 1969.

84. J. Garriga, A. Vilenkin. Many worlds in one. *Phys. Rev. D.*, 64(043511):043511, 2001. e-print arXiv.org/abs/gr-qc/0102010.

85. J. Siewert, R. Fazio. Implementation of the Deutsch–Jozsa algorithm with Josephson charge qbits. *J. of Mod. Opt.*, 90, 2002. e-print quant-ph/0112135.

86. J. W. Cooley, J. Tukey. An algorithm for the machine calculation of complex Fourier series. *Mathematics for Computation*, 19(90):297–301, 1965.

87. J-Y. Hsieh, C-M. Li. A general su(2) formulation for quantum searching with certainty. *Phys. Rev. A*, 65(052322), 2002. e-print quant-ph/0112035.

88. J. A. Jones, M. Mosca, R. H. Hansen. Implementation of a quantum search algorithm on a nuclear magnetic resonance quantum computer. *Nature*, (393):344–346, 1998. e-print quant-ph/9805069.

89. R. Jozsa. Quantum algorithms and the Fourier transform. *Proc. Roy. Soc. London Ser. A*, 454:323–337, July 1998. e-print quant-ph/9707033.

90. K. Dorai, D. Suter. Efficient implementations of the quantum Fourier transform: An experimental perspective. 2002. e-print quant-ph/0211030.

91. A. Yu. Kitaev. Quantum measurements and the Abelian stabilizer problem. 1995. e-print quant-ph/9511026.

92. D. E. Knuth. *The Art of Computer Programming, Vol. 3. (Sorting and searching)*. Addison-Wesley, 1973.

93. L. M. Duan, G. C. Guo. Probabilistic cloning and identification of linearly independent quantum states. *Phys. Rev. Lett.*, 80:4999–5002, 1998. e-print quant-ph/9804064.

94. F. M. Lev. An integral version of Shor's factoring algorithm. 2001. e-print quant-ph/0109103.

95. L. F. Wei, F. Nori. Quantum phase estimation algorithms with delays: How to avoid dynamical phase errors. 2003. e-print quant-ph/0305038.

96. L. F. Wei, X. Li, X. Hu, F. Nori. Phase-matching approach to eliminate the dynamical phase error in Shor's factoring algorithm. 2003. e-print quant-ph/0305039.

97. L. M. K. Vandersypen, M. Steffen, G. Breyta, C. S. Yanonni, M. H. Sherwood, I. L. Chuang. Experimental realization of Shor's quantum factoring algorithm using nuclear magnetic resonance. *Nature*, (414):883–887, December 2001. e-print quant-ph/0112176.

98. L. M. K. Vandersypen, M. Steffen, G. Breyta, C. S. Yanonni, R. Cleve, I. L. Chuang. Experimental realization of an order-finding algorithm with an NMR quantum computer. *Phys. Rev. Lett*, 85(25):5452–5455, December 2000. e-print quant-ph/0007017.

99. G. L. Long. Grover algorithm with zero theoretical failure rate. *Phys. Rev. A*, 64(022307), 2001. e-print quant-ph/0106071.

100. L. R. Hales. *The Quantum Fourier Transform and Extensions of the Abelian Hidden Subgroup Problem*. PhD Thesis, University of California at Berkeley, 2002. e-print quant-ph/0212002.

101. W. W. Lu. *Broadband Wireless Mobile: 3G and Beyond*. J. Wiley & Sons, 2002.

102. E. Knill, M. A. Nielsen, R. Laamme. Complete quantum teleportation using nuclear magnetic resonance. *Nature*, 396:52–55, 1998.

103. M. Ban, K. Kurukowa, R. Momose, O. Hirota. Optimum measurements for discrimination among symmetric quantum states and parameter estimation. *Int. J. Theor. Phys.*, 36:1269–1288, 1997.

104. M. Boyer, G. Brassard, P. Hoyer, A. Tapp. Tight bounds on quantum searching. *Proceedings 4th Workshop on Physics and Computation*, 46(4–5):36–43, 1996. Also in Fortschritte der Physik, Vol. 46, No. 4–5, 1998, pp. 493–505 quant-ph/9605034.

105. M. Clarke, R. B. M. A. Chefles, S. M. Barnett, E. Riis. Experimental demonstration of optimal unambiguous state discrimination. *Phys. Rev. A*, 63:040305, 2001. e-print quant-ph/0007063.

106. M. Dušek, V. Bužek. Quantum multimeters: A programmable state discriminator. *Phys. Rev. A.*, 66(1-5):022112, 2002. e-print quant-ph/0201097.

107. M. Mosca, A. Ekert. *The Hidden Subgroup Problem and Eigenvalue Estimation on a Quantum Computer*, volume 1509 of *Lecture Notes in Computer Science*, pages 174–188. Springer, 1998. e-print quant-ph/9903071.

108. M. Mosca, C. Zalka. Exact quantum Fourier transforms and discrete logarithms. 2003. e-print quant-ph/0301093.

109. M. Varnashi, B. Aazhang. Multistage detection for asynchronous code-division multiple access communication. *IEEE Trans. on Communication*, 38(4):509–519, April 1990.

110. J. Mullins. Making unbreakable code. *IEEE Spectrum*, 39(5):40–45, 2002.

111. N. Alon, V. Gurushwami, T. Kaufman, M. Sudan. Guessing secrets efficiently via list decoding. *Proceedings of the 13th Annual ACM-SIAM SODA*, pages 254–262, 2002. e-print http://www.math.tau.ac.il/~nogaa/PDFS/guessproc2.pdf.

112. N. Bhattacharya, H. B. van Linden van den Heuvell, R. J. C. Spreeuw. Implementation of quantum search algorithm using classical Fourier optics. *Phys. Rev. Lett.*, 88(137901), 2002. e-print quant-ph/0110034v3.

113. N. Gisin, G. Ribordy, W. Tittel, H. Zbinden. Quantum cryptography. 2001. e-print quant-ph/0101098.

114. M. Nathanson. Quantum guessing via Deutsch–Jozsa. 2003. e-print quant-ph/0301025.

115. M. A. Nielsen. Rules for a complex quantum world. *Scientific American*, 287(5):49–57, 2002.

116. P. Hausladen, R. Jozsa, M. Westmoreland, W. K. Wooters. Classical information capacity of a quantum channel. *Phys. Rev. A.*, 54:1869–1876, 1996.

117. P. Hausladen, W. K. Wooters. A 'pretty good' measurement for distingushing quantum states. *J. Mod. Opt.*, 41:2385–2390, 1994.

118. J. D. Parsons. *The Mobile Radio Propagation Channel*. J. Wiley & Sons, 2nd edition, 2001.

119. A. Peres. How to differentiate between two non-orthogonal states. *Phys. Lett. A*, 128(19), 1988.

120. A. Peres. Neumark's theorem and quantum inseparability. *Found. Phys.*, 20(12):1441–1453, 2000.

121. I. Peterson. Guessing secrets - applying mathematics to the efficient delivery of Internet content. *Science News*, 161(14):216, 2002. e-print http://63.240.200.111/articles/20020406/bob8.asp.

122. P. W. Shor. Algorithms for quantum computation: Discrete logarithms and factoring. *Proc. 35th Annual Symposium on Foundations of Computer Science, Santa Fe*, pages 124–134, November 20-22 1994.

123. R. B. Griffiths, C. S. Niu. Semiclassical Fourier transform for quantum computation. *Phys. Rev. Lett.*, 76(17):3228–3231, 1996. e-print quant-ph/9511007.

124. R. Cleve, A. Ekert, C. Macciavello, M. Mosca. Quantum algorithms revisited. *Proc. R. Soc. London, Ser. A*, 454:339–354, 1998. e-print quant-ph/9708016.

125. R. Cleve, J. Watrous. Fast parallel circuits for the quantum Fourier transform. 2000. e-print quant-ph/0006004.

126. R. J. Hughes, J. E. Nordholt, D. Derkacs, C. G. Peterson. Practical free-space quantum key distribution over 10 km in daylight and at night. *New Journal of Physics*, 43(4), 2002. e-print quant-ph/0206092.

127. R. L. Rivest, A. Shamir, L. M. Adlemann. New directions in cryptography. *IEEE Transactions on Information Theory*, 22:644–654, 1976.

128. R. L. Rivest, A. Shamir, L. M. Adlemann. A method of obtaining digital signatures and public-key cryptosystems. *Communications of the ACM*, 21:120–126, 1978.

129. S.-I. Amari, A. Cichocki. Adaptive blind signal processing-neural network approaches. *Proc. IEEE*, 86(10), October 1998.

130. S. Imre, F. Balázs. Positive operation valued measurement based multiuser detection in DS-CDMA systems. *IX. Int. Conference on Software Telecommunications and Computer Networks (SoftCOM'01)*, 1:421–429, October 09-12 2001. e-print quant-ph/0201039.

131. S. Imre, F. Balázs. Non-coherent multi-user detection based on quantum search. *IEEE International Conference on Communication (ICC), New York, USA*, April 28 – May 2 2002.

132. S. Imre, F. Balázs. Performance evaluation of quantum based multi-user detector. *IEEE International Symposium on Spread Spectrum Techniques and Applications (ISSTA'02)*, pages 722–725, September 2-5 2002.

133. S. Imre, F. Balázs. A tight bound for probability of error for quantum counting based multiuser detection. *IEEE International Symposium on Information Theory (ISIT'02)*, page 43, June 30 – July 5 2002. e-print quant-ph/0205138.

134. S. J. Lomonaco JR, L. H. Kauffman. A continuous variable Shor algorithm. 2002. e-print quant-ph/0210141.

135. E. Schrödinger. Die gegenwartige situation in der quantenmechanik. *Naturwissenschaftern.*, 23:807–812; 823–823, 844–849, 1935. English translation: John D. Trimmer, *Proceedings of the American Philosophical Society*, 124:323–38 (1980), Reprinted in *Quantum Theory and Measurement*, p. 152 (1983).

136. C. E. Shannon. Communication theory of secrecy systems. *Bell System Technical Journal*, 28:656–715, 1949.

137. P. W. Shor. Polynomial-time algorithms for prime factorization and discrete logarithms on a quantum computer. *SIAM Journal on Computing*, 26(5):1484–1509, October 1997. e-print quant-ph/9508027.

138. P. W. Shor. Quantum computing. *Documenta Mathematica*, 1998. Extra Volume ICM 1998.

139. P. W. Shor. Introduction to quantum algorithms. *AMS PSAPM*, 58:143–159, May 2002. e-print quant-ph/0005003.

140. D. R. Simon. On the power of quantum computation. *Proceedings of the 35th Annual IEEE Symposium on the Foundations of Computer Science*, pages 116–123, 1994. Also in *SIAM Journal on Computing*, 26:1474–1483.

141. S. L. Braunstein, H. J. Kimble. A posteriori teleportation. *Nature* 394:840–841, 1998. e-print *http://www-users.cs.york.ac.uk/~schmuel/papers/bkB98.pdf*.

142. S. L. Braunstein, H. J. Kimble. Teleportation of continuous quantum variables. *Phys. Rev. Lett.*, 80:869–872, 1998. e-print *http://www-users.cs.york.ac.uk/~schmuel/papers/bk98.pdf*.

143. T. H. Cormen, C. E. Leiserson, R. L. Rivest, C. Stein. *Introduction to Algorithms*. The MIT Press/McGraw Hill, 4th edition, 2003.

144. K. Tachikawa, editor. *W-CDMA Mobile Communications System*. J. Wiley & Sons, 2002.

145. M. Tegmark. Parallel universes. *Scientific American*, 288(5):30–41, 2003.

146. S. Verdu. *Multiuser Detection*. Cambridge University Press, 1998.

147. G. Vermes. *The Dead Sea Scrolls*. Penguin USA, 1998.

148. G. S. Vernam. Cipher printing telegraph systems for secret wire and radio telegraphic communications. *Journal of American Institute of Electrical Engineers*, 45:109–115, 1926.

149. I. V. Volovich. Quantum computing and Shor's factoring algorithm. 2001. e-print quant-ph/0109004.

150. W. T. Buttler, R. J. Hughes, P. G. Kwiat, S. K. Lamoreaux, G. G. Luther, G. L. Morgan, J. E. Nordholt, C. G. Peterson, C. Simmons. Practical free-space quantum key distribution over 1 km. *Phys. Rev. Lett.*, 81:3283–3286, 1998. e-print quant-ph/9805071.

151. W. Tittel, J. Brendel, H. Zbinden, N. Gisin. Violation of Bell inequalities by photons more than 10 km apart. *Phys. Rev. Lett.*, 81:3563–3566, 1998. e-print quant-ph/9806043.

152. www.research.ibm.com/quantuminfo/teleportation/.

153. Y. C. Eldar, A. V. Oppenheim. Quantum signal processing. *IEEE Signal Processing*, 19(6):12–32, 2002.

154. Y. C. Eldar, G. D. Forney. On quantum detection and the square-root measurement. *IEEE Trans. Inform. Theory*, 47(3):858–872, 2001. e-print quant-ph/0005132.

155. Y. H. Shih, C. O. Alley. *Phys. Rev. Lett.*, p. 2921.

156. Y. S. Weinstein, S. Lloyd, D. G. Cory. Implementation of the quantum Fourier transform. *Phys. Rev. Lett.*, 86:1889–1891, 2001. e-print quant-ph/9906059.

157. Z. Y. Ou, L. Mandel. Violation of Bell's inequality and classical probability in a two-photon correlation experiment. *Phys. Rev. Lett.*, 61:50–53, 1988.

158. C. Zalka. Fast versions of Shor's quantum factoring algorithm. 1998. e-print quant-ph/9806084.

159. C. Zalka. Simulating quantum systems on a quantum computer. *Phys. Rev. A.*, 454:313–322, 1998.

160. C. Zalka. Grover's quantum searching algorithm is optimal. e-print quant-ph/9711070v2, 1999.

Solutions of Exercises

Exercise 2.1: Prove in several different ways that $HH = I$.
  Solution: First we use matrix algebraic multiplication

$$HH = \frac{1}{\sqrt{2}} \begin{bmatrix} 1 & 1 \\ 1 & -1 \end{bmatrix} \frac{1}{\sqrt{2}} \begin{bmatrix} 1 & 1 \\ 1 & -1 \end{bmatrix} \begin{bmatrix} 1 & 0 \\ 0 & 1 \end{bmatrix} = I.$$

Next we utilize the superposition principle which claims that performing a linear operator on a superposition is equivalent to computing the outcomes with each individual computational basis state as an input and than adding the results together. Since $HH|0\rangle = |0\rangle$ and $HH|1\rangle = |1\rangle$ therefore two consecutive Hadamard gates act as an identity transform on their arbitrary superpositions.

Finally we remember that Hadamard gates are Hermitian ($H^\dagger = H$) and unitary ($H^\dagger = H^{-1}$) thus $HH = HH^\dagger = HH^{-1} = I$.

Exercise 2.2: Prove that $HXH = Z, HYH = -Y$ and $HZH = X$.
  Solution:

$$HXH = \frac{1}{\sqrt{2}} \begin{bmatrix} 1 & 1 \\ 1 & -1 \end{bmatrix} \frac{1}{\sqrt{2}} \begin{bmatrix} 0 & 1 \\ 1 & 0 \end{bmatrix} \begin{bmatrix} 1 & 1 \\ -1 & 1 \end{bmatrix} \frac{1}{\sqrt{2}} \begin{bmatrix} 1 & 1 \\ 1 & -1 \end{bmatrix} \begin{bmatrix} 1 & 0 \\ 0 & -1 \end{bmatrix} = Z$$

$$HYH = \frac{1}{\sqrt{2}}\begin{bmatrix} 1 & 1 \\ 1 & -1 \end{bmatrix}\frac{1}{\sqrt{2}}\overset{\begin{bmatrix} 0 & -j \\ j & 0 \end{bmatrix} \quad \frac{1}{\sqrt{2}}\begin{bmatrix} 1 & 1 \\ 1 & -1 \end{bmatrix}}{\begin{bmatrix} j & -j \\ -j & -j \end{bmatrix}}\begin{bmatrix} 0 & j \\ -j & 0 \end{bmatrix} = -Y$$

$$HZH = \frac{1}{\sqrt{2}}\begin{bmatrix} 1 & 1 \\ 1 & -1 \end{bmatrix}\frac{1}{\sqrt{2}}\overset{\begin{bmatrix} 1 & 0 \\ 0 & -1 \end{bmatrix} \quad \frac{1}{\sqrt{2}}\begin{bmatrix} 1 & 1 \\ 1 & -1 \end{bmatrix}}{\begin{bmatrix} 1 & 1 \\ 1 & -1 \end{bmatrix}}\begin{bmatrix} 0 & 1 \\ 1 & 0 \end{bmatrix} = X.$$

Exercise 2.3: Perform the analysis of the generalized interferometer using the superposition principle.

Solution: We start from $|0\rangle$ according to Fig. 2.7. The first Hadamard gate produces

$$|0\rangle \rightarrow \frac{|0\rangle + |1\rangle}{\sqrt{2}}.$$

The phase shifter introduces delays independently along the two paths

$$\frac{|0\rangle + |1\rangle}{\sqrt{2}} \rightarrow \frac{e^{j\alpha_0}|0\rangle + e^{j\alpha_1}|1\rangle}{\sqrt{2}}.$$

Finally we apply the second Hadamard gate for the computational basis vectors $|0\rangle$ and $|1\rangle$ independently ($|0\rangle \rightarrow \frac{|0\rangle+|1\rangle}{\sqrt{2}}$ and $|1\rangle \rightarrow \frac{|0\rangle-|1\rangle}{\sqrt{2}}$) and the outcomes have to be added together

$$\frac{e^{j\alpha_0}|0\rangle + e^{j\alpha_1}|1\rangle}{\sqrt{2}} \rightarrow e^{j\alpha_0}\frac{\frac{|0\rangle+|1\rangle}{\sqrt{2}}}{\sqrt{2}} + e^{j\alpha_1}\frac{\frac{|0\rangle-|1\rangle}{\sqrt{2}}}{\sqrt{2}}$$

$$= \frac{e^{j\alpha_0} + e^{j\alpha_1}}{2}|0\rangle + \frac{e^{j\alpha_1} - e^{j\alpha_1}}{2}|1\rangle.$$

Exercise 2.4: Calculate the matrix of the two-qbit SWAP gate.

Solution: One possible easy way to reach the requested matrix is if we consider the transitions of the computational basis states

$$|00\rangle \rightarrow |00\rangle, \quad |01\rangle \rightarrow |10\rangle, \quad |10\rangle \rightarrow |01\rangle, \quad |11\rangle \rightarrow |11\rangle$$

and taking into account the role of U_{ij} (see the remark to the 2nd Postulate in Section 2.2) thus

$$\mathbf{CNOT} = \begin{bmatrix} 1 & 0 & 0 & 0 \\ 0 & 0 & 1 & 0 \\ 0 & 1 & 0 & 0 \\ 0 & 0 & 0 & 1 \end{bmatrix}.$$

Exercise 2.5: Show that $AC + AD + BC - BD = \pm 2$.
Solution: Since $A, B, C, D \in \pm 1$ and

$$AC + AD + BC - BD = A(C + D) + B(C - D)$$

therefore either $(C + D)$ or $(C - D)$ is always zero from which the statement holds.

Exercise 2.6: Show that $\frac{1+e^{j\alpha}}{2} = e^{j0.5\alpha}\cos(0.5\alpha)$ and $e^{j0.5\pi}\frac{1-e^{j\alpha}}{2} = e^{j0.5\alpha}\sin(0.5\alpha)$.

Solution:

$$\frac{1 + e^{j\alpha}}{2} = \frac{1 + e^{j0.5\alpha}e^{j0.5\alpha}}{2} = e^{j0.5\alpha}\frac{e^{j0.5\alpha} + e^{-j0.5\alpha}}{2} = e^{j0.5\alpha}\cos(0.5\alpha),$$

$$e^{j(0.5\pi)}\frac{1 - e^{j\alpha}}{2} = \underbrace{e^{j(0.5\pi)}}_{\frac{1}{-j}}e^{j0.5\alpha}\frac{e^{-j0.5\alpha} - e^{-j0.5\alpha}}{2} = e^{j0.5\alpha}\sin(0.5\alpha).$$

Exercise 3.1: Construct the measurement operators providing sure success in the case of the following set $|\varphi_0\rangle = \frac{|0\rangle+|1\rangle}{\sqrt{2}}$ and $|\varphi_1\rangle = \frac{|0\rangle-|1\rangle}{\sqrt{2}}$.

Solution: Applying the rule of thumb for projective measurement

$$\mathbf{P}_0 = |\varphi_0\rangle\langle\varphi_0| = \frac{|0\rangle + |1\rangle}{\sqrt{2}} \otimes \frac{\langle0| + \langle1|}{\sqrt{2}}$$

$$= \frac{|0\rangle\langle0| + |1\rangle\langle0| + |0\rangle\langle1| + |1\rangle\langle1|}{2} = \frac{1}{2}\begin{bmatrix} 1 & 1 \\ 1 & 1 \end{bmatrix},$$

$$\mathbf{P}_1 = |\varphi_1\rangle\langle\varphi_1| = \frac{|0\rangle - |1\rangle}{\sqrt{2}} \otimes \frac{\langle0| - \langle1|}{\sqrt{2}}$$

$$= \frac{|0\rangle\langle0| - |1\rangle\langle0| - |0\rangle\langle1| + |1\rangle\langle1|}{2} = \frac{1}{2}\begin{bmatrix} 1 & -1 \\ -1 & 1 \end{bmatrix}.$$

In order to avoid trouble we check the completeness relation

$$\mathbf{P}_0 + \mathbf{P}_1 = \frac{1}{2}\begin{bmatrix} 1 & 1 \\ 1 & 1 \end{bmatrix} + \frac{1}{2}\begin{bmatrix} 1 & -1 \\ -1 & 1 \end{bmatrix} = \begin{bmatrix} 1 & 0 \\ 0 & 1 \end{bmatrix} = \mathbf{I}.$$

Exercise 4.1: Check whether the $CNOT(H \otimes I)$ gate really returns the wanted classical states.

Solution: The brute force method to prove the proper functionality is if we perform linear algebraic operations with the matrix of the proposed circuit and all the four $|\beta_{ab}\rangle$ states. Instead we follow a more clever way based on the superposition principle. Equation (2.12) says that

$$|\beta_{ab}\rangle = \frac{|0, b\rangle + (-1)^a|1, NOT(b)\rangle}{\sqrt{2}}.$$

Applying first the CNOT gate it retains $|0, b\rangle$ while inverts $NOT(b)$ on the data wire because of the control with 1

$$(-1)^a|1, NOT(b)\rangle \rightarrow (-1)^a|1, b\rangle,$$

hence the output of the CNOT gate will be

$$|\beta_{ab}\rangle = \frac{|0, b\rangle + (-1)^a|1, b\rangle}{\sqrt{2}} = \frac{|0\rangle + (-1)^a|1\rangle}{\sqrt{2}}|b\rangle.$$

Next the Hadamard gate acts on the control qbit

$$\left(H|0\rangle \longrightarrow \frac{|0\rangle + |1\rangle}{\sqrt{2}}, H|1\rangle \longrightarrow \frac{|0\rangle - |1\rangle}{\sqrt{2}} \right)$$

resulting in

$$\frac{\frac{|0\rangle+|1\rangle}{\sqrt{2}} + (-1)^a \frac{|0\rangle-|1\rangle}{\sqrt{2}}}{\sqrt{2}}|b\rangle = \left(\frac{1 + (-1)^a}{2}|0\rangle + \frac{1 - (-1)^a}{2}|1\rangle \right)|b\rangle = |a\rangle|b\rangle.$$

Exercise 4.2: Using teleportation Bob obtains a replica of an arbitrary one-qbit state in Alice's hand. Explain why quantum teleportation cannot be used in this way as a cloning machine.

Solution: The answer is simple but a bit tricky. Bob requires the two classical measurement result bits from Alice to produce $|\psi\rangle$. However, while Alice is measuring her qbits she is demolishing $|\psi\rangle$ thus there is no moment when both $|\psi\rangle$ exist.

Exercise 5.1: Prove that $U_f : |x\rangle_N|y\rangle \rightarrow |x\rangle_N|y \oplus f(x)\rangle$ is unitary.

Solution: We have several equivalent definitions for unitary operators. The most suitable one in this case claims that unitary operators are reversible and save the unit length. Thanks to the superposition principle it is enough to check these properties for computational basis states. Since the output of U_f contains x we are able to compute $f(x)$. Observing $y \oplus f(x)$ we can deduce y in possession of $f(x)$ which proves the reversible nature of U_f. Furthermore the input computational basis vector has obviously unit length and the output proves to be another computational basis vector therefore both requirements have been satisfied.

Exercise 5.2: Prove that $|f(x)\rangle - |1 \oplus f(x)\rangle = (-1)^{f(x)}(|0\rangle - |1\rangle)$.

Solution: There are two scenarios to be considered either $f(x) = 0$ or $f(x) = 1$. Substituting these values the equivalence is obvious.

Exercise 6.1: Prove that operator F is unitary.

Solution: We have several equivalent definitions for unitary operators. The most suitable one in this case claims that the rows/columns of unitary matrices form an orthonormal vector set. Definition (6.4) ensures trivially that the columns are normalized because $F|i\rangle$ is nothing more than the ith column of the matrix (cf. **Exercise** 6.2). Next we calculate the inner product of the ith and l^{th} columns

$$\langle l|F^\dagger F|i\rangle = \sum_{k=0}^{N-1} \frac{1}{\sqrt{N}} e^{-j\frac{2\pi}{N}lk} \frac{1}{\sqrt{N}} e^{j\frac{2\pi}{N}ik} = \sum_{k=0}^{N-1} \frac{e^{j2\pi \frac{k}{N}(i-l)}}{N},$$

which trivially equals 1 if $i = l$ and 0 else ($i \neq l$) due to (6.55).

Exercise 6.2: Determine the matrix of QFT.

Solution:

$$F = \frac{1}{\sqrt{N}} \begin{bmatrix} 1 & 1 & 1 & \cdots & 1 \\ 1 & B & B^2 & \cdots & B^{(N-1)} \\ 1 & B^2 & B^4 & \cdots & B^{2(N-1)} \\ \vdots & \vdots & \vdots & \ddots & \vdots \\ 1 & B^{(N-1)} & B^{2(N-1)} & \cdots & B^{(N-1)^2} \end{bmatrix}$$

where $B = e^{\frac{j2\pi}{N}}$. The reader may recognize that B is periodic in N and $1 = B^0$ thus F becomes symmetric

$$F = \frac{1}{\sqrt{N}} \begin{bmatrix} 1 & 1 & 1 & \cdots & 1 & 1 & 1 \\ 1 & B & B^2 & \cdots & B^{(N-3)} & B^{(N-2)} & B^{(N-1)} \\ 1 & B^2 & B^4 & \cdots & B^{(N-6)} & B^{(N-4)} & B^{(N-2)} \\ \vdots & \vdots & \vdots & \ddots & \vdots & \vdots & \vdots \\ 1 & B^{(N-3)} & B^{(N-6)} & \cdots & B^9 & B^6 & B^3 \\ 1 & B^{(N-2)} & B^{(N-4)} & \cdots & B^6 & B^4 & B^2 \\ 1 & B^{(N-1)} & B^{(N-2)} & \cdots & B^3 & B^2 & B^1 \end{bmatrix}.$$

Exercise 6.3: Prove that $\left|1 - e^{j\gamma}\right|^2 = 4\sin^2(\frac{\gamma}{2})$.
Solution: Using the following identities: $|z|^2 \equiv zz^*$ if $z \in \mathbb{C}$, $e^{j\gamma} \equiv \cos(\gamma) + j\sin(\gamma)$ and $\sin^2(\gamma) + \cos^2(\gamma) \equiv 1$ we get

$$\left|1 - e^{j\alpha}\right|^2 = (1 - \cos(\alpha) - j\sin(\alpha))(1 - \cos(\alpha) + j\sin(\alpha))$$
$$= 2 - 2\cos(\alpha) = 4\frac{1 - \cos(\alpha)}{2} = 4\sin^2\left(\frac{\alpha}{2}\right).$$

Exercise 6.4: Prove that $|1 - e^{j\gamma}| \le 2$.
Solution: The explanation of this inequality can be traced back to Fig. 1, where $e^{j\gamma} = \cos(\gamma) + j\sin(\gamma)$ is depicted as a unit vector in the complex plain. It points to $[\cos(\gamma), \sin(\gamma)]$. $|1 - e^{j\gamma}|$ is nothing more than the distance between this point and $[1,0]$. Since $e^{j\gamma}$ sweeps the unit circle in function of γ this distance (the length of the chord) cannot exceed the diameter of the circle which is equal trivially to 2.

Exercise 6.5: Prove $|1 - e^{j\gamma}| \ge \frac{2|\gamma|}{\pi}$ if $\gamma \in [-\pi, \pi]$.
Solution: If one rewrites the inequality in the following manner

$$\frac{|1 - e^{j\gamma}|}{2} \ge \frac{|\gamma|}{\pi},$$

then it is easy to recognize on the left-hand side the fraction of the actual chord and the related maximum value (i.e. the diameter 2) while on the right-hand side the arc belonging to the current chord divided with the maximum arc (π). Since both sides are symmetrical on the vertical axis it is enough to investigate the inequality on $[0, \pi]$. Let us replace the right-hand side with $\frac{|\gamma|}{a}$, where a is a real free parameter. This can

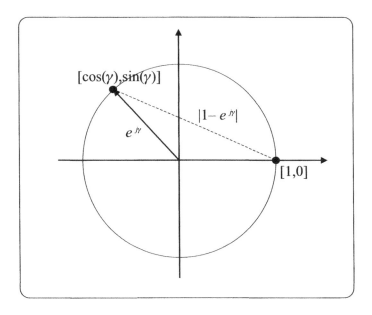

Fig. 1 Geometrical interpretation to **Exercise** 6.4 and **Exercise** 6.5

be regarded as a linear function in γ with slope $\frac{1}{a}$

$$\frac{|1 - e^{j\gamma}|}{2} \geq \frac{|\gamma|}{a}.$$

The equality holds trivially if $\gamma = 0$. Since both sides of the above inequality are strongly monotonic increasing functions without inflection it is enough to check $\gamma = \pi$. If in this case the inequality is satisfied then it is also valid for any other γ. Substituting $\gamma = \pi$ one yields that $a = \pi$ still fulfils the requirements, i.e. the inequality turns to equality.

Exercise 6.6: Factorize $A = 66$! To find the order use an exhaustive search.

Solution: Since 66 is even we divide it by 2. $N = 33$ is a composite odd integer and it is easy to see that 33 does not prove to be a prime power. Therefore we cast a 32-faced dice and we get say $x = 5$. Now we are seeking for the order r of 5 in modulo 33 sense using an exhaustive search, i.e. we try to determine $r : x^r \bmod N = 1$

$$\begin{aligned}
5^1 \bmod 33 &= 5, & 5^6 \bmod 33 &= 16, \\
5^2 \bmod 33 &= 25, & 5^7 \bmod 33 &= 14, \\
5^3 \bmod 33 &= 26, & 5^8 \bmod 33 &= 4, \\
5^4 \bmod 33 &= 31, & 5^9 \bmod 33 &= 20, \\
5^5 \bmod 33 &= 23, & 5^{10} \bmod 33 &= 1.
\end{aligned}$$

So $r = 10$ is even thus $y = x^{\frac{r}{2}} = 5^5$. Next we have to calculate $b_{+1} = (y+1) \bmod N = 24$ and $b_{-1} = (y-1) \bmod N = 22$. Fortunately neither of them equals zero (i.e. $x^{\frac{r}{2}} \bmod N \neq \pm 1$), which enables us to compute nontrivial factors $c_{+1} = \gcd(24, 33) = 3$ and $c_{-1} = \gcd(22, 33) = 11$. In order to check the results it is worth calculating $3 \cdot 11 = 33$.

Exercise 6.7: Derive the matrix of operator $U : |q\rangle \to |(qx) \bmod N\rangle$.

Solution: Let us first determine the original $N \times N$ matrix denoted here by U'. This operator has the special property that each output vector depends only on one input vector. This fact means that matrix element $U'_{iq} = 1$ if $|i\rangle = |(qx) \bmod N\rangle$ else $U'_{iq} = 0$ or more plausible: the columns of U' from left to right correspond to the input vectors form $|0\rangle$ to $|N-1\rangle$, while rows from top to bottom to the output vectors $|0\rangle$ to $|N-1\rangle$, respectively. Setting $U'_{iq} = 1$ results that operator U' transforms input vector $|q\rangle$ to output vector $|i\rangle$. Therefore we get a matrix with rows/columns having a single entry since U' is unitary. In order to save unitary nature for $U_{2^t \times 2^t}$ we were advised to join rows/columns with 1s in the main diagonal. In order to illustrate U we prepared an example for $N = 5 \Rightarrow t = \lceil \mathrm{ld}(5) \rceil = 3$ and $x = 3$

$$U = \begin{bmatrix} 1 & 0 & 0 & 0 & 0 & 0 & 0 & 0 \\ 0 & 0 & 1 & 0 & 0 & 0 & 0 & 0 \\ 0 & 0 & 0 & 0 & 1 & 0 & 0 & 0 \\ 0 & 1 & 0 & 0 & 0 & 0 & 0 & 0 \\ 0 & 0 & 0 & 1 & 0 & 0 & 0 & 0 \\ 0 & 0 & 0 & 0 & 0 & 1 & 0 & 0 \\ 0 & 0 & 0 & 0 & 0 & 0 & 1 & 0 \\ 0 & 0 & 0 & 0 & 0 & 0 & 0 & 1 \end{bmatrix}.$$

Exercise 6.8: Prove that if the order-finding circuit initialized with $|\varphi_0\rangle = |0\rangle|0\rangle$ and its gate V is replaced by $V' : |k\rangle|q\rangle \to |k\rangle|(q + x^k) \bmod N\rangle$ then it produces $|\varphi_2\rangle = \frac{1}{\sqrt{2^n}} \sum_{k=0}^{2^n-1} |k\rangle|x^k \bmod N\rangle$, too.

Solution: Applying the Hadamard gate for the upper qregister we get in accordance with (6.45)

$$|\varphi_1\rangle = \frac{1}{\sqrt{2^n}} \sum_{k=0}^{2^n-1} |k\rangle \otimes |0\rangle.$$

When V' acts on each computational basis states of $|\varphi_1\rangle$ in the spirit of the superposition principle

$$|\varphi_2\rangle = \frac{1}{\sqrt{2^n}} \sum_{k=0}^{2^n-1} |k\rangle|(0 + x^k) \bmod N\rangle.$$

Exercise 6.9: Prove that $|u_b\rangle = \sum_{s=0}^{r-1} \frac{e^{-j2\pi \frac{b}{r} s}}{\sqrt{r}} |x^s \bmod N\rangle$, $b = 0 \ldots r-1$ are eigenvectors of $U : |q\rangle \to |(qx) \bmod N\rangle$.

Solution:

$$U|u_b\rangle = \sum_{s=0}^{r-1} \frac{e^{-j2\pi\frac{b}{r}s}}{\sqrt{r}} U|x^s \bmod N\rangle = \sum_{s=0}^{r-1} \frac{e^{-j2\pi\frac{b}{r}s}}{\sqrt{r}}|xx^s \bmod N\rangle$$

$$= \sum_{s=0}^{r-1} \frac{e^{-j2\pi\frac{b}{r}s}}{\sqrt{r}} \underbrace{e^{-j2\pi\frac{b}{r}}e^{j2\pi\frac{b}{r}}}_{1}|x^{s+1} \bmod N\rangle$$

$$= e^{j2\pi\frac{b}{r}} \sum_{s=0}^{r-1} \frac{e^{-j2\pi\frac{b}{r}(s+1)}}{\sqrt{r}}|x^{s+1} \bmod N\rangle$$

$$= e^{j2\pi\frac{b}{r}} \sum_{s=1}^{r} \frac{e^{-j2\pi\frac{b}{r}s}}{\sqrt{r}}|x^s \bmod N\rangle = e^{j2\pi\frac{b}{r}}|u_b\rangle,$$

where we utilized in the last row that the following two sets are the same $\{|x^s \bmod N\rangle, s = 0 \ldots r-1\} \equiv \{|x^s \bmod N\rangle, s = 1 \ldots r\}$ because r is the period of function $x^s \bmod N$.

Exercise 6.10: Assuming 2^n is a multiple of r (r is a power of 2) prove that quantum inaccuracy disappears from $|\varphi_3\rangle$.

Solution: We start from (6.61) and realize that $Z_k = \frac{2^n}{r} - 1$, next $e^{-j\frac{2\pi}{2^n}ik}$ is pulled out from the summation over z

$$|\varphi_3\rangle = \sum_{i=0}^{2^n-1}\sum_{k=0}^{r-1}\underbrace{\left(\sum_{z=0}^{\frac{2^n}{r}-1} \frac{1}{2^n}e^{-j2\pi\frac{i(zr+k)}{2^n}}\right)}_{\varphi_{ik}}|i\rangle|x^k \bmod N\rangle$$

$$= \sum_{i=0}^{2^n-1}\sum_{k=0}^{r-1}\underbrace{\left(e^{-j2\pi\frac{ik}{2^n}}\frac{1}{r}\sum_{z=0}^{\frac{2^n}{r}-1} \frac{1}{2^n/r}e^{-j2\pi\frac{z}{2^n/r}i}\right)}_{\varphi_{ik}}|i\rangle|x^k \bmod N\rangle.$$

Because of (6.55)

$$\sum_{z=0}^{\frac{2^n}{r}-1} \frac{e^{-j2\pi\frac{z}{2^n/r}i}}{2^n/r} = \delta\left(i - b\frac{2^n}{r}\right),$$

therefore only those i have to be considered for which $i = b\frac{2^n}{r} \Rightarrow b = 0 \ldots r-1$ (remember that b stands for the index of eigenvalues see (6.57)), other values for i are cancelled by constructive interference, i.e. quantum uncertainty has disappeared, $m_b/2^n = b/r$

$$|\varphi_3\rangle = \sum_{b=0}^{r-1}\sum_{k=0}^{r-1}\underbrace{\left(\frac{1}{r}e^{-j2\pi\frac{bk}{r}}\right)}_{\varphi_{bk}}|b\frac{2^n}{r}\rangle|x^k \bmod N\rangle.$$

Finally let us calculate the probability $P(i = m_b)$

$$P(i = m_b) = P(b2^n/r = m_b) = \sum_{k=0}^{r-1} |\varphi_{bk}|^2 = \frac{1}{r^2} \underbrace{\sum_{k=0}^{r-1} \left| e^{-j2\pi \frac{bk}{r}} \right|^2}_{\equiv 1} = \frac{1}{r},$$

which does not depend on b at all and which is in consonance with our expectations – since the initial state $|\psi_2\rangle$ consists of eigenvectors of a superposition with uniform probability amplitudes, eigenvalues belonging to different eigenvectors are expected to be measured according to a uniform distribution on $[0 \ldots r)$.

Exercise 6.11: Determine the eigenvectors and eigenvalues of operator X.
Solution: Based on the definitions introduced in Section 12.2.4 we solve the characteristic equation

$$\det(X - qI) = 0.$$

$$\mathbf{X} - q\mathbf{I} = \begin{bmatrix} 0 & 1 \\ 1 & 0 \end{bmatrix} - \begin{bmatrix} -q & 0 \\ 0 & -q \end{bmatrix} = \begin{bmatrix} -q & 1 \\ 1 & -q \end{bmatrix},$$

from which $q = \pm 1$. Now in possession of the eigenvalues we turn to the eigenvectors. Assuming $|u\rangle$ in the form of $|u\rangle = a|0\rangle + b|1\rangle$ and demanding $X|u\rangle = q|u\rangle$ one obtains $b = a$ or $b = -a$ which leads to

$$|u\rangle = \frac{|0\rangle \pm |1\rangle}{\sqrt{2}}.$$

Eigenvalues and eigenvectors allow us to formulate the spectral decomposition of X in the following manner

$$X = (+1)\frac{|0\rangle + |1\rangle}{\sqrt{2}} \frac{\langle 0| + \langle 1|}{\sqrt{2}} + (-1)\frac{|0\rangle - |1\rangle}{\sqrt{2}} \frac{\langle 0| - \langle 1|}{\sqrt{2}}.$$

Exercise 6.12: Calculate the probabilities (P_0 and P_1) of measuring $m = 0$ and $m = 1$ for the phase estimator circuit in Fig. 6.18 using linear algebraic operations if the eigenvector input has been initialized to $|0\rangle$.
Solution: The initial state of the circuit is trivially $|\varphi_0\rangle = |0\rangle \otimes |0\rangle = |00\rangle$. The first Hadamard gate on the upper wire prepares an equiprobable superposition of $|0\rangle$ and $|1\rangle$, which corresponds to the following state of the system

$$|\varphi_1\rangle = \frac{|0\rangle + |1\rangle}{\sqrt{2}} \otimes |0\rangle = \frac{|00\rangle + |10\rangle}{\sqrt{2}} = \frac{1}{\sqrt{2}}[1, 0, 1, 0]^T.$$

Applying the controlled X gate, i.e. a CNOT gate which swaps computational basis states $|10\rangle$ and $|11\rangle$ while the others are left unchanged

$$|\varphi_2\rangle = \text{CNOT}|\varphi_1\rangle = \frac{1}{\sqrt{2}}[1, 0, 0, 1]^T = \frac{|00\rangle + |11\rangle}{\sqrt{2}}.$$

The next Hadamard gate on the upper wire acts on the first qbit

$$|\varphi_3\rangle = (H \otimes I)|\varphi_2\rangle = \frac{\frac{|0\rangle+|1\rangle}{\sqrt{2}} \otimes |0\rangle + \frac{|0\rangle-|1\rangle}{\sqrt{2}} \otimes |1\rangle}{\sqrt{2}} = \frac{1}{2}(|00\rangle+|11\rangle+|10\rangle-|11\rangle).$$

Measuring the first qbit we get $|0\rangle$ and $|1\rangle$ with the same probability

$$P_0 = \left(\tfrac{1}{2}\right)^2 + \left(\tfrac{1}{2}\right)^2 = \tfrac{1}{2} \quad \text{and} \quad P_1 = \left(\tfrac{1}{2}\right)^2 + \left(-\tfrac{1}{2}\right)^2 = \tfrac{1}{2}.$$

Exercise 6.13: Determine the transformation rule of controlled operator U applied in gate V_f.

Solution: Let us be a bit pragmatic and exploit the technique used in **Exercise** 6.9 instead of using linear equation systems. As we know from Section 6.5.1 when generalizing order finding to search for period r of function f one has to replace the special $f(k) = x^k \mod N$ with general $f(k)$. We can deduce an important conclusion of **Exercise** 6.9, namely U increases the exponent k of x by 1, i.e. it shifts function f. Therefore it seems to be reasonable to propose $U : |f(k)\rangle \to |f(k+1)\rangle$. Now let us validate our conjecture

$$U|u_b\rangle = \sum_{s=0}^{r-1} \frac{e^{-j2\pi\frac{b}{r}s}}{\sqrt{r}} U|f(s)\rangle = \sum_{s=0}^{r-1} \frac{e^{-j2\pi\frac{b}{r}s}}{\sqrt{r}}|f(s+1)\rangle$$

$$= \sum_{s=0}^{r-1} \frac{e^{-j2\pi\frac{b}{r}s}}{\sqrt{r}} \underbrace{e^{-j2\pi\frac{b}{r}}e^{j2\pi\frac{b}{r}}}_{1}|f(s+1)\rangle$$

$$= e^{j2\pi\frac{b}{r}} \sum_{s=0}^{r-1} \frac{e^{-j2\pi\frac{b}{r}(s+1)}}{\sqrt{r}}|f(s+1)\rangle$$

$$= e^{j2\pi\frac{b}{r}} \sum_{s=1}^{r} \frac{e^{-j2\pi\frac{b}{r}s}}{\sqrt{r}}|f(s)\rangle = e^{j2\pi\frac{b}{r}}|u_b\rangle,$$

where we utilized in the last row that the following two sets are the same $\{|f(s)\rangle, s=0\ldots r-1\} \equiv \{|f(s)\rangle, s=1\ldots r\}$ because r is the period of function $f(s)$. Finally we point out that actually one uses U repeatedly several times in gate V_f (see Fig. 6.5), i.e. $U^{2^{n-l}} : |f(k)\rangle \to |f(k+2^{n-l})\rangle$ gates are used.

Exercise 6.14: Show that $F^{\otimes n} \otimes F^{\otimes n} \equiv F^{\otimes 2n}$.

Solution: Let $\{|i\rangle\}$ and $\{|l\rangle\}$ be two orthonormal N-dimensional computational basis vector sets for spanning the Hilbert spaces that the Fourier transforms acting on. Applying the definition of the QFT (see (6.4)) and the 4th Postulate we get

$$\left(F^{\otimes n}|i\rangle\right) \otimes \left(F^{\otimes n}|l\rangle\right) = \left(\frac{1}{\sqrt{N}} \sum_{k=0}^{N-1} e^{j\frac{2\pi}{N}ik}|k\rangle\right) \otimes \left(\frac{1}{\sqrt{N}} \sum_{m=0}^{N-1} e^{j\frac{2\pi}{N}lm}|m\rangle\right)$$

$$= \frac{1}{N} \sum_{k=0}^{N-1} \sum_{m=0}^{N-1} e^{j\frac{2\pi}{N}ik} e^{j\frac{2\pi}{N}lm}|k\rangle|m\rangle$$

$$= \frac{1}{N} \sum_{z=0}^{N^2-1} e^{j\frac{2\pi}{N^2}(i\otimes l)z}|z\rangle = F^{\otimes 2n}\left(|i\rangle \otimes |l\rangle\right)$$

where $\{|z\rangle\}$ form an orthonormal basis for the N^2-dimensional merged Hilbert space.

Exercise 7.1: Show that the transformation of the Oracle can be represented as $O = I - 2|x_0\rangle\langle x_0|$.

Solution: As we already know the outer product of a computational basis vector with itself results in an $N \times N$ matrix with elements $A_{ij} \equiv 0$ except $A_{x_0,x_0} = 1$. Subtracting the double of this matrix from the identity matrix we get almost an identity matrix, the only deviation is that $A_{x_0,x_0} = 1$ has been replaced by $A_{x_0,x_0} = -1$ which is in consonance of the original definition (7.3).

Exercise 7.2: Determine the matrix of the Oracle in the case of an $N = 4$ database assuming $x_0 = 2$.

Solution I: If we start from the definition (7.3) of the Oracle then we need an identity matrix with diagonal elements $A_{ii} = 1$ except $A_{x_0,x_0} = -1$.

Solution II: $|x_0\rangle = \begin{bmatrix} 0 & 0 & 1 & 0 \end{bmatrix}^T$. Using operator formalism in accordance with (7.14) the matrix $\mathbf{O}$ representing the Oracle can be calculated as

$$\mathbf{O} = I - 2 \begin{bmatrix} 0 \\ 0 \\ 1 \\ 0 \end{bmatrix} \begin{bmatrix} 0 & 0 & 1 & 0 \end{bmatrix} = \begin{bmatrix} 0 & 0 & 0 & 0 \\ 0 & 0 & 0 & 0 \\ 0 & 0 & 1 & 0 \\ 0 & 0 & 0 & 0 \end{bmatrix} = \begin{bmatrix} 1 & 0 & 0 & 0 \\ 0 & 1 & 0 & 0 \\ 0 & 0 & -1 & 0 \\ 0 & 0 & 0 & 1 \end{bmatrix}.$$

Exercise 7.3: Show an example scenario when a single application of G ensures sure success for measuring $|x_0\rangle$.

Solution: Using the geometrical interpretation from (7.23) with $i = 0$ one can easily spot the initial angle $\Omega_\gamma/2$ for a single query, which is $\Omega_\gamma = 60°$. This leads to a special relation between the size N of the database and the number of marked states M (see (7.20)) which is

$$N = 4M.$$

The reader is advised to compare this result with that of **Exercise** 7.5.

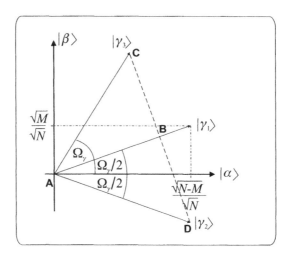

Fig. 2   Geometrical interpretation of the Grover operator

Exercise 7.4: Prove that inversion about the average is equivalent to a reflection about $|\gamma_1\rangle$ in the two-dimensional geometrical interpretation.

Solution: In order to support the explanation of the solution, Fig. 7.5 has been extended according to Fig. 2.

If we were able to prove that the projection of $|\gamma_3\rangle$ onto $|\gamma_1\rangle$ and that of $|\gamma_2\rangle$ onto $|\gamma_1\rangle$ has the same length, i.e. we get a single intersection point B, then triangles $ABC_\triangle$ and $ADB_\triangle$ are the same and thus $BC = DB$. This follows from the fact that both rectangular triangles have a common leg AB and hypotenuse of unit length.

To compute the projections we exploit the fact that all the vectors in question have unit length, thus we are interested in whether $|AB| = |\langle\gamma_1|\gamma_2\rangle| = |\langle\gamma_1|\gamma_3\rangle|$.

First let us determine the two-dimensional representations of the vectors in question. $|\gamma_1\rangle$ is available from (7.19). $|\gamma_2\rangle$ can be regarded as an arbitrary vector in the form of

$$|\gamma_2\rangle = k|\alpha\rangle + l|\beta\rangle$$

with the condition $|k|^2 + |l|^2 = 1$. In order to obtain $|\gamma_3\rangle$ we calculate the N-dimensional probability amplitudes γ_{3x} utilizing

$$\gamma_{2x} = k\frac{1}{\sqrt{N-M}}; \quad x \in \overline{S},$$

$$\gamma_{2x} = l\frac{1}{\sqrt{M}}; \quad x \in S$$

(see definitions (7.17) and (7.18)) and (7.10) therefore

$$\gamma_{3x} = 2\bar{a} - \frac{k}{\sqrt{N-M}}; \quad x \in \overline{S},$$

$$\gamma_{3x} = 2\bar{a} - \frac{l}{\sqrt{M}}; \quad x \in S.$$

Next we produce coordinates of $|\gamma_3\rangle$ in the two-dimensional space

$$|\gamma_3\rangle = (2\bar{a}\sqrt{N-M} - k)|\alpha\rangle + (2\bar{a}\sqrt{M} - l)|\beta\rangle.$$

Now, let us determine the projections in possession of the three vectors

$$AB_1 = |\langle\gamma_1|\gamma_2\rangle| = k\sqrt{\frac{N-M}{N}} + l\sqrt{\frac{M}{N}}.$$

Furthermore

$$AB_2 = |\langle\gamma_1|\gamma_3\rangle| = \sqrt{\frac{N-M}{N}}(2\bar{a}\sqrt{N-M} - k) + \sqrt{\frac{M}{N}}(2\bar{a}\sqrt{M} - l)$$

$$= 2\bar{a} - k\sqrt{\frac{N-M}{N}} - l\sqrt{\frac{M}{N}}.$$

If one substitutes the above results on γ_{2x} into definition (7.9) of $\bar{a}$ then we obtain

$$\bar{a} = \frac{1}{N}\sum_{x=0}^{N-1}\gamma_{2x} = \frac{1}{N}\left((N-M)\frac{k}{\sqrt{N-M}} + M\frac{l}{\sqrt{M}}\right) = k\frac{\sqrt{N-M}}{N} + l\frac{\sqrt{M}}{N}$$

and therefore AB_2 becomes equal to AB_1, i.e. we have managed to prove that the inversion about the average operation reflects $|\gamma_2\rangle$ over $|\gamma_1\rangle$ to $|\gamma_3\rangle$.

Exercise 7.5: – single marked state case – Assuming $N = 4$, $M = 1$ and $x_0 = 2$ determine the matrices of O, U_f and G, the optimal number of iterations and the probability of error.
Solution: **O** is already known from **Exercise** 7.2

$$\mathbf{O} = \begin{bmatrix} 1 & 0 & 0 & 0 \\ 0 & 1 & 0 & 0 \\ 0 & 0 & -1 & 0 \\ 0 & 0 & 0 & 1 \end{bmatrix}.$$

$\mathbf{U}_\gamma$ can be computed bearing in mind (7.13)

$$\mathbf{U}_\gamma = \begin{bmatrix} \frac{2}{4} - 1 & \frac{2}{4} & \frac{2}{4} & \frac{2}{4} \\ \frac{2}{4} & \frac{2}{4} - 1 & \frac{2}{4} & \frac{2}{4} \\ \frac{2}{4} & \frac{2}{4} & \frac{2}{4} - 1 & \frac{2}{4} \\ \frac{2}{4} & \frac{2}{4} & \frac{2}{4} & \frac{2}{4} - 1 \end{bmatrix} = \begin{bmatrix} -1/2 & 1/2 & 1/2 & 1/2 \\ 1/2 & -1/2 & 1/2 & 1/2 \\ 1/2 & 1/2 & -1/2 & 1/2 \\ 1/2 & 1/2 & 1/2 & -1/2 \end{bmatrix}.$$

Considering $\mathbf{G} = \mathbf{U}_\gamma \mathbf{O}$ we can utilize that $\mathbf{O}$ originates from an identity matrix whose third column was multiplied by -1 therefore the same transformation will happen in $\mathbf{U}_\gamma$ if it is multiplied by $\mathbf{O}$ from right

$$\mathbf{G} = \begin{bmatrix} -1/2 & 1/2 & -1/2 & 1/2 \\ 1/2 & -1/2 & -1/2 & 1/2 \\ 1/2 & 1/2 & 1/2 & 1/2 \\ 1/2 & 1/2 & -1/2 & -1/2 \end{bmatrix}.$$

As the next step one should find out the angle between the initial state $|\gamma_1\rangle$ and the basis vector $|a\rangle$. Applying (7.20)

$$\frac{\Omega_\gamma}{2} = \arcsin\left(\frac{1}{4}\right) = 30°,$$

from which follows that $\Theta_1 = \Theta_2 = 0$ and the required number of iterations (see (7.24)) is

$$L_{opt_0} = l_{opt_0} = 1.$$

Performing a single turn of the Grover operator on $|\gamma_1\rangle$ the outcome becomes

$$\mathbf{G}|\gamma_1\rangle = \begin{bmatrix} 0 & 0 & 1 & 0 \end{bmatrix}^T.$$

This indicates that a measurement in the computational basis states will find the marked state after a single iteration with probability of error

$$P_\varepsilon = 0.$$

The reader is advised to compare this result with that of **Exercise 7.3**.

Exercise 7.6: – multiple marked state case – Assuming $N = 8$, $M = 3$ and marked states $x = 1, 4, 7$ determine the matrices of O, U_f and G, the optimal number of iterations and the probability of error.
Solution: Following the line of thought used in **Exercise 7.5**

$$\mathbf{O} = \begin{bmatrix} 1 & 0 & 0 & 0 & 0 & 0 & 0 & 0 \\ 0 & -1 & 0 & 0 & 0 & 0 & 0 & 0 \\ 0 & 0 & 1 & 0 & 0 & 0 & 0 & 0 \\ 0 & 0 & 0 & 1 & 0 & 0 & 0 & 0 \\ 0 & 0 & 0 & 0 & -1 & 0 & 0 & 0 \\ 0 & 0 & 0 & 0 & 0 & 1 & 0 & 0 \\ 0 & 0 & 0 & 0 & 0 & 0 & 1 & 0 \\ 0 & 0 & 0 & 0 & 0 & 0 & 0 & -1 \end{bmatrix},$$

$$
\mathbf{U}_\gamma =
\begin{bmatrix}
-3/4 & 1/4 & 1/4 & 1/4 & 1/4 & 1/4 & 1/4 & 1/4 \\
1/4 & -3/4 & 1/4 & 1/4 & 1/4 & 1/4 & 1/4 & 1/4 \\
1/4 & 1/4 & -3/4 & 1/4 & 1/4 & 1/4 & 1/4 & 1/4 \\
1/4 & 1/4 & 1/4 & -3/4 & 1/4 & 1/4 & 1/4 & 1/4 \\
1/4 & 1/4 & 1/4 & 1/4 & -3/4 & 1/4 & 1/4 & 1/4 \\
1/4 & 1/4 & 1/4 & 1/4 & 1/4 & -3/4 & 1/4 & 1/4 \\
1/4 & 1/4 & 1/4 & 1/4 & 1/4 & 1/4 & -3/4 & 1/4 \\
1/4 & 1/4 & 1/4 & 1/4 & 1/4 & 1/4 & 1/4 & -3/4
\end{bmatrix},
$$

$$
\mathbf{G} =
\begin{bmatrix}
-3/4 & -1/4 & 1/4 & 1/4 & -1/4 & 1/4 & 1/4 & -1/4 \\
1/4 & 3/4 & 1/4 & 1/4 & -1/4 & 1/4 & 1/4 & -1/4 \\
1/4 & -1/4 & -3/4 & 1/4 & -1/4 & 1/4 & 1/4 & -1/4 \\
1/4 & -1/4 & 1/4 & -3/4 & -1/4 & 1/4 & 1/4 & -1/4 \\
1/4 & -1/4 & 1/4 & 1/4 & 3/4 & 1/4 & 1/4 & -1/4 \\
1/4 & -1/4 & 1/4 & 1/4 & -1/4 & -3/4 & 1/4 & -1/4 \\
1/4 & -1/4 & 1/4 & 1/4 & -1/4 & 1/4 & -3/4 & -1/4 \\
1/4 & -1/4 & 1/4 & 1/4 & -1/4 & 1/4 & 1/4 & -1/4
\end{bmatrix},
$$

$$
\frac{\Omega_\gamma}{2} = \arcsin\left(\sqrt{\frac{3}{8}}\right) = 37.76^\circ,
$$

hence $L_{opt} = 1$ and the final state before the measurement is

$$
\mathbf{G}|\gamma_1\rangle = \begin{bmatrix} -0.176 & 0.53 & -0.176 & -0.176 & 0.53 & -0.176 & -0.176 & 0.53 \end{bmatrix}^T.
$$

Summing up the appropriate squared probability amplitudes we conclude an error with probability

$$
P_\varepsilon = 5 \cdot |-0.176|^2 \simeq 0.155.
$$

Exercise 7.7: Determine the matrix of the Grover operator in the basis of $|\alpha\rangle$ and $|\beta\rangle$.

Solution: It is clear from Fig. 7.5 that $|\gamma_1\rangle$ and $G|\gamma_1\rangle$ can be expressed in the basis of $|\alpha\rangle$ and $|\beta\rangle$ as

$$
|\gamma_1\rangle = \begin{bmatrix} \cos(\frac{\Omega_\gamma}{2}) \\ \sin(\frac{\Omega_\gamma}{2}) \end{bmatrix}, \quad |\gamma_3\rangle = G|\gamma_1\rangle = \begin{bmatrix} \cos(\Omega_\gamma + \frac{\Omega_\gamma}{2}) \\ \sin(\Omega_\gamma + \frac{\Omega_\gamma}{2}) \end{bmatrix}.
$$

Therefore applying the unknown

$$
\mathbf{G} = \begin{bmatrix} G_{11} & G_{12} \\ G_{21} & G_{22} \end{bmatrix},
$$

we get

$$
G|\gamma_1\rangle = |\gamma_3\rangle \Rightarrow \begin{bmatrix} G_{11} & G_{12} \\ G_{21} & G_{22} \end{bmatrix} \begin{bmatrix} \cos(\frac{\Omega_\gamma}{2}) \\ \sin(\frac{\Omega_\gamma}{2}) \end{bmatrix} \begin{bmatrix} \cos(\frac{\Omega_\gamma}{2})G_{11} + \sin(\frac{\Omega_\gamma}{2})G_{12} \\ \cos(\frac{\Omega_\gamma}{2})G_{21} + \sin(\frac{\Omega_\gamma}{2})G_{22} \end{bmatrix} = \begin{bmatrix} \cos(\Omega_\gamma + \frac{\Omega_\gamma}{2}) \\ \sin(\Omega_\gamma + \frac{\Omega_\gamma}{2}) \end{bmatrix}.
$$

Having in sight basic trigonometric calculus

$$\sin(\alpha + \beta) = \sin(\alpha)\cos(\beta) + \cos(\alpha) + \sin(\beta),$$
$$\cos(\alpha + \beta) = \cos(\alpha)\cos(\beta) - \sin(\alpha) + \sin(\beta)$$

we reach

$$\mathbf{G} = \begin{bmatrix} \cos(\Omega_\gamma) & -\sin(\Omega_\gamma) \\ \sin(\Omega_\gamma) & \cos(\Omega_\gamma) \end{bmatrix}.$$

Exercise 7.8: Determine the eigenvalues and corresponding eigenvectors of the Grover operator on the basis of $|\alpha\rangle$ and $|\beta\rangle$.

Solution: Based on Section 12.2.4 in the mathematical background we start with the characteristic equation related to $\mathbf{G}$

$$\det(\mathbf{G} - \omega\mathbf{I}) = \det\left(\begin{bmatrix} \cos(\Omega_\gamma) - \omega & -\sin(\Omega_\gamma) \\ \sin(\Omega_\gamma) & \cos(\Omega_\gamma) - \omega \end{bmatrix}\right) = 0,$$

from which

$$(\cos(\Omega_\gamma) - \omega)^2 + \sin^2(\Omega_\gamma) = \omega^2 - 2\omega\cos(\Omega_\gamma) + 1 = 0.$$
$$\omega_{1,2} = \frac{2\cos(\Omega_\gamma) \pm \sqrt{4\cos^2(\Omega_\gamma) - 4}}{2} = \cos(\Omega_\gamma) \pm j\sin(\Omega_\gamma) = e^{\pm j\Omega_\gamma}.$$

According to our expectations $\omega_{1,2}$ correspond to the form of eigenvalues of a unitary matrix.

Having the eigenvalues in our hands we determine the eigenvectors $|g\rangle = \begin{bmatrix} a \\ b \end{bmatrix}$:

$$\mathbf{G}|g\rangle = e^{\pm j\Omega_\gamma}|g\rangle$$

$$\mathbf{G}|u\rangle = e^{\pm j\Omega_\gamma}|u\rangle \Rightarrow \begin{bmatrix} \cos(\Omega_\gamma) & -\sin(\Omega_\gamma) \\ \sin(\Omega_\gamma) & \cos(\Omega_\gamma) \end{bmatrix} \overset{\begin{bmatrix} a \\ b \end{bmatrix}}{\begin{bmatrix} a\cos(\Omega_\gamma) - b\sin(\Omega_\gamma) \\ a\sin(\Omega_\gamma) + b\cos(\Omega_\gamma) \end{bmatrix}}$$
$$= \begin{bmatrix} a(\cos(\Omega_\gamma) \pm j\sin(\Omega_\gamma)) \\ b(\cos(\Omega_\gamma) \pm j\sin(\Omega_\gamma)) \end{bmatrix},$$

which leads to a homogeneous equation system with the following solutions

$$|g_1\rangle = \frac{e^{j\xi}}{\sqrt{2}}\begin{bmatrix} j \\ 1 \end{bmatrix}, \quad |g_2\rangle = \frac{e^{j\xi}}{\sqrt{2}}\begin{bmatrix} -j \\ 1 \end{bmatrix},$$

where $\alpha \in \mathbb{R}$. $|g_1\rangle$ and $|g_2\rangle$ are orthogonal ($\langle g_1|g_2\rangle = 0$) as we have learned for unitary matrices.

Exercise 7.9: Prove that the probability of failing in seeking for the marked entry ($M = 1$) after putting L queries to the database classically is $P_{\varepsilon C}(L) = \frac{N-L}{N}$.

Solution: The probability of failing in the first step is trivially $P_{\varepsilon C}(1) = 1 - P_{sC}(1) = 1 - \frac{1}{N} = \frac{N-1}{N}$. We learned from basic probability theory that for events

A and B the following rule is valid: $P(A \wedge B) = P(A|B) \cdot P(A)$. If the first attempt was unsuccessful then the probability of failing again in the second step is $P_{\varepsilon C}(l = 2|l = 1) = \frac{N-2}{N-1}$ thus

$$P_{\varepsilon C}(2) = P_{\varepsilon C}(l = 2 \wedge l = 1) = P_{\varepsilon C}(l = 2|l = 1)P_{\varepsilon C}(1) = \frac{N-2}{N-1}\frac{N-1}{N}.$$

Generalizing this line of thought we get

$$P_{\varepsilon C}(L) = \prod_{l=1}^{L} \frac{N-l}{N-l+1} = \frac{N-1}{N}\frac{N-2}{N-1}\cdots\frac{N-L}{N-L+1} = \frac{N-L}{N} = 1 - \frac{L}{N}.$$

Exercise 7.10: Let us consider a database with $N = 2^{20}$ and $M = 8$. Calculate the optimal number of rotations L which minimizes the expected number of required Grover gates $\mathbb{E}(z|M \wedge l)$ when using the cycle repetition based searching. Compare the optimal number of Grover operators in the case of the original Grover algorithm to $\mathbb{E}(z|M \wedge L)$.

Solution: We know from (7.33) that

$$\Omega_\gamma(M) = 2\arcsin\left(\sqrt{\frac{M}{N}}\right) = \Omega_\gamma(8) = 2\arcsin\left(\sqrt{\frac{8}{2^{20}}}\right) = 0.0055,$$

from which using (7.43)

$$\mathbb{E}(z|8 \wedge l) = \frac{l+1}{\sin^2\left((2l+1)\,0.011\right)}.$$

Solving (7.44)

$$\frac{d\mathbb{E}(z|8 \wedge l)}{dl} = 0 \Rightarrow \tan\left((2l+1)\,0.011\right) = 2(l+1)0.0055 \Rightarrow L = 211,$$

therefore $\mathbb{E}(z|8 \wedge 211) = 249$ while from (7.24)

$$L_{opt_0} = \left\lfloor \frac{\frac{\pi}{2} - \frac{\Omega_\gamma(M)}{2}}{\Omega_\gamma(M)} \right\rfloor = \left\lfloor \frac{\frac{\pi}{2} - 0.011}{0.0055} \right\rfloor = 284.$$

If we would like to be fair this 284 has to be increased to 285 because we have to check the index coming from the Grover algorithm. This result is a bit surprising because the expected value-based solution seems to be more efficient. However, do not forget that the original solution gives back one of the marked states with high probability (see (7.28))

$$P_s = \sin^2\left(\frac{(2L_{opt_0} + 1)\,\Omega_\gamma(M)}{2}\right) = \sin^2\left(\frac{(2 \cdot 284 + 1)0.0055}{2}\right) = 0.99998,$$

after 284 rotations while the new proposal provides this 249 iterations only on average!

Exercise 9.1 Encrypt and decrypt the following message *'QUANTUM COMPUTING'* using the following alphabet: space, A, B, C, D, E, F, G, H, I, J, K, L, M, N, O, P, Q, R, S, T, U, V, W, X, Y, Z.

Solution: First we realize that our alphabet comprises $N = 27$ different letters including the space. Therefore we enumerate them from 0 up to 26.

space	A	B	C	D	E	F	G	H	I	J	K	L	M
0	1	2	3	4	5	6	7	8	9	10	11	12	13
	N	O	P	Q	R	S	T	U	V	W	X	Y	Z
	14	15	16	17	18	19	20	21	22	23	24	25	26

Next we construct a 17-symbol random secret key according to the length of the plain text and compute the encrypted message using (9.1).

message	Q	U	A	N	T	U	M		C	O	M	P	U	T	I	N	G
P[·]	17	21	1	14	20	21	13	0	3	15	13	16	21	20	9	14	7
K[·]	26	10	20	12	4	14	2	12	1	22	15	5	4	16	24	17	5
E[·]	16	4	21	26	24	8	15	12	4	10	1	21	25	9	6	4	12
E[·]	P	D	U	Z	X	H	O	L	D	J	A	U	Y	I	F	D	L

It is easy to see that by applying (9.2) we get back the original plain message.

Exercise 11.1 Show that $(a + b)^2 \leq 2(a^2 + b^2)$.

Solution: Let us start from the indirect assumption $(a + b)^2 > 2(a^2 + b^2)$ and show that it leads to contradiction

$$(a + b)^2 = (a^2 + b^2) + 2ab > 2(a^2 + b^2) = (a^2 + b^2) + a^2 + b^2$$

$$2ab > a^2 + b^2$$

$$0 > a^2 - 2ab + b^2 = (a - b)^2 \geq 0.$$

Index

Printed and bound by CPI Group (UK) Ltd, Croydon, CR0 4YY

12/01/2025

14624501-0003